Advance praise for Defining Critical Animal Studies

"*Defining Critical Animal Studies* is the type of book that everyone should read—not just animal rights activists, but also the naysayers, fence-sitters, and uninformed. And why? Because this book is educational, enlightening, and transformative. It literally alters how we see and understand the issues of human and nonhuman relations, equality, democracy, food, consumption, activism, and social movements. And the book accomplishes this task by practicing what it preaches: bringing together a variety of scholars and activists, both old and new, that address the theoretical, practical, political, and personal intersections of animal liberation."

—Jason Del Gandio, Author of *Rhetoric for Radicals: A Handbook for 21st Century Activists*

"Through their work in this excellent volume, the editors and contributors give me hope that perhaps all is not lost for our species. But then I think, what kind of society marginalizes, harasses, and surveils these kinds of people as terrorists, but valorizes and rewards the real radicals and the real terrorists whose blood-lust for profits has normalized the systematic torture, oppression, and genocide of creatures unfortunate enough not to have been born human? As long as the latter group retains the backing of state violence, they'll continue super-sizing us toward extinction."

—David Gabbard, Professor of Education, Boise State University

"*Defining Critical Animal Studies* comes at a moment when the devastating effects of climate change, the loss of species in the current sixth mass extinction, the overconsumption of the earth's resources, endless toxic wars, and the exponential increase in human population are converging far more quickly than scientists predicted to create a multitude of crises—not in the distant future—but right here and now. This book reveals the necessity of reframing social justice and animal rights thought to forge new visions and creative movements to end human and corporate domination and exploitation of other humans, other forms of life, and the Earth."

—Julie Andrzejewski, Professor, St. Cloud State University

"This is a must-read for anyone concerned with the interconnectedness of struggles for justice and liberation. It is against single-issue politics. It is for the rights of all animals, irrespective of species, age, sex, race, class, and ability. What an exciting book!"

—Piers Beirne, Author of *Confronting Animal Abuse: Law, Criminology, and Human-Animal Relationships*

More advance praise for **Defining Critical Animal Studies**

"As radical means 'root,' *Defining Critical Animal Studies* is a radical book that explores the social, historical, and political roots underlying the oppression and exploitation of human and nonhuman animals alike. The book is also radical in advocating for the connection between scholarship and activism, and in promoting interdisciplinary and intersectional approaches to 'the question of the animal.' Students, scholars, activists, and citizens interested in engaging social justice across the species boundary will find these essays confronting many of the key issues of the twenty-first century, where what is at stake is survival itself."

—Dan Featherston, Assistant Professor, Temple University;
Editor, Lexington Critical Animal Studies Book Series

"Critical Animal Studies is a spreading academic discipline that brings much-needed activist and radical perspectives to classrooms globally—just the kind of thing that breathes life and real substance into higher education."

—Leslie James Pickering, former Earth Liberation Front Press Officer

"There is an urgent need for a broader analysis in the animal liberation movement. The contributors to *Defining Critical Animal Studies* grapple with questions our movement will have to engage in order to move forward."

—Erin Marcus, Event Coordinator and Co-Founder, Open the Cages Alliance

"Finally, a collection of work that details the rapidly growing field of Critical Animal Studies. Scholars and activists will find much-needed intersectional analysis that calls for nonhuman animal liberation, dismantlement of human oppression, and the end of environmental exploitation. *Defining Critical Animal Studies* should not be read by anyone who wishes to continue the status quo."

—Jessica Ison, Director, Institute for Critical Animal Studies Oceania

Defining Critical Animal Studies

Studies in the Postmodern Theory of Education

Shirley R. Steinberg
General Editor

Vol. 448

The Counterpoints series is part of the Peter Lang Education list.
Every volume is peer reviewed and meets
the highest quality standards for content and production.

PETER LANG
New York • Washington, D.C./Baltimore • Bern
Frankfurt • Berlin • Brussels • Vienna • Oxford

Defining Critical Animal Studies

An Intersectional Social Justice Approach for Liberation

Edited by
Anthony J. Nocella II, John Sorenson,
Kim Socha, and Atsuko Matsuoka

PETER LANG
New York • Washington, D.C./Baltimore • Bern
Frankfurt • Berlin • Brussels • Vienna • Oxford

Library of Congress Cataloging-in-Publication Data

Defining critical animal studies: an intersectional social
justice approach for liberation / edited by Anthony J. Nocella II,
John Sorenson, Kim Socha, Atsuko Matsuoka.
pages cm. — (Counterpoints: studies in the postmodern theory of education; v. 448)
Includes bibliographical references and index.
1. Animal rights. 2. Environmental ethics. 3. Critical theory.
I. Nocella, Anthony J., editor of compilation.
HV4708.C7495   179'.3—dc23   2013038188
ISBN 978-1-4331-2137-1 (hardcover)
ISBN 978-1-4331-2136-4 (paperback)
ISBN 978-1-4539-1230-0 (e-book)
ISSN 1058-1634

Bibliographic information published by **Die Deutsche Nationalbibliothek**.
Die Deutsche Nationalbibliothek lists this publication in the "Deutsche
Nationalbibliografie"; detailed bibliographic data is available
on the Internet at http://dnb.d-nb.de/.

Cover photo: zackembree.com

© 2014 Peter Lang Publishing, Inc., New York
29 Broadway, 18th floor, New York, NY 10006
www.peterlang.com

All rights reserved.
Reprint or reproduction, even partially, in all forms such as microfilm,
xerography, microfiche, microcard, and offset strictly prohibited.

DEDICATION

This book is dedicated to those born into this world only to experience exploitation, torture, and death at the hands of their overseers. It is also dedicated to those who seek to end oppression and domination through critical self-reflection, radical ideas, grassroots actions, and community engagement.

CONTENTS

Foreword..ix
    David Nibert

Preface...xiii
    Ronnie Lee

Acknowledgments.. xvii

Introduction: The Emergence of Critical Animal Studies:
The Rise of Intersectional Animal Liberation............................xix
    Anthony J. Nocella II, John Sorenson, Kim Socha, and Atsuko Matsuoka

Part I: Interdependency

1 An Overview of Anthropocentrism, Humanism, and Speciesism
    in Critical Animal Theory 3
    Adam Weitzenfeld and Melanie Joy

2 Ecological Defense for Animal Liberation:
    A Holistic Understanding of the World........................ 28
    Amy J. Fitzgerald and David Pellow

Part II: Unity

3 Until All Are Free: Total Liberation through Revolutionary
    Decolonization, Groundless Solidarity, and a Relationship Framework 51
    Sarat Colling, Sean Parson, and Alessandro Arrigoni

4 One Struggle 74
    Stephanie Jenkins and Vasile Stănescu

Part III: Critical Scholarship

5 The Ivory Trap: Bridging the Gap between Activism and the Academy 89
    Carol L. Glasser and Arpan Roy

6 Critical Animal Studies as an Interdisciplinary Field:
    A Holistic Approach to Confronting Oppression 110
    Kim Socha and Les Mitchell

Part IV: Radical Education

7 Radical Humility: Toward a More Holistic Critical Animal Studies Pedagogy . . . 135
   Lauren Corman and Tereza Vandrovcová

8 Engaged Activist Research: Challenging Apolitical Objectivity 158
   Lara Drew and Nik Taylor

Part V: Taking It to the Streets

9 From the Classroom to the Slaughterhouse:
   Animal Liberation by Any Means Necessary 179
   Jennifer Grubbs and Michael Loadenthal

10 Taking it to the Streets: Challenging Systems of Domination from Below 202
   Richard J. White and Erika Cudworth

Afterword: From Animal Oppression to Animal Liberation:
A Historical Reflection and the Growth of Critical Animal Studies 221
   Karen Davis

List of Contributors 229

Index 237

FOREWORD

by
David Nibert

The oppression of humans and other animals always has been deeply entangled. When humans began routinely to hunt large animals—primarily a male pursuit—they could do so only by creating weapons. Those who were most successful at such killing exerted growing power; social hierarchy began to emerge and the status of women began to decline.

The beginning of systemic human exploitation and social stratification can be traced to the advent of agricultural society roughly 10,000 years ago. Agricultural systems were tied to the exploitation of large social animals—including cows, horses, sheep, pigs, and goats—who were captured and exploited as laborers and for their hair, skin, body fluids, and flesh. The possession of large numbers of these other animals became a sign of wealth and dominance, and elite males' treatment of them as property was extended to women and devalued people. Countless people were relegated to the socially constructed position of peasant, serf, and slave. Growing numbers of men on the backs of horses, armed with weapons—originally created for killing other animals—were dispatched by elites to raid other peoples for their captive animals and other sources of wealth.

Some societies relied almost entirely on animal exploitation for subsistence, such as the patriarchal and highly aggressive nomadic pastoralists of the Eurasian steppe. They rampaged across the continent for centuries in search of the fresh grazing land and water needed to sustain enormous numbers of captive, exploited animals. Invasions led by such murderous men as Attila the Hun and Genghis Khan destroyed countless communities and entire societies; people not murdered by nomadic warriors or forced into slavery died from deadly zoonotic diseases such as smallpox, which had developed from the crowding together of large numbers of other animals. Sexual violence against women became a standard military practice, and countless women were enslaved by elite warriors. Rulers of autocratic empires—empires made possible only by the exploitation of animals as laborers, rations, and instruments of war—invaded weaker societies while battling each other for supremacy. Eurasian customs and institutions, debauched by incessant and widespread violence that was both promoted and enabled by animal oppression, were spread through imperialism and soon overwhelmed the rest of the world.

Using horses as instruments of war and the salted flesh of other animals as rations, aggressive European elites dispatched their minions to ravage the Earth in search of wealth—much of which was in the form of the skins, hair, body fat, and tusks of other animals and the land and water needed to expand profitable ranching operations. Countless indigenous people in the Americas, Africa, Australia, and other regions were murdered, enslaved, or displaced while others perished from the zoonotic disease brought by the invaders. The destructive invasions relied on state power, and the carnage was rationalized by the use of racism, sexism, speciesism, and other reprehensible ideologies. The resulting ill-gotten wealth allowed the rise of capitalism, a system birthed and continually nourished by the bloody, entangled oppression of the great mass of humans and other animals.

The predacious nature of human society at the start of the twentieth century would have been quite recognizable to Genghis Khan. Adhering to patriarchal and aggressive worldviews cultivated by centuries of violence linked to the oppression of other animals, elites in powerful capitalist nations conscripted millions of people to slaughter each other in wars over resources and markets. While horses no longer were indispensable for warfare after World War I, the flesh of other animals continued to be viewed as essential rations for "fighting men."

By the mid-twentieth century, the expansion of the oppression of other animals as food through the Animal Industrial Complex (AIC), and the convergence and growth of the Military Industrial Complex (MIC) began to generate enormous profits. The MIC and the AIC became mutually reinforcing systems of domination—continuing the inextricable link between the oppression of other animals and human violence that plagued the history of the world.

For example, financial and military support and intervention provided by the MIC has been used to expropriate enormous areas of land in Latin America for ranching and feed-grain operations and to secure the blood-stained oil on which the AIC remains so dependent. And the AIC, broadly defined, has provided military forces with publicly subsidized rations of animal flesh and endless supplies of other animals for use in military experiments. It supports continued recreational hunting and individual access to deadly weaponry, which complement the agenda of the vast armaments industry.

Now in the twenty-first century, as the destructive trajectory of capitalism is leading to hyper-predatory practices, the rolling back of modest social reforms, and the normalization of state surveillance and repression, the AIC is striving to profitably double the consumption of animal products globally by midcentury. To that end, dwindling vital resources such as fresh water, topsoil, and fossil fuel, all crucial for supporting a growing world human population, are being massively squandered. Moreover, raising other animals for food is responsible for as much as

51 percent of anthropic greenhouse gas emissions. Global warming already is producing violent storms, floods, severe droughts, wildfires, and record temperatures, all of which reduce harvests and make future food shortages all but certain. While hedge funds, global corporations, and other investors in the AIC are partaking in land grabs, appropriating tens of millions of acres in Africa and Latin America for future ranching and feed-grain ventures, the MIC and entrenched "national security" advisors are planning a military response to a future of scarce resources, food shortages, and global violence.

Forestalling such a calamitous future will require a greater awareness of the historically destructive—and future-threatening—nature of the entangled oppression of humans and other animals. The growing field of Critical Animal Studies (CAS) stands as the only area of study that promotes scholarly examination of entangled oppression of humans and other animals; places this investigation in the context of historical and social structural forces; recognizes the role of capitalism in promoting systemic oppression of all types; and proposes strategies for purposeful action. This highly important book, and the works of CAS scholars and activists to come, will be essential reading for social justice advocates of all stripes and for concerned people everywhere. It is only through the coordinated efforts of everyone throughout the world who is opposed to oppression in any form that capitalism, the AIC, the MIC, and all profit-driven systems of domination can be transcended and a more socially just, sustainable, and peaceful future can develop.

~ PREFACE ~

by
Ronnie Lee

Congratulations to Anthony, John, Kim, and Atsuko for producing this excellent work and to all the other outstanding contributors, too.

My involvement in the animal liberation movement has been a long one, more than 40 years to date, and I have experienced much in that time. I think it is vitally important that we learn from our experiences of life and of human behaviour and I have tried to do that, in a continuous quest to become a better advocate for animal liberation. After becoming a vegetarian at the age of nineteen and a vegan two years later, I turned very quickly to direct action, first with the hunt saboteurs and then with the Animal Liberation Front (ALF), as a founder member, which resulted in me spending a total of about nine years in prison for "crimes" against the industries of animal abuse.

On release from my third prison sentence in 1992, I embarked on a campaign of public education, setting up street stalls, often several times a week, to educate people to go vegan and oppose all the various forms of animal persecution. Five years later, my wife, Louise, founded a national campaign against the greyhound racing industry and I became more and more involved with this as it attracted increasing interest and support.

In 2011 the administration of the greyhound campaign was taken on by others, leaving me free to become much more involved in vegan outreach, which I had wanted to do for quite some time. I now help run both a county and a local vegan outreach group and was recently one of the founders of the Encouraging Vegan Education network, which exists to help with the setting up and effective operation of vegan outreach groups. I am also an active member of the Green Party, both locally and nationally, where I am involved in a group that works to improve the party's animal protection policies.

Although it is my belief that ALF actions have contributed significantly to a huge reduction in the fur trade and a big decline in animal experiments here in the UK, I now have doubts as to the value of this type of activity in terms of bringing about widespread animal liberation.

For a start, if direct action was ever to reach a scale or an intensity these days where it posed a real threat to the most powerful animal abuse industries, the state would move very quickly to crush those groups and individuals involved—and this is provided only if enough individuals became involved to bring direct action to such a high level, which I feel is extremely unlikely given the intrinsic passivity of most people, including those who are opposed to animal abuse.

Therefore, the only way in which widespread animal liberation, or anything approaching it, can be achieved, is by changing the behaviour of ordinary people towards animals. This means first, vegan education, to attempt to alter the attitudes of a very large percentage of the population, and, second, legislation, to force those who refuse to change to comply. Hence my involvement both in vegan outreach and political campaigning.

My early years in the struggle for animal liberation were spent with a movement that did not engage with the public, but sought to bypass them in its direct war against animal abusers. I now recognise the limitations of this approach, as engagement with ordinary people counts for everything if we are to radically change their attitudes towards other animals. And engagement with ordinary people also means engagement in the struggle for a fair and just society for human beings, as well as for other animals. This is, of course, the moral thing to do in any event, but it is also essential for the achievement of animal liberation, because our movement cannot bring in a political regime sympathetic to the cause of the oppressed on its own, but only in conjunction with other groups that are campaigning against oppression. Public education can take many forms: street stalls, stalls at community events, free food fairs, film shows, talks at schools and colleges, letters in local newspapers, and so on, and it's important that local vegan outreach groups are involved in all of these. Campaigning to change the existing education system is also important so that we can bring about a situation where students are no longer taught vivisection and farming practices that result in the suffering and slaughter of animals.

Local vegan outreach groups should, in my view, give support to and make allegiances with other local groups campaigning against discrimination and oppression. For instance, the local group I help to run recently took part in a Gay Pride march, and we are involved with our local Green Party and other groups in campaigns to protect the environment, against racism, and in opposition to government and local authority cuts that would harm vulnerable people.

We in the animal liberation movement also need to show more love, care, and respect for one another and to try to find compromise and understanding in those few small areas where we might not all agree on everything. There have been far too many instances of vegans tearing one another's throats out over what amounts to only minor differences of opinion in the overall scheme of things, and this causes deep wounds that are tremendously damaging to our movement.

Finally, please remember that it is not enough just to read this book, because no matter how eloquent the words contained in it or how persuasive the arguments, these things amount to very little unless they result in an increase in our efforts to get out in the world and to campaign and educate for animal liberation.

ACKNOWLEDGMENTS

We are honored and excited to publish the first book on the foundational principles of Critical Animal Studies (CAS), which lays out the history and theory of this important field. We hope this book aids in the growth of CAS to become a truly global academic-activist resistance force against all forms of oppression, especially speciesism. We first and foremost thank the Earth for allowing us a home with so much beauty. We would next like to thank our families. Thank you to everyone at Peter Lang, especially Chris Myers, Stephen Mazur, Sophie Appel, and Bernadette Shade, for all their hard work and for believing in this project. We also would like to thank Shirley Steinberg, the Series Editor of Counterpoints: Studies in the Postmodern Theory of Education, who believed in this project and wanted to publish this book in her series. We are so grateful for the passionate collaboration and outstanding, radical work of each of the contributors to this collection. Finally, we thank those who reviewed this book: Jason Del Gandio, David Gabbard, Julie Andrzejewski, Dan Featherston, Piers Beirne, Leslie James Pickering, Erin Marcus, and Jessica Ison.

INTRODUCTION

The Emergence of Critical Animal Studies

The Rise of Intersectional Animal Liberation

Anthony J. Nocella II, John Sorenson,
Kim Socha, and Atsuko Matsuoka

Great social movements arise from compelling ideas and theories. Sociopolitical action arises from those moments when one or one thousand individuals put theory into practice. The animal liberation, advocacy, and rights movements have emerged out of ideas, theories, and actions based upon the seemingly simple, but profoundly radical, premise that nonhuman animals are subjects with agency, not objects to be used as humans see fit. Today, the movement's foundational theories and ideas are being expanded, challenged, and enmeshed with those of other movements and struggles. Critical Animal Studies (CAS) springs from this history.

Although it has much deeper roots, the modern animal advocacy movement is often seen as a development of the 1970s, following publication of utilitarian philosopher Peter Singer's seminal monograph *Animal Liberation*. Singer compared the animal rights movement to Black, gay and women's liberation movements. As Singer (1975) acknowledged, virtually all of the key arguments in *Animal Liberation* had been stated almost a century before in Henry Salt's classic work *Animals' Rights Considered in Relation to Moral Progress* (1894). Salt was a founder of the Humanitarian League, created in 1891 in England to create a broad coalition among radical thinkers who espoused not only animal rights but socialist alternatives to industrial capitalism, prison and education reform, and other progressive causes. Despite this important historical precedent for intersectionality, animal activists' concerns often remained disconnected from other social justice movements. There are two reasons for this. First, many animal advocates focused on nonhumans because it seemed that these concerns were overlooked while so many groups challenged various forms of human oppression. Second, other social justice movements were affected by speciesism prejudice and scorned concern for nonhumans as a waste of time and resources that would be better used to help humanity. Of course, there were exceptions to this dichotomy, as many animal activists supported other social struggles such as the women's rights and antiwar movements of the late 1960s–early 1970s in the West.

Nevertheless, while the animal rights movement was progressive in seeking liberation for other animals as well as humans, some of the movement's assumptions, campaigns, and rhetoric were flawed by unintended and unconscious ableism, classism, racism, and sexism (as were those of other social movements). One example would be vegetarian or vegan advocacy that ignores those without ready access to healthy diets, especially those living in poverty-stricken areas where fast food restaurants and convenience stores are the only places to obtain food. While veganism does provide a moral baseline for the animal rights movement, it is important to recognize the structural conditions that make this more challenging for some groups. Of course, the most well-known examples of failure to recognize the complexity of these issues are seen in some of the campaigns by People for the Ethical Treatment of Animals, where women's bodies and slavery, genocide, and Holocaust rhetoric are used to encourage concern for other animals. These analogies are not invalid but must be used carefully. Sexism and misogyny in the animal rights movement are particularly troubling given that women have played major roles historically and still make up the majority of the movement as organizers, fundraisers, and "street-level" volunteers (see Adams, 1990; Gaarder, 2011). Nevertheless, as is the case with other social movements, major national organizations are run by men and the theoretical "voice" of the movement is still dominated by men.

These sorts of contradictions have affected the animal rights movement because of a flawed analysis that fails to see these forms of oppression as fundamentally entangled (Nibert, 2002). Recognizing the intersectionality of oppression is fundamental to a CAS approach. This book continues this project of seeking the connections among oppressions by encouraging the global social justice movement to be more inclusive by incorporating nonhuman animal issues. Animal advocates do not need to keep "creating" a movement. Rather, we need to renew and expand the principles that motivated Henry Salt and other members of the Humanitarian League and to join an increasingly global chorus that challenges capitalism, racism, heteronormativity, ableism, sexism, ageism, classism, and so forth. Of course, it is not simply the case that animal activists have been oblivious to other social and political struggles: those engaged in these other struggles must challenge their own speciesism and their willingness to overlook or benefit from the oppression of other animals (Sorenson, 2011).

A *Very* Brief Historical Overview of Animal Advocacy

Although the animal rights movement is often regarded as a modern development, the philosophical, moral, and ethical foundation of animal advocacy can be traced back to the great Eastern religions of Jainism, Buddhism, and Hinduism, along with numerous early Western philosophers such as Pythagoras (ca. 552–496 BCE), Hesiod (eighth century BCE), and Draco (621 BCE), each calling for the protection of nonhuman animals in some manifestation.

These early religious thinkers and philosophers played a major role in establishing the fundamentals of our ethics and morality, including questions of what we as humans owe to nonhuman animals. Concern for animals has been an undercurrent in various forms of religious thought, finding expression in Christian works such as Humphrey Primatt's 1776 book *A Dissertation on the Duty of Mercy and Sin of Cruelty to Brute Animals*. In some Eastern religions, saving the lives of sentient beings constitutes the highest form of virtue. Vegetarianism is an important concept not only for these religions but also among some Christian groups such as Seventh Day Adventists. The Vegetarian Society, formed in England in 1874, developed among members of the Bible Christian Church founded by William Cowherd in the early nineteenth century. Such concerns have continued right up to the present and some contemporary authors have made religious arguments for improving our treatment of animals (Linzey, 2000; Scully, 2003).

Despite these tendencies, religious thought is dominated by anthropocentric views that legitimize human domination of other animals. The most notorious is the concept of dominion stated in the Christian Bible and usually interpreted as a supernatural authorization for exploitation. Of the monotheistic powerhouse that is Christianity, Dunayer (2004) bluntly states: "Extremely human-centered and hierarchical, Christian doctrine is incompatible with animal equality" (p. 11). Even those religions that are more putatively "animal friendly," such as Buddhism and Hinduism, largely argue for kindness to animals as a pathway to human enlightenment. As Sharma (2013) acknowledges of the Hindu-Buddhist philosophy with which she grew up: "Human actions had karmic consequences; by inflicting pain and suffering upon other beings, we would ensure reciprocity . . . blocking ourselves from a higher consciousness (p. 158). While she states this as a positive aspect of Eastern religions, one can also see that while kindness to nonhumans has been suggested in world religions, it is most often done upon the premise that such behavior will have spiritual benefits. There is not a single religion that argues for animal rights, liberation, or advocacy upon the supposition that humans and nonhumans are allied. Thus, Socha (2012) argues that even where religious arguments do endorse animal rights, they fail to "shak[e] off the assumption of human divinity and species-specific natural rights" (p. 199).

Still, while the foundation of animal advocacy is ancient and grounded in religious dogma to some extent and has remained a persistent theme in Western philosophy (Preece, 2005, 2008), the actual movement per se dates only to the early 1800s, with specific cruelty laws dating back to the mid-1600s. The movement began to take formal shape in 1824 with the founding of the Society for the Prevention of Cruelty to Animals (SPCA) in England. While some of these activists supported welfare reforms in the treatment of animals, others such as Lewis Gompertz outlined a rights-based approach in his 1824 book *Moral Inquiries on the Situation of Man and of Beasts*. The animal advocacy movement asks that nonhuman animals be respected and free from cruelty and exploitation of any kind (Regan, 1983; Singer, 1975). To varying degrees, this profound concept of providing rights, protection, and even liberation to all sentient beings has been supported by many peacemakers including Mahatma Gandhi, Anna Kingsford, Henry David Thoreau, Albert Einstein, and Leo Tolstoy.

In sum, the "animal question" has been asked, in different ways, for quite a long time. Therefore, it is not surprising that in recent decades, the movement has developed not one but several fields of study that argue from different intellectual vantage points for the protection and/or liberation of nonhumans. These fields include Human-Animal Studies (HAS), established by the Animals and Society Institute; green criminology (Beirne & South, 2007); ecopedagogy (Kahn, 2010); humane education, championed by the Institute for Humane Education; and CAS, advanced globally by the Institute for Critical Animal Studies (ICAS).

The Emergence of Critical Animal Studies

As social movements develop, some activists seek to create a change in consciousness by working in the classroom. For example, the women's liberation struggle created women's studies, the Black liberation struggle created African and Black studies, and the environmental movement created environmental studies as both programs and academic departments. Similarly, CAS, rooted in critical theory, anarchism, ecopedagogy, and social justice, argues for an interdisciplinary and multidisciplinary intersectional and multi-movement approach for a total liberation field of study, encouraging specialized departments, degrees, and programs. Consequently, CAS and scholar-activists within CAS tend to find it difficult to work in the traditional rigid disciplinary academic structure because the field strives to break down individualism, competition, and walls within higher education that limit education, innovation, and discovery.

One group that sought to further these objectives was the Center on Animal Liberation Affairs (CALA), cofounded in 2001 by Anthony J. Nocella II and Steve Best; this was renamed ICAS in 2006. CALA, now ICAS, was founded post–September 11, 2001, to obtain creditability for animal and Earth liberation activists stigmatized as terrorists, which Nocella terms "terrorization" (Nocella II, 2013). As explained on ICAS's website:

> The term Critical Animal Studies (CAS) emerged out of a great deal of dialogue by many animal rights/liberation academics and activists around the world in 2006 and 2007 facilitated by Anthony J. Nocella II, Steve Best, Richard Kahn of ICAS, and John Sorenson, a sociology professor at Brock University who founded the first Critical Animal Studies minor and concentration. (n.d.)

At Brock University, the academic concentration in CAS was inspired by and developed in association with a local grassroots activist group, Niagara Action for Animals, which promotes animal advocacy through education and community outreach. CAS was integrated into the Department of Sociology's focus on possibilities for progressive social change and its attention to political economy, political ecology, critical race theory, post-colonial theory, queer paradigms, and critical criminology. CAS also became a focus area for graduate students in Brock's Critical Sociology and Social Justice and Equity Studies programs. Brock students and faculty have continued to work with local activists and to support animal advocacy. While CAS developed independently at Brock and at ICAS, its Canadian and American proponents realized that collaborative efforts would be productive and have engaged in a number of joint conferences that have attracted international scholarly participation.

As Sorenson (2010) notes, CAS draws on the essentially emancipatory character of the animal rights movement:

> Mobilization for animal rights is a serious social justice movement, sharing fundamental elements of other progressive social movements: a sense of compassion and fairness, a focus on power relations and a critique of domination, inequality and hierarchy, along with efforts to alleviate conditions of exploitation. (p. 16)

CAS developed to challenge two specific fields of theory: (1) Animal Studies (AS), rooted in vivisection and animal testing in the hard sciences and (2) HAS, which reinforces the socially constituted human-animal binary through which detached scholars look at animals as objects without agency that exist to be theoretically studied and examined. (In fairness, not all AS and HAS scholars agree with this characterization, though we argue that an overview of such scholarship renders the assessment self-evident.) Scholars working in these fields do not explicitly challenge the exploitation of other animals and may collaborate in forums and conferences with vivisectors and others who directly harm animals. Further, AS and HAS scholars lack a well-developed sense of holistic social justice (as do many in the animal advocacy movement). Further, some even promote injustice by being part of oppressive organizations, corporations, cultural traditions, and personal practices. Most scholars in these fields speak about animals not as individuals but as objects, with nary a mention of the torture and murder inflicted upon nonhumans by the billions each year.

To quote Margo DeMello, Human-Animal Studies Program Director with the Animals and Society Institute and author of *Animals and Society: An Introduction to Human-Animal Studies*, the field promotes the "study of the interactions and relationships between human and nonhuman animals" (2012, p. 5). In contrast, DeMello defines CAS as an "academic field of study dedicated to the abolition of animal exploitation, oppression, and domination" (p. 5). In the field of HAS, there are a number of centers, including the New Zealand Centre for Human-Animal Studies and the Finnish Society for Human-Animal Studies. DeMello defines AS as "generally used, at least in the natural sciences, to refer to the scientific study of, or medical use of, nonhuman animals, as in medical research. In the humanities, it is the preferred term for what the social sciences calls HAS" (p. 5). Humanities scholars such as postmodernists use the term "animal studies" rather than "human-animal studies" or "critical animal studies" because they are not interested in analysis or research that investigates the oppression, exploitation, or liberation of nonhuman animals; they do not agitate for the end of that subjugation. Such perspectives render the animal unreal and important only insofar as what they and their interactions say about the human animal. Some scholars working in this area feel no ethical or political commitment to other animals but regard our relationships with them merely as interesting problems of academic exploration. Others affect a radical pose but trade in jargon-filled, elitist theories characteristic of post-humanist approaches.

Post-humanism, influenced by postmodernism and continental philosophy, generally lacks any discussion about activism and liberation. Scholars such as Donna Haraway are characteristic of this field, dealing in elaborate wordplay but disdaining activism on behalf of other animals while continuing to engage in their exploitation (Weisberg, 2009). New York University, Wesleyan University, and Michigan State University offer AS degrees, departments, and centers in the sciences. One could argue that those in the humanities self-relating to AS or post-humanism are theoretical vivisectors while AS in the sciences are physical vivisectors; neither are engaged with real-world theory and praxis focused on the liberation or oppression of nonhuman animals. While science-based vivisectors test and conduct hands-on research on nonhuman animals such as pigs, monkeys, rabbits, dogs, and cats, theoretical vivisectors detach themselves by using an apolitical objectivist methodology when discussing the concept and status of nonhuman animals. CAS is not only opposed to the physical exploitation, torture, and murder of nonhuman animals by scientists, but it also is strongly opposed to the theoretical analytical dissection of nonhuman animals, which is not concerned with their oppression.

A recent addition to scholarship concerned with the animal question is McCance's (2013) misleadingly titled *Critical Animal Studies: An Introduction*. While an interesting read for academics, McCance erroneously credits 1970s Oxford scholars Roslind Godlovitch, Stanley Godlovitch, and John Harris as founding CAS—a term they never used but that McCance attributes to them—by influencing a young scholar named Peter Singer through their publication of *Animals, Men, and Morals* (1972). Early in the text, McCance asserts that most "contributors to critical animal studies would agree that . . . modern Western ways of knowing nonhuman animals, inseparable from violent techniques practiced on them, have turned animals into 'stone,' that is, into inert objects" (p. 2). This assessment is valid; however, being critical of human use of nonhuman animals does not a CAS scholar-activist make. Our book clarifies this point.

To illustrate, McCance allies Jacques Derrida within her exploration of CAS because he critically questions human dominion over nonhumans in *The Animal That Therefore I Am* (2008, p. 65). Consequently, CAS scholars have often cited Derrida, just as they might cite Karl Marx, in their exploration of the animal condition. However, this does not make Derrida or Marx CAS scholars, while McCance tacitly infers that this is the case for Derrida. While CAS scholars in the vein of ICAS try—admittedly with varying degrees of success—to write tracts that are accessible to the activist as well as the academic, McCance has no such agenda. An unintentional irony of *Critical Animal Studies: An Introduction* is that it simultaneously *simplifies* what it means to be critical, which goes beyond mere theoretical posturing, while relying on *complex*, esoteric, jargon-laden rhetoric that would surely be off-putting to anyone not firmly situated in the Ivory Tower. McCance clearly states that CAS is "properly philosophical" (p. 122) with nary a mention of activism, only *one* mention of veganism as a moral baseline, and absolutely no acknowledgment of the existence of CAS as a field that claims its own institute overflowing with intersectional scholarship, conferences, and activism.

In her introduction, McCance gives a three-pronged explanation of how she defines the term "critical," replete with references to Greek and Latin vernacular roots (pp. 4–5). But again, the book as a whole leaves out the most important element of being critical: to use criticism to enact change as activists, advocates, radicals, and street-level scholars, to be critical in the pedestrian sense of criticizing—calling out—tyrannical norms. In sum, *Critical Animal Studies: An Introduction* is decidedly apolitical, which is the antithesis of CAS. From another perspective, McCance's book is quite interesting, and we hope that it influences academics to investigate CAS proper from the scholar-activists at ICAS. And lest one think this overview of McCance's book is an example of sour grapes for our being left out of her history, that is not the case. *Critical Animal Studies: An Introduction* is a direct example of the fears early ICAS founders held: that CAS, once part of the academic industrial complex, would have the radicalism and praxis written out of it, that it would become another pathway from which one can simply obtain tenure; all the while, nonhumans are tortured and slaughtered by the billions. Abstruse rhetoric will not expose these grave injustices; in fact, it may only succeed in further hiding it.

In contrast to these approaches, CAS promotes justice for all animals and challenges the socially constructed dominant relationship between humans and nonhuman animals. To confront this dominion, CAS argues against all systems of domination such as capitalism, standardization, and normalcy. ICAS defines CAS as "rooted in animal liberation. CAS is a radical, interdisciplinary field dedicated to establishing a holistic total liberation movement for humans, nonhuman animals, and the Earth. CAS is engaged in an intersectional, theory-to-action politics, in solidarity with movements to abolish all systems of domination" (n.d.). Best (2009) writes, "CAS seeks to abolish not only animal exploitation, but also the exploitation of humans and the natural world" (p. 44). Best (2007) explains:

> As a *critical* animal studies, however, we seek to avoid the scholasticism, jargon-laden language, apolitical pretense, and theory-for-theory's sake style and mentality that infects so much academic writing, including the field of animal studies. A concept we have coined for an approach we hope to spread, CAS takes shape in awareness of historically-constructed ideologies and systems of power and domination in which humans have oppressed and exploited animals. Rejecting the masks of objectivity and neutrality that in fact hide covert commitments and by default support systems of oppression, CAS is informed by a normative commitment—such as grounded in ethology, ecology, and the moral philosophy of animal rights to animal liberation. CAS has a broad and holistic understanding of hierarchical power systems (e.g., racism, sexism, classism, and speciesism) and their intricate interrelationships, explores the systemic destructive effects of capitalism on all life and the earth, and views animal liberation and human liberation as inseparably interrelated projects. Most generally, CAS uses theory as a means to the end of illuminating and eliminating domination. (p. 3)

Helena Pedersen (2010), in *Animals in Schools: Processes and Strategies in Human-Animal Education*, the first book that explicitly discusses CAS, writes a concise definition of the field: "Critical animal studies is a field of research dealing with issues related to the exploitation and liberation of animals; the inclusion of animals in a broader emancipatory struggle; speciesism; and the principles and practices of animal advocacy, animal protection, and human-related policies" (p. 2). Another apt definition is offered by Best (2009):

> CAS emerges in conditions in which positivism is still a prevalent ideology in academia, and sophisticated sociological critiques of positivism replicate its separation of theory from values and practice. Apolitical values reign, as even "radicals" vie for respectability within the rules and logic of academia, and as the professionalization of discourse has transformed language from a potential medium of clarity into an opaque tool of obfuscation that ultimately reinforces systems of power. (p. 39)

Against positivism, CAS argues for an engaged critical praxis (i.e., theory and action interwoven) that promotes listening to, following, and working with the oppressed. CAS argues against the notion that nonhuman animals do not have voices while agitating against their domination because those voices are not human. CAS stresses that nonhuman animals do have agency, thus arguing for a nonhuman animal standpoint (Adams & Donovan, 1999; Best, 2009; Donovan, 2006; Kahn, 2010), perhaps not one that can be fully articulated or understood by humans, but one that must be respected, nevertheless. Moreover, CAS does not only argue for a nonhuman animal advocacy movement but, like the Humanitarian League, instead promotes a holistic social justice struggle that includes and respects nonhuman animals. This is precisely the approach undertaken in the Critical Animal Studies Concentration at Brock University. Therefore, CAS is a struggle that conterminously argues and fights for the liberation of all oppressed groups. Indeed, it can properly be seen as an anti-oppression movement.

In 2007, Steven Best, Anthony J. Nocella II, Richard Kahn, Carol Gigliotti, and Lisa Kemmerer developed "The Ten Principles of Critical Animal Studies," which follow here:

1. Pursues interdisciplinary collaborative writing and research in a rich and comprehensive manner that includes perspectives typically ignored by animal studies such as political economy.

2. Rejects pseudo-objective academic analysis by explicitly clarifying its normative values and political commitments, such that there are no positivist illusions whatsoever that theory is disinterested or writing and research is nonpolitical. To support experiential understanding and subjectivity.

3. Eschews narrow academic viewpoints and the debilitating theory-for-theory's sake position in order to link theory to practice, analysis to politics, and the academy to the community.

4. Advances a holistic understanding of the commonality of oppressions, such that speciesism, sexism, racism, ableism, statism, classism, militarism and other hierarchical ideologies and institutions are viewed as parts of a larger, interlocking, global system of domination.

5. Rejects apolitical, conservative, and liberal positions in order to advance an anti-capitalist, and, more generally, a radical anti-hierarchical politics. This orientation seeks to dismantle all structures of exploitation, domination, oppression, torture, killing, and power in favor of decentralizing and democratizing society at all levels and on a global basis.

6. Rejects reformist, single-issue, nation-based, legislative, strictly animal interest politics in favor of alliance politics and solidarity with other struggles against oppression and hierarchy.

7. Champions a politics of total liberation which grasps the need for, and the inseparability of, human, nonhuman animal, and Earth liberation and freedom for all in one comprehensive, though diverse, struggle; to quote Martin Luther King Jr.: *"Injustice anywhere is a threat to justice everywhere."*

8. Deconstructs and reconstructs the socially constructed binary oppositions between human and nonhuman animals, a move basic to mainstream animal studies, but also looks to illuminate related dichotomies between culture and nature, civilization and wilderness and other dominator hierarchies to emphasize the historical limits placed upon humanity, nonhuman animals, cultural/political norms, and the liberation of nature as part of a transformative project that seeks to transcend these limits towards greater freedom, peace, and ecological harmony.

9. Openly supports and examines controversial radical politics and strategies used in all kinds of social justice movements, such as those that involve economic sabotage from boycotts to direct action toward the goal of peace.

10. Seeks to create openings for constructive critical dialogue on issues relevant to Critical Animal Studies across a wide range of academic groups; citizens and grassroots activists; the staffs of policy and social service organizations; and people in private, public, and non-profit sectors. Through—and only through—new paradigms of ecopedagogy, bridge-building with other social movements, and a solidarity-based alliance politics, it is possible to build the new forms of consciousness, knowledge, and social institutions that are necessary to dissolve the hierarchical society that has enslaved this planet for the last ten thousand years (pp. 4–5).

CAS has two further goals beyond those ten principles within higher education: (1) to abolish nonhuman animal oppression, exploitation, and murder on college and university campuses, and (2) to provide space and place for the advocacy of all oppressed groups including nonhuman animals. Richard Twine, a highly significant foundational CAS scholar who helped develop ICAS Europe and authored the first book fully dedicated to CAS, *Animals as Biotechnology: Ethics, Sustainability and Critical Animal Studies*, writes, "CAS scholars stress ethical veganism and may work with those civil society groups or individuals who campaign against animal exploitation" (p. 8). Having learned from so many other movements that have taken political struggle from the streets and into the academy, ICAS wants to stress forms of critical theory that promote engaged activist scholarship in the community. ICAS argues for clear, direct, simple principles that are less likely to be misconstrued or misinterpreted, rather than drawing out a lengthy and complex set of theoretical concepts accessible only to academics well-versed in obscure argot (e.g., see McCance, 2013). "The Ten Principles of Critical Animal Studies" were designed so activists in the community would be willing to reprint them in books, articles, 'zines, and flyers and repost them on their blogs and websites.

To further understand the CAS sense of history, we should add that its proponents theoretically support the Animal Liberation Front's (ALF) anarchic-style philosophy, tactics, strategies, and decentralized nonhierarchical organizational structure. The ALF grew out of the hunt saboteurs movement, founded in 1964 by John Prestidge, to stop the slaughter of wildlife in England. In 1972, Ronnie Lee and others created Band of Mercy to take more direct action against hunting. They took their name from the nineteenth-century youth association within the RSPCA that was created by antislavery activist Catherine Smithies. In 1973, the modern Band of Mercy took direct action against the vivisection industry, destroying buildings and rescuing animals; they also shut down the seal hunt in Norfolk and a Wiltshire farm breeding guinea pigs for experimentation. In 1974, Lee and Cliff Goodman were arrested at Oxford Laboratory in Bicester and sentenced to prison. However, public opinion and media coverage was sympathetic both to their efforts to save animals from torture and death and to Lee's prison hunger strike, intended to draw attention to the plight of animals and to the government's biological and chemical warfare experiments. Paroled after a year, Lee renewed his efforts to save animals by creating the Animal Liberation Front in 1976. Recognizing that considerable public support existed for activists' compassionate efforts, the animal exploitation industries directed their enormous resources into a propaganda campaign that would transform efforts to save animals from harm into "terrorism." By 2005, the Federal Bureau of Investigation (FBI) had labeled the ALF as a top domestic terrorist threat in the United States. However, the ALF is not an organization but a set of ideas grounded in the following principles:

- To inflict economic damage on those who profit from the misery and exploitation of animals.
- To liberate animals from places of abuse, i.e., laboratories, factory farms, fur farms, etc., and place them in good homes where they may live out their natural lives, free from suffering.
- To reveal the horror and atrocities committed against animals behind locked doors, by performing nonviolent direct actions and liberations.

- To take all necessary precautions against harming any animal, human and non-human.

- Any group of people who are vegetarians or vegans and who carry out actions according to ALF guidelines have the right to regard themselves as part of the ALF (Best & Nocella II, 2004, p. 8).

With these guidelines in place, Best (2009) explains their application to the rise of an academic-activist field of study:

> CAS is unique in its defense of direct action tactics, its willingness to engage and debate controversial issues such as anti-capitalism, academic repression, and the use of sabotage as a resistance tactic; its emphasis on the need for total liberation stressing the commonalities binding various oppressed groups; and the importance of learning from and with activists. (p. 13)

CAS demands that all nonviolent tactics are considered as a possibility for successful social change. ALF activists have played an important role in showing the public the tremendously abusive conditions under which nonhuman animals are forced to live out their abbreviated lives, while also physically liberating those beings from a life of torture and violent murder. CAS, beyond promoting total liberation, also supports alternatives to dominant and oppressive systems such as the current criminal justice system that has stigmatized the ALF through repressive laws such as the Animal Enterprise Terrorism Act (AETA) in the United States. In contrast, we see the ALF as a compassionate "organization," for lack of a better term, that has given the world its first images of animal cruelty in laboratories, factory farms, fur farms, and other places where animal torture occurs. They have also offered the world images of liberated nonhuman animals, joyously acting more in accordance with their natures. Because CAS does not support the prison industrial complex, its proponents do not demand the incarceration of animal abusers. Rather, CAS seeks avenues for transformative justice, a non-punitive justice process that addresses oppression, interpersonal injustices, and accountability for wrongs committed (Davis, 2003; Nocella II, 2012).

Since its inception, the ALF has been controversial within the animal advocacy movement. In the post–September 11 landscape, the Human Society of the United States (HSUS) launched a public call for anyone knowing about any ALF activity to give information to law enforcement. Rather than focus on the end of oppression of nonhuman animals and social justice, groups and individuals in the animal advocacy movement, since the founding of the ALF, have spent their time speaking out against these freedom fighters. So often, the worst opponents are those in one's own social movement. If everyone in the movement agreed that a diversity of tactics will win, rather than believing that one tactic will, there would be far fewer divisive conflicts and more successful campaigns.

The Implementation of Critical Animal Studies

CAS argues for solidarity and alliance with human activists and academics with nonhumans for total liberation to end all oppression, domination, and authoritarianism, not only in a theoretical way by simply writing about alliance politics but also by directly organizing and participating in other movements beyond nonhuman animal liberation. This includes supporting locally grown, organic, fair-trade veganism. As Sorenson (2010) points out:

> Veganism is not just a personal choice but a political one. It is the logical outcome of the recognition that animals are not property but individual beings who have their own interests, which should be considered. It is an ethical commitment, a symbolic gesture and a statement of principle, the rejection of hierarchy, domination and oppression, an acknowledgement of the inherent value of other beings. Veganism is expression of animal rights philosophy through the effort to reduce, as much as possible, the exploitation of animals. Becoming vegan expresses a commitment to minimize harm and avoid a diet based on misery and demonstrates compassion and concern for the well-being of others. (p. 174)

DeMello notes that ICAS has put this into practice by engaging

> in university-based activist activities such as bringing vegan food onto college campuses or working to end academic animal research . . . [whereas in contrast] there is nothing in the field of HAS that demands that researchers, instructors, or students take an advocacy or political position of any kind. (2012, pp. 17–18)

To give an example of the more politically committed and activist approach of those working in CAS, the editors of and contributors to this book have not only been engaged in activism on behalf of other animals but also have taken part in antiwar activities, helped to feed homeless people through groups such as Food Not Bombs, worked on prison abolition projects, supported LGBTQIA rights, engaged in anti-sweatshop campaigns, advocated for disability rights, and a variety of other social justice issues.

ICAS is conscious of the institutionalization of social movements when they are embraced by academia; for this reason CAS challenges imperialism, capitalism, and all other forms of authoritarian institutions in a multi-movement praxis approach. Higher education is one of these systems of domination that represses students, staff, faculty, and nonhuman animals (Nocella II, Best, & McLaren, 2010). CAS encourages all activists to be concerned about and engaged with other issues, effectively putting an end to single-issue activism. In order for systems of domination to be abolished, a total global justice activist movement must be fostered.

Furthermore, CAS today can be seen through the ideas, dialogues, and actions of members of ICAS. Since the founding of CAS in 2006, much has developed. ICAS is now active in Europe, North America, South America, Asia, Oceania, and Africa with events, annual conferences, and research committees. Moreover, ICAS, still a fully-volunteer organization, now has hundreds of members, a board of more than fifteen active scholars and activists, a newsletter, regular board meetings, three intersectional journals—*Journal for Critical Animal Studies*, *Peace Studies Journal*, and the *Green Theory and Praxis Journal*—a YouTube channel, and a blog that covers the latest news and events within the field of CAS. ICAS has also founded a Center for Scholarship that hosts workshops, provides annual awards, and manages a robust internship program. CAS has inspired many new initiatives and theories such as eco-ability (Nocella II, Bentley, & Duncan, 2012), while continuing to draw issues such as prison abolition, Black liberation, and native sovereignty into the dialogues about animal liberation.

At CAS conferences, we include panels that appear to have nothing directly to do with nonhuman animals. These panels focus on youth advocacy as presented by the Save the Kids organization, ending racism as presented by A. Breeze Harper, food justice as presented by Lauren Ornelas, and defending political prisoners such as Jalil Muntaqim, Mumia Abu-Jamal, Eric McDavid, Marie Mason, Walter Bond, Steve Murphy, Justin Solondz, Sundiata Acoli, Cuban Five, Move9, Leonard Peltier, Mutulu Shakur, and so many others. We do this because true intersectionality will be achieved not only by teaching, writing books, and giving lectures at universities but also by organizing and actively participating in struggles such as the occupy movement and those related to prison abolition, Black liberation, LGBTQIA liberation, disability liberation, youth liberation, and women's liberation, among others. Becoming part of these and other movements is critical if we are to end the oppression of human and nonhuman animals. With its goal of total liberation, CAS offers an important and valuable perspective that we encourage all readers of this book to seriously consider and then act upon.

Philosophical Structure of the Book

This book was somewhat difficult to put together but also unique, because it asked that all participants—barring those writing pre- and afterword pieces—to write in collaboration with one or more additional activist-scholar(s). Higher education gives the most credit to single-authored articles, books, and presentations. Collaborating with fellow colleagues is difficult, even impossible in some departments. Those who have spent any time in colleges and universities have heard stories of (or even engage in) intra-departmental sabotage, jealousy, and backstabbing.

Most see conflict as something to avoid, rather than as an opportunity for personal and collaborative growth; for this reason, many academics choose not to work together, as the academy fosters a competitive and individualistic environment. *This book has not been the exception to the rule.* Some initial authors had to leave the project because of over-commitments, work obligations, and personal issues. Others left because of political differences. Within these conflicts, however, arise new collaborative opportunities that will aid in the growth of CAS, total liberation, and, we hope, lasting friendships.

Organization of the Book

This book is organized into five parts. In their respective chapters, contributors address the ten principles of CAS, as delineated above. However, we have chosen not to address the principles numerically but to divide the book into parts, which open themselves up to inclusion of particular principles.

Adam Weitzenfeld and Melanie Joy open "Part I: Interdependency" by addressing Principle 8. In their chapter, "An Overview of Anthropocentrism, Humanism, and Speciesism in Critical Animal Theory," they review and critique key concepts such as speciesism, anthropocentrism, humanism, post-humanism, and human-animal dualism and examine the phenomenon of carnism to deconstruct individual and institutional levels of speciesism. They conclude by offering forms of praxis to counter the speciesist–carnist paradigm.

As discussed above, CAS takes the position that various forms of oppression such as speciesism, sexism, racism, and classism are fundamentally interconnected. Using critical feminist, critical race, environmental justice, and green criminological perspectives, Amy Fitzgerald and David Pellow address Principle 4. They begin their chapter, "Ecological Defense for Animal Liberation: A Holistic Understanding of the World," by examining dichotomies—culture-nature dichotomies, in particular—as foundations of oppression in Western societies. They argue the deconstruction of such interlocking oppressions is essential for the achievement of social justice and present the total liberation frame.

In Part II, Unity, Sarat Colling, Sean Parson, and Alessandro Arrigoni dedicate their chapter, "Until All Are Free: Total Liberation through Revolutionary Decolonization, Groundless Solidarity, and a Relationship Framework," to analysis of Principle 7. They effectively argue that "no one is free while another is oppressed" by applying Steven Best's work to various examples of subjugation. They rightly conclude Western values and society need radical restructuring to face interconnections of oppression and to bring about total liberation.

Unity is essential for making significant changes to overcome speciesism. Stephanie Jenkins and Vasile Stănescu title their chapter "One Struggle," identifying Principle 6 as the most important guiding principle, one struggle against the social injustice that affects all animals. They introduce the idea of engaged veganism as praxis to counteract commodity fetishism and to work against the interweaving oppression of multiple "-isms" to bring total global justice.

One of two articles in Part III: Critical Scholarship is "The Ivory Trap: Bridging the Gap between Activism and the Academy," by Carol L. Glasser and Arpan

Roy. By addressing Principle 3, they argue for the importance of a politics of liberation in CAS. They maintain that CAS is the field that can best promote such politics productively within academia by avoiding what they call the "ivory trap."

Related themes are taken up in "Critical Animal Studies as an Interdisciplinary Field: A Holistic Approach to Confronting Oppression," by Kim Socha and Les Mitchell, who argue that true understanding of issues of power and oppression must come from interdisciplinary collaboration in research, writing, and praxis. Drawing from their own experiences of working against rhino poaching and of developing innovative English and social studies/history/civics lesson plans for teachers, they demonstrate how Principle 1 can meaningfully manifest when put into action.

In Part IV: Radical Education, Lauren Corman and Tereza Vandrovcová dedicate "Radical Humility: Toward a More Holistic Critical Animal Studies Pedagogy" to Principle 10. They argue that pedagogy for CAS includes theory and activism, which addresses heterogeneous representations of animals' subjectivities and intersectional analysis beyond human animals. They discuss ways to help students gain new consciousness and knowledge to develop just relationships, and share teaching strategies from their own experiences.

Again drawing on their own experience as CAS scholars and activists, Lara Drew and Nik Taylor address Principle 2 in "Engaged Activist Research: Challenging Apolitical Objectivity." They propose that critical pedagogy can be used as a framework to make scholar-activist roles complementary and to develop research as resistance.

The final section, Part V: Taking It to the Streets, begins with "From the Classroom to the Slaughterhouse: Animal Liberation by Any Means Necessary," by Jennifer Grubbs and Michael Loadenthal. Based on Principle 9, the authors argue against single-issue politics and for the importance of reflexivity, collaboration, and countering neoliberalism in both activism and academia to reclaim the space for total liberation.

The final chapter, "Taking It to the Streets: Challenging Systems of Domination from Below," is dedicated to Principle 5. Richard J. White and Erika Cudworth guide us on how we can take ourselves to the streets by introducing anarchist thought that helps to fill the lacuna of liberal critiques of animal exploitation and provides the key for bottom-up strategies of animal liberation, which is, indeed, human liberation.

References

Adams, C. J. (1990). *The sexual politics of meat: A feminist-vegetarian critical theory*. New York: Continuum.

Adams, C. J., & Donovan J. (1995). *Animals & women*. Durham, NC: Duke University Press.

Animal Rights History. (n.d.). *Animal rights-humane timeline*. Retrieved on January 10, 2010, from http://www.animalrightshistory.org/animal-rights-law/law-antiquity.htm

Beirne, P., & South, N. (2007). *Issues in green criminology: Confronting harms against environments, humanity, and other animals.* Portland, OR: Willian.
Best, S. (2009). The Rise of Critical Animal Studies: Putting Theory into Action and Animal Liberation into Higher Education. *Journal for Critical Animal Studies, 7*(1), 9–52.
Best, S. (2007). Introduction. *Journal of Critical Animal Studies, 5*(1), 2–3.
Best, S., & Nocella II, A. J. (2006). *Igniting a revolution: Voices in defense of the Earth.* Oakland, CA: AK.
Best, S., & Nocella II, A. J. (2004). *Terrorists or freedom fighters?: Reflections on the liberation of animals.* New York: Lantern.
Best, S., Nocella II, A. J., Kahn, R., Gigliotti, C., & Kemmerer, L. (2007). Introducing Critical Animal Studies. *Journal of Critical Animal Studies, 5*(1), 4–5.
Davis, A. (2003). *Are prisons obsolete?* New York: Seven Stories.
DeMello, M. (2012). *Animals and society: An introduction to human-animal studies.* New York: Columbia University Press.
Derrida, J. (2008). *The animal that therefore I am.* (Marie-Louise Mallet, Ed.; David Wills, Trans.). New York: Fordham University Press.
Donovan, J. (2006). Feminism and the treatment of animals: From care to dialogue. *Signs: Journal of Women in Culture and Society, 31*(2), 305–330.
Dunayer, J. (2004). *Speciesism.* Derwood, MD: Ryce.
Gaarder, E. (2011). *Women and the animal rights movement.* New Brunswick, NJ: Rutgers University Press.
Godlovitch, S., Godlovitch, R., & Harris, J. (Eds.). (1972). *Animals, men, and morals: An enquiry into the maltreatment of non-humans.* New York: Taplinger.
Institute for Critical Animal Studies. (n.d.). *About ICAS: History.* Retrieved on July 17, 2011, from http://www.criticalanimalstudies.org/about/
Kahn, R. (2010). *Critical pedagogy, ecoliteracy, & planetary crisis: The ecopedagogy movement.* New York: Peter Lang.
Kemmerer, L., & Nocella II, A. J. (2011). *Call to compassion: Religious perspectives on animal advocacy.* New York: Lantern.
Linzey, A. (2000). *Animal theology.* Norwich: SCM.
McCance, D. (2013). *Critical animal studies: An introduction.* Albany, NY: SUNY Press.
Nibert, D. (2002). *Animal rights human rights.* Lanham, MD: Rowman & Littlefield.
Nocella II, A. J. (2013). The rise of the terrorization of dissent. In M. Nagel & A. J. Nocella II (Eds.), *The end of prisons: Reflections from the decarceration movement* (pp. 13–29). New York: Rodopi.
Nocella II, A. J. (2012). An overview of the history and theory of transformative justice. *Peace & Conflict Review, 6*(1), 1–10.
Nocella II, A. J., Bentley, J. K. C., & Duncan, J. M. (2012). *Earth, animal, and disability liberation: The rise of the eco-ability movement.* New York: Peter Lang.
Nocella II, A. J., Best, S., & McLaren, P. (2010). *Academic repression: Reflections from the academic industrial complex.* Oakland, CA: AK.
Pedersen, H. (2010). *Animals in schools. Processes and strategies in human-animal education.* West Lafayette, IN: Purdue University Press.
Preece, R. (2008). *Sins of the flesh.* Vancouver: University of British Columbia Press.
Preece, R. (2005). *Brute souls, happy beasts, and evolution.* Vancouver: University of British Columbia Press.
Regan, T. (1983). *The case for animal rights.* Los Angeles: University of California Press.
Salt, H. (1894). *Animals' rights considered in relation to moral progress.* London: Macmillan.
Scully, M. (2003). *Dominion.* New York: St. Martin's.

Sharma, V. (2013). Knowing ignorance. In K. Davis & W. Lee (Eds.), *Defiant daughters: 21 women on art, activism, animals, and the sexual politics of meat* (pp. 157–166). New York: Lantern.

Singer, P. (1975). *Animal liberation.* New York: Ecco.

Socha, K. (2012). Why I am not religious . . . and what that has to do with being vegan. In B. Lehto (Ed.), *Atheist voices of Minnesota: An anthology of personal stories* (pp. 195–204). St. Paul, MN: Freethought House.

Sorenson, J. (2011). Constructing extremists, rejecting compassion: Ideological attacks on animal advocacy from Right and Left. In J. Sanbonmatsu (Ed.), *Critical theory and animal liberation* (pp. 219–238). Lanham, MD: Rowman & Littlefield.

Sorenson, J. (2010). *About Canada: Animal rights.* Halifax: Fernwood.

Twine, R. (2010). *Animals as biotechnology: Ethics, sustainability and critical animal studies.* New York: Routledge.

Weisberg, Z. (2009). The Broken Promises of Monsters. *Journal of Critical Animal Studies, 7*(2), 22–62.

PART I

Interdependency

ONE

An Overview of Anthropocentrism, Humanism, and Speciesism in Critical Animal Theory

Adam Weitzenfeld and Melanie Joy

This chapter serves as an overview of the conceptualization of human existence as something superior and opposed to animals and animality. While previously given independent treatments, the concepts of anthropocentrism, humanism, speciesism, and carnism in this chapter will be differentiated and discussed as having mutually reinforced one another through constructing, legitimating, and reproducing a human-animal hierarchy and binary.

As shall be argued, anthropocentrism, which has narcissistically privileged humans as the center of all significance, is not an innate disposition but a historical outcome of a distorted humanism in which human freedom is founded upon the unfreedom of human and animal others. Nonetheless, the humanist aspiration to ground knowledge in reason through modern science has undermined the tenability of a human-animal binary and hierarchy, thus resulting in a critique of speciesist beliefs and institutions. Yet still, residue of anthropocentric thought is retained in the work of humanistic thinkers opposed to speciesism who take for granted the presuppositions of classical humanism.

Critical Animal Theory (CAT) scholars, including posthumanists and feminists, reevaluate the significance of dependencies, emotions, and the specificity of animal being and agency. Further, they aim to dismantle the structures of speciesism at the politico-economic, sociocultural, and psychosomatic levels of existence. Of all the ways humans are subject to speciesism, carnism—the unrecognized ideology that legitimates the killability and edibility of animal others—is arguably the deepest, most pervasive and catastrophic in modern Western cultures. Vegan praxis is one means of embodying CAT and challenging the hegemony of speciesist institutions and anthropocentrist ideology that keep the human-animal binary and hierarchy alive.

Anthropocentrism, Humanism, and the Human-Animal Dualism: The Anthropocentric and Anthropocentrism

> Once upon a time, in some out of the way corner of that universe which is dispersed into numberless twinkling solar systems, there was a star upon which clever beasts invented knowing. That was the most arrogant and mendacious minute of "world history," but nevertheless, it was only a minute . . . [Humans regard their intellect] so solemnly—as though the world's axis turned within it. But if we could communicate with the gnat, we would learn that he likewise flies through the air with the same solemnity, that he feels the flying center of the universe within himself. (Nietzsche, 2000, p. 53)

For several millennia, humans—at least those of Western cultures—have assumed a staunch anthropocentric orientation, the effect of positioning humans as the center of meaning, value, knowledge, and action. While the character of the West's anthropocentric orientation is very explicit, some degree of an anthropocentric orientation is inescapable simply by the fact that as humans, humans perceive the world within the limits of human bodies and cognition. Even if one absolutely rejects anthropocentrist ethics—in which "moral consideration is only properly granted to humans"—anthropocentric metaethics, "the view that [human] conceptions of morality are constrained to human perspectives and sensibilities," is a condition of any human moral system (DeLapp, 2008, p. 40). Anthropocentric orientations are thus not exclusive to cultures in which humans are classified as categorically distinct and superior to animal others. Many indigenous cultures, even those that celebrate human-animal hybrids and becomings, are also anthropocentric to varying degrees in privileging the value of (local) humans and the meanings and values they assign to all other animal life (Noske, 1997b).

Anthropocentrism, on the other hand, is more than the consequence of privileging humans' knowledge and values. Anthropocentrism is a belief system, an ideology of human supremacy that advocates privileging humans (and those who approximate humanity). Anthropocentrism, as an ideology, functions to maintain the centrality and priority of human existence through marginalizing and subordinating nonhuman perspectives, interests, and beings. Anthropocentrism requires that a society have a concept of humanity, assign privileged value to it, and measure all other beings by this standard. Meaning and value are partial to the idea of humanity and not partial to certain human beings over others so long as they are not "less human" (i.e., subhuman). Further, anthropocentrism may assume a variety of forms such as a human-animal dualism or continuum. A human-animal dualism posits humans over and above all other animals, radically separated into two homogenous, opposing kinds. Alternatively, a human-animal continuum hierarchically ranks humans and animal others along a scale by the degree to which they are "human," with some human capacity—usually reason— privileged as the most essential and valuable (Ingold, 1994).

Although the cultural hegemony of anthropocentric ideologies and institutions has been present for at least five thousand years—such as in creation stories and sacrificial rites whereby humans are ordained to have dominion over other creatures in the service of the divine—these stories and rites were grounded and centered in something beyond humans (i.e., deities) that were believed to have mediated and constrained human knowledge and action. Not until modernity would deities be widely regarded as antiquated justifications for humanity's rule, and humans could rule the world with no external constraints set by a nonhuman actor (Bell, 2011). Anthropocentrism, in its purest and most pervasive form, could only come into being with humanism—a belief system that defines human beings as ontologically free through a universally shared essence such as reason, and considers humans as the source of knowledge and value. Anthropocentrism is not the effect of inescapable, ahistorical constraints of human sensibilities, but rather it is a historic development born from specific institutional and philosophical traditions.

Anthropocentrist Humanism and the Human-Animal Dualism

"Humanism," a term coined in the nineteenth century, contemporarily has a variety of definitions. With care, the term can be used anachronistically to characterize ideological and cultural movements from antiquity to modernity. The first precursors of humanistic thought in Europe were Ancient Greeks such as Protagoras who famously proclaimed, "Man is the measure of all things." Humanism, however, was an unpopular belief system in Europe until interest in classical texts, pedagogy, and independent inquiry were renewed during the Italian Renaissance. During the eighteenth-century Age of Enlightenment, humanism reduced the religiosity of the Renaissance and broadened its project to the utopian ambition of universal human progress through rational inquiry (i.e., the natural and human sciences), the demystification of the natural world, and the self-authorization of the nation state (i.e., democracy).

The dominant tradition of humanist thought since the Enlightenment may be characterized as anthropocentrist humanism due to its ideological commitment to conceptualizing human being over and against animal being, and privileging human consciousness and freedom as the center, agent, and pinnacle of history and existence. The human-animal dualism and hierarchy of anthropocentrist humanism is supported by at least three premises: human exceptionalism, perfection, and dignity. First, human beings are defined by a capacity assumed to be exclusive to humans such as speech, reason, or consciousness itself. Second, human consciousness is conceptualized as an individual and autonomous entity capable of freethinking and thus also self-realization and self-determination. Third, all beings capable of self-determination possess dignity (i.e., intrinsic self-worth). Since only humans have the potential for self-determination due to their exclusive capacity for reasoning, human beings alone possess intrinsic value.

In contrast to the self- and world-forming character of human being, all nonhuman beings are regarded as merely in the world, bound by natural law. As a result, nonhumans have no dignity to violate and, thus, are owed little to no direct moral consideration. Normally, nonhuman animals deserve basic welfare, but only indirectly. Gratuitous cruelty and excessive exploitation are not wrong because of the effect they have on animals, but rather on humans (e.g., harm to the human whose companion was damaged, the development of an inhumane character, the diminishment of the utility of resources). These conclusions lead to the attitude that nonhumans are bare nature upon which to exercise human freedom, to project human values, and actualize human potential. In other words, the aimlessness of other species—in so far as they don't have aspirations that transcend and reform their existences—only achieves meaning instrumentally through human consciousness. For humans to assert their species-being upon the world, to optimize nature's utility for human interests, is not merely an option, but a historical destiny to be fulfilled (Linzey & Clarke, 1990).

The Ironies of Anthropocentrist Humanism:
The Irrational Dualism and Inhumane Hierarchy

Anthropocentrist humanism's dualism and hierarchy have "largely been seen, even by its opponents, as part of an ideology that has benefited human beings," writes Aaron Bell (2011); however, in reality, its latent contradictions "have manifested themselves in a violent and self-destructive manner, fatal both to human and nonhuman life" (p. 163). The violent manifestation of anthropocentrist humanism is due to at least two ironies. The first is anthropocentrist humanism's dogmatic, irrational adherence to human exceptionalism despite the empirical evidence of a continuum and multitude of species capabilities. The second is the inhumane history of exclusionary violence arising from the ranking, ordering, and molding of humankind. What is called dehumanization is made possible by defining the essence of humanity over and against all other animals. The human-animal binary and hierarchy has historically produced and may continue to reproduce a bloody margin of subhumans, thus contradicting humanism's premise of the universality of freedom and dignity.

The most glaring irony of humanism is that the dogmatism of human exceptionalism contradicts humanism's commitment to truth based in human experience and empiricism. Shortly after anthropocentrism came into full force through humanism, it was immediately undermined by humanistic endeavors in modern science: the Copernican revolution, evolutionary theory, and psychoanalysis. Consciousness of these three discoveries—heliocentrism, humanity's descent from animals, and the unconscious—destroyed humanity's self-image as a purposeful creation at the center of the universe with the exceptional capacity of free will (Davis, 2011). Without an ultimate meaning, and subject to unconscious processes, humanity could no longer have the same confidence in its God-given or self-directed dominion over being.

While Western humans learned that they were not quite as "human" as they thought they were, they later (re)discovered that animal others were much more "human" than they gave them credit. In the last half century, the modern science that once had ideologically dismissed considering animal others as anything other than objects has generated a great many studies that conclude just how untenable human exceptionalism and the human-animal dichotomy is. Nonhumans from ants to apes demonstrate that capabilities that were previously—for a relatively short time by only a fraction of the people on Earth—thought to be exclusive to humans are actually shared with others: planning for a future, long-term memory, deception, a sense of fairness, abstract reasoning, tool use, material culture, agriculture, language use, self-recognition, and even a relationship with the dead (Noske, 1997a).

For centuries, the belief that animal others possessed such capabilities was considered anthropomorphic, attributing the mental experiences and capabilities supposedly exclusive to humans to nonhuman others. However, contemporary scholars such as Franz de Waal characterize the stigmatization of anthropomorphism as anthropodenial—"the willful blindness to the human-like characteristics of animals, or the animal-like characteristics of ourselves" (quoted in Weil, 2012, p. 45). The anthropocentrist commitments of some scholars, however, have prompted them not to concede these capabilities to animal others, but rather to redefine them, especially "language." As Stephen Clark writes, "It is not that we have *discovered* them to lack a language but rather that we define and redefine, what language is by discovering what beasts do not have" (quoted in Shapiro, 1990, p. 23). The boundary project of delimiting "the human" from "the animal" has been in a steady retreat since the 1970s and will in all likelihood continue to be so long as humans presuppose themselves as an exclusive class in which what is essential to and valuable about humanity is defined by what all animal others lack.

The Anthropological Machine and Hegemonic Centrisms

The *anthropos* in the anthropocentrism of humanism can never be purified of its own so-called animality without redrawing an ontological and ethico-political boundary that risks casting out members of the human species. Through what

Giorgio Agamben (2004) calls the "anthropological machine," each attempt to identify human being through its ontological difference from animal being results in an excision *within* human being itself as well as the production of an ethico-politically privileged inside and sacrificial outside. In other words, human being is not so much a value-neutral biological fact as a violent political fiction. The historic and fictitious human-animal dualism that is thought to protect the sovereignty of humans is also ironically the very mechanism that legitimates their sacrifice. What are believed to be the mutually exclusive moral categories of expendable animalized lives (e.g., broiler hens) and sacred humanized lives is betrayed "by the furious line drawing at work in the hybrid designations" of the humanized animals (e.g., pets) exempt from slaughter and the animalized humans (e.g., prisoners at Abu-Ghraib) exempted for it (Wolfe, 2003, p. 101).

To this end, the anthropological machine commits at least four forms of violence. First, the anthropological machine performs what Bell (2011) calls an "auto-vivisection," the violence in the creation of a human-animal binary that alienates humans not only from themselves—their bodies, passions, and experiences—but also from fellow creatures who co-inhabit their world (p. 166). Second, homogenizing all nonhuman sentient life under the term "animal" is a representational violence that negates the specificity and positive attributes of each being by defining them generically through something "human" they all lack. This classification does not define animals on their own terms, but contingently on the desire of the human animal to exercise its power over them and recognize itself as special and superior (Derrida, 2008). Third, by abstracting the non-substitutable subjectivity of "human" life from the anonymous facticity of bare life—a life reduced to mere biological persistence stripped of distinction and integrity—"animal" life becomes an object to be ordered, ranked, aggregated, and molded to economic and political ends. Fourth is the final material and political manifestation of the exclusionary and sacrificial logic of anthropocentrist humanism: the institutionalization of the noncriminal management and destruction of animal life in the service of the state and economy risks extending into the management and sacrifice of the "animal life" of humans (e.g., Nazi Germany's eugenics and mass slaughter of humans) (Patterson, 2002).

What is considered most definitely human in its uniqueness and its superiority is not objective, fixed, and universal. On the contrary, the concept of what we now call "the human" has been selectively, adaptively, and partially defined according to a particular form of embodiment and culture against others. The definition of humanity has been a reflection of a particular group of elite men's perception of themselves in opposition to those they ruled over and classified as their others: animals, women, foreigners, disabled people, and more. In ancient times, women and slaves were considered unfit to participate in the proto-humanist democracy in ancient Greece (duBoise, 1982). The development of natural/human rights in modern times fared little better. According to Lynn Hunt (2007), "Claims about the natural equality of all mankind called forth equally global assertions about natural difference" that "inadvertently opened the door to more virulent forms of sexism, racism, and anti-Semitism" (p. 187).

Joseph Slaughter (2007) explains that while the fictitious creation of human rights "expresses certain laudable aspirations" of egalitarianism, "human rights" obscures its role in practices and discourses of inequality as it became a universalized common sense under liberal ideology (p. 5). In the present, Western societies—and the scientific, legal, and economic systems they are built upon—colonize other lands and minds, conforming them to the West's own image of "the human." Many people of non-European descent continue to be either culturally assimilated into Western civilizations or be managed by it, if such people have not already been exterminated for interfering with human "progress" and "freedom" as heralded by Western civilizations. Jean-Paul Sartre (2007) warned of such a humanist "theory that takes man as an end and as the supreme value" (p. 50). When the remarkable achievements of a few humans signal the greatness of all humanity, the value of one individual's achievement is assumed to give value and identity to the collective "us." A humanism that praises and condemns humans through a fixed, unitary meaning and goal of an "us" "leads ultimately to . . . Fascism" (p. 51). Just as whiteness was invented and deployed to divide and conquer the multiracial working class—preventing them from uniting to overthrow class hierarchy (Allen, 2012)—so too may the "cult of humanity" function to maintain the market and cultural imperialism of white supremacist, capitalist patriarchy through people's complicity with and celebration of its technological, globalizing "progress."

The hypocrisies of anthropocentrist humanism are not historical accidents, but the logical outcome of the production of subjectivities (e.g., identities and consciousnesses) founded on the negation of others. Val Plumwood (2002) argues that one cannot properly address the injustices against human and animal others independently since they are rooted in hegemonic centrisms—widespread and often unquestioned cultural practices of understanding and evaluating the world through the experiences and norms of an exclusive, elite population. Predicated upon the dominant understanding of the human "us," anthropocentrism fundamentally intersects with other centrisms such as androcentrism and ethnocentrism. Together, they operate through a self-referencing conceptual system of oppositional dualisms (e.g., human-animal, man-woman, civilized-savage) in which the implicit, taken-for-granted associations between subordinated identities mutually reinforce one another's subordination as Others. Given the intersections of various oppressions based upon a hegemonic human subjectivity, Matthew Calarco (2008) argues that anthropocentrism ought to be the primary target for critical theory since it is "always one version or another of *the human* that falsely occupies the space of the universal and that functions to exclude [others] . . . from ethical and political consideration" (p. 10).

Liberal Humanist, Posthumanist, and Feminist Anti-speciesism: Multiple Theoretical Fronts Against Speciesism

Theoretically, humanism can retain its central project to nourish and protect human reason and freedom without defining human being over and against animals and animality. Humanism can recognize both animal others' similarities and their differences by attending to their perspectives, experiences, and desires and the moral limits these place on human action. Yet, in practice, many humanists continue to insist that humans and all other animals inhabit mutually exclusive moral categories despite the continual scientific undermining of any clear and distinct line between humans and (at least certain) other animals. To continue to insist on the anthropocentrist human-animal dualism and hierarchy in spite of the empirical and phenomenological evidence against them is an act of speciesism—defined recently by Oscar Horta (2010) as "the unjustified disadvantageous consideration or treatment of those who are not classified as belonging to one or more [privileged] species" (p. 244). While one need not be anthropocentrist to be a speciesist (e.g., an alien race could be speciesist by privileging its own kind, and some humans may categorically favor dolphins over humans), anthropocentrism is the most pervasive ideological form of humanism and speciesism in the modern Western world.

The violent contradictions of anthropocentrist humanism—the irrational dogmatism of human exceptionalism and the inhumane ordering and ranking of human and animal beings—are addressed by multiple, diverging theoretical orientations. The most mainstream orientation is that of liberal humanist anti-speciesists who recognize that the human-animal dichotomy is a false and unjust one, and advocate that the moral and legal principles of liberalism—the privileging of the autonomy of the individual—be extended logically and consistently to each individual, regardless of their species classification. They decry the irrational inconsistency of anthropocentrism and speciesism's correspondence to other prejudices though deductive logic and moral reasoning. Those with alternative orientations like—but not exclusive to—feminist and posthumanist anti-speciesists are critical of the ontology and epistemology of humanist moral and political philosophy, considering the demand for the logical consistency of present thought and politics insufficient. A radical transformation in thought and politics, they believe, is necessary for challenging the dominant and dominating ways of conceptualizing humans, animals, and morality that are at the very root of the world's problems.

Anthropocentric Bias and Consistency in Liberal Humanism

Just as modern science has come to undermine its (anthropocentrist) humanist origins, so has humanism's commitment to its own principles demanded that it recognize its moral failure in excluding animal others from equal consideration for being assigned to different biological classes. Enlightenment humanism's distaste for appeal to authority and tradition, arbitrary prejudices, and nonrational sources of morality delegitimized previous justifications for human supremacy. Humanist values (e.g., reason, liberty, equality, individuality) could not be fairly advocated without extending moral consideration to each individual, regardless of one's species identity. "With the spread of universalist and egalitarian ideals," writes John Sanbonmatsu (2011), "it did not take a great leap of logic for some far-sighted individuals to see how other animals too might have an interest in freedom, liberty, and fraternity" (p. 14). Beginning amid the civil rights, feminist, peace, and environmental movements of the late 1960s, a movement on the behalf of animal others deployed humanist rhetoric to demand that equal consideration be properly and consistently extended to individuals across species, challenging the unquestioned anthropocentrist ideology. In 1975, Peter Singer articulated what would become the most canonized argument for the equal consideration to animal others in his book *Animal Liberation*.

In *Animal Liberation*, Singer wrote that the advocacy for equality is not an appeal to the fact that everyone is one another's equal in status and performance. Clearly, each being is superior and inferior to other beings in different capacities and by different standards. The advocacy for equality is a moral prescription that each being's interests count equally to the like interest of another, regardless of their present status and performance. The failure to administer equal moral consideration to a sentient being for not belonging to a privileged species is speciesism, a prejudice as irrational and unjust as racism and sexism. One example of speciesism Singer deploys is that nonhuman animals with greater cognitive capabilities than severely brain-damaged orphans are regularly subjected to painful, invasive research while the orphans are not merely because of their biological classification. Singer's conclusion is not that the use of human and nonhuman animals as research equipment for medical progress is morally wrong, but that it is morally inconsistent to accept the exploitation of animal others and not also the humans with comparative cognitive capabilities.

Although he does not rank preferences as did John Stuart Mill (1993), who wrote "better to be a human being dissatisfied than a pig satisfied" (p. 164), Singer only recognizes the value of a being's future existence if that being is aware of it and has preferences that extend into the future. Those beings (e.g., chickens and severely cognitively impaired humans) who are incapable of projecting themselves and their desires into the future, he concludes, are not harmed by early deaths. Their lives are substitutable and their deaths are not only justified but also potentially "good" if that means their substitutes will live richer, happier lives (Singer, 1993). A strictly utilitarian approach like Singer's may regard genetically engineering animals without consciousness as a moral improvement that resolves the present suffering of billions of animals exploited for food and science (Shriver, 2009).

Tom Regan (1983) critiques Singer for inadequately addressing the violation of the integrity of animal others' individuality. According to utilitarianism, since the preferences of sentient beings can be abstracted from their singularity in order to be aggregated and weighed against one another, lives may be sacrificed and exploited for the greater many. The interests of human and animal others are to their personal integrity as liquid is to a receptacle: alienable, quantifiable, and exchangeable. Regan proposes that moral agents have a duty to respect the integrity of "subjects-of-a-life"—sentient beings with rich desires, emotions, experiences, and thoughts. Animals with complex cognition such as mammals and perhaps birds ought to have equal moral rights because of the inherent worth of their inner lives, not simply because they have preferences.

Gary Francione (2000, 2009), while sympathetic to Singer's attack on speciesism and Regan's advocacy of rights, take issues with both Singer's and Regan's privileging of human consciousness in which animal others are due equal moral consideration only in proportion to how closely they correspond to humans. Singer and Regan represent an anthropocentric anti-speciesism—privileging "normal," adult human cognition by which all other beings are consistently judged regardless of assigned species. In lifeboat scenarios, both Singer and Regan would unquestioning sacrifice a dog—even a million in Regan's scenario—for an able-bodied adult human. Francione upholds that no capacity (such as advanced cognitive functioning) beyond sentience has comparable moral relevancy. A being is due equal moral consideration for sentience alone. Joan Dunayer (2004) takes the principle of equal consideration to its most radical conclusion, advocating not only equal moral rights and the right not to be property, but also equal legal protection and penalties when humans violate animals' rights to bodily integrity, self-determination, labor, and habitat.

Posthumanist and Feminist Challenges to the Autonomous Humanist Subject

While Singer and Regan challenged traditional humanism's speciesism, but retained its anthropocentric presuppositions, Francione and Dunayer challenged the anthropocentric cognitive prejudices of Singer and Regan in an attempt to push liberal humanism to its limits. Yet Francione and Dunayer, like Singer and Regan, never challenged their liberal humanism's own presuppositions. According to Cary Wolfe (2009a), while ethicists from Singer to Dunayer say they challenge the anthropocentric bias of their predecessors, they are humanist at "the performative level of what philosophy *does* (and thinks it *can* do) on a methodological level . . . via the autonomy and impartiality of 'reason'" (p. 58). Their humanist metaphysics and epistemology, Wolfe boldly declares, are "part of the very problem it wants to think through. It wants to be anti-speciesist, but only because it is already humanist, it really can't be—or rather, it can, but only in a strategic, pragmatic way" (p. 58). Posthumanist and feminist theorists have challenged humanist anti-speciesist presuppositions such as the autonomous human subject, morality as a set of universalizable principles, disembodied reasoning as the origin and sole arbiter of moral values, and the marginalization of animal others' specificity and participation in morality and society (Donovan & Adams, 2007; Wolfe, 2009b). Posthumanist and feminist theorists conceive of the human subject as embodied and relational, and morality as embodied care and situational response to the particularities of the multitudes of animal bodies and contexts.

Posthumanist theories open both the traditional objects of discourse ("the animal") as well as the subjects of discourse ("the human") to continual reassessment and revision. Posthumanism regards "the autonomous, domineering, atomistic subject of modernity" as a myth of Enlightenment thinking; it describes a subject alternatively as a "witness to and bearer of an event that exceeds and calls the singular subject into being" (Calarco, 2008, p. 12). Consciousness is not an intangible, fixed entity on-the-scene independent of and prior to the material and discursive constitution of the world. Rather consciousness is the effect of the institutions and discourses to which it responds. To be a subject is at once to be an active participant in constituting the world and to be subjected to the institutions and discourses one is thrown into. Further, according to Wolfe (2009b), posthumanism names the present moment in which "human nature" is thrown into question by technologies and discourses (e.g., cognitive ethology, neurobiology, bioengineering, cybernetics, global capitalism) (p. xv). Posthumanists may describe a present human condition to be carefully responded, but they do not prescribe a future human kind to be militantly attained. Neither is posthumanism a total rejection of humanism; it is an understanding of how humanist aspirations like reason and equality "are undercut by the philosophical and ethical frameworks used to conceptualize them" (p. xvi).

Like posthumanist theory, postmodern (Haraway, 2007; Oliver, 2009) and radical feminist theory (Adams & Donovan, 1995; Donovan & Adams, 2007) contests the universality of the assertive, atomistic, autonomous subject that is foregrounded and sustained only through the disavowal of the "feminine" vulnerabilities of embodiment, dependency, and affect. The liberal humanist subject is not a benign myth but a foundational figure that dominating discourses and institutions are built upon. The myth of the autonomous subject both legitimizes the exploitation of women (and other others) due to the cultural construction of women as partially autonomous while also producing ignorance of the conditions that both limit their autonomy and prop up the illusion of men's full autonomy: inequity in leadership roles and women's expected, co-opted, or undercompensated physical and emotional labor.

According to Emily Clark (2012), feminist theory is uniquely and strategically adept at addressing the human-animal binary and hierarchy because of its

> commitment to the materiality of the body, to attending to those bodies most vulnerable to abuse, to exposing the logic of exclusion and the politics of abjection, and… in its commitment to thinking about, and critiquing its own participation in, the ethics of representation and "speaking for." (p. 516)

Posthumanism and feminist theory have different genealogies and orientations to overthrowing anthropocentrist norms that divide and conquer, but they sometimes converge in ecofeminist theory, which exposes the material, conceptual, and historical interconnections between the exploitation and degradation of women and nonhuman others (Gaard, 1993; Plumwood, 2002). Yet, the important connections made by ecofeminists among sexism, anthropocentrism, racism, colonialism, militarism, and capitalism continue to be relatively ignored despite having preceded the articulation of similar connections described in recent Human-Animal Studies literature by twenty-five years (Gaard, 2012).

Posthumanist and feminist critiques of the illusion and injustices of the liberal subject is a challenge simultaneously to the ontology of Enlightenment humanism as well as its moral rhetoric of "rights" and "interests." Feminist critics Josephine Donovan and Carol Adams (2007) list several issues with rights-based and utilitarian orientations. First, these theories are founded upon centuries-old liberal humanism that served to protect the territorial interests of competitive, atomistic individuals, mainly those of landowning white men. Kelly Oliver (2009) explains that liberal humanist theories have not only an exclusionary logic "whereby one class has rights and the other has none," but also a competitive logic that "leads to calculations of whose interests are more important and whose rights trump others" (p. 36). Thus, equal protection under the law is insufficient since "it pits interests or rights against each other without considering differential power structures" (p. 35).

Second, these theories extend moral considerability to animal others, not on their own terms but in correspondence (i.e., conformity) to their similarity to the "gender-neutral" liberal human subject free of dependency. Extentionist ethics only question the inconsistent application of the values and principles of the present system, not the criteria (i.e., content) and methodology (i.e., form) of judgment. As Catharine MacKinnon (2004) writes, "If qualified entrance into the human race on male terms has done little for women . . . how much will being seen as humanlike, but not fully so, do for other animals?" (p. 271). Third, liberal humanist ethics "devalues, suppresses, or denies the emotions" in order to codify ethics into a formalistic moral calculus, marginalizing the on-the-ground context of moral deliberation (Donovan & Adams, 2007, p. 6). Oliver (2009) contends that basing ethics in principles rather than response to "the ambiguities and uncertainties of our experience"(p. 36) is paradigmatic of "the powerful speaking for the powerless," which replicates, but does not change, "the power structure itself," as it amounts to silencing lived experiences of both the moral agents and subjects (p. 38).

Rationality, Rule-based Ethics, and the Marginalization of Embodiment and Care

The marginalization (i.e., silencing) of the agency and experience of (human and nonhuman) animal bodies becomes salient when one dissects the self-authorization of humanist ethics extending from humanist ontology. As Traci Warkentin (2010) lucidly articulates, humanist morality assumes "that humans already have the right to 'grant' moral status to others, which implies that humans have both the ability and authority to pre-judge who counts morally and who does not" (p. 107). Even moral theorists who attempt to empty moral theory of its traditional anthropocentric standards still accept humanism's anthropocentric orientation that moral valuation and judgment originate and are grounded in the locus of (human) reason. Cora Diamond (2008) interprets the reason-based humanist methodology to moral consciousness and action as a deflection from the difficulty of reality—"something in reality resistant to our thinking it, or possibly to be painful in its inexplicability" (p. 45–46). The moral argumentation of humanist anti-speciesists ironically reproduces the human-animal binary by deflecting attention from the difficulty of reality produced by two finitudes humans share with animal others: the finitude of flesh (i.e., embodiment and vulnerability) and the finitude of thought (i.e., the non-correspondence between our concepts and reality) (Wolfe, 2009b).

First, methodologically approaching the issue of the unjust suffering and exploitation of animals from deductive reasoning fails "to see how 'debate' as we understand it may have built into it a distancing of ourselves from our sense of our own bodily life and our capacity to respond to and to imagine the bodily life of others" (Diamond, 2008, p. 53). The philosophical vocabulary and methodology of humanist anti-speciesism is "a deflection which makes our own bodies mere facts—facts which may or may not be thought of as morally relevant" (p. 59). Whereas a moral theory that begins ethics with "being a live [animal] body . . . transfers the burden of proof" to anthropocentrism to justify excluding animals from moral consideration, notes Ralph Acampora (2006), rationality-based approaches to ethics tend to place the burden of proof on those advocating moral consideration for animals (p. 5). The humanist methodology holds that the powerlessness one experiences in the face of suffering—one's subjection to the power of the powerlessness of another's body—is distorting, and so one must remain at a distance not only from the suffering animal other, but also one's own suffering.

Second, the powerlessness that one experiences as a witness to injustices, the horror, and deep woundedness, is doubled as a feeling of powerlessness to represent it in thought and language: "The words fail us, the words don't do what we are trying to get them to do" (Diamond, 2008, p. 67). The powerlessness from the woundedness may even be tripled when one's struggle to give testimony to an injustice is invalidated as irrationality by another to whom "my powerlessness presents itself as ignorance—a metaphysical finitude as an intellectual lack" (p. 68). The humanist anti-speciesist then is not so far from the anthropocentrist humanist in the "shared desire for a 'because'; because animals are this kind of being . . . thus-and-such is their standing for our moral thought" that amounts to "a form of skepticism in the desire for something better than what we are condemned to (as the kind of animal we are)" (p. 71).

The humanist disavowal of and distancing from the finitude of embodiment and language is a performance of a "humanity" defined against the imperfect transcendence and reasoning of animal and human others. For millennia, women (and other human Others) have been excluded from full and equal citizenship due to their discursive and institutional construction as less capable of articulating themselves in speech and being unreasonably moved by external and bodily events. Their finitude, vulnerability, and passivity were thus marked as if powerful normalized males uniquely transcended these limitations. Beings with anything less than full autonomy place less demand on one's enlightened self-interest since they lack the power to fully reciprocate and self-actualize. To care about the exploitation and suffering of those institutionally or intrinsically less capable of reciprocating and self-actualization (such as animals) is considered irrational and sentimental. By this logic, caring for animals is childish, primitive, and feminine—identities the modern, rational subject is defined against.

Brian Luke (2007) argues that liberal rights- and interests-based theories, grounded in (the universalizability or contractual reciprocity of) self-interest, treat caring about dependent and nonreciprocating others as "the unreliable quirk of a few" versus "the normal state of humans generally" (p. 134). Animal liberation, however, is not obstructed because people are naturally selfish and unmoved by animals' well-being but because "enormous amounts of social energy are expended to forestall, undermine, and override sympathies for animals" (p. 134). Donovan and Adams (2007) have sought to reevaluate the role relationships and emotions play in ethics with a feminist ethics of care, which places emphasis on the sociopolitical context of relationships and the specificity of responsibilities for caring. While care is a fundamental capability for being human, care is a skill that "requires effort, courage and discipline" (p. 4). An animal care ethics, however, does not preclude an attention to justice, for to care for another is to care about the conditions of their existence, the structures of their oppression, and opposing those structures that exploit and marginalize their existence.

Universal, Individual-based Ethics, and the Marginalization of Ecology and Dependency

The humanist anti-speciesist tradition has generally marginalized not only the embodiment and finitude humans share with animal others but also humans' embedding and interdependency in ecological societies. Ecofeminist and post-humanists critique not only the human-animal dualism but also the civilization-wilderness dualism that helps maintain it. They advocate (re)situating humans as ecologically embedded and embodied subjects of interspecies communities (Plumwood, 2002). Humans did not evolve apart from other animals but rather over time as inhabitants in mixed species communities (Midgley, 1984). Donna Haraway (2008) deploys the term "companion species" to describe the species with whom humans have been entangled in their natural (i.e., material) and cultural (i.e., semiotic) evolution. The concept of companion species punctuates the reality that we have never been human. Humans have always been part of co-constitutive relationships with other species. Recognizing that humans and animal others are always already entangled, Sue Donaldson and Will Kymlicka (2012) advocate perceiving animal others "not solely as vulnerable and suffering individuals but also as neighbors, friends, co-citizens, and members of communities . . . [in which] animals and humans can co-exist, interact, and even cooperate on the basis of justice and equality" (p. 24).

Liberal humanist anti-speciesists favor the moral concepts of the individual, interests, and rights over those of the mixed communities, companion species, and nature cultures. Some liberal humanists are utilitarians who advocate the hyper-management of ecology and eradicating predation to reduce aggregative individual suffering (Cowen, 2003). Others who, on the contrary, respect the integrity and autonomy of animals identify as abolitionists—animal rights activists who consider all welfare reform as immoral and ineffective at abolishing institutionalized animal exploitation. For many abolitionists, write Donaldson and Kymlicka (2012), "It is the very fact of interaction and interdependency that is the problem" (p. 63). Some conceive of the status of domesticated animals "as a kind of deviation from their true or natural community in the wild," perceiving their lack of freedom from human dependency not only as a condition enabling their continued exploitation but also as an indignity (p. 100). Because domestic animals have been bred for neoteny (e.g., juvenile traits such as submissiveness) and have lost any ecologically viable niche in which to be free outside of human society, abolitionists like Francione (2000) and Hall (2010) advocate ending the existence of domestic animals.

While Donaldson and Kymlicka (2012) acknowledge that the majority of animals are institutionally bred without agency in ways not in the interest of them or their children, they are also concerned that Francione and Hall's abolitionist-extinctionist position supports "a massive [sexual] intervention" and that they make "no attempt to justify [it] in relation to the individuals whose liberty is being restricted" (p. 81). While neither would advocate "policing nature" through eradicating animal predation as some utilitarians have (Cowen, 2003), they seem to have no problem, at least theoretically, with policing animal sexuality until animal cohabitation is eradicated. Kari Weil (2012) interprets this extinctionist position as the sacrifice of domestic animals for the "idea of the world" (p. 136) despite the possibility that animal others "may accept those [human-animal] bonds as the price (and sometimes the point) of life" (p. 134). Instead of practicing a dialogical, attentive care, as advocated by feminist anti-speciesists, to attempt to understand what particular animals may want, some humanist anti-speciesists are more concerned with the consistent application of their transcendental ideas. Indeed, some liberals like Siobhan O'Sullivan (2011) would accept an overall decrease in animal welfare so long as it was "internally consistent" across nonhuman animal species as part of "legitimate" democratic decision making (p. 171). Anti-speciesists do not always attend to animal others "on their own terms"; occasionally they project their humanist aspirations for consistency and full autonomy upon them.

Ironically, what seems to result from the eradication of domestic human-animal relations is a more radical segregation of human and animal societies. This domestic-human/wild-animal dualism is itself part of the very problems humanist anti-speciesists want to address: the reproduction of a human-animal dichotomy and the human exceptionalism of agency. First, the domestic-wild dichotomy treats the two as ontologically distinct entities, ignoring liminal animals such as migrating birds (e.g., Canadian Geese) and urban dwellers (e.g., coyotes) who require no direct human care yet who are partially dependent upon urban habitat (Donaldson & Kymlicka, 2012). Second, the dichotomy insinuates the human exceptionalist idea that humans are the intentional and sole authors of history, outside or above the influence and agency of animal others as if the presence of companion species hasn't facilitated and undermined (human) imperialism (Weil, 2012, p. 132). By recognizing these limits and inconsistencies in liberal humanist anti-speciesism, posthumanist, and feminist theory advance anti-speciesist theory and practice by resisting the inclination to merely extend the dominant discourse that has historically served to justify the subjugation of animal others.

The Critical Animal Turn: The Theoretical Analysis of and Opposition to Speciesism

Some anti-speciesists are critical of both liberal humanists' limited understanding of speciesism and posthumanists' reluctance to prescribe norms and strategy.

Liberal humanism, they argue, attacks the symptoms of the structural violence of capitalism and other dominating regimes without a broader historical and sociological critique of their sources, while posthumanists "often seek to bracket, postpone, or eradicate questions of ethics" despite the fact that "ethico-political and practical questions regarding animal exploitation" are an inevitable consequence of deconstructing the human-animal binary (Jenkins, 2012, p. 506). These critical anti-speciesists gravitate toward CAT, which shares the posthumanist critique of modernity with the humanist advocacy of freedom, engaging in interdisciplinary theory and coalition building for the total liberation of all those oppressed by anthropocentrism and other hegemonic centrums (Best, 2009).

John Sanbonmatsu (2011) writes that critical theory originates from the intuition that the present world is unfree and "shares with other emancipatory traditions the desire to redeem the conscious living subject, or person, from thoughtlessness, violence, and domination" (p. 5). Accusations that critical theory's commitment to defend the "universal freedom" of persons from the indignities wrought by oppressive systems like capitalism is humanistic would be correct, as two of critical theory's major sources are neo-Marxist and existential humanism (p. 6). Kenneth Shapiro (1990), Sanbonmatsu (2007), and Gary Steiner (2013) argue that humanism need not be a lost cause if it is dissociated with its anthropocentrist ideological commitments. The problem with past humanisms is not the dignity they recognize in human experience and freedom, but the exclusivity of what counts as freedom (e.g., reason) and whose ought to be respected (e.g., *Homo sapiens*). Previous formulations of humanism were unjust and illusory because they subordinated what humans share with animal others (e.g., human embodiment and desire) to transcendence and instrumental reasoning, and founded a violent antagonism in which human freedom is enacted through the subjection of all that is nonhuman.

The central disjuncture between (humanist) CAT and posthumanist theory is that, methodologically, the former begins with human (and animal) others' originary freedom and wholeness before alienation, repression, and fragmentation under capitalist patriarchy, whereas the latter is suspicious of "natural," prediscursive, pre-institutionalized bodies. The former accepts anthropological and normative universals that define and advocate mutual human and nonhuman animal freedom, while the latter is wary that a call for global unity under the name of "freedom," "liberation," and "progress" would only serve as another pretense for empire. Yet, what the two orientations share in common—their critique of anthropocentrism, human exceptionalism, instrumental reason, and the transcendence of the finitude and passions of embodiment—overshadow their divergences. Posthumanism and critical theory need not be opposed in their efforts to address speciesism's "rootedness in our minds, bodies, practices, discourses, institutions, [and] identities" (Sanbonmatsu, 2011, p. 29).

Both critical animal and posthumanist theorists understand that attitudes and practices founded on human-animal dualism and hierarchy in spite of the empirical and phenomenological evidence against them are not merely human chauvinism—a militant and bigoted patriotism to humanity. Human chauvinism insinuates that the violence against human and animal others is an individual's irrational prejudice; it fails to capture the ideological nature of anthropocentrism, the institutional and discursive mechanisms that ensure its reproduction and entangle it with other centrisms. "Speciesism," as a neologism, more effectively addresses interspecies injustices by analogy to and in complicity with other oppressive (e.g., sexist and racist) discourses and practices than "human chauvinism." David Nibert (2002) addresses speciesism sociologically as an ideology that naturalizes and rationalizes the present unequal political-economic relationships based upon competition and exploitation of animal others that are upheld by the state. Speciesism, accordingly, is not the source but the symptom of oppression that lies in hierarchical material relationships whereby power and capital—fiscal, social, cultural, and spiritual—are accumulated through the exploitation of animals.

Speciesism is not mere prejudice but a composite of interspecies injustices within material institutions, discursive regimes, and embodied affects. Speciesism is a complex of material institutions that systematically, non-criminally sacrifice the lives and interests of animals (Noske, 1997a; Nibert, 2002; Torres, 2007; Twine, 2012) as well as cultural discourses and narratives, speech and stories that circulate misrepresentations of animal others as inferiors and proper objects of sacrifice (Dunayer, 1995). The institution and discourse are part of a positive feedback loop, in which the existence of one validates the existence of the other. Material and discursive relations transmitted through human and animal other bodies also become habituated in embodied affect—a visceral force (e.g., anxiety, disgust, rage, lust, joy) that moves bodies toward actions and relations with others. Affect provides explanatory power for how humans both become subject to speciesism through family meals (e.g., the communal enjoyment and performance of [human] family through eating animals) as well as how they may be freed from it through witnessing—(e.g., grief and rage from the exposure to speciesism's violence as violence). CAT thus requires an awareness of and opposition to the larger political-economic structures that manifest oppression, the discourse and narratives that legitimate these institutions, and the exclusionary affects that may ensue when these institutions and discourses are challenged.

Carnism: A Case Study of Structural Speciesism

From a CAT standpoint, speciesism is to be understood as a complex of institutions, discourses, and affects that structure human existence on a false, pathological reality. The most grand and omnipresent occurrences of speciesism are ironically the most banal: the exploitation, objectification, and consumption of animals as food. Carnism—a sub-ideology of speciesism that dichotomizes nonhuman animals into "edible" and "inedible" categorizations and legitimates the exploitation and consumption of animal others—thus presents an apt case study of speciesism. Carnism is used here for several other reasons as well. First, carnism is structurally similar to speciesism but, while most examinations of speciesism have been theoretical, there is empirical research examining the psychological and social dimensions of carnism (Angyal, 1941; Beardsworth & Keil, 1993; Holm & Mohl, 2000). Naming and deconstructing carnism, therefore, may enable us to make invisible naturalized and normalized practices and affects of speciesism visible objects to challenge and transform. Moreover, carnism enables the oppression of the majority of nonhuman beings who are exploited for human ends. And finally, the perpetual, intimate, and deeply symbolic act of eating animals in large part defines the human-nonhuman relationship.

Given the profound impact of carnism on the structure of human-nonhuman relations, vegan praxis—a counternarrative and practice in which nonhuman beings are not viewed or treated as appropriate for human consumption—is perhaps the most effective and direct way to subvert the speciesist complex. Deconstructing carnism is a significant step in moving toward such a praxis. This final and most important point reflects a central tenet of Critical Animal Studies: that theoretical understanding must be grounded in and geared toward practical application to bring about real change in individual lives and to cultivate a genuine shift in social consciousness.

Carnism is the ideology that conditions people to eat (certain) animals and it is a sub-ideology of speciesism, in that it exists within a speciesist ethos (Joy, 2001, 2010). Carnism (like speciesism) is structural and internalized, shaping individual attitudes and behaviors toward those animal others who are classified as "edible." Carnism is a global phenomenon; in animal-eating cultures around the world, a select group of animal others are classified as edible while all other species are classified and thus perceived as inedible and disgusting to consume (Farb & Armelagos, 1980; Fessler, Navarrette, & Navarrette, 2003; Simoons, 1961).

The mechanisms of carnism are defenses that are disseminated by and inform material institutions and individual human consumers of animals in an invisible yet potent feedback loop. Such defenses are necessary to maintain the carnist system or complex, as the tenets and practices of carnism are diametrically opposed to fundamental human motivations and values (e.g., compassion, reciprocity, justice). Carnistic defenses enable gross cognitive and affective distortions in order for human consumers to support the system. Indeed, the empathic response to witnessing the suffering of others has been demonstrated to be a normal, biological reaction through the discovery of mirror neurons (Blakeslee, 2006; Ramachandran, 2006). Mirror neurons are neurons in the brain that are activated when a subject witnesses the experience of another, and the subject actually feels with the other. Though studies on motor neurons have focused on the witnessing of human beings, there is no reason to assume that mirror neurons are not activated when humans witness the experience of nonhuman beings as well. The dominant, carnistic narrative appears to be constructed to obstruct the authentic human empathy and compassion that would disable the system. In short, exploitative systems such as carnism must use a set of institutional and discursive mechanisms that enable otherwise empathic people to participate in violent practices without fully realizing what they are doing.

Carnistic defenses operate on two levels: they are institutionalized and internalized, and each level reinforces the other. Carnistic defenses exist to construct fictitious cultural narratives that both validate carnism and invalidate veganism. These narratives tell the respective stories that "eating animals is the right thing to do" and "not eating animals is the wrong thing to do." Carnistic defenses are at once discrete and interrelated; they are distinct but overlap with and reinforce one another, the whole they create becoming greater than the sum of its parts.

The primary carnistic defense is denial: denying that there is a problem in the first place erases any responsibility for addressing it. The main cultural narratives told by denial are "there is no problem," "there is no system," "there is no oppression," and "there is no counternarrative." Denial is expressed largely through invisibility, and the main way carnism remains invisible is by remaining unnamed: if carnism is not named, it cannot be conceptualized, questioned, or challenged. The invisibility of carnism is why eating animals appears to be a given rather than a choice. Thus, carnism strips human consumers of animal others of their freedom of choice, because without awareness, there is no free choice.

Carnism also remains invisible by keeping its victims out of sight and thus conveniently out of public consciousness. Indeed, carnism is a system of victimization, in that it victimizes all participants in different ways. Some victims are obvious and direct, such as the 10 billion (land) animals who are slaughtered annually in the United States alone for their flesh and other body parts (as cited by FARM, 2013), and the environment, the degradation of which the United Nations says is caused largely by animal agriculture (United Nations, 2006). Other victims are indirect, such as vegans, who one could argue comprise an ideological minority in a repressive dominant culture; or nonvegans who are at once perpetrators and victims, supporting a system that has conditioned them to act against their core values and their own interests, as eating animals increases one's risk for some of the most serious diseases in the Western world today (Campbell & Campbell, 2006) and requires a fundamental psycho-emotional disconnection.

While all carnistic institutions utilize denial, the institution that relies most heavily on this defense is animal agriculture itself. The blatant denial of animal agriculture can be seen through its wildly misleading discourse (e.g., carnistic advertising campaigns promoting the "happy-to-be-eaten" farmed animal) and its refusal to retract the invisibility of its practices, an act most notably manifested in the enactment of new laws that criminalize any attempt to challenge or expose carnistic denial. The denial of carnism and the embodied experience of farmed animals—the fact that "meat," "eggs," and "dairy" are from once-conscious and sentient beings—becomes internalized by human consumers of animal others who end up viewing corpses as cuisine and thus feel delight rather than disgust. Moreover, carnistic denial obscures and minimizes the vegan counternarrative. The vegan movement is obfuscated, and vegan advocates are often silenced and stereotyped.

Denial-invisibility is in no way sufficient to maintain the entire carnistic system; hints of the truth are omnipresent, from the palpable vein in the chicken "drumstick" to the dismembered bodies of dead animals that line the aisles of supermarkets and fill the plates of the majority of consumers. Thus, consumers of animal others must be able to justify their participation in carnism. Justification provides consumers a "good reason," a set of dominant, fictitious narratives, to be participating in an ideological system that in fact runs counter to what are likely their authentic narratives.

There is a vast mythology surrounding eating animals, but all myths arguably fall under the Three Ns of Justification: eating animals is normal, natural, and necessary (Joy, 2010). The Three Ns are of course the same narratives that prop up all ideological complexes. Narratives of justification essentially normalize, naturalize, and mandate adherence to an ideology, thus legitimizing the system and forcing widespread discursive and affective conformity. Put differently, carnistic justifications provide a rationale that shapes the way human consumers of animal others think and feel about eating animals and reinforce the human-over-animal dynamic that marks such a relationship.

Within the past several years, there has been a shift in cultural attitudes toward eating animals, at least in parts of the affluent West. As public awareness of CAFOs and veganism has increased, three distinct trends in the consumption of animals have emerged: "humane," "sustainable/local," and "nutritional" meat, dairy, and eggs. Each of these trends may be understood as part of a backlash against the vegan counternarrative; as such a counternarrative has sufficiently raised awareness of the impact of animal agriculture on animals, the environment, and human health. The new pro-carnism arguments may thus be seen as an attempt to defend the weakened animal-eating establishment against the very real threat posed by an increasingly powerful vegan movement.

The aforementioned arguments have morphed into new ideologies—neocarnisms—that are organized around the invalidation of the vegan counternarrative (Joy, 2011). Neocarnist narratives promote the fictions that not eating animals—veganism—is abnormal, unnatural, and unnecessary. In other words, the neocarnisms exist to provide "rational" arguments to invalidate veganism, largely by invalidating the three pillars of the vegan argument: animal welfare-rights, the environment, and human health. Moreover, because veganism is framed as a (subjective) ideology while the neocarnisms are framed as (objective) ideas, vegan arguments are portrayed as biased and thus invalid. Neocarnisms are reminders that social movements do not grow along a straight trajectory. The radical change demanded by vegan praxis will not come about without great resistance. And finally, neocarnism is a manifestation of the fact that (at least the majority of) those who participate in animal exploitation do in fact care about nonhuman beings; the neocarnisms would not have emerged if eating animals did not trigger a deep moral unease. This last point is easily overlooked or forgotten but it is essential to grasp if people are to move toward vegan praxis.

Carnistic discourse and affect are perhaps best understood through a deconstruction of the carnistic schema. The carnistic schema is organized around defensive cognitive processes that distort perceptions and therefore cultivate pro-carnist affect. Carnistic cognitive processes include objectification, de-individualization/abstraction, and dichotomization (creating a perceived binary and enabling a speciesist-carnist hierarchy). Farmed animals are objectified in unique and powerful ways; they are "livestock" and "broilers" (before they are even killed). They are seen as abstract members of a group about which humans have made generalized assumptions ("a pig is a pig and all pigs are the same"). And they are placed in rigid cognitive categories, classified as "edible" and thus less worthy, or unworthy, of moral concern (Adams & Donovan, 1995).

Carnistic discourse plays a key role in reinforcing carnistic ideology, largely through the use of an inaccurate and misleading lexicon. For instance, the phrase "meat eater" describes a behavior as though it were divorced from a belief system (hence vegans are not referred to as "plant eaters"), in essence reinforcing the invisibility of the ideology. And both "omnivore" and "carnivore" refer to one's biological predisposition rather than one's ideological choice; these terms reinforce the assumption that eating animals is natural, one of the most entrenched and compelling carnistic justifications. Because of the power of discourse to construct perceptions and affect to reinforce the dominant narrative, it is particularly important that the vegan counterdiscourse not mirror the language of oppression. In other words, moving toward total liberation means examining internal and external structures and taking steps toward shifting such ways of seeing, communicating, and being.

Dominant ideologies and narratives, and the complexes they inevitably form, maintain power largely by remaining invisible. The invisibility of the carnist-speciesist complex—and of its defenses—form some of the central pillars on which the system stands. The transformative vegan counternarrative discourses and practices must therefore not only provide alternative narratives but explicitly expose the fictions of the speciesist-carnist narratives. In other words, as mentioned earlier, vegan praxis cannot replace the speciesist-carnist complex without first exposing normalized practices and affects of these systems, making such practices visible objects to confront and transform.

Vegan praxis must incorporate a discourse and affect that reflect not only animal liberation but also total liberation. Vegan praxis must be oriented toward challenging all oppressive power structures, externally—in the realm of material institutions—and internally—in discourse/perception/affect. It must embody and promote the opposing qualities and practices of anthropocentrism, binary and hierarchical categorization, and, thus, othering. A vegan praxis, ideally, is an ever-changing way of understanding and relating to oneself and all other beings based on empathy, authenticity, reciprocity, justice, and integrity—the principles that underscore true freedom.

References

Acampora, R. R. (2006). *Corporal compassion: Animal ethics and philosophy of the body*. Pittsburgh: University of Pennsylvania Press.
Adams, C. J., & Donovan, J. (Eds.). (1995). *Animals and women: Feminist theoretical explorations*. Durham, NC: Duke University Press.
Agamben, G. (2004). *The open: Man and animal*. (W. Hamacher, Ed.; K. Attel, Trans.). Stanford, CA: Stanford University Press.
Allen, T. W. (2012). *The invention of the white race, vol. 2: The origins of racial oppression in Anglo-America*. London: Verso.
Angyal, A. (1941). Disgust and related aversions. *Journal of Abnormal and Social Psychology, 36*, 393–412.
Beardsworth, A., & Keil, T. (1993). Contemporary vegetarianism in the U.K.: Challenge and incorporation?" *Appetite, 20*, 229–234.
Bell, A. (2011). The dialectic of anthropocentrism. In J. Sanbonmatsu (Ed.), *Critical theory and animal liberation* (pp. 163–175). Lanham, MD: Rowman & Littlefield.
Best, S. (2009). The rise of critical animal studies: Putting theory into action and animal liberation into higher education. *Journal for Critical Animal Studies, 7*(1), 9–54.
Blakeslee, S. (2006, January 10). Cells that read minds. *New York Times*. Retrieved from http://www.nytimes.com/2006/01/10/science/10mirr.html?pagewanted=all
Calarco, M. (2008). *Zoographies: The question of the animal from Heidegger to Derrida*. New York: Columbia University Press.
Campbell, T. C., & Campbell, T. M. (2006). *The china study*. Dallas: Benbella.
Clark, E. (2012). Returning the ethical and political to animal studies. *Hypatia, 27*(3), 516–520.
Cowen, T. (2003). Policing nature. *Environmental Ethics, 25*(2), 169–182.
Davis, D. (2011). Creaturely rhetoric. *Philosophy and Rhetoric, 44*(1), 88–94.
DeLapp, K. (2011). The view from somewhere: Anthropocentrism in metaethics. In R. Boddice (Ed.), *Anthropocentrism: Human, animals, environment* (pp. 37–57). Boston: Brill.
Derrida, J. (2008). *The animal that therefore I am*. (M. Mallet, Ed.; D. Wills, Trans.). New York: Fordham University Press.
Diamond, C. (2008). The difficulty of reality and the difficulty of philosophy. In S. Cavell (Ed.), *Philosophy and animal life*. New York: Columbia University Press.
Donaldson, S., & Kymlicka, W. (2012). *Zoopolis: A political theory of animal rights*. New York: Oxford University Press.

Donovan, J., & Adams, C. J. (Eds.). (2007). *The feminist care tradition in animal ethics: A reader.* New York: Columbia.

duBois, P. (1982). *Centaurs and amazons: Women and the prehistory of the great chain of being.* Ann Arbor: University of Michigan Press.

Dunayer, J. (2004). *Speciesism.* Derwood, MD: Ryce.

Dunayer, J. (1995). *Animal equality: Language and liberation.* Derwood, MD: Ryce.

Farb, P., & Armelagos, G. (1980). *Consuming passions: The anthropology of eating.* Boston: Houghton Mifflin.

Farm Animal Rights Movement. (2013). Retrieved May 31, 2013, from http://farmusa.org/statistics11.html

Fessler, D., Navarrette, M. T., & Navarrette, C. D. (2003). Meat is good to taboo: Dietary proscriptions as a product of the interaction of psychological mechanisms and social processes. *Journal of Cognition and Culture, 3*(1), 1–40. Retrieved from http://www.sscnet.ucla.edu/anthro/faculty/fessler/pubs/MeatIsGoodToTaboo.pdf

Francione, G. (2009). *Animals as persons.* New York: Columbia University Press.

Francione, G. (2000). *Introduction to animal rights: Your child or your dog?* Philadelphia: Temple University Press.

Gaard, G. (2012). Speaking for animal bodies. *Hypatia, 27*(3), 520–526.

Gaard, G. (1993). *Ecofeminism: Women, animals, nature.* Philadelphia: Temple University Press.

Hall, L. (2010). *On their own terms: Bringing animal rights philosophy down to earth.* Darien, CT: Nectar Bat.

Haraway, D. (2008). *When species meet.* Minneapolis: University of Minnesota Press.

Hare, R. D. (1999). *Without conscience.* New York: Gilford.

Holm, L., & Mohl, M. (2000). The role of meat in everyday food culture: An analysis of an interview study in Copenhagen. *Appetite,* (34), 277–283.

Horta, O. (2010). What is speciesism? *Journal of Agriculture and Environmental Ethics,* (23) 243–266.

Hunt, L. (2007). *Inventing human rights, a history.* New York: W. W. Norton.

Ingold, T. (1994). Introduction. In T. Ingold (Ed.), *What is an animal?* (pp. 1–16). New York: Routledge.

Jacobsen, K., & Riebel, L. (2002). *Eating to save the earth: Food choices for a healthy planet.* Berkeley, CA: Celestial Arts.

Jenkins, S. (2012). Returning the ethical and political to animal studies. *Hypatia, 27*(3), 504–512.

Joy, M. (2011, July 29). Understanding neocarnism. *One Green Planet.* Retrieved from http://www.onegreenplanet.org/lifestyle/understanding-neocarnism/

Joy, M. (2010). *Why we love dogs, eat pigs, and wear cows: An introduction to carnism.* San Francisco: Conari.

Joy, M. (2001). From carnivore to carnist: Liberating the language of meat. *Satya, 8*(2), 26–27.

Linzey, A., & Clarke, P. A. B. (Eds.). (1990). *Animal rights: A historical anthology.* New York: Columbia University Press.

Luke, B. (2007). Justice, caring, and animal liberation. In J. Donovan & C. J. Adams (Eds.), *The feminist care tradition in animal ethics* (pp. 125–152). New York: Columbia University Press.

MacKinnon, C. A. (2004). Of mice and men: A feminist fragment of animal rights. In C. R. Suunstein & M. Nussbaum (Eds.), *Animal rights: Current debates and new directions* (pp. 263–276). Oxford: Oxford University Press.

Midgley, M. (1984). *Animals and why they matter.* Athens: University of Georgia Press.

Mill, J. S. (1993). *On liberty and utilitarianism.* Random House Digital.

Nibert, D. (2002). *Animal rights/Human rights: Entanglements of oppression.* New York: Rowman & Littlefield.

Nietzsche, F. (2000). Truth and lies in an extra-moral sense. In C. Cazeaux (Ed.), *The continental aesthetics reader* (pp. 53–62). New York: Routledge.
Noske, B. (1997a). *Beyond boundaries: Humans and animals*. New York: Black Rose.
Noske, B. (1997b). Speciesism, anthropocentrism, and non-Western cultures. *Anthrozoös, 10*(4), 183–190.
Oliver, K. (2009). *Animal lessons: How they teach us to be human*. New York: Columbia University Press.
O'Sullivan, S. (2011). *Animals, equality, and democracy*. New York: Palgrave Macmillan.
Patterson, C. (2002). *Eternal Treblinka: Our treatment of animals and the Holocaust*. New York: Lantern.
Plumwood, V. (2002). *Environmental culture: The ecological crisis of reason*. New York: Routledge.
Ramachandran, V. S. (2006, January 10). Mirror neurons and the brain in the vat. *Edge: The Third Culture*. Retrieved from http://www.edge.org/3rd_culture/ramachandran06/ramachandran06_index.html
Regan, T. (1983). *The case for animal rights*. Berkley: University of California Press.
Robbins, J. (2010). *The food revolution*. San Francisco: Conari.
Sanbonmatsu, J. (2011). *Critical theory and animal liberation*. Lanham, MD: Rowman & Littlefield.
Sanbonmatsu, J. (2007). The subject of freedom at the end of history: Socialism beyond humanism. *American Journal of Economics and Sociology, 66*(1), 217–235.
Sartre, J. P. (2007). *Existentialism is a humanism*. (J. Kulka, Ed.; C. Macomber, Trans.). New Haven, CT: Yale University Press.
Shapiro, K. J. (1990). Animal rights versus humanism: The charge of speciesism. *Journal of Humanistic Psychology, 30*(2), 9–37.
Shriver, A. (2009). Knocking out pain in livestock: Can technology succeed where morality has stalled? *Neuroethics, 2*, 115–124.
Simoons, F. J. (1961). *Eat not this flesh: Food avoidances in the old world*. Madison: University of Wisconsin Press.
Singer, P. (1993). *Practical ethics*. Cambridge: Cambridge University Press.
Singer, P. (1975). *Animal liberation*. New York: Avon.
Slaughter, J. R. (2007). *Human rights, inc.: The world novel, narrative form, and international law*. New York: Fordham University Press.
Steiner, G. (2013). *Animals and the limits of postmodernism*. New York: Columbia University Press.
Torres, B. (2007). *Making a killing: The political economy of animal rights*. Oakland, CA: AK.
Twine, R. (2012). Revealing the "Animal Industrial Complex"—A concept and method for critical animal studies? *Journal for Critical Animal Studies, 10*(1), 12–39.
United Nations Food and Agriculture Organization. (2006). *Livestock's long shadow: Environmental issues and options*. Retrieved from http://www.fao.org/docrep/010/a0701e/a0701e00.htm
Warkentin, T. (2010). Interspecies etiquette: An ethics of paying attention to animals. *Ethics & Environment, 15*(1), 101–121.
Weil, K. (2012). *Thinking animals: Why animal studies now?* New York: Columbia University Press.
Wolfe, C. (2009a). Humanist and posthumanist anti-speciesism. In P. Cavaliere (Ed.), *The death of the animal: A dialogue* (pp. 45–58). New York: Columbia University Press.
Wolfe, C. (2009b). *What is posthumansim?* Minneapolis: University of Minnesota Press.
Wolfe, C. (2003). *Animal rites: American culture, the discourse of species, and posthumanist theory*. Chicago: University of Chicago Press.

TWO

Ecological Defense for Animal Liberation

A Holistic Understanding of the World

Amy J. Fitzgerald and David Pellow

> *Injustice anywhere is a threat to justice everywhere.*
> —Martin Luther King Jr.

There is now widespread acknowledgment in the social sciences that social inequalities are interconnected. It has become increasingly common to refer to the intersections among race, class, gender, and sexuality (among other social locations) using metaphors, including prism of differences and matrix of inequalities. The implication of this way of understanding inequality is that individuals are multiply situated and that understanding one's social positioning requires analyzing an array of intersecting hierarchies. It has become evident that we can no longer assume that the experience of sexism, for example, is the same for all racial-ethnic groups and social classes. These conceptual developments are constructive and have made our understanding of social inequalities more sensitive and nuanced.

Another axis of inequality, however, remains obscured in the vast majority of analyses. This axis is constructed with humans as agential subjects creating culture on one hand and nonhuman animals and the environment as objects and cast as "nature" on the other. Although a growing number of academics and activists are attending to this specific axis of inequality, it is critical to conceptualize and engage with it as intersecting with other forms of inequality. Failure to do so obscures the ways in which these forms of inequality are interdependent and mutually reinforcing and makes successful praxis elusive. We suggest here more holistic analyses that move us in the direction of critically examining the power relations that undergird these forms of inequality.

In this chapter we trace what a holistic understanding of inequality and power dynamics vis-à-vis animal liberation would look like. This is admittedly a large task, and what we can accomplish in this chapter is certainly more modest. We therefore focus on insights that can be drawn from critical feminist, critical race, environmental justice, and green criminology perspectives, all of which have examined—albeit from different vantage points—how forms of oppression are grounded in and derive support from problematic dichotomies prevalent in Western societies. The culture-nature dichotomy is particularly pernicious and relevant to the topic of this chapter. We begin with an examination of this dichotomy and its implications. We then move on to explore the intersecting forms of oppression grounded in this specific dichotomy, including speciesism, sexism, racism, and classism. We make a case for why Critical Animal Studies (CAS) must confront these forms of oppression, and we conclude with a discussion of how the environmental and animal liberation movements are integrating insights about the intersections of inequality.

Interlocking Forms of Oppression

Like other dichotomies, the culture-nature dichotomy is encountered as hierarchical, such that the dominant category (culture) is rendered normal and is privileged over its perceived opposite (nature). Nonhuman animals and ecosystems have been largely subsumed under the nature category in this dichotomy, yet the reality of how we engage with other animals and the environment is more complicated than that. This dichotomy rationalizes and perpetuates the belief that humans are unique and vastly different than (and superior to) nonhuman animals: humans are believed to belong exclusively to the realm of culture, whereas other beings are considered simply as nature (Noske, 1989).

It is important to note, however, that membership in the realm of the cultural has not been equally afforded to humans: hegemonic conceptions of masculinity have been associated with culture, whereas women and subordinated masculinities (e.g., those who belong to racialized or impoverished groups) have been largely identified with nature. As a result, nature and those associated with it have been constructed as the other and of lesser value than those associated with culture. This othering process undergirds numerous forms of human oppression (such as sexism, racism, and classism) as well as the oppression of nonhuman animals. The result vis-à-vis nonhuman animals is pervasive speciesism and anthropocentrism.

It is worth briefly digressing here to explore the concepts of speciesism and anthropocentrism because they are often utilized to draw parallels between the oppression of nonhuman animals and human groups. "Speciesism" is generally conceptualized as prejudice or discrimination based on species, although philosophers have debated the parameters of the term (e.g., Fjellstrom, 2002). The term was coined by Richard Ryder (1975), who employed it as "a deliberate 'wake-up call' to challenge the morality of current practices where non-human animals are being exploited in research, in farming, domestically and in the wild" (p. 1). His underlying argument is that physical characteristics, such as species, are not relevant in making moral decisions. By extension, speciesism is conceptually analogous to racism, sexism, and so forth; however, not everyone agrees with that comparison. Some argue that it could trivialize the suffering of specific human groups (see Cushing, 2003, for a description of this position, although it is not one that he personally subscribes to), while others assert that species is a different dividing line than sex or race because there are inherent differences between humans and animals, such as intelligence (e.g., Brennan, 2003; Steinbock, 1978). Scientific research, however, is continuously demonstrating that nonhuman animals have capabilities we once assumed they did not possess, and picking qualities that presumably distinguish human from nonhuman animals increasingly appears rather arbitrary. Against the claim that such comparisons trivialize the suffering of human groups, we argue that in order to redress oppression rooted in the culture-nature dichotomy we cannot simply attempt to "elevate" certain human groups from the nature side of the dichotomy to the culture side. Instead, we must deconstruct the entire dichotomy.

We find the speciesism concept useful for two main reasons. The first we have alluded to above: it reminds us of the similarities and interconnectedness of the forms of oppression experienced by human groups and nonhuman animals. This is an important conceptual maneuver: "From this perspective, using non-human animals for food, clothing, biomedical experiments, product testing and entertainment is reconceptualized as comparable to the worst atrocities committed against humans" (Sorenson, 2010, p. 12). Second, the term reminds us that the harming of animals extends beyond individual, socially prohibited actions (e.g., "animal cruelty")—it is institutionalized, and in many cases socially accepted. Like racism, sexism, and classism, this type of institutionalized oppression legitimizes the uses and abuses of the less powerful.

The privileging of humans over nonhuman animals and the environment, referred to as "anthropocentrism," is related to discrimination based on species. Although some scholars have suggested the use of other terms, such as "human racism" (see Eckersley, 1998), the term "anthropocentrism" remains ascendant. Three types or gradations of anthropocentrism can be delineated, ranging from the strongest to weakest forms: (1) dominionism, which is based on the belief that God gave humans dominion over nature; (2) stewardship, which gives humans the responsibility of managing nature; and (3) evolutionary, which posits that humans have gained ascendancy through competition and human progress will benefit nature (Arluke & Sanders, 2008). Each of these gradations defines humans as the single most important species on Earth.

In Western cultures both anthropocentrism and speciesism reinforce one another and are used to rationalize the perceived boundary between nature and culture. Even though at times we witness some blurring of this boundary, nonetheless it remains staunchly guarded. For instance, research on media depictions in Canada and the United States of the expansive recall of "pet" food in 2007 that killed countless animals found that even when the most culturally beloved animals—dogs and cats—are harmed, it is not enough to transgress the culture-nature binary and earn them the status of victim in a meaningful way. Instead media discourses about the recall became focused on the culture side of the dichotomy, fixating on the potential risk to humans and obfuscating the actual harm to the nonhuman animals who had ingested the tainted "pet" food (Fitzgerald, 2010).

For CAS to challenge the culture-nature dichotomy and develop a holistic analysis of the intersections of forms of oppression it is useful to draw insights from various perspectives that have been engaged in deconstructing this dichotomy and proposing analytical ways forward. These perspectives include critical feminist, critical race, environmental justice, and green criminology. We examine key insights from each that CAS might usefully draw on in turn below.

Critical Feminist Theory

Two schools of feminist theorizing are particularly useful for developing a holistic analysis of intersecting human and nonhuman forms of oppression: intersectional or multiracial feminism and ecofeminism. Due to space constraints we cannot provide an exhaustive review of each here; instead we focus on the insights we think are most germane in understanding how speciesism is interconnected with forms of human oppression and the praxis that emerges from this interconnectedness.

Intersectional-Multiracial Feminism

This perspective integrates several interrelated concepts that will prove useful in CAS. More specifically, the concept of intersectionality assists us in appreciating how forms of oppression intersect and are experienced as simultaneous, as opposed to the additive model of experiencing differences. The simultaneous intersection of hierarchies at all levels of social life places individuals in different locations within the social structure, with differing degrees of access to power. Intersectionality reminds us that we cannot understand one form of oppression without understanding others and that various forms of inequality interrelate and work together to produce advantages and disadvantages for individuals and groups.

The concepts of marked and unmarked categories are also interrogated from this perspective. Marked categories have been examined critically for years; critical examinations of unmarked categories are more recent. Some of the unmarked categories examined in the literature include men (Hearn & Collinson, 1994; Kaufman, 1994), heterosexuality (Messner, 2000), and whiteness (Frankenberg, 1996). Even scholars who do not take up such unmarked categories as the focus of their work are increasingly cognizant of the fact that examining one group requires examining the group against which it has been constructed.

The role of relationality has also been foregrounded in this literature (Brod, 2003; Glenn, 2000; Hearn & Collinson, 1994). The concept of relationality is crucial for understanding categories such as gender, race, and class for three main reasons (Glenn, pp. 10–11). First, this concept helps to problematize the dominant or unmarked categories against which the subjugated and marked categories are constructed. Second, the relationality concept assists us in appreciating the ways in which differences among groups are related and how different groups are interconnected. Finally, the relationality concept:

> helps to address the critique that social constructionism, by rejecting the fixity of categories, fosters the postmodern notion that race and gender categories and meanings are free-floating and can mean anything we want them to mean. Viewing race and gender categories and meanings as relational partly addresses this critique by providing "anchor" points that are not, however, static. (p. 11)

Baca Zinn and colleagues (Baca Zinn, Hondagneu-Sotelo, & Messner, 2000; Baca Zinn & Thornton Dill, 2000) have also raised this point, highlighting the concept of relationality as a safeguard against "empty pluralism." Relationality reveals how various social categories are developed, defined, and measured against one another. Furthermore, race, class, gender, and sexuality are also what feminist theorist Anne McClintock (1995) calls "articulated categories"—that is, we define each of these categories through the others. We would add humanness and species to this list. For example, if we define race, class, gender, and sexuality through each other, do we not also define these categories by drawing on images and popular understandings of nature, land, and nonhuman animals, and vice versa?

As the above statement by Glenn demonstrates, the theme of relationality in the intersectionality literature is at least partially connected to another theme that emerges in this literature—that the categories and the meanings that they are imbued with are socially constructed. Scholars have addressed the social construction of sexuality and gender (Lorber, 2000), masculinities (Hearn & Collinson, 1994), and race (Glenn, 2000). These scholars not only direct our attention to how groups of people are socially constructed, they also emphasize that these groups are situated very differently in the social power structure and, therefore, these social constructions have very concrete meanings in people's lives.

These scholars have also interrogated the assumptions that result from simplistic, dichotomous thinking. Glenn (2000) eloquently describes why dichotomous thinking is particularly problematic:

> Because the dichotomy is imposed over a complex "reality", it is inherently unstable. Stability is achieved when the dichotomy is made hierarchical—that is, one term is accorded primacy over the other. In race and gender dichotomies, the dominant category is rendered "normal" and therefore "transparent", whereas the other is the variant and therefore "problematic". Thus white appears to be raceless and man appears to be genderless. (p. 10)

Such dichotomous thinking is not only apparent in discussions about race and gender, it is also evident in discussions of sexuality (Lorber, 2000) and in Western science (Hill Collins, 2000).

In sum, intersectional-multiracial feminists have contributed to our understandings of inequalities by articulating how the intersections of forms of oppression mean that people are situated differently in society in relation to power. They have emphasized the importance of examining unmarked categories and the role of relationality, delineated how the meanings given to these categories are socially constructed, and challenged dichotomous thinking that reifies these intersecting forms of inequality. There is one form of privilege, however, that this body of literature has not interrogated or challenged: the unmarked category of humanness has escaped critical scrutiny. That is, the culture-nature dichotomy has not been thoroughly challenged here, and the ways in which groups of people have been positioned in relation to nonhuman animals and nature has been overlooked (recent notable exceptions include Deckha, 2008; Hovorka, 2012).

Ecofeminism

The human-nonhuman animal dichotomy is intertwined with other dichotomies that have been attended to within the intersectional literature, as evidenced by the fact that women, people of color, and people of less privileged social classes frequently have been relegated to the animal side of the dichotomy while privileged white men have been equated with humanity on the other side. Yet sharp boundaries have been drawn in the literature between humans and nonhuman animals. Ecofeminists, such as Carol Adams, have been at the forefront of examining this type of boundary work. Adams explains, "The emphasis on differences between humans and animals not only reinforces fierce boundaries about what constitutes humanness, but particularly what constitutes manhood. That which traditionally defined humans from animals—qualities such as reason and rationality—has been used as well to differentiate men from women" (1994, p. 11). Adams has also been at the forefront of exploring how speciesism is interrelated with forms of human oppression, particularly sexism.

Attending to the relationship between speciesism and forms of human oppression contributes to a more thorough critique of the culture-nature dichotomy, as doing so attends to the very base of the dichotomy and draws attention to speciesism as another form of interlocking oppression. Attending to all forms of these interlocking oppressions is really the only way to undermine them and, for many scholars, will constitute the only true form of liberatory politics (Birke, 2002; Nibert, 2002).

The insights of ecofeminism point to other limitations of the intersectionality perspective. For instance, despite the call within intersectional-multiracial feminism to critically examine unmarked categories, they have been blinded to the unmarked category of human within which they are situated, thus limiting their analyses. Additionally, scholars who have emphasized the social construction of categories (especially those allegedly rooted in biology) have failed to acknowledge the ways in which the categories of animal and human have both been socially constructed. These categories are imbued with assumptions. For instance, it has been demonstrated that assumptions related to gender are often written into our narratives about animals and nature (Birke, 2002; Haraway, 1989).

Sadly, many of the same scholars who have drawn attention to the relationality between categories have seemingly turned their backs on the relation between humans and nonhuman animals. As Noske (1992) explains,

> There are very few social scientists who seem willing to ask what animal-human continuity might mean in terms of their own field. Thus sociologists [generally] do not bother about a sociology of animals. Neither do social scientists question the common hierarchical subject-object approach to the human-animal relationship, least of all do they pose questions as to the ways in which animal subjects might relate to human subjects. By far the majority of social scientists tend to treat our continuity with animals as some kind of purely material residue from a remote pre-historical past. (pp. 80–81)

The simplistic, dichotomous thinking that feminists have been at the forefront of critiquing is rendered acceptable by many feminists when the focus shifts to animals. Adams (2008) describes the difficulty faced when trying to address the issue of animals with non-ecofeminist feminists: "The problem that an analysis such as mine faces is that these divisions continue to be accepted even by many feminists when the issue is animals; and the response by dominant groups is to banish the issue back to a zone of discursive privacy" (p. 192). The issue of how one ought to treat animals (e.g., should feminists be vegetarian or vegan) is depoliticized as a matter of individual choice.

Clearly, although the intersectional perspective represents a step in the right direction, it has stopped short of its logical conclusion. The work of ecofeminists can serve to fill the gaps in current intersectional thinking. Since the 1970s, ecofeminists have been theorizing the connection between the oppression of women and the "natural" world. And recently, some ecofeminists have focused specifically on the relationship between the oppression of women and nonhuman animals. These scholars argue that the oppression of women and animals can be traced back to the same patriarchal social structure whereby women and animals (and children) are considered chattel and men are taught that they are to be in control and have a right to dominate others. Ecofeminists further point to the similar ways in which women and animals have been constructed as the other to privileged masculinity. These classes of other have been relegated to the devalued side of many normative dualisms in patriarchal culture, including culture-nature, public-private, and mind-body (see Adams, 1991; Kheel, 1995; King, 1991; Noske, 1989).

Patriarchal-speciesist culture goes beyond just devaluing nature and those associated with it. Adams (1994) argues that this culture is also characterized by a reverence for and promotion of dominance and control. The abuse of animals is one mechanism through which one can accomplish this culturally prescribed pursuit of dominance and control. In fact, research indicates that the desire for control is a common motivator of animal abuse, particularly among serial animal abusers (Hensely & Tallichet, 2005). Research also indicates that animal abuse can be a vehicle for establishing dominance and control over people. This dynamic has been prominent in the research on intimate partner violence (IPV). Studies in Canada and the United States have found that anywhere from 25 percent (Simmons & Lehmann, 2007) to 86 percent (Strand & Faver, 2005) of abused women with pets report their pet was also mistreated by their abuser. In addition to finding significant overlap between these forms of abuse, research indicates that animal abuse is most likely to be present in the more severe cases of IPV (e.g., Ascione et al., 2007; DeGue & DiLillo, 2008; Simmons & Lehmann, 2007) and that batterers who abuse pets tend to use more forms of violence and exhibit more controlling behaviors (Simmons & Lehmann). Interview-based research with abused women indicates that they believe that the abuse of their pets by their abusive partners did not originate from their partner's loss of control and uncontrollable aggression as many might assume; instead they report the mistreatment of their pets was used as a tool to further abuse them and their children. Animal abuse can be a particularly useful tool because many of these women and children form very close relationships with their pets (Fitzgerald, 2005; Flynn, 2000a, 2000b).

A combination of the intersectional and ecofeminist perspectives assists us in understanding how sexism and speciesism are interrelated, both conceptually and in applied ways. Women and animals have been relegated to the devalued, nature side of the culture-nature binary. This devaluation, along with the valorization of control and dominance within patriarchal culture, puts women and animals at risk of harm. This combination places animals at risk of socially approved violence (e.g., being used as natural resources) and socially disapproved violence, where they can be abused to satisfy someone's desire to exert control and dominance over them or as a vehicle to establish control and dominance over a human victim. The intersectionality of oppression and the pernicious role played by the culture-nature dichotomy are further explored by other perspectives.

Critical Race Theory

At the core of critical race theory is the view that racism and racialization are normal, central, driving forces in society. That is, racism is not an aberration, it is not episodic or temporary; rather society is deeply and unavoidably imbued with racial meaning and power, particularly in the United States (Bell, 1992). This includes but is not limited to the way that race is involved in shaping the state, legal systems, educational institutions, labor markets, the economy, language, and national identity (Delgado & Stefancic, 2012; Goldberg, 2002; Kurtz, 2010). Because race is so central to the way human societies operate (particularly in the West), it is a major factor that shapes the way that environmental injustices unfold and impact human populations, and it is deeply implicated in the ways we use nature and constructions of nonhuman animal traits to define differences among human populations. Drawing from the concept of intersectionality, critical race theory is also quite conscious of and attentive to the ways in which class, gender, and sexuality intersect with race to produce advantages and disadvantages for individuals and groups (Delgado & Stefancic, 2012). This suggests that Earth and animal justice activists and theorists must grasp the centrality of inequalities among human populations if we are to build stronger movements and more robust theoretical frameworks for understanding and responding to socioecological crises.

Critical race theorists and legal scholars Lani Guinier and Gerald Torres's book *The Miner's Canary* (2002) makes two key arguments of importance here. The first is that the experiences of those of us who are marginalized by virtue of being people of color in a racist society are an early warning system for the rest of us who ignore racism at our peril. Racism certainly offers benefits to certain individuals and groups, but Guinier and Torres contend that, ultimately, it harms us all, economically, politically, socially, culturally, and psychologically. The second argument Guinier and Torres present is in response to the first: in order to address the collectively destructive effects of racism and white supremacy, we must enlist the support of a diverse cross section of humanity to embrace social justice in all forms. This "political race" project is a model of coalition building across groups of people that begins with attention to race, extends to class, gender, and other social categories, but never loses sight of race and the role of antiracist theory and politics (Guinier & Torres). In other words, this model of politics begins with the understanding that race is a central organizing principle and anchor around which people of color and white allies can mobilize. Whites and others who enjoy privileges will have to consciously reject those social systems and practices that support their gains while people of color and whites will have to expand their conception of social justice to include multiple categories beyond race.

We see productive parallels between this idea and the goals of CAS. Accordingly, melding Guinier and Torres's concept with insights from CAS, we offer four related proposals. First, while human privilege has produced seemingly infinite benefits and gains for a single species on Earth, it has also led to catastrophic impacts on nonhuman species and ecosystems. Second, as a direct and indirect result of the exercise of human privilege, humans themselves have and will continue to suffer from the effects of harm to ecosystems and nonhuman animals (Beck, 1995). This human suffering results from our inseparable relationship to nonhuman natures and our dependence upon land, air, water, and other species for our existence. Third, we embrace a model of politics that begins with humans taking responsibility for practicing transformative ecological political work, and extends to understanding inequalities across species and space in order to imagine and struggle for a more respectful and egalitarian relationship of human beings to the broader nonhuman world. In this way, we destabilize the notion of the human as a biological category that places humans at the apex of a human-nature hierarchy and embrace it as a political category that extends to include more than human natures as part of the broader ecological community (Schlosberg, 2007). This model of politics also rejects the state as an arbiter of justice as well as any uncritical efforts at inclusion of marginalized humans and nonhumans into the state's sphere of influence. The power and role of the state in classifying and producing racial, gender, and humanist categories for centuries should be reason enough to embrace an anarchist approach to social change. The state has managed, included, excluded, homogenized, and controlled humans and nonhuman natures for the benefit of a small elite and therefore underscores the importance of thinking and acting beyond the state. This model of politics must approach the question of the agency of the other in a distinct fashion. Namely, while nonhuman species and ecosystems may not engage in politics the way humans tend to, they can and do exert power and influence in a myriad of ways and we must be more observant and respectful of that fact and seek ways to work with rather than always against them (Braun & Whatmore, 2010). Finally, the preceding argument suggests that we might expand Guinier and Torres's notion of the miner's canary to include vulnerable humans, nonhuman species, and ecosystems. In a sense, we argue for extending that metaphor literally to include the miner, the canary, the mine itself, and the ecosystem in which all three are situated.

Environmental Justice

The basis of environmental justice (EJ) studies and politics is that human communities that experience political, cultural, social, and economic marginalization also tend to confront disproportionately intense exposure to pollution and other risks associated with industrialization. The terms "environmental racism" and "environmental injustice" capture this relationship wherein many people of color, immigrant, indigenous, and working-class communities are targeted by the state and industry for negative environmental externalities, which produce greater public health risks as well. For decades, the EJ movement has risen up to respond to these disparities, challenging governments, corporations, and affluent communities to remove, reduce, and rethink the toxic approach to policymaking that reinforces existing social hierarchies.

As scholars working to document and explore the expanding field and politics of environmental injustice, we adopt the recent use of the term "critical environmental justice studies" (Adamson, 2011; Pellow & Brulle, 2006). This concept is meant to capture more recent, "second generation" scholarship in EJ studies that questions assumptions and blind spots of earlier work in the field, by embracing greater interdisciplinarity and moving toward post-positivist methodologies and epistemologies. The second generation of EJ studies is also characterized by an expansion of social categories under consideration, particularly a stronger attention to gender, sexuality, and, increasingly, nonhuman natures. There is also a greater depth with which scholars are envisioning the question of justice and sustainability (Agyeman, 2005). Thus, critical EJ studies draws from several fields (including political economy, feminist theory, ethnic-racial studies, and postcolonial-transnational scholarship) for the purpose of providing more robust, complex, and nuanced explanations for why environmental injustices exist, how human and nonhuman forces produce and are impacted by them, and what environmental justice might look like.

With its primary focus on the public health of communities fighting for social and environmental justice, one might think that there is little in common between a CAS politics and the movement for environmental justice. However, EJ and CAS do have a good deal in common. For example, both movements challenge and oppose myriad forms of hierarchy, inequality, and domination, which can include racism, nativism, classism, heterosexism, patriarchy, colonialism, speciesism, and naturism-dominionism. Not only do these movements reject multiple forms of hierarchy, they also challenge the violence those hierarchies embody and authorize. The list is long and includes war, the slaughter and consumption of nonhumans, and the appropriation or destruction of forests, rivers, and compromises to air and water quality. These movements may oppose such violence for different reasons and with difference emphases, but their focus on these practices suggests possibilities not for recruitment and movement building, but for cross-movement conversation, analysis, and collaborative action.

Both movements also oppose the violence associated with states and dominant economic systems like capitalism and socialism. While the EJ movement tends to take a reformist approach to these social institutions, it nevertheless refuses to stand for their excessive abuses of vulnerable human populations and their associated ecosystem bases. The EJ movement's support of human rights, civil rights, and the sacredness of nonhuman nature reflects these values. The Principles of Environmental Justice are a sort of founding document of the EJ movement and contain several statements that speak to these intersecting concerns. Principle #2 reads: "Environmental Justice demands that public policy be based on mutual respect and justice for all peoples, free from any form of discrimination or bias," and Principle #3 states: "Environmental Justice mandates the right to ethical, balanced and responsible uses of land and renewable resources in the interest of a sustainable planet for humans and other living things." Principle #15 "opposes military occupation, repression and exploitation of lands, peoples and cultures, and other life forms." These three principles embrace the idea of nonhierarchical relations between and among all beings, both human and nonhuman—a cornerstone of CAS.

Both movements also view human society as the source or point of origin for the harm visited upon vulnerable bodies, whether they are human or nonhuman. In that sense, both movements adopt a biocentric or anti-speciesist orientation to varying degrees. While the CAS movement pursues a thoroughly anti-speciesist worldview, the EJ movement is perhaps best described as a hybrid of biocentrism and anti-speciesism.

Both movements broadly view threats to ecological sustainability as harmful to all life forms. While much of the animal rights movement has been rightly criticized for its general lack of attention to ecosystem defense, the CAS movement makes clear connections among risks to ecosystems, nonhumans, and humans. As an activist told one of the authors of this chapter, "I'm an animal liberation activist, but that means I must also be in favor of forest protection and preservation because that's home for countless animals." As for the EJ movement, the first of seventeen Principles of Environmental Justice affirms "the interdependence of all species," underscoring that movement's commitment to protecting the future of all life forms.

Finally, both the CAS and environmental justice movements are important actors in broader efforts to attribute accountability and responsibility for harms visited upon ecosystems, nonhumans, and marginalized people—all of which are key concerns of the field of green criminology (Beirne & South, 2007a, 2007b; White, 2008).

Green Criminology

The term "green criminology" was coined by Lynch (1990) and has since been defined as "the study of those harms against humanity, against the environment (including space) and against non-human animals committed by both powerful institutions (e.g., governments, transnational corporations, military apparatuses) and also by ordinary people" (Beirne & South, 2007a, p. xiii). A central premise of green criminology is that the purview of criminology should not be determined by rather arbitrary legalistic boundaries. Green criminology is therefore framed around a social harm approach that expands traditional disciplinary boundaries beyond what is officially defined as criminal.

Although there are divergent perspectives within the field of green criminology, the general field has produced important insights that CAS could draw from. The first is the understanding that it is important to examine socially approved of and even institutionalized harms against the environment and animals, and not just focus on individual acts of cruelty against animals (particularly pets) or egregious forms of environmental damage (see Beirne, 2007). Important to note, this critical focus on socially injurious action instead of strictly illegal behavior is also applied to harms against people. Part of this focus is a critical interrogation and assessment of why certain harmful behaviors (and some arguably harmless behaviors) are defined as illegal by the state while others (sometimes even more injurious) are not.

Second, there is a dedication to praxis within green criminology that CAS could draw on for support. Although green criminologists may at times engage in seemingly esoteric debates and analyses, the central question that these analyses culminate in is "how do we engender a system of regulation and human intervention that will provide the best outcome for human and non-human" (White, 2008, p. 26). South and Beirne (2006) have described this mandate as an attempt "to 'make a difference' for the common good" (p. xxv). Important, the "common good" referred to by green criminologists is not restricted only to human populations but also extends to the natural environment and other species of animals.

Third, green criminology also includes a critical political economic analysis. Green criminological analyses focus on the roles played by nation-states, global capitalism, and corporations in understanding the harms suffered by the environment, animals, and disproportionately by certain groups of humans (Fitzgerald, 2012; Fitzgerald & Baralt, 2010). The animal-industrial complex concept, originally introduced by Barbara Noske (1989) and revived by Twine (2012), could be particularly useful in integrating the insights of green criminology into CAS. The concept can be useful in highlighting and interrogating the various interconnections at play in the commodification and objectification of animals. Twine provides us with the following useful definition of the animal-industrial complex: it is "a partly opaque and multiple set of networks and relationships between the corporate sector, governments, and public and private science. With economic, cultural, social and affective dimensions it encompasses an extensive range of practices, technologies, images, identities and markets" (2012, p. 23). Green criminological analyses might be particularly useful here in critically examining the various actors in the animal-industrial complex and additionally how harms against animals, the environment, and groups of people are tightly integrated and stem from the same sources.

We can use the example of the production and consumption of meat to illustrate how the political-economic system creates the conditions that can produce significant suffering for humans and other animals. Although not a self-identified green criminologist, David Nibert's work in the area of political economy and animal rights is instructive. In his book *Animal Rights/Human Rights* (2002), Nibert traces the ways in which the oppression of animals has been linked historically and geographically with the oppression of marginalized groups of people. In his own words,

> The oppression of humans and other animals developed in tandem, each fuelling the other . . . to hunger generated by the elite's feeding and consumption of "domestic" animals, to warfare necessitated by the need for new grazing areas (with the added "bonus" of claiming women and other animals as the spoils) . . . to the debasement and extermination of the Irish by the British (in large part for the appropriation of land to raise sheep and cows), to the exploitation and extermination of indigenous Americans (in part for the skins and hair of other animals and for acquisition of grazing land), to the violence and discrimination against humans of Mexican descent (for land acquisition for increased populations of cows raised for slaughter)—the oppression of devalued groups of humans has been intimately and thoroughly tied to the oppression of other animals. (pp. 51–52)

The production of animals for human consumption, and the misery wrought for animals and humans, increased dramatically in the twentieth century. This increase was fostered by policies of the state and the expansionary drive of capitalism. After WWII, agricultural policy in the United States promoted increased meat consumption as a solution to dealing with the oversupply of grain: the glut of grain could be fed to an increased number of livestock animals, which could then be slaughtered and sold to consumers (Winders & Nibert, 2004). Dealing with the overproduction of grains was not simply about managing the food supply and feeding the masses; rather, it is an economic solution to a (manufactured) problem. Not only were more livestock animals being produced and slaughtered, the conditions of their living and dying also were deteriorating. The production of livestock animals is no longer for use value; instead it is for exchange value: "the primary purpose of rearing livestock today is *not to create food*, but *to make money*" (Gunderson, 2011, emphasis in original). In this type of system, the suffering of the animals becomes a concern only when it impacts productivity.

Although some minor welfare changes are afoot (such as increases in cage sizes for chickens in some jurisdictions), the size of the industry globally and the number of animals subjected to harm within it is expected to increase. Novek (2003) frames the increase in industrial animal agriculture in North America as part of an international treadmill of production. In the pursuit of profits, the industry has to continually increase production and stimulate demand. The international demand for meat is growing, and the transition to a meat-based diet, especially in Asia, is expected to increase demand even further. Using the expansion of the hog industry in Manitoba as an example, Novek points to some of the outcomes of this treadmill of production:

> The expansion of the hog industry in Manitoba presents a useful case study of the global treadmill of production in agriculture. It has been characterized by the ascendancy of large-scale, specialized producers allied with meat processors, suppliers and other corporate interests. Smaller hog producers and more traditional mixed farmers have found themselves at a disadvantage compared to factory farms. (p. 19)

Thus, the "factory farm" or confined animal feeding operation (CAFO) becomes hegemonic. It subjects greater numbers of animals to harm in the name of productivity and profit. But animals are not the only ones who suffer under this system. The CAFO system is associated with environmental problems and worker illnesses, as is industrialized animal slaughter (see Fitzgerald, 2012).

The example of the production and consumption of animal flesh illustrates how some of the strengths of green criminology can be brought to bear on the subjects of interest to CAS: the importance of examining both socially approved and disapproved of forms of harm, the politics of such definitions, questioning the role of the state in preventing and regulating such harms, and engaging in critical political economic analyses.

Toward Social-Environmental-Species Justice: The Total Liberation Frame

Some of the theorizing discussed in this chapter is becoming apparent in the environmental and animal rights–liberation movements, which can also be instructive for CAS scholars. The total liberation frame emerged during the 1990s among radical environmental and animal liberation activists who were influenced by the politics of social justice that permeated many other social movements, social change organizations, and academic disciplines on university campuses. Ideas and concepts like intersectionality, multiple and linked oppressions, and social privilege took hold in many of these spaces, and had a noticeable effect on the language and practices of social movements. The idea that we can no longer understand, analyze, or resist a single form of oppression in isolation from other forms materialized in feminist and antiracist circles, and we began seeing these discourses appear in the writings, speeches, and alongside the actions of radical animal liberation and environmental activists, although not yet central to these movements. Radical Earth and animal liberation groups drew from these ideas as a key component of the total liberation frame in their movement struggles and continue to utilize it today.

In 2010, professor and activist Steven Best gave a presentation at the International Meeting for Environmental Ethics, in which he employed the term "total liberation" to describe the concept embodied in his earlier use of the term "revolutionary environmentalism":

> It is imperative that we no longer speak of human liberation, animal liberation, or earth liberation as if they were independent struggles; rather, we need to speak of total liberation. By "total liberation" . . . I refer to the theoretical process of holistically understanding movements in relation to one another, to capitalism, and to other modes of oppression, and to the political process of synthetically forming alliances against common oppressors, across class, racial, gender, and national boundaries, as we link democracy to ecology and social justice to animal rights. A truly revolutionary social theory and movement will not just emancipate members of one species, but rather all species and the earth itself. It will merge animal, earth, and human liberation in a total liberation struggle against global capitalism and domination of all kinds. It must dismantle all asymmetrical power relations and structures of hierarchy, including that of humans over animals and the earth. It must eliminate every vicious form of prejudice and discrimination—not only racism, sexism, homophobia, and ablism, but also the scientifically false and morally repugnant lies of speciesism and humanism.

Best's words partially echo the well-established concept of intersectionality discussed earlier, and parallel the ways in which ecofeminists have extended this idea to include nonhuman species and ecosystems, essentially embracing a total liberation framework (Gaard, 1993; Sturgeon, 1997).

Environmental and animal rights movements have rightly been accused of prioritizing the protection of animals and ecosystems over the needs of human beings, particularly communities of color, working-class populations, immigrants, and indigenous peoples. While elitism and exclusion are certainly intertwined within the histories of the environmental and animal rights movements (Seager, 1994; Smith, 2005), members of the radical wings of each movement have recently begun to grapple with issues like whiteness, racism, patriarchy, class inequalities, homophobia, nativism, and social privilege. In other words, these activists are integrating a serious social justice critique into their politics, which is a core element of the total liberation frame.

Many activists are learning from the difficult lessons of past (and ongoing) tensions with indigenous communities, women, LGBTQ communities, and people of color arising from offensive and insensitive campaigns, tactics, language, and behavior by environmentalists and animal rights activists, and they have decided that one of the most important approaches to movement building should be developing anti-oppression and antiracist principles and practices within their ranks. Without question, radical environmentalists have had much more success and achieved greater depth with these efforts than have animal rights movements, but there is significant evidence that this is changing. For example, we do not see this kind of language in animal rights publications or within the discourse or documents produced by most contemporary animal rights groups (although this was not always the case historically). It is the more recently formed groups that organize around total liberation where we see support for these ideas. Thus, there are anti-oppression panels at various animal rights conferences and gatherings, and the North American Animal Liberation Front Press Office's communiqués regularly articulate the discourse of total liberation.

EarthFirst! formalized this idea into an official Earth First! Anti-Oppression Policy, which was published in a 2007 edition of the *EarthFirst! Journal* and reads in part:

> The *Earth First! Journal* editorial collective recognizes that the institutional, economic, political, social and cultural dynamics of hierarchy, power and privilege that define mainstream society also permeate the radical environmental movement. These dynamics are expressed in various interlocking systems of oppression (e.g., racism, sexism, classism, heterosexism, ageism, ableism, speciesism, etc.), which prevent equal access to resources and safety, disrupt healthy communities and movement building, and severely—sometimes irreparably—harm our allies, our friends, our loved ones and ourselves. Over the years, the *Journal* has featured a growing number of articles addressing the need to challenge these systems of oppression. This is a reflection of the editorial collective's understanding that implicit in our desire to stop the domination and exploitation of the Earth is a need to create communities that are free of oppressive social relations. We understand that failing to address oppressive behavior not only weakens our movement by alienating and further victimizing our friends and allies, it also calls into question our commitment to a better world and our qualification as a radical movement. For these reasons, the *Earth First! Journal* editorial collective has drafted this policy of active opposition to oppressive behavior of all kinds within the editorial collective, the *Journal* community and the pages of the *Journal* itself. (Earth First!, 2007, p. 13)

The animal rights movement offers another instance of how an anti-oppression policy was applied to an offender. The North American Animal Liberation Press Office (NAALPO) issued a press release titled "In Defense of Total Liberation" that castigated a group of animal liberation activists for racist language directed at people of Chinese descent. The Chinese Business Association of Toronto received a letter from Animal Liberation Canada/USA concerning a recent successful legal ban on the sale of shark fins, considered a delicacy by many restaurant goers. The press release also articulated the total liberation view that multiple forms of oppression are linked:

> The "communiqué" was shamefully shot through with slurs, crude generalizations and racially charged rhetoric directed towards Toronto's Chinese community and Chinese communities worldwide. In light of this blatant and disturbingly racist "communiqué," we wish to put forth the following assertions as human beings and animal liberation activists . . . Racism and racial generalizations perpetuate speciesism, and vice versa, due to the fact that such stereotypes and classifications have been closely intertwined throughout history and have been used to degrade one group or another. People are compared to "undesirable" non-human animals and associated with their perceived behaviors e.g. the Jewish Holocaust and rat references, with similar slurs also prevalent in the U.S. during WWII towards Japanese people. . . . As liberationists, we must embrace the fight and

struggle for liberation of all oppressed beings on the planet. Since our struggles are interconnected, the liberation of one cannot be achieved without the liberation of the other. We would only continue to perpetuate a hierarchical ordering of beings if we fought to eradicate speciesism but not racism, sexism but not classism, heterosexism not speciesism, so on and so forth. We have one common goal: to liberate ourselves and others from the systemic injustices of modernity. (Sheen, 2011)

Radical environmentalists and animal liberationists are not only getting the message that their movements must support an agenda of anti-oppression and justice for humans, they also are promoting these ideas inside and outside their movement circles. The total liberation frame is an extension of many of the concepts in CAS and is largely consistent with the perspectives outlined in this chapter. Further, it reminds us that the liberatory goal of bridging the perceived gulf between culture and nature cannot be accomplished by attempting to elevate those associated with nature to the level of the cultural. Attempting to do so "perhaps unwittingly reproduces the conception that culture and nature are distinct, a view that grounds much of patriarchal thinking. Failing to challenge this distinction undermines a more complete understanding of the workings of oppression" (Gruen, 1993, p. 77). Instead—whether through a politics of total liberation or other projects—academics and activists alike need to challenge the denigration of "nature" and those associated with it; doing so is necessary to achieving the stated goals of CAS (Best, Nocella, Kahn, Gigliotti, & Kemmerer, 2007), particularly understanding and challenging the power relations that have institutionalized speciesism and anthropocentrism.

References

Adams, C. (2008). The feminist traffic in animals. In A. Arluke & C. Sanders (Eds.), *Between the species: A reader in human-animal relationships*. Boston: Allyn & Bacon.

Adams, C. (1994). *Neither man nor beast: Feminism and the defense of animals*. New York: Continuum.

Adams, C. (1991). *The sexual politics of meat: A feminist-vegetarian critical theory*. New York: Continuum.

Agyeman, J. (2005). *Sustainable communities and the challenge of environmental justice*. New York: New York University Press.

Arluke, A., & Sanders, C. (Eds.). (2008). *Between the species: A reader in human-animal relationships*. Boston: Allyn & Bacon.

Ascione, F., Weber, C., Thompson, T., Heath, J., Maruyama, M., & Hayashi, K. (2007). Battered pets and domestic violence: Animal abuse reported by women experiencing intimate violence and by nonabused women. *Violence against Women, 13*(4), 354–373.

Baca Zinn, M., Hondagneu-Sotelo, P., & Messner, M. A. (2000). Introduction: Sex and gender through the prism of difference. In M. Baca Zinn, P. Hondagneu-Sotelo, & M. A. Messner (Eds.), *Gender through the prism of difference* (2nd ed., pp. 1–9). Boston: Allyn & Bacon.

Baca Zinn, M., & Thornton Dill, B. (2000). Theorizing difference from multiracial feminism. In M. Baca Zinn, P. Hondagneu-Sotelo, & M. A. Messner (Eds.), *Gender through the prism of difference* (2nd ed., pp. 23–29). Boston: Allyn & Bacon.

Beck, U. (1995). *Ecological Enlightenment: Essays on the politics of the risk society*. Amherst, N.Y.: Prometheus Books.

Beirne, P. (2007). Animal rights, animal abuse, and green criminology. In P. Beirne & N. South (Eds.), *Issues in green criminology: Confronting harms against environments, humanity, and other animals* (pp. 55–83). Portland, OR: Willan.

Beirne, P., & South, N. (2007a). Approaching green criminology. In P. Beirne & N. South (Eds.), *Issues in green criminology: Confronting harms against environments, humanity, and other animals* (pp. xiii–xxii). Portland, OR: Willan.

Beirne, P., & South, N. (Eds.). (2007b). *Issues in green criminology: Confronting harms against environments, humanity, and other animals*. Portland, OR: Willan.

Bell, D. (1992). *Faces at the bottom of the well: The permanence of racism*. New York: Basic.

Best, S. (2010). Animal liberation, human liberation and the future of the left. Retrieved on June 1, 2012, from http://www.drstevebest.org/RethinkingRevolution.htm

Best, S., Nocella, A., Kahn, R., Gigliotti, C., & Kemmerer, L. (2007). Introducing critical animal studies. *Journal for Critical Animal Studies, 5*(1), 4–5.

Birke, L. (2002). Intimate familiarities? Feminism and human-animal studies. *Society & Animals, 10*(4), 429–436.

Braun, B., & Whatmore, S.J. (Eds). 2010. *Political Matter: Technoscience, Democracy, and Public Life*. University of Minnesota.

Brennan, A. (2003). Humanism, racism and speciesism. *Worldviews, 7*(3), 274–302.

Brod, H. (2003). Scholarly studies of men: The new field is an essential complement to women's studies. In E. Disch (Ed.), *Reconstructing gender: A multicultural anthology* (pp. 355–358). Mountain View, CA: Mayfield.

Cushing, S. (2003). Against "humanism": Speciesism, personhood, and preference. *Journal of Social Philosophy, 34*(4), 556–571.

Deckha, M. (2008). Intersectionality and posthumanist visions of equality. *Wisconsin Journal of Law, Gender & Society, 23*(2), 249–267.

DeGue, S., & DiLillo, D. (2008). Is animal cruelty a "red flag" for family violence? Investigating co-occurring violence toward children, partners, and pets. *Journal of Interpersonal Violence, 24*(6), 1036–1056.

Delgado, R., & Stefancic, J. (2012). *Critical race theory: An introduction* (2nd ed.). New York: New York University Press.

Earth First! Editorial Collective. (2007, September–October). EF! Anti-Oppression Policy. *Earth First! Journal*.

Eckersley, R. (1998). Beyond human racism. *Environmental Values, 7*, 165–182.

Fitzgerald, A. (2012). A social history of the slaughterhouse: From inception to contemporary implications. *Human Ecology Review, 17*(1), 58–69.

Fitzgerald, A. (2010). The "underdog" as "ideal victim"? The attribution of victimhood in the 2007 pet food recall. *International Review of Victimology, 17*, 131–157.

Fitzgerald, A. J. (2005). *Animal abuse and family violence: Researching the interrelationships of abusive power*. Lewiston, NY: Edwin Mellen.

Fitzgerald, A., & Baralt, L. (2010). Media constructions of responsibility for the production and mitigation of environmental harms: The case of mercury-contaminated fish. *Canadian Journal of Criminology and Criminal Justice, 52*(4), 341–368.

Fjellstrom, R. (2002). Specifying speciesism. *Environmental Values, 11*, 63–74.

Flynn, C. (2000a). Woman's best friend: Pet abuse and the role of companion animals in the lives of battered women. *Violence against Women, 6*(2), 162–177.

Flynn, C. P. (2000b). Battered women and their animal companions: Symbolic interaction between human and nonhuman animals. *Society and Animals, 8*(2), 99–127.

Frankenberg, R. (1996). Whiteness as an unmarked cultural category. In K. E. Rosenblum & T.-M. C. Travis (Eds.), *The meaning of difference* (pp. 62–68). New York: McGraw-Hill.
Glenn, E. N. (2000). The social construction and institutionalization of gender and race: An integrative framework. In M. M. Ferree, J. Lorber, & B. B. Hess (Eds.), *Revisioning Gender* (pp. 3–43). New York: AltaMira.
Goldberg, D. T. (2002). *The racial state*. Malden MA: Blackwell.
Gruen, L. (1993). Dismantling oppression: An analysis of the connection between women and animals. In G. Gaard (Ed.), *Ecofeminism: Women, animals, nature* (pp. 60–90). Philadelphia: Temple University Press.
Guinier, L., & Torres, G. (2002). *The miner's canary: Enlisting race, resisting power, transforming democracy*. Cambridge, MA: Harvard University Press.
Gunderson, R. (2011). From cattle to capital: Exchange value, animal commodification, and barbarism. *Critical Sociology, 39*(2), 259–275.
Haraway, D. (1989). *Primate visions: Gender, race, and nature in the world of modern science*. New York: Routledge.
Hearn, J., & Collinson, D. L. (1994). Theorizing unities and differences between men and between masculinities. In H. Brod & M. Kaufman (Eds.), *Theorizing masculinities* (pp. 97–118). Thousand Oaks, CA: Sage.
Hensely, C., & Tallichet, S. (2005). Learning to be cruel? Exploring the onset and frequency of animal cruelty. *International Journal of Offender Therapy and Comparative Criminology, 49*(1), 37–47.
Hill Collins, P. (2000). Moving beyond gender: Intersectionality and scientific knowledge. In M. M. Ferree, J. Lorber, & B. B. Hess (Eds.), *Revisioning gender* (pp. 261–284). New York: AltaMira.
Hovorka, A. (2012). Women/chickens vs. men/cattle: Insights on gender-species intersectionality. *Geoforum, 43*(4), 875–884.
Kaufman, M. (1994). Men, feminism, and men's contradictory experiences of power. In H. Brod & M. Kaufman (Eds.), *Theorizing masculinities* (pp. 142–163). Thousand Oaks, CA: Sage.
Kheel, M. (1995). License to kill: An ecofeminist critique of hunters' discourse. In C. Adams & J. Donovan (Eds.), *Animals & women: Feminist theoretical explorations*. Durham, NC: Duke University Press.
King, R. J. H. (1991). Environmental ethics and the case for hunting. *Environmental Ethics, 13*(1), 59–85.
Kurtz, H. (2010). Acknowledging the racial state: An agenda for environmental justice research. In R. Holifield, M. Porter, & G. Walker (Eds.), *Spaces of environmental justice*. Malden, MA: Wiley-Blackwell.
Lorber, J. (2000). Embattled terrain: Gender and sexuality. In M. M. Ferree, J. Lorber, & B. B. Hess (Eds.), *Revisioning gender* (pp. 416–448). New York: AltaMira.
Lynch, M. (1990). The greening of criminology. *Critical Criminologist, 2*, 1–5.
McClintock, A. (1995). *Imperial Leather: Race, Gender, and Sexuality in the Colonial Contest*. New York: Routledge.
Messner, M. A. (2000). Becoming 100% straight. In M. Baca Zinn, P. Hondagneu-Sotelo, & M. A. Messner (Eds.), *Gender through the prism of difference* (2nd ed., pp. 205–210). Boston: Allyn & Bacon.
Nibert, D. (2002). *Animal rights/Human rights: Entanglements of oppression and liberation*. Lanham, MD: Rowman & Littlefield.
Noske, B. (1992). Animals and anthropology. In E. K. Hicks (Ed.), *Science and the human-animal relationship* (pp. 79–90). Amsterdam: SISWO.
Noske, B. (1989). *Humans and other animals: Beyond the boundaries of anthropology*. London: Pluto.

Novek, J. (2003). Intensive hog farming in Manitoba: Transnational treadmills and local conflicts. *Canadian Review of Sociology, 40*(1), 3–26.
Pellow, D.N., & Brulle, R. J. (Eds). (2006). *Power, justice and the environment: A critical appraisal of the environmental justice movement.* Cambridge, MA: MIT Press.
Ryder, R. (1975). *The victims of science.* London: Davies Pointer.
Schlosberg, David. 2007. *Defining Environmental Justice: Theories, Movements, and Nature.* Oxford University Press.
Seager, J. (1994). *Earth follies: Coming to feminist terms with the global environmental crisis.* New York: Routledge.
Sheen, N. (2011, December 4). In defense of total liberation: A response to Animal Liberation Canada/USA's racialized rhetoric. North American Animal Liberation Front Press Office.
Simmons, C., & Lehmann, P. (2007). Exploring the link between pet abuse and controlling behaviors in violent relationships. *Journal of Interpersonal Violence, 22*(9), 1211–1222.
Smith, A. (2005). *Conquest: Sexual violence and American Indian genocide.* Cambridge, MA: South End.
Sorenson, J. (2010). *About Canada: Animal rights.* Halifax; Winnipeg: Fernwood.
South, N., & Beirne, P. (2006). Introduction. In N. South & P. Beirne (Eds.), *Green criminology* (pp. xiv–xxvii). Burlington, VT: Ashgate.
Steinbock, B. (1978). Speciesism and the idea of equality. *Philosophy, 53*(204), 247–256.
Strand, E. B., & Faver, C. A. (2005). Battered women's concern for their pets: A closer look. *Journal of Family Social Work, 9*(4), 39–58.
Sturgeon, N. (1997). *Ecofeminist natures: Race, gender, feminist theory, and political action.* New York: Routledge.
Twine, R. (2012). Revealing the "animal-industrial complex"—A concept and method for critical animal studies? *Journal for Critical Animal Studies, 10*(1), 12–39.
White, R. (2008). *Crimes against nature: Environmental criminology and ecological justice.* Devon; Portland, OR: Willan.
Winders, B., & Nibert, D. (2004). Consuming the surplus: Expanding "meat" consumption and animal oppression. *International Journal of Sociology and Social Policy, 24*(9), 76–96.

PART II

Unity

THREE

Until All Are Free

Total Liberation through Revolutionary Decolonization, Groundless Solidarity, and a Relationship Framework

Sarat Colling, Sean Parson, and Alessandro Arrigoni

On April 28, 2012, about one thousand activists descended on the Green Hill breeding facility, a supplier of animals owned by U.S.-based multinational Marshall Bioresources, located in Northern Italy. After a torchlight vigil, one activist managed to climb over the fence and reach the gate of the farm. Although there were riot police deployed outside the fence, once activists were inside they were able to reach the cages and remove the dogs. The action culminated in the now iconic moment in which beagles were lifted over the wire fencing, over the heads of police officers, and into the hands of activists and caring veterinarians. The public outcry in Italy against Green Hill is only one incidence in a growing movement against the practice of vivisection. Activists in Italy against Green Hill, in the United States against Huntingdon Life Sciences, and in Asia against bear-bile farming are not only resisting the torture of animals but also are protesting capitalism, state power, and the structures of contemporary life that keep us all oppressed. It is this intersection that this chapter looks to examine.

Earth, animal, and human liberation: there have been many movements and organizations under the banner of each, but fewer that have given equal attention to all three, despite the pressing need to do so. Critical Animal Studies (CAS) "champions a politics of total liberation which grasps the need for, and the inseparability of, human, nonhuman animal, and Earth liberation and freedom for all in one comprehensive, though diverse, struggle; to quote Martin Luther King Jr.: 'Injustice anywhere is a threat to justice everywhere' (Best, Nocella, Kahn,

Gigliotti, & Kemmerer, 2007, p. 5). When we pollute and destroy the ecosystem, we no longer have a healthy habitat; when we neglect others we damage our own psyche and numb our society; when we factory farm billions of animals every year, we destroy their lives, our own health, and the environment. These connections between the oppression of humans, nonhumans, and the natural world are often obfuscated by those in power to the detriment of us all.

In this chapter we propose three guiding principles, enacted collectively and through individual self-transformation, upon which a total liberation movement forms. Our guidelines are rooted in a historical understanding of recent global movements for social change, and how each of these constitutes a piece in the great mosaic of total liberation. First, revolutionary decolonization as a method of decolonizing through self-transformation and revolutionary action; second, what Richard Day calls groundless solidarity, which looks to find a politics of solidarity, not in shared beliefs but in a shared sense of struggle and resistance; and third, what Zainab Amadahy calls the relationship framework, an indigenous- and anarchist-based understanding that how we act in the world naturally impacts others.

These principles are a requirement for a paradigm of total liberation intended to counteract the dominant paradigm of global capitalism that runs counter to solidarity, decolonization, and mutual aid. The neoliberal model values competition over caring and cooperation, assimilation over diversity, and ownership over mutual aid. At a time when arctic ice caps are melting at an unprecedented rate, drought and hurricanes are shattering communities, and already vulnerable countries are the first to be hit by drastic human-induced climate change, a transnational, all encompassing, mass movement of total liberation is needed to stop the complete destruction of human and nonhuman life on the planet. Because animal and human oppression and liberation are inseparable, liberation must entail not only abolishing capitalism but also dismantling the animal industrial complex (Noske, 1997).

Toward a Comprehensive Total Liberation: Expanding the Scope of Total Liberation

The concept of "total liberation" that we are using in this paper was largely developed by animal rights activist and ethical philosopher Steven Best (2010, 2011a, 2011b). According to Best, total liberation emerges as an ethical imperative for radical activists because of the inherent failures of Western progressive rationalism. To Best, this progressive rationalism, which is best expressed through Plato, Bacon, Descartes, Marx, and the entire liberal political tradition, has led to a culture bent on economic growth, technological progress, and increasing standards of living. This "progress" has historically been created through the expansion of domination and control over humans, nonhuman animals, and the natural world. In this regard, progress only exists for a subset of the planet; only humans benefit from this progress, not nonhumans or ecological systems; and only a small subset of humans even benefit (the ruling classes, multinational corporations, and Western imperialists). Over the few thousand years in which "progress" as an ideology has dominated human culture, the planet has been forced to the brink of ecological collapse, the vast majority of humans currently live in precarious conditions, and yearly we perpetuate a holocaust against nonhumans in order to feed ourselves, expand scientific knowledge, and generate profit.

In response to this zero-sum account of progress, Best argues for the concept of total liberation. This approach, which has its roots in Aldo Leopold's land ethic and deep ecology's biocentrism, posits that "no viable conception of progress can be dominionist, anthropocentric, and speciesist, or can ignore the evolutionary and ecological unity and coherence of the social and natural worlds" (2011a). In effect, Best wishes to expand our understanding of liberation to include not only oppressed humans but oppressed nonhuman animals and ecological systems. In this respect

> a sound concept of progress is necessarily holistic, and grasps the interrelations and evolutionary continuity among the natural, animal, and human worlds. It abandons hackneyed hierarchies, pseudo-separations, and indefensible prejudices of all kinds, as it views nonhuman animals as sentient subjects of life entirely of their own purpose and value. (Best, 2011a)

In other words, the concept of "total liberation" requires us to understand the connections among human, nonhuman, and ecological liberation. It posits that human liberation is incomplete—as it would still be rooted in domination and oppression—if it does not include these other facets.

Best's conception of total liberation is not completely unique but it does add complexity, militancy, and ethical rigor to concepts that were developed by others. Most important, and not covered by Best, his conception of total liberation is heavily rooted in the ecological and animal rights politics of Élisée Reclus. Reclus, a late nineteenth-century French anarchist activist and academic geographer, claimed throughout his work that human freedom requires ecological wellness and requires humans to ethically relate to nonhuman nature. In his short piece "On Vegetarianism" (1901a), Reclus proudly explains his conversion to vegetarianism and his understanding that the slaughter of animals and the mistreatment of other humans are inherently connected. He claims, "It is not a digression to mention the horrors of war in connection with the massacre of cattle and carnivorous banquets. The diet of individuals corresponds closely with their manners. Blood demands blood." Reclus does not end with this connection but also notes that the treatment of the natural world is connected with our treatment of other animals and other humans. He states:

> We turn with dislike from the engineer who robs Nature of her beauty by imprisoning a cascade in conduit-pipes, and from the California woodsman who cuts down a tree, four thousand years old and three hundred feet high, to show its rings at fairs and exhibitions. Ugliness in persons, in deeds, in life, in surrounding Nature—this is our worst foe. Let us become beautiful ourselves, and let our life be beautiful! (1901a)

Expanding on this, Reclus, in "The Great Kinship of Humans and Fauna" (1901b), contends that humans might have "progressed" in some ways but we have also moved markedly backward in our ethical responsibilities to animals and the environment. Expressing this, Reclus claims that "we may say that in many respects the domestication of animals, as we practice it today, exhibits a veritable moral backsliding, for, far from having improved them, we have deformed, degraded and corrupted them."

In effect, Reclus, through his geographic academic work and his anarchist activism, came to understand that there was a complex and important relationship among humans, nonhuman animals, and the natural world. He contended that barbarity in one of these realms will lend itself to barbarity in the others. In effect, Reclus understood what Best has developed as total liberation, more than one hundred years prior. What Reclus was unable to adequately understand was how to rectify the horrible behaviors of humans. Reclus saw the treatment of animals and the natural world as being addressed only through individual ethical choices and education. While these aspects are essential for expanding the concept of total liberation, Best correctly notes that rarely have humans expanded ethical rights without external pressure—from John Brown's raid on Harpers Ferry, to Animal Liberation Front (ALF) activists liberating mink, to the shutting down of ministerial meetings in Seattle, Washington, during the World Trade Organization (WTO) protests in 1999.

Best also expands on the arguments developed in the 1980s and 1990s by ecofeminists who noted the intersections between the destruction of the natural world and the domination that white patriarchal societies impose on women, people of color, and third world countries. The connection between women and nonhuman animals is made explicit by Lori Gruen in her piece "Dismantling Oppression: An Analysis of the Oppression of Women and Animals" (1993) in which she argues that ecofeminism needs to understand the intersections the dominant culture engages in with its treatment of women, nature, and animals. She contends that women and animals are both deemed irrational, more passionate, and, therefore, exempt from the political world men inhabit. She contends that instead of trying to become more masculine women should reject the logic that justifies oppression toward women, the natural world, and animals. Likewise, Carol Adams, in her book *The Sexual Politics of Meat* (1990), contends that the deforming power of patriarchy is also present in the deforming and degrading practice of animal slaughter and that in order to overcome patriarchy we also have to overcome speciesism.

That said, there are certain strains of ecofeminism—most are rooted in work of Mary Daly—that promote an essentializing notion of woman that embraces transphobia. This happens, especially in her book *Gyn/Ecology* (1990), when theorists claim that there is an inherently biological connection between women and the natural world. As such, the connection that ties women and the natural world is not a byproduct of socialization or lived experiences of oppression but biological. Thus male-born individuals, even those who are gender queer or trans, are unable to have the same lived experiences as women and are therefore not as closely connected to the natural world nor as oppressed by patriarchy. This approach also fails to adequately address differentiating factors such as race, culture, queerness, and ability.

Some feminists and sex workers have contested the "anti-sexual expression and anti-erotica" that is predominant in animal rights discourse and analysis, as well as the lack of inclusion of voices of sex workers to represent themselves in the discourse (Furry Girl & Ross, 2004). *The Sexual Politics of Meat*, for instance, is hinged upon

> particular constructions of women and animals as victims. Indeed, the analogy between the exploitation of animals in the meat industry and women's exploitation within patriarchy (exemplified by women's social construction as "hookers" and "whores" inside and outside sex work) only holds if both groups are understood as similarly regarded and treated. (Corman, 2012, p. 33)

This assumption has been contested by some sex workers themselves, who argue that they don't feel oppressed but rather enriched by their work. Furry Girl, who runs the sites Veg Porn and SWAAY ("sex work activists, allies, and you") explains that part of her goal is to "keep letting people know that yes, it's ok to be interested in sex, it's ok if you want to cross dress, if you want to be queer, whatever it is, that's great" (Furry Girl & Ross, 2004). In her argument Adams does not include positions of those such as Furry Girl and Ross who not only enjoy being sex workers but become empowered through it. To suggest that their experiences are the same as nonhuman animals being systematically exploited and murdered for meat suggests that those sex workers who are satisfied with their work are experiencing false consciousness. This denies the women agency, when the goal is to empower the women to fight back.

This all said, there are many ecofeminist theorists—from Greeta Gaard (1997) to Vandana Shiva (2010)—who seem to overcome this radical essentializing notion of "womanness" by understanding the constructed nature of not only gender but also gender roles. These ecofeminists understand that patriarchal society has constructed a conception of the "feminine" that is directly tied to a sexist understanding of "womanness," which allows them to critique the structure of patriarchy in such a way as to shatter and dismantle the logic that gives it power instead of attempting to "turn patriarchy on its head" as Mary Daly does. The connection by ecofeminists concerning the treatment of women, the natural world, and nonhuman animals is an important theoretical step for understanding and developing a concept of total liberation. However, because our culture exploits women and animals through a perverse system of domination, many commentators view any form of sex work as merely women working with their oppressors and engaging in self-victimizing themselves. A total liberation framework has to engage in solidarity with all oppressed peoples fighting domination—whether nonhuman animals who fight back against their oppressors or sex workers who try to reclaim power from their exploiters.

Overall, the conception of total liberation we are using throughout this paper is rooted in Best's conception of the term but we are attempting to move beyond his formulations. By discussing the connection between total liberation and postcolonial theories we are not only expanding the historical legacy and tradition of total liberation but also connecting the struggle for liberation to the lived experiences of indigenous and colonized people the world over. In addition, total liberation needs to fight to end the oppression of women, alter-abled individuals, trans-identified people, and racialized minorities if it ever hopes to be truly liberatory. Included in this need to expand the scope of total liberation, to actually make it "total," we have to be openly aware of the dichotomies and essentializing discourse that often emerges in discussions around environmental, animal, class, gender, and racial politics. In the end we need to shatter and dismantle the logic of the colonizer, and that means shattering the binaries that the hegemonic worldview has imposed on the world.

Roots of Total Liberation: Franz Fanon and Revolutionary Decolonization

The use of "total liberation" to describe a political movement was first articulated by Franz Fanon, a socialist and early anticolonial thinker who called for colonized and working-class people to free their minds from, and fight back against, colonial enslavement. In his revolutionary work, *The Wretched of the Earth* (1968), Fanon argues that freedom can only be taken and that the oppressed must use violence to free themselves from the colonizer. The psychological dimension to freedom is central for Fanon who writes, "Total liberation is that which concerns all sectors of the personality" (p. 310). In other words, total liberation can only occur if the consciousness of colonized peoples is first liberated. As exiled Black Panther Assata Shakur (n.d.) explains, "Our problem [in the United States] is that we want to belong to a society that wants to oppress us. We want to be the plantation owner." Instead, we should work toward a community that seeks to abolish the plantation. In contradistinction, any freedom that involves negotiated settlements and economic dependency on a neocolonial system is pseudo freedom that amounts to puppet independence. Total liberation can only be achieved through a commitment to the destruction of the colonial system through armed resistance and radical self-transformation.

In the struggle against the colonizer, Fanon (1968) calls for the colonized to fight for their humanity and no longer be turned "into an animal" (p. 42) and thus exhibits the inherent rejection of being animal that CAS deconstructs. Adam Weitzenfeld (2011) explains the role of nonhuman animals in Fanon's work:

> Fanon's characterization of the relationship between decolonization and animals is complex: on the one hand, animal being is to be transcended, if not negated through self-assertion and violence, yet the animal virtues of spontaneity, ferocity, and pack-forming are crucial for the overthrow of the colonizers.

The demand to be seen as "human" (and not "animal") is prevalent in anticolonial writings because oppressors have long devalued colonized peoples by reducing them to a homogenized, derogatory notion of animals (Armstrong, 2002; Derrida, 2008; Harper, 2010; Patterson, 2002; Spiegel, 1996). Humanness has long been associated with the white, "civilized," European male while non-white people have been characterized as animalistic. This is seen in Enlightenment thinkers like Kant, who viewed Africans, native peoples, women, and nonhuman animals as being inherently unreasonable and therefore not worthy of equal moral consideration. The speciesist hierarchy has been used to subordinate humans as well as nonhuman animals.

One of the most effective reactions to the destruction of nature and of human-nature relationships comes from the Frankfurt School and its representatives, such as T. W. Adorno. Adorno (1951) is clear when it comes to animal exploitation and human slavery (*pogrom*):

> The recurring statement that the savages [sic], the blacks, the Japanese resemble animals, or monkeys, already contains the key to the pogroms. . . . The possibility of pogroms is decided at the time when the eye of a wounded animal affects humans. The stubbornness with which man deviates from the gaze of the dying is repeated endlessly in the atrocities committed upon men, in which the performers must always confirm to themselves that their victims are nothing more than animals. (p. 117)

Adorno, when he talks about subjects and objects, refers to the human subject objectified by exploitation and violent behaviors but, since he does not exclude animalization of humans as a cognitive, moral, and practical path to the extermination of other humans, we can affirm that since all sentient beings are killed and exploited, all humans are exposed to the same dangers.

While Adorno's concept of the "dialectical animal," as well as Gilles Deleuze and Félix Guattari's "anarchistic process" of "becoming-animal" (Weitzenfeld, 2011), which destabilizes the neoliberal subject and challenges the binary system that upholds human domination, should be pursued in place of humanism, the anticolonial roots of total liberation do lie with Fanon and have significance for a total liberation framework of CAS. Jennifer Hales (2006) defines colonization as including "all forms of dominating and oppressive relationships that emerge from structures of power and privilege inherent and embedded in our contemporary social relations" (p. 244). While oppression manifests from different sources of privilege and power, colonial conquests have led to many human and nonhuman injustices. These include encouraging ownership of and colonizing people of color, women, children, queers, the poor, those with disabilities, forests, seeds, and non-human animals, as well as imposing on traditionally egalitarian cultures such as the capitalist conception of private property (Nibert, 2007). True liberation, as Fanon concludes, involves breaking down the structures that uphold the colonial system—including the colonial ideologies imposed on indigenous peoples.

This total destruction must occur through revolutionary decolonization, which has two central tenets that are closely connected: that of liberating consciousness through self-transformation, and revolutionary action against the structures of colonialism. First, self-transformation must occur because, particularly for Fanon, Africans and African Americans are psychologically enslaved under colonialism and must liberate their consciousness. All colonized peoples experience this psychological oppression that manifests in material violence. As Amy Breeze Harper (2010) explains, liberating consciousness and decolonization is closely tied with acts of bodily autonomy that create nondominating, alternative ways of living, such as those belonging to communities traditionally subordinated under colonialism rejecting the unhealthy—high in animal product—diets imposed on them (p. 37). Linda Fisher (2011) makes a similar argument regarding the influence of Europeans on increased meat consumption for indigenous peoples in North America. Before the colonialists arrived,

> the Americas were a rich and fertile land, providing plentiful berries, vegetables, nuts, beans, squash, roots, fruits, corn, and rice. Most tribal people survived comfortably eating meat sparingly, while thriving on the cornucopia of the land . . . Only recently has meat become an important staple.

Further, Fisher suggests that today's meat-centered diet is "harming native cultures and causing health problems such as diabetes, cancer, and heart disease." Rejecting the legacy of the colonial system by refusing to consume the products of its slaughterhouses also means rejecting the multiple oppressions that arise from that site: from the horrific treatment of workers, including migrant workers, devastating environmental pollution, and the systematic murder of nonhuman animals whose very bodies and labor have been the material for colonial expansion (Hribal, 2003).

Decolonization is a responsibility of all who fight for social justice. Given that all non-natives who live in North America and other colonial countries live on land that is appropriated and contested, as Harsha Walia (2012) writes, "Any serious attempt by non-natives at allying with indigenous struggles must entail solidarity in the fight against colonization." In an intersectional, antiracist, antispeciesist praxis, it is important to recognize that European settlers have engaged in the project of empire building for the last five hundred years and that the wealth of North America is dependent on the genocide of millions of indigenous peoples and the many nonhuman animals who are also indigenous to the land (Nibert, 2007). The entanglements of oppression rising from colonialism are found around the world; for instance, the French exploited Algerians "as laborers and developed an extensive export industry based on grazing animals like goats and sheep" (Davis, 2008, as cited in Urbanic, 2012, p. 108). In North America, indigenous people are stereotyped, removed from their families, thrown into prisons, and subject to ongoing military invasions. Along with other marginalized communities, they are subject to environmental racism with pipelines, nuclear waste dumps, coal plants, and slaughterhouses being imposed on their communities. To prevent such practices, non-natives need to become educated about the lands they occupy and listen to members of communities that are some of the most marginalized under colonialism.

A second tenet of revolutionary decolonization is the collective struggle against the oppressor. As Fanon (1968) states, "Decolonization is always a violent phenomenon" (p. 35). Colonization is a violent process, and likewise so is decolonization because many of those who benefit from it will violently uphold their positions of power and privilege. While he argues that a process of decolonization should reverse power relations, it may be more accurate to suggest that we must transform these relations, although this process requires upheaval and subversive actions, as seen, for instance, in Pascua Yaquis activist Rod Coronado's (2000) extensive actions to destroy the fur industry with Operation Bite Back. Coronado explains that the fur trade is another incarnation of the colonial project that has devastated both human and nonhuman nations with traders introducing gunpowder, alcohol, new diseases, and corporations, such as the Hudson Bay Company, into indigenous communities.

Building Alliances for Revolutionary Decolonization: Connecting Civil and Animal Rights

While the theoretical foundation of total liberation is important in developing a comprehensive understanding of the idea, as a movement we can only move forward by understanding lessons from past social movements that advocated various forms of "total liberation," and the similarities found in the repression of movements today. This is essential in building an inclusionary and cohesive total liberation movement based on the principle of revolutionary decolonization.

In the United States, early coalitions for total liberation are found in the Black power movement and their allies. Black Panther members such as Huey Newton and Bobby Seale were impressed by Fanon's revolutionary argument. The Black Panther Party for Self Determination (BPP) emerged in 1966 amid the tide of revolutions, independence struggles, and guerrilla warfare of third world peoples. During the late 1960s and early 1970s, inspired by these struggles and the work of Fanon, Malcolm X, and other revolutionaries, they called for total liberation and world revolution of Africans. They built coalitions with other third world and indigenous groups such as the Young Lords, Chicago Brown Berets, I Wor Kuen, American Indian Movement, and groups led by poor and working-class whites such as JOIN Community Union, the Young Patriots, and Rising Up Angry in Chicago, White Lightning in New York, and the October 4th Organization in Philadelphia.

Combining several of these disparate groups in mid-1969 was a political merger known as the Rainbow Coalition. Initiated by BPP members Fred Hampton and Bobby Lee, the Rainbow Coalition included Chicago's Black Panther Party, the Young Patriots, and the Young Lords. The coalition worked on social justice causes including Rainbow food programs and unity across race, class, and gender. As poor whites, the Young Patriots were often assumed to be too uneducated or racist to participate in leadership roles of social justice movements, but they proved these stereotypes wrong. These radical self-identified hillbillies were distinguished by their political buttons: "Free Huey" and "Resurrect John Brown" (Sonnie & Tracy, 2011, p. 67). Their inclusion in this alliance was "proof of the era's revolutionary vision" (Sonnie & Tracy, p. 100).

Also connected to this struggle was John Africa's MOVE organization (formed originally as the Christian Movement for Life), which promoted an urban back-to-the-land philosophy. While the organization is mostly known through the bombing of their communal home by Philadelphia police in 1985, the philosophy promoted by John Africa connected resistance to capitalism, white supremacy, environmentalism, and animal rights. Expressing this connection, MOVE's website (2012) states:

> We have seeds for the birds, nuts for the squirrels, raw meat for the dogs and cats, and fruits and vegetables for the people. We love all life. It is tremendously upsetting for us to see someone mistreat an animal and we will take immediate action to stop anyone from beating a dog, throwing stones at birds, or causing similar impositions on innocent life.

To members of MOVE, these intersections are noted because they all cause harm to life. To MOVE, all forms of life have intrinsic value and should be respected.

Founding this reverence for life in spirituality, John Africa and his followers pushed to preserve and promote the flourishing of life. This was done mainly by living according to tenants of John Africa's teaching, which included eating raw and vegan food, taking care of stray animals, by embracing and engaging in cooperative organic gardening, and radical simplicity.

The allegiances of the Rainbow Coalitions and other alliances—responding to concerns of the draft, racism, and drugs, poor living and working conditions, unemployment or women's rights—were strengthened in their common fight against the state-corporate-complex and neoliberal capitalist powers. For these poor and working-class communities, "the police were a common enemy" (Sonnie & Tracy, 2011, p. 77). Indeed, the coalitions proved a threat to the state. Hampton was murdered during a police raid six months after the coalition formed while Martin Luther King Jr. was murdered on April 4, 1968, soon after calling for a meeting of eighty leaders in Atlanta (including Cesar Chavez, Reies Lopes Tijerina, Tillie Walker, and Big Dovie). King had called for collaboration from "representatives of all radical, religious and ethnic groups" but was murdered before the meeting could occur (Sonnie & Tracy, p. 58). This was during a time when Counter Intelligence Program (COINTELPRO) initiatives, aimed to contain the movements' effectiveness and growth, were taking place (Churchill, 2001, p. 89). With the backlash against these movements, it became increasingly clear that the prison system is an institution of slavery that imprisons people who are racialized. African Americans make up the largest number of inmates in the United States, often for minor "crimes." Civil rights lawyer and academic Michelle Alexander (2012) has even called this carceral state "the new Jim Crow."

The prison system is tied with the global imprisonment of animals as, like imprisoned humans, nonhuman animals are also institutionally confined for economic purposes. In a special "Prison and Animals" issue of the *Journal for Critical Animal Studies*, the editors write of how the connections have "developed out of noticing the eerily similar trajectories of the prison industrial complex and factory farms" (Shields & Thomas, 2012, p. 4). Speciesism and racism are both manifestations of oppression that serve to maintain white supremacy, neocolonialism, gender, and class privileges and capital. As Anthony Nocella (2012) writes in an article published in the same issue, "One easy way for animal advocates to challenge racism is to support prison abolition and engage in true total liberation and justice for all" (p. 114). The increasing recognition of animals as subjects, awareness of their plight under capitalism, and the negative health effects of meat consumption inspired some 1960s revolutionaries and those heir to their struggles to become vegans and include animal suffering in their articulations of social justice. Angela Davis has discussed how chickens are oppressed and caged alongside humans under capitalism (Harper, 2012); while Martin Luther King Jr.'s son Dexter Scott King has been vegan for more than twenty years, which he sees as an extension of his father's nonviolent legacy; and Martin Luther King, Jr.'s wife, Coretta Scott King, was vegan for the last ten years of her life (Messina, 2010). Similarly, meeting with Stop Huntingdon Animal Cruelty (SHAC7) activist Andy Stepanian, who was indicted as a so-called animal rights terrorist, led former BPP member Ashanti Omowali Alston (2006) to state on government repression tactics: "They called us the same names, and we were, and still are, Freedom Fighters" (p. 224). We see history repeating itself today with the "green scare" against environmental and animal activists (Potter, 2011).

The calls for intersectional alliances can be traced to Black feminists such as Esther Cooper Jackson who argues that race, class, and gender are interrelated (McDuffie, 2009, p. 27). In the 1940s, Cooper Jackson founded the vibrant, transnational magazine *Freedomways*, which published many distinguished authors, including Alice Walker who included animals in her analysis of civil rights. In essence, these recognitions of intersectionality and alliances are working toward the perfect storm that Angela Davis (1974) speaks of, that can only arise from a multi-axle struggle, for "all our separate movements—political prisoners, welfare rights, national liberation, labor, women, antiwar—might generate storms here and there. But only a mighty union of them all could beget the great hurricane to topple the whole edifice of injustice" (p. 382).

Nuclear Power, Militarism, Capitalism, and Homelessness: From Intersectionality to Groundless Solidarity

Social movement scholars have stated that starting in the 1970s many U.S. social movements began moving away from the class reductionism that was prevalent within the old left toward what are called the "new social movements." These new social movements are identified as being about "post-material" issues such as environmentalism and ethnic or gender identity and are often mistakenly considered single issue movements. While some identity and postmaterial movements (mostly liberal in their orientation) were single issued, many started to make connections between the intersectional nature of oppression and domination. Barbara Epstein (1993) in her book *Political Protest and Cultural Revolution: Nonviolent Direct Action in the 1970s and 1980s* clearly described the development of radical intersectional politics.

Epstein (1993) explores the complex development of the antinuke movement from the Clamshell Alliance in New England to California's Abalone Alliance. The Clamshell Alliance was formed in 1976 in order to stop the development of nuclear power plants throughout the New England area. The group was made up of environmental activists, Quakers, and anarchists and what made the movement unique was its ability to synthesize these views into a coherent politics. The group borrowed from anarchists the concept of the affinity group and consensus decision making from the Quakers. Organizing through these decentralized, democratic groups the Clamshell Alliance was able to mobilize quickly, alter its plans on a dime, and engage in a diverse range of protests.

Expanding on this was the Abalone Alliance in California. The Abalone Alliance was formed to stop the development of the Diablo Canyon nuclear power plant near San Luis Obispo, California. The group modeled itself after the Clamshell Alliance but expanded its political analysis. According to Epstein, the Abalone Alliance openly combined feminism, anarchism, and environmentalism into a coherent analysis against nuclear power. Stating this, Epstein (1993) writes:

> The anarcha-feminists insisted that an anarchist or revolutionary egalitarian politics must be feminist, meaning that it must transcend the division between public and private by putting its political principles in practice in daily life, and that those principles must include nonviolence, respect for all human beings and the natural environment, and a rejection of the machismo that had undermined the antiwar movement and had infected the Clamshell Alliance. (p. 95)

By combining feminism, anarchism, and environmentalism the feminist activists in the Abalone Alliance set the stage for other anarchists, ecofeminists, and antiwar movements in the 1980s and 1990s. Most notably, the anarchist group Food Not Bombs, which was formed by members of the Clamshell Alliance, is one of the largest and most well-known anarchist banner groups as there are currently more than four hundred chapters of the group existing in every continent other than Antarctica.

The organization, which was founded in 1981, contends that homelessness, militarism, patriarchy, white supremacy, capitalism, and violence are all interconnected. In order to protest militarism, confront homelessness, and provide a prefigurative example of anarchist politics, Food Not Bombs gives away vegan food, openly stating that they chose vegan food because of their desire to reject violence against workers and nonhumans.

By understanding the intersections of militarism, homelessness, capitalism, animal rights, patriarchy, and others, Food Not Bombs was an early precursor to the anarchist politics of the 1990s and the first decade of the twenty-first century. This analysis of power, though, emerged through the dedicated activism of people involved in the 1970s antinuke movement. This same analysis was included in other movements and groups that split off from the antinuclear movement, including the Latin American Solidarity Movement, the antimilitarism movement, and ecofeminist movements of the 1980s.

Some groups with intersectional praxis took actions to another level, such as when Canada's Direct Action went underground and instigated a series of politically motivated bombings in the 1980s on behalf of the "women, animals, Third World people, and the environment [who] are reduced to product and thus are objectified" ("Litton Bombing," 2001, p. 92). The urban guerrillas bombed a British Columbia hydro substation under construction on Vancouver Island, Litton Industries in Toronto that was manufacturing cruise missile components under a U.S. contract, and three Red Hot Video outlets on Vancouver Island that were selling pornographic films of women and children being raped and murdered. Their commitment to multiple concerns reflected a total liberation outlook.

The Zapatistas, the southern Mexico indigenous freedom fighters against neoliberalism, provided a much needed theoretical and practical addition to the concept of total liberation by openly rejecting taking state power and instead fighting for local autonomy. By accepting that local peoples will all have radically different understandings of social and political goals, sociologist Richard Day has referred to the Zapatistas as rejecting the logic of hegemony. In place of a hegemonic politics the Zapatistas embrace a respect for affinity. This politics of affinity, to Richard Day, is the foundation for the practice of "groundless solidarity," a practice that has become the backbone of anarchist organizing in the twenty-first century (Day, 2005).

Groundless solidarity is a realization that there is no grounding to a claim that one form of oppression is central and others merely peripheral. In other words, instead of looking to claim your political struggle is primary, groundless solidarity claims that all resistance to domination is essential and necessary. Embracing this view would mean that environmentalists would realize that animal, queer, Black, and worker liberation is required to adequately dismantle the political structures that keep us oppressed. In essence, groundless solidarity provides a theoretical grounding for the belief that "no one is free while another is oppressed" and imagines resistance to the state, capitalism, or even civilization not as a "movement," which embraces hegemonic thinking, but as movements.

The most well-known example of groundless solidarity in action was the "movement of movements" commonly known as the alter-globalization movement. This movement against neoliberalism and economic globalization had its roots in the Zapatista struggle but quickly expanded to include a multitude of issues—from environmentalists concerned with the trapping and killing of sea turtles, labor unions concerned with decreasing worker wages, and indigenous farmers concerned with the spread of genetically modified organism (GMO) seeds. In essence the alter-globalization movement existed because a multitude of other movements joined together in common struggle with each other under a realization that all who resist globalization and domination are brothers and sisters in the struggle. This conception of groundless solidarity creates an understanding that all those struggling against capitalism and the state—be they human or non-human—need our support, resources, and love.

Nonhuman Animals and Self-liberation: Their Agency, Multiplicity, and Subjectivity

Scholarship on animal liberation often focuses on human roles in liberating animals. While it has occasionally been pointed out that the animals themselves are rebelling against their oppressors, CAS would benefit from more studies that focus on the agency, multiplicity, and subjectivity of other animals. Rather, there is a pervasive discourse of "voicelessness" in the animal advocacy movement (Corman, 2012, p. 187). Attributing voicelessness to nonhuman animals can lead to the denial of nonhuman animals' political voice(s) that "forecloses the possibility that they do participate or influence political realms" (Corman, 2012, p. 198). The notion that nonhuman animals are acted upon—but never act—objectifies and assumes that they are powerless when, as some cognitive ethologists have shown, nonhuman animals have rich and meaningful social and emotional lives and a sense of "wild justice." This wild justice recognizes that qualities typically thought to be possessed by human animals alone, such as cooperation and a sense of empathy, are common among other animals (Bekoff & Pierce, 2009). For instance, western scrub jays will hold funerals by calling out to one another and immediately gathering in a circle around their dead (Walker, 2012), while cows at farm sanctuaries will gather to welcome animals who are new to the farm (Coston, 2011).

As Jason Hribal (2003, 2010) argues, in transgressing boundaries and escaping their confinement and fighting back against oppressors, nonhuman animals demonstrate intentionality and resistance. It should be no surprise that other animals have responded with force and cunning to the systematic violence and domination. They break out of laboratories and zoo enclosures, bash back against their trainers, and escape from transport trucks and slaughterhouses. In some cases, several hundred animals will escape together, whether a group of one hundred rhesus monkeys who broke out of a laboratory (Hribal, 2010, p. 96), more than one thousand turtles who escaped from a turtle farm ("Turtles Escape," 2012), or hundreds of buffalo who fled from a "meat" farm (Pfeiffer, 2012).

Nonhuman animal escapees face great challenges with little space provided for (some) animals in human-mediated society. Take the case of a bear who broke free from a bile farm in China in 2012. On bile farms, moon bears are kept for up to twenty years in small wire cages and have their gall bladders milked daily, a painful procedure that leads to infections and disease. Because of the atrocious conditions, bears may try to kill themselves by punching their own stomachs so they are fitted with iron vests. One day a bear managed to escape her tiny prison after hearing her cub in distress. But the mother and child had nowhere to escape to, and in order to avoid a lifetime of torture, the bear hugged and strangled her cub to death and killed herself by running into a wall ("The ultimate sacrifice," 2012). This story is not so different from that of Margaret Garner, a fugitive slave who killed her own daughter and then tried to kill herself so that they would not have to endure the suffering of slave life (Davis, 1983, p. 21). As this story illustrates, the instances of oppression between humans and nonhumans who are enslaved "share the same essence" (Spiegel, 1996, p. 28), and nonhuman animals are also capable of complex decision making even when subjected to total domination.

Sometimes escapees are fortunate enough to elude their pursuers, or they receive enough media attention so that they find a place to call home. Susie Coston (2011) describes the fortuitous escape of a cow, later named Queenie, who escaped from a live animal market in New York:

> Driven by the fear of the canes, sticks and electric prods, which are commonplace in live markets and stockyards, Queenie made the choice any animal would if given the chance . . . she sprinted for blocks, attracting the attention of surprised and jeering onlookers as she dodged traffic, pedestrians and eventually police cars on the busy New York streets. Her flight to freedom was finally brought to a halt when police shot her with a tranquilizer gun.

Queenie, marked for slaughter, was met by the enforcers of the state. Fortunately Queenie's brave actions attracted national media attention and people called for her freedom. It also led to the freedom of 150 chickens because of subsequent investigations of the live animal market she escaped from (Coston). Queenie's escape illuminates the cognitive dissonance that exists in a society that champions individual animals whom we personalize, while continuing to murder the billions of animals distanced on farms every year. Animal geographers point out that such escapes exhibit a "particularly dramatic act of animal 'out of placeness'" (Philo & Wilbert, 2000, pp. 22–23). The distinctive presence of escapees and resistors can amount to anxiety and feelings of discomfort when they make the secrets of animal enterprises visible, even if for a fleeting moment. Crossing barriers and refusing to stay in their allotted places, these escapees also confirm the urgency to include other animals in struggles for total liberation.

Perhaps, the keyword is *subjectivity*. All sentient beings, human and nonhuman, are subjects, unique and irreducible. We are increasingly seeing nonhumans as subjects in cognitive sciences (e.g., Balcombe, 2007; Bekoff & Pierce, 2009; Marchesini, 2002), social sciences (e.g., Ingold, 1994; Noske, 1997; Rivera, 2000), as members of interspecies relationships (Haraway, 2003; Noske, 1997; Shiva, 1997), and as moral and legal subjects (e.g., Regan, 2004). This ethical and philosophical task was needed in an earlier time to include people with disabilities, women, and people of color into our ethical and political worlds. The questions we must ask: Are we treating all sentient beings as subjects, or are we treating them as objects?

In discussing "animal natures" the anthropologist Barbara Noske (1997) maintains that the biologization of animals has connected their essences to their biology, as happened to women and non-whites during the nineteenth and twentieth centuries. As long as one's identity is connected entirely to their biology, one cannot be an active subject, imbued with agency. Noske's work is concerned about human-animal continue-discontinuity. She asks: "What sort of animal image are we talking about when referring to the biobehavioural conception of animalness? We are talking about deanimalized animals: twentieth century biology is moving fast into the direction of theoretical de-animalization" (1997, p. 83). De-animalization means reification, which is the main way capitalist culture objectifies animals and allows their industrial exploitation. She continues:

> The animal is modified to suit the production system, and its offending parts simply cut off. Moreover, the animal is deprived of its own society which is not replaced in any way. In the earlier stages of domestication humans invaded and became part of animal social systems (seen from the animal point of view), often replacing the original leaders. At the same time there continued to exist a social system, as well as some sort of ecosystem to which the animals could relate. But under industrial capitalism these systems are no longer intact so that animals have become reduced to mere appendages of computers and machines. (p. 20)

This dehumanization and denial of sentience rights is seen in the vivisection of nonhuman animals today, which is continuous with invasive procedures carried out on colonized groups, such as the reproductive experiments inflicted on Black women by founder of gynecology James Marion Sims (Harper, 2011). Explaining how eugenics has been used to justify the systematic murder of people with disabilities, Snyder and Mitchell (2006) write, "Eugenics can be recognized as a quintessential example of hegemony" (p. 73). To this day, those in power have tested on and enslaved humans and nonhuman animals, whether it was experimentation on Jews, Gypsies, queers, those with disabilities, and other marginalized peoples in Nazi Germany; the U.S. government's forced sterilization of people of color and indigenous peoples; birth control testing on Puerto Rican women; experiments within the prison-industrial complex; or the widespread vivisection of nonhuman animals. While the medical industry might argue that animal experimentation is beneficial for people with disabilities, history has shown that states and corporations are more likely to exploit the differently abled than they are to help them. In addition, these practices are rooted in human and white supremacy and attempt to deny humans and nonhumans control of their bodies.

In the end, expanding our understanding of agency to include nonhumans provides a unique challenge to contemporary political activism by forcing us to ask, "What does it mean to act in solidarity with nonhuman animals?" This conception of solidarity moves beyond the simplistic politics of "speaking for those who cannot speak" by actually trying to listen to those who are denied a voice and acting in concerted effort with them. A lesson that one can glean from postcolonial theory is that imposed liberation, or acting as a representative for a marginalized other, can disempower the subaltern community you are trying to help. It is also a re-creation of the colonial mindset, as entitled communities impose their political will and beliefs onto the communities they are trying to liberate. The goal, however difficult it might seem, is to allow the animals the space and agency to resist their oppression and provide solidarity and support to help them.

One solution is to combine a postcolonial mindset with a politics of groundless solidarity. In such a politics, one does not to attempt to take power or impose a hegemonic mindset on others, but instead to create space for others to have autonomy. This means that we must embrace and recognize the need for solidarity with nonhumans and struggle to help them create spaces where they can flourish and develop their own organic relations and communities. This means fighting against animal industries that imprison and slaughter them; struggling against the speciesist mindset that our culture promotes; providing our support and energy to those species and individuals that resist their human oppressors; and stopping human attempts to isolate and marginalize nonhumans geographically as we currently do with deer, bears, and wolves.

Envisioning Community: The Relationship Framework and Mutual Aid

This groundless solidarity among all species makes space for the "relationship framework" within which Zainab Amadahy, a Black-Cherokee writer, suggests basing our activism. She explains, "We don't see ourselves, our communities, or our species as inherently superior to any other, but rather see our roles and responsibilities to each other as inherent to enjoying our life experiences" (cited in Walia, 2012). Taking responsibility for ourselves and each other regardless of individual, community, or species is necessary for building a compassionate and fulfilling society. It is necessary to destroy the multiple oppressive hierarchies that exist in our society, including species hierarchy. The relationship framework is similar to the anarchist conception of mutual aid, which recognizes that in egalitarian human and nonhuman animal societies, those most likely to survive are "those who learn to combine so as mutually to support each other, strong and weak alike, for the welfare of the community" (Kropotkin, 1972, p. 28). This community building should include building autonomous and protected spaces where nonhuman animals may organize themselves and where they are sheltered from violence.

Conclusion: Animal Liberation Is Total Liberation! The Green Hill Beagle Liberation

Green Hill is the largest breeding farm for pharmaceutical companies, universities, and the notorious Huntingdon Life Sciences, running twenty farms around the world. After the closure of the Morini breeding center Green Hill became the most important farm in Italy, delivering about 250 dogs every month to laboratories. The coordinated campaigns of groups such as Occupy Green Hill, the Committee against Green Hill, and the Coordinating Board against Green Hill have brought people from throughout Italy and abroad to protest the facility. At protest demonstrations and other community events, activists have sought to involve locals, who in turn have offered protection and assistance to the demonstrators. While no activists were arrested at the beagle liberation described in the introduction, twelve activists were later arrested for the action (C. G., 2012, personal correspondence).

The Green Hill liberation soon caught the national media's attention. During the following weeks the activists organized two national events in continuity with the protest. Videos of the liberation and a wiretap of a Green Hill employee talking about killing dogs were made available. With the public outcry, two of the major groups of environmental protection, Legambiente, and animal rights, Anti-Vivisection League (LAV), sent formal complaints to the court, and on July 18, 2012, the Judiciary of Brescia established the seizure of the plant and the confiscation of the 2,700 dogs inside. While the court investigated the company for animal abuse, possession of unregistered dogs, and other minor offenses, Legambiente and LAV gained temporary custody of the dogs—including 500 who were pregnant. And as of September 20, all the Green Hill beagles have been freed and released to families, the last being a mother and two puppies, and the facility is now closed.

The case of Green Hill beagle liberation shows not only our chauvinistic attitudes toward nonhuman animals but also our deep ignorance of the animal-industrial complex. As Steve Best (2012) said in a conference presentation in Brescia, "The vivisection battle could be won more easily than the veganism battle." Agreeing with him, Occupy Green Hill declares on its website that once the 99 percent of people learn what vivisection is, they oppose it, as the vast majority of humans are against the torture of dogs. In Europe and the United States, we are trained to see and treat cats and dogs as pets and subjects. They are typically understood as protected animals who deserve our attentions and care, while animals commonly viewed as tools, food, or entertainment are not. But if we look closer, the common zoo-anthropological gap between pets and exploitable animals is not so sharp. The French anthropologist Jean Pierre Digard (1990) argues that our love toward pets is a kind of "counterpass" for feelings of guilt about factory farming and treatment of nature. In fact, speciesism is so deep that Euro-American populations don't even realize that many cats and dogs are used in animal experimentation, animal testing, and vivisection.

The liberation of the Green Hill beagles was progress not only for nonhuman animals but for humans as well. Actions such as these begin to educate the public on these interconnections, in vivisection and beyond. Alongside the barriers that displace other animals, there are ideological barriers such as racism, sexism, and ableism, often functioning through public institutions. For instance, in Italy the endemic presence of architectural barriers excludes those with disabilities from public spaces, similar to how nonhuman animals are excluded behind walls, fences, and locked gates (Arrigoni, 2012). Suicides are common among people with disabilities as is also the case for undocumented workers and immigrants who are often trapped in dangerous occupations—often in animal industries. This devaluation of humans and nonhuman animals through the epistemic and material violence of a society built on domination is why animal liberation must include human liberation, and vice versa.

Today's animal enterprises exist in direct continuity with the Western European colonial project of slavery, genocide, and environmental destruction. The global capitalist paradigm encourages us to live to work instead of working to live, and always at the expense of, or in competition with, our fellow earthlings. Conversely, a relationship framework of mutual aid, aided by ecologically balanced ways of living, would lead to genuine wealth for all. This requires a radical restructuring of Western values and society so that achieving more resources and commodities is no longer the predominant goal. The consumer growth paradigm, which has created the climate and ecological crisis threatening all life on this planet, has failed to ensure prosperity to all humans and has failed to respect the lives of nonhuman animals. Whether building on the rich tradition of indigenous struggles and the new social movements, inspired by actions such as the Green Hill beagle liberation, or in solidarity with the acts of resistance by nonhuman animals, a total liberation based on the revolutionary decolonization, groundless solidarity, and relationship framework could be the paradigm under which we construct the frame of the individual and social ethics required to succeed in the following decades.

References

Adams, C. (1990). *The sexual politics of meat: A feminist-vegetarian critical theory.* New York: Continuum.

Adorno, T. W. (1951/1954). *Minima moralia. Reflexionen aus dem beschädigten Leben.* Frankfurt am Main: Suhrkamp Verlag. Italian Translation: *Minima moralia. Meditazioni della vita offesa.* Torino: Einaudi.

Alexander, M. (2012). *The new Jim Crow: Mass incarceration in the age of colorblindness.* New York: New Press.

Alston, A. O. (2006). Mojo workin'. In S. Best & A. J. Nocella II (Eds.), *Igniting a revolution: Voices in defense of the earth* (pp. 224–231). Oakland, CA: AK.

Armstrong, P. (2002). The postcolonial animal. *Society & Animals, 10*(4), 413–419.

Arrigoni, A. (2012). Institutional and common oppression of people with disabilities, nonhuman species, and the environment in Italy. In A. J. Nocella II, J. K. C. Bentley, & J. M. Duncan (Eds.), *Earth, animal and disability liberation: The rise of the eco-ability movement.* New York: Peter Lang.

Balcombe, J. (2007). *Peaceable kingdom: Animals and the nature of feeling good.* New York: Macmillan.

Bekoff, M., & Pierce, J. (2009). *Wild justice: The moral lives of animals*. Chicago: University of Chicago Press.
Best, S. (2011a). Total liberation and moral progress: The struggle for human evolution. Retrieved from http://drstevebest.wordpress.com/2011/06/22/total-liberation-and-moral-progress-the-struggle-for-human-evolution-3/
Best, S. (2011b). Manifesto for radical liberationism: Total liberation by any means necessary. Retrieved from http://drstevebest.wordpress.com/2011/07/14/manifesto-for-radical-liberationism-total-liberation-by-any-means-necessary/
Best, S. (2010). Total liberation: Revolution for the 21st century. Retrieved from http://drstevebest.wordpress.com/2010/12/31/total-liberation-revolution-for-the-21st-century-4/
Best, S., Nocella, A. J., Kahn, R., Gigliotti, C., & Kemmerer, L. (2007). Introducing critical animal studies. *Journal for Critical Animal Studies, 5*(1), 4–5.
C. G. (2012). Personal correspondence. Italy.
Churchill, W. (2001). "To disrupt, discredit and destroy": The FBI's secret war against the Black Panther Party. In K. Cleaver (Ed.), *Liberation, imagination, and the Black Panther Party* (pp. 78–117). New York: Routledge.
Corman, L. (2012). *The ventriloquist's burden? Animals, voice, and politics*. PhD dissertation. Toronto: York University.
Coronado, R. (2000). Indigenous traditionalist and earth warrior. [Podcast]. Animal Voices. Toronto, ON: CIUT 89.5FM. Retrieved from http://animalvoices.ca/2000/06/15/indigenous-traditionalist-and-earth-warrior-rod-coronado/
Coston, S. (2011, August 22). Queenie. *Farm Sanctuary*. Retrieved from http://farmsanctuary.typepad.com/sanctuary_tails/2011/08/queenie.html
Daly, M. (1990). *Gyn/Ecology: The metaethics of radical feminism*. Boston: Beacon.
Davis, A. (1983). *Women, race, and class*. New York: Random House.
Davis, A. (1974). *Angela Davis: An autobiography*. New York: Random House.
Day, R. (2005). *Gramsci is dead: Anarchist currents in the newest social movements*. London: Pluto.
Derrida, J. (2008). *The animal that therefore I am*. New York: Fordham University Press.
Digard, J. P. (1990). *L'homme et les animaux domestiques. Anthropologie d'une passion*. Paris: Fayard.
Epstein, B. (1993). *Political protest and cultural revolution: Nonviolent direct action in the 1970s and 1980s*. Berkeley & Los Angeles: University of California Press.
Fanon, F. (1968). *The wretched of the earth*. New York: Grove.
Fisher, L. (2011, August 14). On the "right to hunt" by a Native American vegan. *Scavenger*. Retrieved from http://www.thescavenger.net/animals/on-the-right-to-hunt-by-a-native-american-vegan-768.html
Furry Girl, & Ross, M. (2004). Plants and pornography and sex work, oh my! [Podcast]. Animal Voices. Toronto, ON: CIUT 89.5FM. Retrieved from http://animalvoices.ca/2004/06/29/plants-and-pornography-and-sex-work-oh-my/
Gaard, G. (1997). Toward a queer ecofeminism. *Hypatia, 12*(1), 137. Retrieved from http://www.lespantheresroses.org/textes/ecology_toward_a_queer_ecofeminism.pdf
Gruen, L. (1993). Dismantling oppression: An analysis of the connection between women and animals. In G. Gaard (Ed.), *Ecofeminism: Women, animals, nature* (pp. 60–90). Philadelphia: Temple University Press.
Hales, J. (2006). An anti-colonial critique of research methodology. In G. J. Sefa Dei & A. Kempf (Eds.), *Anti-colonialism and education: The politics of resistance* (pp. 243–256). Rotterdam, Netherlands: Sense.
Hansen, A. (2001). *Direct action: Memoirs of an urban guerrilla*. Oakland, CA: AK.
Haraway, D. J. (2003). *The companion species manifesto*. Chicago: Prickly Paradigm. Italian translation: *Compagni di specie. Affinità e diversità tra esseri umani e cani*. Milano: Sansoni.

Harper, A. B. (2012, February 23). Angela Davis on eating chickens, Occupy, and including animals in social justice initiative of the 99%. Sistah Vegan Project. Retrieved from http://sistahvegan.com/2012/02/23/angela-davis-on-eating-chickens-occupy-and-including-animals-in-social-justice-initiative-of-the-99/

Harper, A. B. (2011, June 11). Critical vegan interventions: Black female slave vivisection, non-human animal experimentation, and the foundation of Western gynecology. Sistah Vegan Project. Retrieved from http://sistahvegan.com/2011/06/11/critical-vegan-interventions-black-female-slave-vivisection-non-human-animal-experimentation-and-the-foundation-of-western-gynecology/

Harper, A. B. (2010). Social justice beliefs and addiction to uncompassionate consumption. In A. B. Harper (Ed.), *Sistah vegan: Black female vegans speak on food, identity, health and society* (pp. 20–41). New York: Lantern.

Hribal, J. (2010). *Fear of the animal planet: The hidden history of animal resistance*. Petrolia, CA: Counterpunch.

Hribal, J. (2003). "Animals are part of the working class": A challenge to labor history. *Labor History, 44*(4), 443–444.

Ingold, T. (1994). *What is an animal?* London: Routledge.

Kropotkin, P. A. (1972). *Mutual aid, a factor of evolution*. London: Allen Lane.

The Litton Bombing Communiqué, October 14, 1982. (2001). In A. Hansen, *Direct action: Memoirs of an urban guerilla* (pp. 477–486). Oakland, CA: AK.

Marchesini, R. (2002). *Posthuman. Towards new models of existence* (ITA). Torino: Bollati Boringhieri.

McDuffie, E. S. (2009). "No Small Amount of Change Could Do": Esther Cooper Jackson and the making of a Black left feminist. In D. F. Gore, J. Theoharis, & K. Woodard (Eds.), *Want to start a revolution? Radical women in the Black freedom struggle* (pp. 25–46). New York: New York University Press.

Messina, V. (2010, January 18). A vegan lifestyle honors Martin Luther King, Jr. Examiner.com. Retrieved from http://www.examiner.com/article/a-vegan-lifestyle-honors-martin-luther-king-jr

MOVE. (2012). Beliefs. Retrieved from http://www.onamove.com/belief/

Nibert, D. (2007). Cows, colonialism, and capitalism: Interview with David Nibert. [Podcast]. Animal Voices. Toronto, ON: CIUT 89.5FM. Retrieved from http://animalvoices.ca/2007/04/03/cows-colonialism-and-capitalism-interview-with-david-nibert/

Nocella, A. J. II. (2012). Animal advocates for prison and slave abolition: A transformative justice approach to movement politics for an end to racism. *Journal for Critical Animal Studies, 10*(2), 112–199.

Noske, B. (1997). *Beyond boundaries: Humans and animals*. New York: Black Rose.

Patterson, C. (2002). *Eternal Treblinka: Our treatment of animals and the holocaust*. New York: Lantern.

Pfeiffer, E. (2012, May 17). 200 buffalo escape Iowa farm, spotted across five counties in two states. Yahoo News. Retrieved from http://news.yahoo.com/blogs/sideshow/200-buffalo-escape-iowa-farm-spotted-across-five-211235677.html

Philo, C., & Wilbert, C. (2000). Introduction. In C. Philo & C. Wilbert (Eds.), *Animal spaces, beastly places: New geographies of human-animal relations*. New York: Routledge.

Potter, W. (2011). *Green is the new red: An insider's account of a social movement under siege*. San Francisco: City Lights.

Reclus, É. (1901a). On vegetarianism. Retrieved from http://theanarchistlibrary.org/library/elisee-reclus-on-vegetarianism

Reclus, É. (1901b). The great kinship of humans and fauna. Retrieved from http://theanarchistlibrary.org/library/elisee-reclus-the-great-kinship-of-humans-and-fauna

Regan, T. (1987/2005). *The struggle for animal rights*. Clarks Summit, PA: International Society for Animal Rights. Italian translation: *La mia lotta per i diritti animali*, Ed. Torino: Cosmopolis.

Regain, T. (2004). *The case for animal rights*. Berkeley, CA: University of California Press.

Rivera, A. (Ed.). (2000). *Homo sapiens and Mad Cow. Anthropology of relationships with nonhuman world*. Bari: Dedalo.

Shakur, A. (n.d.). Assata Shakur speaks: In her own words. *Melanian News*. Retrieved from http://melaniannews.wordpress.com/2011/10/14/assata-shakur-speaks-in-her-own-words/

Shields, L., & Thomas, S. (2012). Prison studies and critical animal studies: Understanding interconnectedness beyond institutional comparisons. *Journal for Critical Animal Studies, 10*(2), 4–11.

Shiva, V. (2010). *Staying alive: Women, ecology, and development*. Brooklyn, NY: South End.

Shiva, V. (1997). *Biopiracy: The plunder of nature and knowledge*. Toronto: Between the Lines.

Snyder, S. L., & Mitchell, D. T. (2006). *Cultural locations of disability*. Chicago: University of Chicago Press.

Sonnie, A., & Tracy, J. (2011). *Hillbilly nationalists, urban race rebels, and Black power: Community organizing in radical times*. New York: Melville House.

Spiegel, M. (1996). *The dreaded comparison: Human and animal slavery*. New York: Mirror.

Turtles escape captivity, make a beeline for nearby ponds. (2012, July 19). *Huffington Post*. Retrieved from http://www.huffingtonpost.com/2012/07/19/summerville-georgia-turtle-escape-_n_1685898.html

The ultimate sacrifice: Mother bear kills her cub and then herself to save her from a life of torture. (2011, August 12). *Daily Mail Reporter*. Retrieved from http://www.dailymail.co.uk/news/article-2025388/China-Tortured-mother-bear-kills-cub-herself.html

Urbanic, J. (2012). *Placing animals: An introduction to the geography of human-animal relations*. Lanham, MD: Rowman & Littlefield.

Walia, H. (2012, January 1). Decolonizing together: Moving beyond a politics of solidarity toward a practice of decolonization. *Briarpatch Magazine*. Retrieved from http://briarpatchmagazine.com/articles/view/decolonizing-together

Walker, M. (2012, September 1). Birds hold "funerals" for dead. *BBC Nature*. Retrieved from http://www.bbc.co.uk/nature/19421217

Weitzenfeld, A. (2011, January 16). Decolonization and animal liberation: Love, violence, and becoming-other-wise. *Staying Healthy*. Retrieved from http://doctoralazerius.blogspot.ca/2011/01/decolonization-and-animal-liberation.html

↠ FOUR ↞

One Struggle

Stephanie Jenkins and Vasile Stănescu

Critical Animal Studies (CAS) rejects the exploitation of animal life as an ontological, epistemological, and ethico-political strategy. It disrupts the anthropocentrism that produces the "human" as a set of cognitive and morphological criteria for moral considerability. Furthermore, it requires the rejection of three key assumptions that govern ethical and political theory: (1) the dichotomy between theory and practice, (2) the ethico-political significance of species membership, and (3) the isolation of animal liberation movements from human concerns (Best, 2009; Jenkins, 2012). Specifically, this chapter explains the sixth principle of CAS. Namely it:

> rejects reformist, single-issue, nation-based, legislative, strictly animal interest politics in favor of alliance politics and solidarity with other struggles against oppression and hierarchy. (Best, Nocella, Kahn, Gigliotti, & Kemmerer, 2007, p. 5)

Stated differently, CAS scholars champion the "one struggle" against all forms of domination. We contest the naturalness of the human-animal dichotomy and reveal how the interlocking of classicism, ableism, nationalism, gender norms, and racism contribute to the oppression of all animals, whether human or nonhuman. CAS articulates the call to respond to the violence perpetuated in the name of such norms; veganism is the corresponding commitment to minimizing violence against all (human or nonhuman) animal life.

In responding to this one struggle against exploitation, CAS deploys veganism as a stratagem for practicing and cultivating the experience of freedom; it is a technology for caring for oneself and others that explicitly problematizes the boundaries of the moral community (Taylor, 2010). Engaged veganism does not treat moral considerability as a uniquely human characteristic. Instead it understands the idea of "moral community" to represent only a construct of historically contingent power relations. Treating the human as a naturally superior species rather than a cognitive and morphological norm conceals how the idea of a "divine chain of being" isolates humans from caring relations with other-than-human worlds. The biological criteria used to justify anthropocentric ownership and management of life on Earth are not neutral, ahistorical facts, but rather only human-made rationalizations for perpetuating and intensifying our exploitation of both human and nonhuman animals (Twine, 2010).

Anthropocentrism

Anthropocentrism reinforces itself through the naturalization and valorization of human superiority. Nonhuman animals are de-individualized as generic natural kinds (i.e., animals in general or species rather than individuals) and disembodied as parts or products (i.e., meat or leather). "[Human] superiority," as Chloë Taylor (2010) explains, "is something which we construct through our instrumentalization of other species" (p. 75). Both nonhuman animal, and so-called subhuman lives, become classified as only what Agamben and Heller-Roazen (1998) term "bare life," or biological resources that humans can use to pursue their own desires, goals, and projects. Existing merely as equipment or raw material, the less-than-human world becomes rendered as an amoral realm that cannot be harmed or violated because such descriptive categories demand the ethico-ontological judgment that nonhuman creatures are worthy of moral consideration. Deviation from the species-typical norms of *Homo sapiens* becomes evidence of animal others' inferiority or justification for their instrumentalization; difference is denigrated rather than respected.

In addition to the production of nonhuman animals as deprived of morally valuable human characteristics, human subjects are constituted so that they understand moral community as membership in an elite class of life; "natural rights" and dignity exclusively belong to animals with the privilege of being born human. Moral status is granted through the capacity (or potential capacity) to perform functions definitive of humanness, such as self-consciousness, cognitive rationality, vision-centric perception, and so forth (Jenkins, 2012). Consequently, while extraordinary animals with unusual and "advanced" abilities may charitably be granted some degree of citizenship in the moral community (e.g., primates, whales, or companion animals), moral standing functions as a finite commodity that can be taken away from humans or nonhumans deemed incapable of passing membership requirements (Wolfe, 2008).

Moral considerability, defined as the recognition that another being intrinsically requires respect and attention, hinges on unconsciously selective habits of perception, affect, and response. Through repeated performance, patterns of care disguise, transmit, and perpetuate unexamined beliefs about what sorts of bodies are relevant to ethico-political decision making. Moral citizens ignore the suffering of beings recognized only as tools available for humanity's entertainment, education, or consumption. Moral concern, as the prerequisite to responsibility, determines the difference between a hamburger and a corpse, animal husbandry and systematic murder, and a circus or compulsory labor. However, because these judgments act at the level of unconscious, habituated bodily reactions, CAS must continually challenge these norms of moral considerability.

Anthropocentric privilege defines the criteria for inclusion in the moral community through the glorification of human-centric capacities. As the judge and jury of moral worth, humanity controls the terms and outcomes of the competition for moral consideration. Consequently, other life forms become valuable only insofar as they are similar to us. As a power-knowledge regime, the animal industrial complex masks the horrifying deaths of innumerable nonhuman animals through appeals to their inferior existence (i.e., animal deaths are not grievable because their lives do not count), subhuman capacities (i.e., those who cannot fear death cannot "die"), and necessary demise (i.e., human survival justifies their death) (Noske, 1997; Stănescu, 2012).

Critical Animal Studies as Practice: Engaged Veganism

This chapter proposes that "engaged veganism" is a counter-discipline informed by CAS principle 6. However, engaged veganism represents not simply abstention from nonhuman animal food sources. Instead, engaged veganism refuses complicity with and symbolically disrupts the instrumentalization and hierarchizing of animal life. Insofar as its practice necessitates a micro-political revolution at the level of embodied perception, aesthetic tastes, and affective responses, engaged veganism enacts a radical care ethics that explicitly investigates socially given assumptions about who counts as recipients of moral concern. CAS scholars, as engaged vegans, do not accept the predefined boundaries of respect, even when these standards are presented as naturally determined accounts of universal rights, biological capacities, or socio-political organization. Engaged veganism begins from the assumption that intellectual inquiry and ethical action must be held accountable for the (often unacknowledged) rift they create between subjects worthy of the rights to life and self-determination and amoral beings whose interests need not be considered in ethical judgment. As a self-transformation via counter-discipline, engaged veganism catalyzes a gestalt shift that dissolves the territorialized boundaries of the moral community. CAS principle 6 requires that ethical practice and moral theory begin from the presupposition of the inherent value of animal life; those who seek to instrumentalize animals, whether human or other-than-human, carry the burden of justifying exceptions to their presumed inviolability.

The key and wholly motivating purpose of principle 6 is a firm, unwavering normative commitment to ending the exploitation of all animals for human consumption and pleasure. An animal lives as not merely a concept or a metaphor but instead a real, living, and embodied organism who requires our respect, support, and solidarity; nonhuman animals are not property (Kelch, 2007). Consequently, they should not be bought and sold at the whim of their "owners" nor raised and killed for human consumption as meat, as leather, as fur, or in any other product. Additionally, nonhuman animals should not be experimented on for cosmetics, for household products, or for supposed scientific or medical benefits.In fact, engaged vegans even go so far as to oppose all the "harmless" daily humiliations and examples of speciesist privilege that are visited on nonhuman animals every day— being forced to perform in circuses, used to sell products, forced into movies for humanity's amusement, and objectified through speciesist terminology and jokes. In short, engaged vegans reject and live opposed to all examples of anthropocentric privilege and human exceptionalism. And we would suggest that any text, no matter how well written, how insightful, or how compelling, that violates these core ideas, while it may (or may not) be classified as an example of animal studies, animality studies, or human-animal studies, is not and could never become *critical* animal studies (Pedersen & Stănescu, 2012). For us "critical" refers not only to the use of critical theory but also an engaged commitment to be critical of anything that purports to study animals and at the same time fails to engage, support, protect, and stand with them (Jenkins, 2012; Pedersen & Stănescu, 2012). In other words, CAS reveals that ontological inquiry cannot be isolated from ethico-political engagement. This is, for us, the most basic and necessary prerequisite for any work that attempts to reside in the field of CAS.

Capitalism and the Commodity Fetish

Engaged veganism is not (only) about abstaining from eating animals but instead also represents an entire social justice worldview of which individual dietary choice represents the visible tip of the iceberg. To make an analogy, the boycott of segregated business in the U.S. civil rights movement (lunch counters, buses) was not only about segregation-based practices at lunch counters and buses but also about a holistic rejection of racism, Jim Crow, and segregation-based politics (West, 1984). So, too, we wish to offer our condemnation of the meat, dairy, and egg industries as not (only) about the violence and exploitation inherent in the production of meat, dairy, and eggs but also as a rejection of speciesism and anthropocentric-based ethics. For these reasons, engaged veganism extends into any point of contact with the animal industrial complex, including entertainment, scientific research, and clothing, among others, and challenges the commodification of life via global capitalism.

As Noelie Vialles (1994) has argued in *Animal to Edible* and Nicole Shukin (2009) has explicitly built on Vialles' work in *Animal Capital*, the animal industrial complex commodifies life, renders bodies as isolated and disembodied structures (the leg of lamb, the arm of the worker), and fetishizes the body, and the suffering of both worker and animal vanish into a single consumable product. As principle 6 proclaims, engaged veganism and anti-capitalist advocacy mutually inform and reinforce each other; they are two aspects of one original and shared, ethical, and ontological engagement in the world. Hence, for advocates of CAS, the difference between the structural violence to the human slaughterhouse worker engaged in the disassembly lines is a difference in degree (but not of kind) to the structural violence rendered around the bodies of the animals who represent the slaughterhouse end "product" (Shukin, 2009).

This chapter distinguishes engaged veganism from boycott veganism, because the latter's main activist effort is abstention from the consumption of nonhuman animal products, without consideration of human or environmental costs. Boycott veganism conflates conspicuous consumption with ethical action and political change. Simply replacing animal with plant-based products only transfers capital to global corporations through different mechanisms; boycott veganism serves to reinforce capitalist institutions and neoliberal social structures that promote the commodification of life and disguise market forces as neutral, amoral means of distributing social goods. Furthermore, limiting activism to an economic boycott undercuts the moral force of veganism by reducing it to an individual lifestyle choice (Twine & Jenkins, forthcoming); promoting moral progress by "voting" with dollars leaves ethical responses to the exploitation of human and nonhuman animals to the will of the market. As a practice promoting CAS principle 6, engaged veganism refuses to treat moral considerability and virtue as commodities that can be purchased, traded, or given as charity.

The choice to be vegan or to remain complicit with everyday anthropocentrism is not an amoral lifestyle, dietary, or any other mode by which human individuals can freely stylize their existence; it is not a decision that can be characterized as a matter of preference. We do not consider human freedoms to be limited in any meaningful sense by prohibitions against murder. Refusals to engage in rape or consume chocolate produced using involuntary child labor are not considered ascetic deprivation, precisely because, as morally indefensible actions, rape and child slavery are not available as free choices. In a similar manner, engaged veganism cannot be understood as only the abstention from animal products.

Rather, this practice is an ethico-political strategy through which we create ways of being, kinds of pleasures, communities, and institutions that cultivate new practices of care that are not dependent on the exploitation of nonhuman animal life as a raw material.

Within a CAS framework, an individual could refrain from eating animal products, for example for human-oriented health reasons, and not constitute a vegan in this engaged, ontological articulation of the practice. This represents perhaps the most valuable contribution to the field of "critical" animal studies: an all-encompassing, shared rejection of any social justice paradigm premised on the micro-fascist assumption that "might makes right." Engaged vegans oppose all commodity culture and commodity fetishism, as well as ethically opposing the notion that life—human or otherwise—can, or should, ever be rendered as a buyable or sellable commodity (Twine, 2010).

Consequently, engaged vegans hold that any idea or articulation of "humanely" raised meat is an inherent and impossible oxymoron. And it makes no difference to us if this slaughter is marketed as "locavorism" (a geographic distinction); "slow food" (a communal eating experience); "compassionate" carnivore (ethical distinction); "free range," "organic," or "pasture raised" (distinctions based on specific practices of animal husbandry). Such practices offend because, fundamentally at their core, they still treat animals as only buyable and sellable commodities wholly at the whims of their "owners" rather than beings with inherent moral considerability (Stănescu, 2010).

Admittedly, in terms of pure numbers, a focus on the locavore movement may seem ill-placed since 99 percent of all animals killed for human consumption within the United States are killed in the factory farm system (Stănescu, forthcoming). So to focus on the locavore movement is to focus on the 1 percent exception that, merely, "proves the rule." Second, it seems misplaced in that no matter how much actual suffering occurs on these supposedly humane farms no one, including engaged vegans, could argue that the animals suffer as much as those housed in factory farm conditions. However, as a CAS framework demonstrates, focusing on these statistically unrepresentative examples—of the theoretical ideal farm—conceals the suffering of the overwhelming majority of nonhuman animals. Locavore farms represent a manner in which the inherent power relations of anthropocentrism becomes masked in a, now literal, rhetoric of "pastoral care" and supposed benevolence. The reality is that the locavore movement could never function on any scale beyond its current tokenistic existence, since it utilizes more land per pound of meat than the current factory farm system (Stănescu, 2010). Consequently, the locavore movement does not currently help virtually any animals at all, and cannot do so in the future. But this is not the essence of our critique. It is instead to suggest that even if, via the suspension of the laws of ecology and physics, the entire 60 (and soon to be 120) billion land animals currently raised and killed could be transferred from factory farms to local, free-range, and "humane" farms, such a practice would only serve to help render the staggering level of speciesist violence as even more naturalized and therefore invisible. In other words, rather than being critiques of the current speciesist system, the locavore or free range movement and the factory farm systems work in tandem. The locavore movement helps to set up a false (but viewable) proxy for what is supposedly occurring throughout all meat production, and, at the exact same time, the statistical reality that a "humane farming" system is wholly impractical and would in practice render 99 percent of all meat consumption as unviable is, in turn, rendered invisible via the universal nature of the factory farm system (Stănescu, 2010).

Therefore, all that seems to occur, in reality, is that consumers of higher socioeconomic status purchase overpriced "humane meat," which they consume to "atone" for the factory farmed animals that they continue to consume as the vast majority of their diets. And, indeed, this is exactly the case with advocates of local humane farming such as Michael Pollan (2006) who repeatedly assures his readers that there are no strict rules and that small steps constitute actual change, or Catherine Friend, who in exactly parallel fashion not only assures readers that they are wholly free to continue to purchase factory farm meat (as long as they also purchase some "happy meat" as well) but even assures us that she herself continues to consume factory farm meat for at least 25 percent of all her meals because it is so "convenient" (2008, p. 197).

Our point is that the locavore and humane meat movement is not a different system or a critique of the factory farm system; it is instead a function of the same system that justifies the instrumentalization of nonhuman animal life. The factory farm cannot be rendered visible; however, via the deceptive lens of the "humane" farm, the killing of animals can be shown. For example, consumers may visit local farms to experience or witness the killing of farm animals even if, in reality, what they are seeing pales in comparison to the atrocities committed against 99 percent of all animals in the animal industrial complex (Stănescu, 2010). Consumers of local and "humane" animal products desire the experience of piercing the commodity fetish and cultural capital afforded to animal welfare activism, even if, in reality, their actions do not alter oppressive institutions.

Engaged veganism reveals how both the locavore movement and the associated DIY slaughter movement represent a similar false and wholly token indictment of the commodity fetish. For example, both writer Michael Pollan and farmer Joel Salatin speak, at length, about the need to go "beyond the bar code" by personally interacting with the farmer, personally raising one's "own" animals, and even personally slaughtering these animals (Pollan, 2010). Indeed, Pollan (2006) personally kills "his" own chickens on Polyface farms and also kills feral pigs in Santa Cruz (an experience he enjoys so much that he compares it to being high). In turn, these practices have spawned cottage industries of individuals raising and then killing their own animals (primarily chickens and rabbits). However, the pastoral romanticization of eating locally, meeting the farmers, and "piercing the bar code" simply obscures the violence of these supposedly happy farms and their retrenchment of commodity culture. For example, as Foer (2010) has pointed out, Salatin uses the same selectively bred birds, who live abnormally short and painful lives, as factory farms do because this practice is more profitable. Likewise Friend (2008) on her supposedly humane farm engages in castration, tail docking, and sexual violation of her lambs (who she then sends to the exact same industrial slaughterhouses). As a result, these consumers purchase at a premium the illusion of authentic knowledge and ethical relationships. So-called humane farmers simply carefully construct the appearance of better care regardless of the actual treatment of animals on such farms.

Engaged vegans acknowledge the reality that one cannot buy one's way out of the commodity fetish, no matter how much one pays for organic or pasture raised meat. And, likewise, we contend that it is equally impossible to kill one's way out of anthropocentrism and human chauvinism, no matter how well the animals are supposedly treated before their murder. CAS advocates reject all calls for animal welfare that still keep the reality of human supremacy left unchecked and unchallenged. For the concept of being a "compassionate carnivore" inherently reduces animal liberation to one of mere charity, which consequently can be ignored, compromised, or abandoned at will. CAS concerns itself with the lives, joys, and suffering of actual animals. In doing so, it refutes, as inherently ironic, paradoxical, and impossible, any reformist method of animal welfarism, locavorism, or humane slaughter. The goal of CAS is the suspension of all animal exploitation.

Interweaving of Oppression: Sexual Violence, Racism, and Speciesism

A current popular meme suggests that one cannot be a meat-eating environmentalist (Shanker, 2010). CAS-informed, engaged veganism supports a similar position that one also cannot be a meat-eating feminist or queer advocate. Feminism and queer theory are absolutely incompatible with any form of ownership, exploitation, and consumption of animals (Kelch, 2007). Deemed unworthy of moral considerability, animal life that departs from predominant norms becomes raw material for management, industrialization, and commodification. The instrumentalization of nonhuman animals as raw material is morally permissible as long as they do not meet anthropocentric performance criteria deemed relevant for inclusion in the moral community (Beckoff, Gruen, Townsend, & Rollin, 1992). Moreover, the commodification of nonhuman animate life is historically inseparable from the exchange of woman as property in Western civilization (Adams, 1990). If similarity to "man" as a stand-in for the human species determines the ethical significance of a life, then all non-normate beings lacking heteronormative characteristics will always be in danger of being denied moral concern (Butler, 2004).

Feminist advocates must not condone the exploitation of female reproductive systems, whether they belong to human or nonhuman animals. Catherine Friend (2008) and her partner Melissa are both self-identified feminists who entered into the farming practice as a way to combat both traditional gender roles and heteronormativity. Despite these convictions, they hold down a female goat and force her to have what is clearly undesired sex for their desired breeding program. In a chapter titled "Let's Just Forget this Ever Happened," this is how Friend (2008) describes the practice:

> At Mary's, we led Ambrosia [Friend's female sheep] to the converted chicken house, into a building about twenty feet by ten feet, with bare board door and Bozeman [the male sheep] came flying in, eyes wild, lip curled at the scent of Ambrosia. Our goat took one look at this creature and began running. I couldn't blame her. Not only do intact bucks reek with an indescribable scent, but this guy's head and neck were oily, greasy, and matted with something foul . . . Ambrosia wasn't buying it. Who could blame her? We watched Bozeman chase in a circle for five minutes. "Is this how goat sex usually goes?" I finally asked. "No," Mary said. "Usually the doe stands still. Ambrosia must be near the end of her cycle. She can still get pregnant, but isn't willing to stand still." She sighed. "I'm afraid we have to hold her." Groaning, we stepped forward. Melissa grabbed Ambrosia's collar but she twisted away. Mary and I cornered her but she slipped past us. Finally it took all three of us to catch Ambrosia. Then, unbelievably, we restrained her head and torso while Bozeman, loopy with lust, flung himself on her and began thrusting his hips. No one said a word as Bozeman concentrated on the task at hand, and Ambrosia grunted indignantly. I held my breath to avoid Bozeman's aroma. Finally I muttered, "Can I still call myself a feminist after this?" (p. 146)

The answer to this rhetorical question for engaged vegans is "No" (Stănescu, forthcoming). Carol Adams (1990) has helped CAS advocates see how the system of the production of meat is part of a shared particular system of mutual exploitation of nonhuman animals and female animals. However, in line with principle 6, CAS would reject eating meat even if it had no impact on female humans. Because the animal industrial complex exploits female reproductive systems through breeding and milking, all forms of eating represents acts of sexual violence. Therefore, all meat always and already is intrinsically incompatible with the core ideas of feminism, queer theory, and sexual autonomy. As such, all nonhuman animal products are always and already a support for sexual violence. For this reason, engaged vegans' insistence that nonhuman animals are members of the moral community is in and of itself already a feminist act. That is, of course, not to suggest that we are so naïve to be unaware of that fact that one can be a boycott vegan and still grossly patriarchal. The advertisements of People for the Ethical Treatment of Animals frequently utilize the objectification of heteronormative women's bodies to market vegan products. CAS, as defined by principle

6, supports the "one struggle" to end animal exploitation and acknowledges the interconnectedness of oppressive institutions. Consequently, engaged vegans refuse to deploy hegemonic norms in the service of single-issue reform. "Selling" (boycott) veganism through (hetero)sexist strategies only displaces, but does not eliminate, systematic cruelty.

Indeed, Joel Salatin's popularized support for the locavore or humane meat movement exemplifies the interweaving of racist and speciesist oppression. For example, Salatin repeatedly admits to his readers that he is "real sexist" (2007, p. 201), that he doesn't support the 1964 Civil Rights Act because he believes it caused "reverse discrimination, forced school busing, and as much if not more racial hatred today than in 1965" (p. 201) and, likewise, fills his writing with multiple nativist diatribes against immigrant labor (Salatin, 2007; Stănescu, 2010). Such insights only make "sense" (if we can stretch that word almost beyond meaning) in a worldview that denigrates women, other races, and immigrants in an Aristotelian worldview of God-ordained "natural order" that held that men should (albeit protectively) rule over women, master should rule over slaves, citizen should rule over barbarians, and humans should rule over animals. In other words, to return to the essential message of this chapter these are not simply oppressions that intersect—they are instead part of a shared worldview of the straight, white, wealthy, abled, Western, male human exceptionalism. Since the oppressions are themselves linked, what is called for are not isolated single issue campaigns, but a shared fight based on a solidarity of shared interests and support. Or, more simply put, we must all fight together in one struggle.

Conclusion: Direct Action

CAS-informed, engaged veganism must acknowledge, support, and sustain direct action taken for the purpose of minimizing violence against animal life. Direct action for animals fits within a long tradition of civil disobedience in social justice activism. CAS supports these activists and their actions. Some feminists, such as Carol Adams (1990) and Marti Kheel (2006), have criticized direct action as a hyper-masculinity approach to social change. Moreover, there are relevant issues of class, race, and citizenship privileges that define the stakes and underpin the ability to engage in any direct action at all. For example, the risks of being arrested are significantly different for an undocumented worker than a full citizen. CAS's support for direct action is not a universal mandate to engage in direct action; direct action should be seen as a higher form of action. Rather, like the anticolonial, anti-apartheid, or anticapitalist movements before it, CAS as a social justice movement can only succeed if it deploys a diversity of tactics. CAS scholars and advocates support engaged vegan activism but remain open to the critique of specific tactics. This is the final, and most important, guiding principal for the oneness of the struggle for human and nonhuman animals. Real, concrete, and direct action is necessary in order to help actual animals and end their suffering. In other words CAS scholars must not only write to activists we must also write as activists. Our overarching goal would be for CAS to echo Foucault's call for his theory to serve as "a kind of tool-box others can rummage through to find a tool they can use however they wish in their own area . . . I don't write for an audience, I write for users, not readers" (1994, pp. 523–524). CAS scholars write for users, including activists, comrades, and supporters. CAS matters because we believe that it is not only our goal; to interpret the world (nonhuman animals, speciesism, global destruction, etc.), the point is for CAS academics and activists, working together, to actually change it.

References

Adams, C. J. (1990). *The sexual politics of meat: A feminist-vegetarian critical theory*. New York: Continuum.
Agamben, G., & Heller-Roazen, D. (1998). *Homo sacer: Sovereign power and bare life*. Stanford, CA: Stanford University Press.
Beckoff, M., Gruen, L., Townsend, S., & Rollin, B. (1992). Animals in science. *Animal Behavior, 44*(3), 473–484.
Best, S. (2009). The rise of critical animal studies: Putting theory into action and animal liberation into higher education. *Journal for Critical Animal Studies, 7*(1), 9–52.
Best, S. (2012, September 8). Steve Best - Conferenza Contro la Vivisezione - Brescia - Green Hill [Video file]. Retrieved from http://www.youtube.com/watch?v=4GtKZu5ttTw&feature=youtu.be
Best, S., Nocella, A. J., Kahn, R., Gigliotti, C., & Kemmerer, L. (2007). Introducing critical animal studies. *Journal for Critical Animal Studies, 5*(1), 4–5.
Butler, J. (2004). *Undoing gender*. New York: Routledge.
Foer, J. S. (2010). *Eating animals*. New York: Little, Brown & Co.
Foucault, M. (1994/1974). *Prisons et asiles dans le mécanisme du pouvoir. Dits et Ecrits, Vol. 11*. Paris: Gallimard.
Friend, C. (2008). *The compassionate carnivore: Or, how to keep animals happy, save Old MacDonald's Farm, reduce your hoofprint, and still eat meat*. Philadelphia: Da Capo Lifelong.
Jenkins, S. (2012). Returning the ethical and political to animal studies. *Hypatia, 27*(3), 13–24.
Kelch, T. (2007). Toward a non-property status for animals. In J. Donovan & C. Adams (Eds.), *The feminist care tradition in animal ethics*. New York: Columbia University Press.
Kheel, M. (2006). Direct action and the heroic ideal: An ecofeminist critique. In S. Best & A. J. Nocella (Eds.), *Igniting a revolution: Voices in defense of the earth* (pp. 306–318). Oakland, CA: AK.
Noske, B. (1997). *Beyond boundaries: Humans and animals*. Buffalo, NY: Blackrose.
Pedersen, H., & Stănescu, V. (2012). What is "critical" about animal studies? From the animal "question" to the animal "condition." In K. Socha (Ed.), *Women, destruction, and the avant-garde: A paradigm for animal liberation* (pp. ix–xi). Amsterdam & New York: Rodopi.
Pollan, M. (2010, June 10). The food movement, rising. *New York Times Book Review*.
Pollan, M. (2006). *The omnivore's dilemma: A natural history of four meals*. New York: Penguin.
Salatin, J. (2007). *Everything I want to do is illegal*. Swoope, VA: Polyface.

Shankar, C. (2010). Can you be a meat-eating environmentalist? *Huffington Post*. Retrieved April 14, 2013, from http://www.huffingtonpost.com/cheri-shankar/can-you-be-a-meat-eating_b_484906.html
Shukin, N. (2009). *Animal capital: Rendering life in biopolitical times*. Minneapolis: University of Minnesota Press.
Stănescu, J. (2012). Species trouble: Judith Butler, mourning, and the precarious lives of animals. *Hypatia, 27*(3), 567–582.
Stănescu, V. (2010). "Green" eggs and ham? The myth of sustainable meat and the danger of the local. *Journal for Critical Animal Studies, 8*(1–2), 8–32.
Stănescu, V. (forthcoming). Why "loving" animals is not enough: A response to Kathy Rudy, locavorism, and the marketing of "humane" meat." *Journal of American Culture*.
Steinfeld, H. (2006). *Livestock's long shadow: Environmental issues and options*. Rome: Food and Agriculture Organization of the United Nations.
Taylor, C. (2010). Foucault and the ethics of eating. *Foucault Studies, 9*, 71–88.
Twine, R. (2010). *Animals as biotechnology*. Washington, DC: Earthscan.
Twine, R., & Jenkins, S. (forthcoming). On the limits of food autonomy—rethinking choice and privacy. In R. Twine & N. Taylor, *The rise of critical animal studies*. New York: Routledge.
Vialles, N. (1994). *Animal to edible*. Cambridge: Cambridge University Press.
West, C. (1984). The paradox of the Afro-American rebellion. *Social Text, 9–10*, 44–58.
Wolfe, C. (2008). Animal studies and disability studies, or, learning from Temple Grandin. *New Formations, 64*, 110–123.

PART III

Critical Scholarship

FIVE

The Ivory Trap

Bridging the Gap between Activism and the Academy

Carol L. Glasser and Arpan Roy

> *Functionally, oppression is domesticating. To no longer be prey to its force, one must emerge from it and turn upon it. This can be done only by means of the praxis: reflection and action upon the world in order to transform it.*
> —Paulo Freire, 2006, p. 51

The place where learning and knowledge are meant to occur is referred to as many things—university, post-secondary education, college, the academy, and, of course, the ivory tower. The term "ivory tower" captures both the glories and pitfalls of study and scholarship within the academy. The term first emerged in biblical sources in the Song of Solomon and later came to be a reference to the figure of Mary. However, by the twentieth century it came into its modern usage—referring to the university and intellectual and artistic work detached from daily life (Shapin, 2012).

The ivory tower in this sense has been both ridiculed and revered. During the Second World War, the ivory tower was associated with artists. While there was a call among many artists and intellectuals to reject insular artistic creation and direct their work toward dismantling fascism and Nazism, others argued that it was precisely because of the turmoil in the world that good art could only be produced in a space detached from these problems (Shapin, 2012). By the second half of the twentieth century the phrase was firmly associated with the American university, and the debate as to the utility of intellectualism detached from social and everyday life has continued. For those concerned with the treatment, rights, and liberation of nonhuman animals, the term has additional significance. Literally, ivory is the direct product of the exploitation and killing of nonhuman animals; further, the university is a space hostile to nonhuman animals, who are welcomed onto campus only insofar as they are used for food, research tools, or to assist the disabled. Similarly, the study of nonhuman animals as subjects is undervalued; there are very few universities that have courses examining nonhuman animals as subjects of study, and AS scholars are often marginalized.

We argue that in this instance, rather than serving as a conduit that allows for the production and dissemination of new knowledge, institutional boundaries and professional indoctrination creates a scenario in which the attempt to produce knowledge goes nowhere. For those of us deeply embedded in and reliant on academic institutions for our livelihood and the expression of our intellectual passions, the ivory tower can unexpectedly become a trap. To ameliorate this problem, we need to strive to produce knowledge with the intent to inform action and speak directly to current social, cultural, or physical realities of the world in a manner that improves society and benefits others. This can be a difficult task, as scholars may struggle to successfully share their work outside of the academy or may be hesitant to push intellectual and institutional barriers for fear of losing professional respect or employment.

This ivory trap keeps knowledge production and dissemination limited. This is problematic because academics should aim to use their privileged position to better society by engaging with current social problems. Further, scholarship should advance an emancipatory ethic, intentionally opposing exploitation and inequality and promoting liberation. This chapter serves as a reminder that academics can, and should, take up the role of activist scholar. Academics are exceptionally privileged—we have a vast amount of knowledge on very specific topics, we are the most (formally) educated members of society, and our degrees give us a platform from which to speak. It is our duty to use our privilege productively for the benefit of our communities.

To address both the lack of research directed toward advocacy for nonhuman animals and research that is often esoteric and inaccessible, a clear line of praxis is needed. Praxis is theory in practice, scholarship for the sake of action and reflection, one supporting the other. Brazilian pedagogist Paulo Freire (2006) is often associated with the philosophy of praxis, which he sees as the only means by which to overturn oppression.

There are both contemporary and historical instances of scholars writing material directed toward activism, as well as engaging in activism in their own lives. One notable example is Marcel Mauss, an early twentieth-century anthropologist whose comparative studies of pre-capitalist gift economies complimented his work running a consumer cooperative in Paris (Graeber, 2004; Hart, 2007). He wrote fiercely in socialist newspapers about the need for an economic system based on syndicalism and mutual insurance. Mauss's objective was for his scholarship to "succeed in throwing a little light upon the path that our nations must follow, both in their morality and in their economy" (1990, p. 78). He advocated an "economic movement from below," words that would be echoed almost verbatim by Zapatistas in the jungles of Chiapas more than half a century later. Mauss provides an exemplary case of a scholar who asked research questions that were directly raised by and applicable to his activism.

The tradition of activist scholars like Mauss continues, but the rift between academia and the street seems larger than ever. Academics were once a part of American cultural life, evident in figures like Franz Boas gracing magazine covers in the 1930s (Eliaeson & Kalleberg, 2008, p. 9) or scholars of the New Left hobnobbing with artists and musicians of their era; but now we see only condensed and scattered mentions of the works of contemporary academics through Facebook feeds and 140-character tweets as individuals struggle to make sense of important events that occur in the world. Clearly, there is a gap between scholars and the street.

The German philosopher Jürgen Habermas (2009) notes that there has been a structural transformation of the public sphere that is hostile to intellectuals, and the academic response has been to become more insular, only exacerbating the problem (p. 53). Feminist theorist bell hooks addresses this same issue, identifying it as a "tug-of-war" between activists, who identify education and theory with "bourgeois privilege," and intellectuals, who create knowledge without a clear practical focus (2000, p. 113). She actively critiqued feminist philosophers and institutions in the early 1980s for their esoteric style and inaccessibility to ordinary women. She, too, made an explicit call for praxis, as Freire defined it:

> This tug-of-war has led to the formation of a false dichotomy between theory (the development of ideas) and practice (the actions of the movement) . . . As a consequence, there is often little congruity between feminist theory and feminist practice . . . From the onset, women's liberation movement participants have struggled to unite theory and practice, to create a liberatory feminist praxis . . . That struggle has been undermined by anti-intellectualism and by elitist academics who believe their "ideas" need not have any connection to real life. (2000, pp. 113–114).

The public sphere is defined by Habermas as "the domain of our social life in which such a thing as public opinion can be formed" (2009, p. 231) but the obvious question is how can an informed public opinion be formed when academics, the keepers and evaluators of information, are excluded from this domain or hoard their knowledge in the private sphere of the ivory tower?

Critical Animal Studies (CAS) has the potential to overcome these problems and advance a praxis of emancipation in regard to nonhuman animals. CAS seeks to professionalize, legitimate, and prioritize the ethic of praxis, to encourage socially relevant, interdisciplinary research that has the potential to overcome disciplinary and institutional barriers, and to create new knowledge and theory with the aim of advancing liberation of nonhuman animals.

Animal Studies

For centuries, nonhuman animals made their way into academic study almost exclusively as a tool of research. Among scientists, in the media, and across academic disciplines today, this is called "animal experimentation." However, this masks the true nature of what is happening. More appropriately this type of research should be called "vivisection." Vivisection is defined as "the cutting of or operation on a living animal usually for physiological or pathological investigation; *broadly*: animal experimentation especially if considered to cause distress to the subject" (Merriam-Webster).

When used as tools of vivisection, nonhuman animals are not simply parts of experiments as humans are when they voluntarily participate in human trials or other studies. Rather, nonhuman animals are forcibly enrolled in studies and their live bodies are manipulated, cut open, exposed to diseases, physical ailments, chemicals, and environments that they otherwise would not have experienced.

There are recorded instances of vivisection for academic learning in ancient Greece in the third century BC by Erasistratus (Orlans, 1993, p. 3) who used pigs to study breathing (ORI, n.d.). In the seventeenth century in France and England, a strong wave of vivisection emerged (Orlans). One of the thinkers associated with this tradition is Réne Descartes, infamous for nailing down live dogs by their paws and cutting them open in front of other scholars and audiences to study the circulatory system. His work, and the work of others in the period, was premised on the belief that nonhuman animals could not feel pain. Even now that it is acknowledged that nonhuman animals do feel pain, vivisection remains the most common way nonhuman animals are present in academic research.

Nonhuman animals are also commonly used as objects of research. When fields such as zoology, ethology, psychology, and evolutionary biology study nonhuman animals they tend to intrusively voyeur into nonhuman animals' environments or their physical bodies to study their genomes, reactions to stimuli, and behaviors. The emergent field of animal studies (AS) represents the first serious attempt to position nonhuman animals as subjects of research. The field has been called by various names, including "Anthrozoology, Animal Studies, Critical Animal Studies, Animals and Society Studies, Humanimalia" (Shapiro, 2008, p. 7) and now has a number of flagship journals in the humanities, arts, and social sciences, including *Anthrozoos, Animals and Society, Journal for Critical Animal Studies*, and *Antennae*.

The launch of the journal *Anthrozoos* in 1987 marked the beginning of the field of human-animal studies (HAS) (Shapiro, 2008, p. 7). HAS is an interdisciplinary field of academic study that "examines the complex and multidimensional relationships between humans and other animals," taking the role of other animals seriously rather than focusing solely on what nonhuman animals can provide to humans. The field has grown exponentially since its inception (Best, 2009; Shapiro, 2008).

HAS seeks to reorient the nonhuman animal away from being a tool or an object of research to test on, physically manipulate, or voyeuristically observe after human interference, and treats them as subjects of study. Crucially, it is explicitly focused on the implications of research and orients itself around specific moral and political outcomes. HAS has largely been developed by the organization Animals and Society Institute (ASI), which has succeeded in formalizing and institutionally embedding this development in animals studies. ASI (n.d.) describes themselves on their website as a:

> nonprofit, independent research and educational organization that advances the status of animals in public policy, and promotes the study of human-animal relationships. The ASI seeks to advance institutional change for animals by helping to establish the moral and legal rights fundamental to a just, compassionate and peaceful society. We are an independent think tank as well as a producer of educational resources, publications and events. Our objectives are to:
> 1. Stop the cycle of violence between animal cruelty and human abuse
> 2. Learn more about our complex relationship with animals
> 3. Promote new and stricter animal protection laws

While it makes important strides in the right direction, ASI does not bring AS to its full potential. Though there is a focus on policy outcomes stemming from research, the politics of liberation are absent from the outset and it tolerates the objectification of nonhuman animals in research.

ASI currently publishes two journals. *Animals & Society* is a peer-reviewed journal that began in 1993, publishing research that addresses nonhuman animals in the humanities and social sciences. The *Journal of Applied Animal Welfare Science* (JAAWS) began in 1998 and, according to ASI, "is the leading peer-reviewed journal on the science of animal welfare for veterinarians, scientists and public policy makers. It presents articles and reports on practices that demonstrably enhance the welfare of wildlife, companion animals and animals used in research, agriculture and zoos."

While the journal may have good intentions by adding to knowledge that can make the life of exploited nonhuman animals less horrific, it fails to fundamentally reorient the role of nonhuman animals in the academy and the social world. Alongside studies that examine nonhuman animals in nonintrusive ways, JAAWS publishes studies that accept the use of nonhuman animals for human means, for example, by examining processes on animal slaughter, housing of nonhuman animals for experiments, and the behavior of specific species in zoos. These studies normalize the study of nonhuman animals as objects and tools and lack any politics of liberation.

CAS seeks to productively work within the academy while being critical of its boundaries, avoiding the limitations of HAS, and openly opposing animal exploitation. At its best, CAS pushes HAS to a point of praxis by

> deconstruct[ing] and reconstruct[ing] the socially constructed binary oppositions between human and nonhuman animals, a move basic to mainstream AS, but also looks to illuminate related dichotomies between culture and nature, civilization and wilderness and other dominator hierarchies to emphasize the historical limits placed upon humanity, nonhuman animals, cultural/political norms, and the liberation of nature as part of a transformative project that seeks to transcend these limits towards greater freedom, peace, and ecological harmony. (Best, Nocella, Kahn, Gigliotti, & Kemmerer, 2007, p. 5)

In other words, CAS has the objective not only to study nonhuman animals and issues of relevance to them but to study them with the purpose of breaking down ideologies that promote their oppression as well. Further, CAS aims to tie these issues to other social and environmental questions.

The above quote is one of the ten orienting principles of CAS as presented in 2007 (Best et al., 2007). In the remainder of this chapter we will discuss the boundaries to liberatory praxis that are embedded in what we call the "ivory trap," and we will present these ten foundational tenets of CAS as a way to potentially overcome those boundaries.

The field of CAS is directly associated with the nonprofit organization Institute for Critical Animal Studies (ICAS). ICAS was originally called the Center on Animal Liberation Affairs (CALA), founded by Anthony Nocella II and Steve Best in 2001. In 2007 it was renamed ICAS and the ten orienting principles were published by Best and Nocella along with Richard Kahn, Carol Gigliotti, and Lisa Kemmerer in the article "Introducing Critical Animal Studies." Also, in 2007, the first CAS college minor was introduced by sociologist John Sorenson at Brock University in St. Catharines, Ontario, Canada. Central to the renaming of the field is the use of the word "critical," which expresses the intent to be critical of the normative position of human dominance over nonhuman animals and nature as well as to be critical of the state of AS. As Best (2009) explains:

> First, [CAS] is critical of (mainstream) *animal studies itself*, for its moral incoherence and aloofness (studying exploited beings without explicit commitment to ending their oppression, and indeed, further exploiting animals for their theoretical worth and career capital) and its overly abstract, esoteric, and jargon-laden language that is inscrutable to the general public and inherently elitist. The version of animal studies promoted by ICAS is critical, second, of the entire social system and complex of oppression and domination, such as has developed throughout the human-established "civilization" of the last ten thousand years, and it seeks a radical political analysis and tactic in response to systemic social and environmental problems.

For CAS to move forward productively and in the manner outlined above, it is imperative to understand what obstacles exist within the academy and to identify how CAS's foundational principles and current practice might overcome these challenges and to develop concrete ways in which individual scholars can maintain their positions in the academy while also creating work that can engender radical praxis.

The Ivory Trap

Most academic work will not reach ordinary people in a manner that can lead to radical or even incremental change due in large part to the confines of academia. Academic research often fails to address issues of relevance to current social issues and, even when it does, the knowledge gained often remains locked in our ivory towers and inaccessible to a general audience—because they don't know it is there, find it too complicated or esoteric to engage with, or simply cannot access it without being embedded in academic environments that provide database access and assistance through libraries. Scholars also often seem confined, limited perhaps by the institutional constraints of the academy or by the likely marginalization of their work, and do not generally conduct research that has direct relevance on the ground for social justice. In the following sections we detail the problems associated with the ivory trap and discuss CAS's potential to surmount them.

Lack of Access

The ivory tower can serve as a barrier to information for those without the desire, need, or socioeconomic status to gain admittance to or attend postsecondary educational institutions. As of 2010, roughly 30 percent of U.S. citizens attained a college degree (U.S. Census Bureau, 2012). Though one need not attend college to know how to conduct research and not all college graduates are adequate researchers, college is the most common way to come into contact with what research is available, where to access it, and how to conduct research. College libraries provide access to journal article databases, where much academic research is published, and are also more likely to purchase research anthologies not available at local libraries. Notably, even those who have attended college are locked out of college libraries after receiving their degree.

CAS attempts to push past this lack of access and acknowledge that activists and academics can learn from each other by making academic venues accessible and welcoming to non-academics, and by recognizing that knowledge can be generated outside of the confines of universities. As one key principle of CAS states:

> [CAS] seeks to create openings for constructive critical dialogue on issues relevant to Critical Animal Studies across a wide-range of academic groups; citizens and grassroots

activists; the staffs of policy and social service organizations; and people in private, public, and non-profit sectors. (Best et al., 2007, p. 5)

Commitment to this principle is evidenced by the annual conferences organized by ICAS that feature activists and academics in the audience and on its panels. Additionally, the *Journal for Critical Animal Studies* (JCAS), currently the only peer-reviewed journal in the field, is available for free online in an open-access (OA) format. Open access is "digital, online, free of charge, and free of most copyright and licensing restrictions" (Suber, 2012) and is important for disseminating scholarly work in a more egalitarian manner. More academic journals are utilizing the open-access publishing format, a sign that academics are seeking alternatives to traditional publishing and that this type of publishing is becoming more accepted.

Open access is reliant on the Internet (Suber, 2012), and while the Internet cannot reach everyone, it is perhaps the most important tool for making research accessible for free. Blogs, articles, research, and videos can all be posted online and seen by anyone with Internet access. The Internet can also be used creatively to allow activists or human subjects of research to engage with research in ways that best serve their needs. Some resources now allow the layperson to access datasets and request specific information. For example, the Humane Research Council (HRC) (2010) maintains the Animal Tracker Graphing Tool, which allows access to the results of their annual survey data in an understandable format. Users can chose which survey question they would like to see responses for and view those responses immediately in a histogram. Two graphs are laid side-by-side so that different years and demographic segments can be compared. This tool can help activists quickly understand social attitudes toward various animal protection issues without a need for prior knowledge about the more complex aspects of research such as survey design or representatively weighting data.

Pedants and Jargon

Academic language is often field specific, filled with jargon, and sophisticated. It may be difficult for a trained person to understand, much less the average person not trained in the field of interest. This means that even when conferences, articles, and books are available to activists and citizens, they can still be so difficult to understand that they remain effectively inaccessible. Academic language is developed as part of the method of establishing credentials and creating clear signals to identify disciplinary insiders. However, this sort of semantic gesturing is problematic if the point of research is to communicate effectively to those both inside and outside of the academy.

CAS, as envisioned by the ten orienting principles, does not directly address the role of semantics in liberatory praxis. We suggest the addition of an eleventh principle. To use the same language as the original tenets of CAS: *We seek to develop a Critical Animal Studies that produces knowledge that is not only relevant to social justice issues, but is also accessible to those whom the research can benefit. Jargon and esoteric language and publication formats are rejected in favor of accessible language, explanations, and formats of transmission.*

One way to achieve this without completely rejecting standard professional formats of publication and language is by producing dual publications. As bell hooks (2000) suggests:

> All too often, educators, especially university professors, fear their work will not be valued by other academics if it is presented in a way that makes it accessible to a wider audience. If these educators thought of rendering their work in a number of different styles, "translations," they would be able to satisfy arbitrary academic standards while making their work available to masses of people. (p. 112)

Academics can continue to write in the technical language of the academy while also writing up results for activists. This solution allows scholars to stay within the linguistic confines of the ivory tower, but also to reproduce the work so that others can access it. Furthermore, these secondary publications can be produced in multiple formats, not all of which rely on the written word. Research can be presented in blogs, news articles, zines, YouTube videos, pamphlets, conferences, workshops, or through live Internet chats. Scholars are increasingly using the Internet to not only bridge the gap between academia and activism but also to widen the scope of what constitutes academic analysis. Presenting work publicly in accessible language and allowing for user commentary on one's personal blog, for example, may allow not only for increased comprehension but also for participation in theory building by non-academics, activists, and, in some instances, by oppressed and marginalized populations themselves.

One scholar who serves as an example is A. Breeze Harper, founder of the Sistah Vegan Project. She not only produces academic work but also posts articles on the blogs Sistah Vegan and Vegans of Color, which reach a wider audience that includes academics, people of color, and animal liberation activists. In addition, she produces and posts videos on these blogs as well as on relevant Facebook pages. The video content includes discussions of her research as well as talks she gives at various venues. The videos reach beyond the written word, making her work more accessible to those for whom listening is easier than reading.

Certain academic publishing formats may also engender increased availability and comprehension. Books are easier to publish in accessible language than peer-reviewed journal articles and are more likely to be accessible for free from public libraries. However, they are not always as attractive to academics as they take longer to produce and may therefore slow publication pace.

As well as making work accessible in cyberspace, academics should also seek to physically bring their research to activists and others outside the academy. Public, semi-public, and other physical spaces, such as parks, metro stations and cafés, are potential meeting grounds for such learning to take place. These spaces should become a target for academics intent on escaping the ivory trap and engaging with the non-academic public; this could include free workshops in public spaces and community centers, developing projects with facilitators of certain public spaces (e.g., libraries), or conducting research directly with activists. Vibrant examples of this approach occurred through the interaction of academics and social movement activists in the occupy encampments in the United States and beyond.

During the occupy movement in the United States in 2011, many encampments created spaces for education. Sergio Ballesteros, cofounder of the People's Collective University in the Los Angeles encampment, noted that the most important lesson he learned was that a physical public space with meaningful proximity among humans was key to bridging the gap between academics and non-academics and creating a dialogue (personal communication). This highlights the need for academics to escape the confines of the ivory tower not only ideologically but also physically. It's worth noting that in the midst of the media's obsession with the role of text messaging and social networking in these movements, or even the 2009–2010 Iranian election protests (dubbed the "Twitter Revolution" by the media), these technologies were only a means by which to physically mobilize human beings in public spaces (Juris, 2012). Public space as an architectural staging ground for diverse human interactions is also a material staging ground for ideology (Delgado, 2011, p. 29), and this is where academics have an opportunity to meaningfully operationalize their knowledge and privilege. Similarly, academics can bring their politics into the ivory tower to radicalize the workplace (see Chatterton, 2008). This could involve introducing more community-based material into their courses or being candid and vocal with their department colleagues about their own activism to validate and normalize the politics of scholarship.

Escaping the Ivory Trap

Just as the ivory tower works to keep activists out, it also works to keep researchers and academics locked into institutional, disciplinary, and professional imperatives. At its most extreme, academic policing occurs through actively repressing certain ideologies. More common and perhaps more insidious than outright repression, however, are institutionalized biases that privilege positivism, quantitative methodologies, and speaking to past research over current social problems. This allows the avoidance of social problems altogether, particularly "fringe" issues like animal liberation. Academics become trapped by what we identify as the fallacy of objectivity, methodological hierarchies, and marginalization.

The Fallacy of Objectivity

There is a privileging of "objectivity," the belief that the scholar should be impartial to the process and outcome of theory building and research. Therefore it is often deemed unwise or inappropriate for people to study movements in which they are involved, for fear they will not be objective. In reality, all research involves subjective elements and pure objectivity on the part of the researcher is not possible.

The idea that a scientific objectivity or a value-free approach is the only means by which to do research is referred to as "positivism." Anthropology is one discipline that has made a self-conscious split with this positivist approach in recent decades. Some criticisms of this approach highlight that the researcher is often deprived of observational and representational authority, becoming mechanized within a limited scientific method (Roscoe, 1995).

The pursuits of the disciplines that are considered more prestigious are erroneously viewed as purely objective. However, researchers have their own biases as to what is an interesting or important topic, which in turn makes even the most technical and mainstream research constrained by the questions being asked. Interestingly, vivisection is viewed as objective science even though the researchers almost always have personal financial gain tied into their research by way of funding from pharmaceutical companies or government agencies. Conversely, CAS scholars, who rarely receive large grants or have any personal monetary gain—and may even suffer negative professional repercussions for their work—are more likely to be deemed problematically subjective, highlighting the fallacy of objectivity.

CAS openly rejects the politics of objectivity and positivism:

> [CAS] rejects pseudo-objective academic analysis by explicitly clarifying its normative values and political commitments, such that there are no positivist illusions whatsoever that theory is disinterested or writing and research is nonpolitical. To support experiential understanding and subjectivity. (Best et al., 2007, p. 4)

Researchers need to acknowledge and embrace that there is a degree of subjectivity or, at the very least, disciplinary, cultural, and biographic influence in all research so that they can be cognizant of their biases. A researcher who rejects a notion that the academy is limited to abstract theorizing or simply speaking to existing scholarly work is free to address the social ills that urgently call for study, theory, reflection, and action.

The Professional Is Political

CAS calls not only for overcoming positivism but also asserts that scholars should have clear political orientation and goals: "[CAS] rejects apolitical, conservative, and liberal positions in order to advance an anti-capitalist, and, more generally, a radical anti-hierarchical politics" (Best et al., 2007, p. 5).

Not only should scholars promote liberatory politics and social movement tactics but they also need to live their values. CAS, in its current iteration, does not explicitly state that scholars should have a personal daily praxis that avoids exploitation and promotes liberation, but it is foundational to this type of work.

For an ethic of scholarship that can be truly beneficial to nonhuman animals—
or any exploited group—scholars need to know their politics and be willing to
embody a living example: the personal is political and our work is personal. Lack
of attachment to personal politics in one's scholarship is accepted in most of the
academy, including HAS, a limitation that CAS seeks to overcome. Tension over
the issue is regularly played out in venues when HAS and CAS scholars interact.
An Internet listserv of HAS scholars, humananimalstudies, sees these debates every year or so. For example, in 2011, after a number of scholars made comments
about veganism and the moral expectations of researchers studying nonhuman
animals, one scholar asked for clarification as to who could participate in a forum
of HAS researchers:

> I am increasingly unsure whether this discussion group is intended for the participation of an omnivorous scientist with a pragmatic/consensus-driven approach to issues. It seems that discussions now typically assume veganism is correct and any other approaches [sic] are abberant [sic] and can be freely insulted. If this group is not open the "animalusers" [sic] and/or does not require respectful discourse, that is totally fine and I can opt out. But as a contributing ASI member I would be interested in clarifying whether or not this is the case.

Some group members e-mailed with support for the inclusion of all voices in the
listserv, regardless of personal ethics and use of nonhuman animals. Though most
also clarified they are vegan and think others should be, no one suggested the
listserv should be a safe space for people who simultaneously study nonhuman
animals and refuse to exploit them to exchange ideas and share information.

HAS openly accepts scholars who assert that the study of nonhuman animals
can be purely "objective" even while millions die daily at the hands of humans
and human interventions. HAS also tolerates human violence toward nonhuman
animals, such as meat eating, by not explicitly demanding personal accountability
for those studying nonhuman animals.

Since all scholarship is influenced by researchers' experiences, biography, and
socioeconomic characteristics, CAS scholars must remain critical of their own actions and lifestyle so that, to the degree possible, their work is less affected by their
experiences as oppressors. As such, we suggest an additional orienting principle
for CAS: *We seek to develop a CAS that insists that scholars remain accountable to
their research subjects. In regard to liberation politics this means that scholars must
not abuse, injure, degrade, exploit, cage, denigrate, or kill oppressed human groups,
nonhuman animals, or the Earth.*

Not only must scholars remain accountable to their research subjects but
when their subjects are exploited or oppressed, the onus is on them to use their
work to advance the rights of their subjects and to take action to engender liberation, when such actions are warranted or desired. Meaningful social change ulti-

mately happens in the streets, not in classrooms or on listservs. This means that academics often have an obligation to be activists as well.

Marginalization

Social hierarchies in the larger culture are also reflected in the privileging of different academic topics of study such that some social justice issues and topics of research are marginalized in academia. For example, women's, minority, and disability studies are not as well supported—often having all faculty members cross-listed in other departments. Also, work in these areas often cannot get into the major disciplinary journals, so a wide academic audience never reads their work or is exposed to their ideas. All of this is especially true for AS. Currently only 5 percent of U.S. universities and colleges offer a single HAS or CAS course (HRC, 2011). This marginalization of the field serves to delegitimize AS, making it particularly difficult for scholars to engage in CAS.

CAS scholars are not only topically peripheral in the eyes of the system but they also produce scholarship that explicitly aims to critique the status quo:

> [CAS] rejects apolitical, conservative, and liberal positions in order to advance an anti-capitalist, and, more generally, a radical anti-hierarchical politics. This orientation seeks to dismantle all structures of exploitation, domination, oppression, torture, killing, and power in favor of decentralizing and democratizing society at all levels and on a global basis. (Best et al. 2007, p. 5)

This marginalization of work that is either expressly political or topically "special interest" comes from within the academy, and it causes many scholars to avoid critical topics such as these out of concern for publication opportunities and space.

At its worst, ideological marginalization is expressed in the form of outright repression, such as Yale University's choice to let go anthropologist David Graeber. Graeber conducted years of ethnographic fieldwork in rural Madagascar and has a strong publication record. While this should have made him an asset in any anthropology department, Yale did not renew his contract in 2005 and provided little explanation as to why. Many, including Graeber himself, attribute this to his outspoken anarchist politics and activism that he engaged in outside of his scholarship. As Graeber explains:

> I've been hearing a lot of stories . . . about radical teachers suddenly being let go for no apparent reason. They don't even have to dig up something offensive you're supposed to have said anymore—at least, in my case no one is even suggesting I did or said anything outrageous . . . We're moving from the neoliberal university to the imperial university. Or at least people are trying to move us there. (quoted in Frank, 2005)

Not only does CAS reject the status quo academically, but it also accepts and defends radical modes of social change:

> [CAS] openly supports and examines controversial radical politics and strategies used in all kinds of social justice movements, such as those that involve economic sabotage from boycotts to direct action toward the goal of peace. (Best et al., 2007, p. 5)

This "radical" orientation leads to repression even from outside the academy. Promoting such politics and pushing for radicalism and a re-envisioning of the quasi-democratic, capitalist underpinnings of Western societies is threatening to governments and elite interests with whom the government is enmeshed, for example, pharmaceutical companies, the military-industrial complex, and agribusiness. The experience of sociologist Rik Scarce illustrates this point. He spent five months in jail for refusing to reveal the names of interviewees for his doctoral dissertation research, individuals to whom he had guaranteed anonymity. Even though the American Sociological Association's code of ethics prohibited his cooperation, he was jailed for contempt of court. CAS cofounder Steven Best has not only had troubles within his own department because of his activism and scholarship, including being suddenly removed as chair of the Philosophy Department at the University of Texas in El Paso, but the British government also banned him from entry to the UK for his scholarship, which was said to "foment, justify, or glorify violence in furtherance of particular beliefs" (Kahn, 2008, p. 7). Spectacular stories such as these proscribe the "appropriate" and limiting boundaries of mainstream scholarship.

Fear of repression and fear of the inability to secure tenure drives many scholars to moderate their own work. The psychology of the panopticon is part of the professionalizing process and molds professors to self-police and to police one another. This is particularly relevant in the case of animal liberation politics, as the issues addressed by scholars in the field may not only critique individual behaviors that one's colleagues regularly engage in (speciesism, meat eating, using animal for entertainment, etc.), but also it actively critiques one of the university's money generators—vivisection. Scholars may worry that funding, classes, and support will be cut for their work. Further, the dominant interpretation of the liberal ideal of being "open-minded," that is, maintaining a personal ethic of political correctness but having an open and accepting attitude toward others, does not sit comfortably with research that makes explicit political and moral claims.

Methodological Hierarchies

The premise of objectivity exists not only topically but also methodologically, leading some methods to be considered more prestigious or legitimate. This creates a hierarchy that places more confidence and value in numeric and technical data over data gained through observation or conversation. The pursuit of hard sciences, quantifiable phenomenon, and historically privileged topics of study are prioritized over venturing into the "messy" world of case-specific studies or current social justice or environmental issues. This has created an odd situation in which the intrusive, violent, and immoral act of vivisection is actually held in higher regard than most work within CAS, as CAS embraces myriad methodologies, many of which are non-quantifiable. That is not to say that there are not quantitative scientists and researchers who engage with CAS, but CAS does not privilege certain methodologies over others, advocating instead a pluralist approach that values the method(s) that can best answer a research question in a non-exploitative manner.

Methodologies are better viewed as tools, with different methods being more or less useful depending on the research question. The larger one's toolbox, the more options are available for understanding a problem. While scholars benefit from being widely trained in methodologies, it is helpful simply to be open to and aware of all methods, and to be willing to collaborate with methodological experts or scholars in other disciplines when useful.

Knowledge for Knowledge's Sake

Academia also accepts and encourages pursuit of knowledge for the sake of knowledge, and offers few incentives to pose research questions of relevance to current social justice issues. In fact, the hurdles of engaging in research that might be deemed unscientific actually discourages theory aimed at praxis in favor of research for the sake of research. In order to achieve tenure or intellectual esteem, academics must first demonstrate a strong knowledge base within their field that they expand upon or contribute to in their own work. This encourages scholars to speak directly to past research and others in their field, but it does not reward venturing into unknown intellectual territory, creating a pattern in which scholars engage in insular conversations with each other. On the other hand, CAS "eschews narrow academic viewpoints and the debilitating theory-for-theory's sake position in order to link theory to practice, analysis to politics, and the academy to the community" (Best et al., 2007, p. 5).

In short, what researchers need to do is to work to avoid being pedantic in favor of being pragmatic. One way that this can be done is by seeking to answer questions that are of direct value to disadvantaged others or their advocates. For example, animal activists are working with a lack of data to take even the most basic steps to help nonhuman animals; there are little to no data regarding the number of nonhuman animals dying in shelters, how many nonhuman animals are currently in zoos and circuses, or the reasons that people choose to become vegan, among other basic questions.

For activists to convince others that these are important issues, basic research is needed to build a foundation. Some research has accomplished this, but it is minimal. For example, Amy Fitzgerald, Linda Kalof, and Thomas Dietz (2009) examined links between slaughterhouse work and violence against humans. Controlling for factors that typically affect arrest rates, they compared the slaughterhouse industry to other major industries and found that slaughterhouse employment increases total arrests and arrests for rape, other sex offenses, and other violent crimes. This study shows a clear link between violence against nonhuman animals and violence against humans, allowing activists to safely and accurately claim that normalized violence against nonhuman animals negatively impacts human society.

The case for veganism was forwarded by one of the largest population studies ever conducted, providing a wealth of information about how dietary habits influence health. Cornell University nutritionist T. Colin Campbell (2005) studied the diets of relatively insular communities across rural China and examined correlations between diet and health outcomes. He found that a variety of dietary choices directly influences development of certain diseases and provides clear evidence in support of the health benefits of a vegan diet.

More work like Fitzgerald and colleagues' and Campbell's is necessary. In some areas, foundational research and theory is needed just to begin measuring and identifying the basic dimensions of a problem. Even though the lack of data about the use of nonhuman animals is often due to animal exploitation industries refusing to release records, it is up to researchers to create ways to estimate and extrapolate this information. Asking basic research questions to accumulate knowledge about topics that have been ignored and looking to those who need the research to determine what research questions to ask will generate praxis by prioritizing pragmatic topics of research that can accomplish at least one of the following: directly helping a disadvantaged population, enabling the development or improvement of social justice programs, enabling the physical needs of a community, or empowering social justice activists or grassroots movements.

Building Bridges

While freeing disciplines from the confines of the ivory trap is a necessary step toward liberatory scholarship, it is not sufficient to engender praxis. While some shackles must be shed, some new bonds must also be built. Specifically, CAS endeavors to connect disciplines within the academy, connect social justice movements to each other, and to connect scholarship to practice. The first orienting principle of CAS states that it:

> pursues interdisciplinary collaborative writing and research in a rich and comprehensive manner that includes perspectives typically ignored by animal studies such as political economy. (Best et al., 2007, p. 4)

Further, CAS:

> seeks to create openings for constructive critical dialogue on issues relevant to Critical Animals Studies across a wide range of academic groups; citizens and grassroots activists;

the staffs of policy and social service organizations; and people in private, public, and non-profit sectors. (Best et al., 2007, p. 5)

Interdisciplinary work is important for topically driven research. If one hopes to fully explore uncharted territory, one must adopt both disciplinary and methodological versatility. Acceptance of interdisciplinary work in the field does not mean that scholars cannot work within a specific discipline, but it does mean that all disciplines must be accepted as viable conduits to bring theory and the academy to practice and the populous. There is an urge in the academy to police the boundaries of one's discipline and to know who is in and who is out so that competition for jobs, classes, and funding can be bounded. However, this is not pragmatic if the desired outcome is liberation. Accordingly, CAS encourages co-authorships and collaborations across disciplines so that scholars can expand the scope of their understanding.

In some cases it may even be appropriate to incorporate the research subject into the research project, though this is more often the case with human animals than it is with nonhuman animals. An encouraging trend that has developed in anthropology over the last several decades is the technique of collaborative ethnography, in which researcher and subject together build research models and theory at various levels of research, with the fullest expression of the technique being co-authorship by researcher and subject. One of the driving tenets of the technique is the idea that "much more than data collection" happens in the field (Rappaport, 2008) and this is perhaps nowhere truer than in cases of academics working with social movements and social justice issues. A sample first question of a scholar working directly with activists or disadvantaged others might be, "What research questions would accommodate *your* work?"

In describing an experience doing field research with the Movement for Global Resistance in Barcelona, Jeffrey Juris (2007) recalls being asked by a miffed activist how activists like him benefit in exchange for the degrees and prestige gained by the researcher for what is really a shared experience. Juris takes this point seriously and notes that most social movement research is myopic in that it is *about* and not *for* movements. A feeling of debt to research subjects can only be mitigated by reciprocity (Pulido, 2008). At a basic level, the researcher's work should in no way disadvantage the research subject, as is regular practice in most disciplines that study nonhuman animals. A more effective way to reciprocate with the research subject is to engage in collaborative activist scholarship or produce work of direct benefit, when it is possible and desired by the subject(s).

A necessary step to bridging the gap between the ivory tower and the street below is humility. Though academics are usually the most privileged keepers of knowledge in society, in many cases nondegree holders know more about a given topic than scholars. It has been pointed out that while social scientists are licensed professionals formulating theories on, for instance, housing issues, a housing activist is likely to be more knowledgeable on this topic than academic researchers (Calhoun, 2008). To recognize that non-academics are prepared and willing to bear the burden of knowledge is to begin dismantling the elitism that isolates the ivory tower from the street.

One fantastic example of this dialogical approach between academic and non-academic is the experiments in pedagogy that emerged during the occupy movement in the United States in late 2011. As the occupy encampments spread across the country, most allocated space for educational purposes. In Los Angeles, the People's Collective University was a tent at the occupy LA encampment that attracted professors from universities in the Southern California region who taught free seminars on everything from civil disobedience movements to veganism. Organizers debriefed instructors to keep academic jargon to a minimum and encouraged the classes to be more dialogical and facilitative rather than lecture based. The classes resembled seminars, with a diverse student body of occupiers, homeless activists, and curious passersby of all ages.

Interlocking Oppressions

There is no liberation without total liberation because all oppressions are rooted in dichotomous thinking that creates arbitrary, but defensible, boundaries (us vs. them; animals vs. humans; man vs. nature) and hierarchical ways of rank ordering and organizing individuals into groups. When it comes to oppression, while everything about each experience of oppression is unique, oppression as a dominating force is not. CAS scholars need to be aware of and make these connections explicit in their work.

No point is discussed more exhaustively in the ten initial orienting principles of CAS than the need to understand all liberation struggles as tied together. For only in understanding that oppressions are working in concert, and in concerning itself with other oppressions, can CAS create liberatory praxis. Specifically, CAS:

> advances a holistic understanding of the commonality of oppressions, such that speciesism, sexism, racism, ablism, statism, classism, militarism and other hierarchical ideologies and institutions are viewed as parts of a larger, interlocking, global system of domination. . . . rejects reformist, single-issue, nation-based, legislative, strictly animal interest politics in favor of alliance politics and solidarity with other struggles against oppression and hierarchy . . . champions a politics of total liberation which grasps the need for, and the inseparability of, human, nonhuman animal, and Earth liberation and freedom for all in one comprehensive, though diverse, struggle; to quote Martin Luther King Jr.: "Injustice anywhere is a threat to justice everywhere." (Best et al. 2007, p. 5)

This need for understanding oppressions as interlocking and mutually reinforcing is not just ideologically or morally sound—it is imperative for the realization of liberation. There is a potential for the disadvantaged to gain a false sense of power by creating a boundary between themselves and other disadvantaged groups or individuals and then using this boundary to assert superiority or, worse, violence.

On another level, we find the tendency for social justice organizations to rank-order their causes and pit them against other social justice issues. In vying for resources or legitimacy some may claim their cause is more important than another. An example of this occurred during the 2008 election in California when two propositions were being voted on—one that would make gay marriage illegal (Proposition 8) and one that would give farmed animals a few minor protections (Proposition 2). Both passed. Outrage ensued and statements such as "animals have more rights than gays" were seen on signs carried during protests. In reality, the two movements were in no way opposed. Farmed animals received gains, which in reality were symbolic and minimal, but these gains in no way led to the discrimination and oppression inherent in Proposition 8. While some of the oppressed turned anger on other liberation causes, energy was diverted away from the unjust economic and political foundations of both oppressions. Further, if the causes had been viewed as linked in the first place, and everyone who voted yes on Proposition 2 had also voted no on Proposition 8, then perhaps such a repressive law may not have passed.

Conclusion: Theory in Action

The best scholarship is fomented in the pragmatic needs of a community and the ultimate realization of scholarship is when it informs action. However, universities and colleges, the institutions charged with the development of new theory, ideas, and invention, have become entrenched in hurdles and boundaries that prevent a privileging of praxis. We have identified key problems within the academy that limit scholars and prevent a bridge between the ivory tower and the street as (1) inaccessibility, (2) a fallacy of objectivity, (3) methodological hierarchies, (4) disciplinary boundary policing, and (5) marginalization. We reject these tendencies in favor of scholarship aimed at having the potential to motivate activists and other citizens in struggles against oppressions.

As vegan scholars focused on the study of social movements, we are particularly concerned with the liberatory potential of praxis in the field of AS. Nonhuman animals typically only make their way into universities by way of the cafeteria or the vivarium, and we see CAS as a way to overcome this. Not only does CAS advocate scholarship that sees nonhuman animals as subjects of research, not to be exploited in the process, but it also pushes for liberatory praxis. CAS clearly delineates ten orienting principles, to which we added two more in this chapter. These twelve tenets, taken together, can allow for a discipline that views the scholar as a bridge builder—someone who takes their privileged position to carry ideas and knowledge back and forth, from cerebral spaces to physical spaces and vice versa.

Though all the tenets of CAS are important, we have centered this chapter on the one principle that can direct all others—for us, the "golden rule" of CAS:

> [Critical Animal Studies] eschews narrow academic viewpoints and the debilitating theory-for-theory's-sake position in order to link theory to practice, analysis to politics, and the academy to the community. (Best et al., 2007, p. 5)

In the end, the goal is to encourage activist-scholars who view the relationship between community members and the academy as symbiotic, recognize the importance of scholarship to their communities, are motivated by justice over institutional politics, and prefer revolution over a promotion.

References

American Association of University Professors (AAUP). (2012). Recommended institutional regulations on academic freedom & tenure. Retrieved December 9, 2012, http://www.aaup.org/AAUP/pubsres/policydocs/contents/RIR.htm

Animals and Society Institute (ASI). (n.d.). About Us. Retrieved October 13, 2012, http://animalsandsociety.net/pages/about-us

Best, S. (2009). The rise of critical animal studies: Putting theory into action and animal liberation into higher education. *State of nature*. Retrieved July 27, 2011, http://www.stateofnature.org/theRiseOfCriticalAnimal.html

Best, S., Nocella, A. J., Kahn, R., Gigliotti, C., & Kemmerer, L. (2007). Introducing critical animal studies. *Journal for Critical Animal Studies, 5*(1), 4–5.

Calhoun, C. (2008). Social science for public knowledge. In S. Eliaeson & R. Kalleberg (Eds.), *Academics as public intellectuals*. London: Palgrave.

Campbell, C. T., & Campbell, T. M. (2005). *The China study*. Dallas: BenBella.

Chatterton, P. (2008). Demand the possible: Journeys in changing our world as a public activist-scholar. *Antipode, 40*, 421–427.

Delgado, M. (2011). *El espacio público como ideologia*. Madrid: Los Libros de la Catarata.

Eliaeson, S., & Kalleberg, R. (2008). Introduction: Academics as public intellectuals. In S. Eliaeson & R. Kalleberg (Eds.), *Academics as public intellectuals* (pp. 1–16). London: Palgrave.

Fitzgerald, A., Kalof, L., & Dietz, T. (2009). Slaughterhouses and increased crime rates: An empirical analysis of the spillover from "The Jungle" into the surrounding community. *Organization & Environment, 22*, 158–184.

Frank, J. (2005, May 13). Without cause: Yale fires an acclaimed anarchist scholar. *CounterPunch*. Retrieved May 31, 2013, http://www.counterpunch.org/2005/05/13/without-cause-yale-fires-an-acclaimed-anarchist-scholar

Freire, P. (2006/1970). *Pedagogy of the oppressed*. New York: Continuum.

Graeber, D. (2004). *Fragments of an anarchist anthropology*. Chicago: Prickly Paradigm.

Habermas, J. (2009). *Europe: The faltering project*. Malden, MA: Polity.

Hart, K. (2007). Marcel Mauss: In pursuit of the whole. *Comparative Studies in Society and History, 49*, 473–485.

hooks, b. (2000/1984). *Feminist theory: From margin to center*. Cambridge, MA: South End.

Humane Research Council (HRC). (2011, August 25). Proportion of universities with human-animal studies courses and animal law programs. *Humane Trends*. Retrieved May 31, 2013, http://www.humanetrends.org/ht/proportion-of-universities-with-human-animal-studies-courses-and-animal-law-programs/

Humane Research Council (HRC). (2010, September 30). Animal tracker graphing tool. *Humane Spot*. Retrieved June 2, 2013, http://www.humanespot.org/content/animal-tracker-graphing-tool

Juris, J. S. (2012). Reflections on #occupy everywhere: Social media, public space, and the emerging logics of aggregation. *American Ethnologist, 39*, 259–279.

Juris, J. S. (2007). Practicing militant ethnography with the movement for global resistance in Barcelona. In S. Shukaitis, D. Graeber, & E. Biddle (Eds.), *Militant investigations, collective theorization* (pp. 164–176). Oakland, CA: AK.

Kahn, R. (2008). Operation Get Fired: A Chronicle of the Academic Repression of Radical Environmentalist and Animal Rights Advocate-Scholars. Retrieved July 27, 2011, http://richardkahn.org/writings/new/OperationGetFiredDraft.pdf

Mauss, M. (1990/1925). *The gift*. New York: W. W. Norton.

Office of Research Integrity (ORI). (n.d.). Pigs. U.S. Department of Health & Human Services. Retrieved October 13, 2012, http://ori.hhs.gov/education/products/ncstate/pig.htm

Orlans, F. B. (1993). *Issues in responsible animal experimentation*. New York: Oxford University Press.

Pulido, L. (2008). Frequently (un)asked questions about being a scholar activist. In C. R. Hale (Ed.), *Engaging contradictions: Theory, politics, and methods of activist scholarship* (pp. 341–365). Los Angeles: University of California Press.

Rappaport, J. (2008). Beyond participant observation: Collaborative ethnography as theoretical Innovation. *Collaborative Anthropologies, 1*, 1–31.

Roscoe, P. B. (1995). The perils of "positivism" in cultural anthropology. *American Anthropologist, 97*, 492–504.

Shapin, S. (2012). The ivory tower: The history of a figure of speech and its cultural uses. *British Journal for the History of Science, 45*, 1–27.

Shapiro, K. (2008). *Human-animal studies: Growing the field, applying the field*. Ann Arbor, MI: Animals & Society Institute.

Suber, P. (2012). Open access overview: Focusing on open access to peer-reviewed research articles and their preprints. Retrieved October 13, 2012, http://bit.ly/oa-overview

U.S. Census Bureau. (2012). 2012 Statistical Abstract, Table 229. Retrieved October 13, 2012, http://www.census.gov/compendia/statab/2012/tables/12s0229.pdf

SIX

Critical Animal Studies as an Interdisciplinary Field

A Holistic Approach to Confronting Oppression

Kim Socha and Les Mitchell

Rhinoceros poaching, Stephen King's fiction, children's rights, Western literature, the sex trade in Thailand, and revolution—both literally and of the mind—might seem to comprise a list of disconnected items with little in common. However, they are just some of the topics we discuss in this chapter about the critical relations of power and how those relations specifically affect those who suffer from the unjust exercise of cultural control. Simultaneously, we call for a response to diverse situations of injustice in terms of acting ethically whenever an individual or group is oppressed, thereby encompassing a greater understanding of how authority is formed and wielded. Only then can we develop a call to action and foster solidarity among social justice movements. And as suggested by the list of seemingly detached ideas with which we begin this paragraph, greater understanding and real change come through looking at the world and its problems holistically.

    Within higher education, interdisciplinary studies (IS) challenges established boundaries between distinct fields of knowledge. In fact, IS is a degree major at colleges and universities that recognize certain problems and questions are too multifarious to address within the confines of one academic field. To wit, the University of California at Berkeley (n.d.) promotes its Interdisciplinary Studies Field major as offering "students the opportunity to develop an individualized cross disciplinary research major utilizing courses from the social sciences, the humanities, and/or the professional schools and colleges." UC Berkeley and other schools are challenging the traditional model of higher education that segments knowledge into narrowly constricted realms.

IS has the potential to transform the academy by enriching texts, classroom interactions, and degrees, while reaching broader audiences. In "Why JIS" (n.d.), the *Journal of Interdisciplinary Studies* explains the value of such multifaceted scholarship, stating that the

> need for interdisciplinary approaches as a key to reinvigorating and integrating both teaching and learning is increasingly recognized in the academy . . . It is becoming increasingly clear that research is interdisciplinary. Hence, higher education should also be more integrative, and thus fulfill the vision of liberal learning—what John Henry Newman called the *idea* of a *uni*versity.

IS brings together seemingly disparate modes of learning and obtaining knowledge. For example, the journal *ISLE: Interdisciplinary Studies in Literature and the Environment* (n.d.), although based in the University of Nevada's English Department, "explore[s] the relation between human beings and the natural world, and publishes articles from literary scholars, environmental historians, specialists in the visual and performing arts, environmental philosophers, geographers, economists, ecologists," and scholars from any field who wish to have a say in the journal's mission.

Similarly, Critical Animal Studies (CAS) is an inherently interdisciplinary field that encourages breaking down classic scholarly divisions within the academy. Indeed, the first core principle of CAS, and the one we explore in this chapter, is to pursue "interdisciplinary collaborative writing and research in a rich and comprehensive manner that includes perspectives typically ignored by animal studies such as political economy" (Best, Nocella, Kahn, Gigliotti, & Kemmerer, 2007, p. 4). As nonhuman communities underlie, to varying extents, all human social customs, institutions, and structures, it is imperative that CAS becomes a filter through which oppression and domination of nonhuman animals, human animals, and the environment are examined and contested. Each academic area has something to contribute to CAS, and CAS can benefit all areas.

Although other authors in this collection have defined CAS, we base our understanding of the field as stated in the mission from the Institute for Critical Animal Studies' (ICAS) website (n.d.): CAS "is the academic field of study dedicated to the abolition of animal and ecological exploitation, oppression, and domination. CAS is grounded in a broad, global, emancipatory, inclusionary movement for total liberation and freedom." Despite the restrictive conclusions one might draw from the word "animal" in CAS—and, to an extent, ICAS's mission statement—the field is concerned with both human and nonhuman animals and the cultural-social institutions through which they navigate—though the presence of nonhuman animals in these institutions is most often by force. As Pedersen (2009) explains in *Animals in Schools*:

> My approach to critical animal studies includes analytic exploration of social structures, institutions, practices and ideologies that define what relations are possible between humans and animals . . . I also seek to scrutinize and problematize a variety of power arrangements by which *both humans and animals* are currently subjected to domination, marginalization, and exploitation. For this purpose, I rely on a critical theoretical and critical pedagogical framework. (p. 3, emphasis added)

Pedersen positions CAS as a pedagogical construction that uses multiple processes to gain vital insights into the powerlessness of nonhuman animals and their treatment as human tools in the academy, corporate world, and entertainment venues. Based on our own anecdotal experiences, CAS as an academic field reflects dilemmas that arise within "street level" animal advocacy, as animal activists are often, and not always unfairly, seen as single issue thinkers who are unwilling to look at the broader implications of animal liberation's connection to other liberatory causes. Of course, this is not necessarily unique to the animal advocacy movement, but to help others see animal liberation as a political issue, it is important that activists of all kinds begin to look at oppression intersectionally, as theorized by Crenshaw (1991) through her analysis of the ways in which "the experiences of women of color are frequently the product of intersecting patterns of racism and sexism" (p. 1243). CAS offers an effective paradigm for animal advocates who work outside of higher education. Further, CAS has wide applicability for identifying and critiquing currents of power and oppression in different academic and social contexts, offering a way to explore traditional disciplines with nontraditional knowledge groupings.

Currently, there is only one school in North America, Brock University in Ontario, Canada, that offers CAS as a minor or concentration. Other colleges and universities will hopefully follow suit. However, scholars should be cautious when developing CAS majors or minors at colleges and universities, as such an approach limits the possibilities of using CAS as a theory—much like feminism, Marxism, and psychoanalysis—with far-reaching applications in putatively nonanimal related academic and cultural fields such as business, medicine, art, literature, and others. This is not to say that CAS majors and minors should not flourish, as students could pursue a CAS minor and use its perspectives within their major fields. Rather, CAS scholars must be vigilant in assuring that CAS does not become depoliticized or appropriated by the academy, thereby losing its ability to enact social change. This has happened in other academic areas that began as social movements. For example, at a recent conference, Birke (2012) noted that women's studies, springing from radical feminism of the 1960s and 1970s, as it exists in higher education today, is disconnected from the real-world issues that women face. Similarly, Best (2009) notes in "The Rise of Critical Animal Studies" that animal studies has grown in higher education, with "at least 40 courses being offered in departments that span [various] disciplines in universities and colleges in North America, the UK and New Zealand" (n.p.). But as he argues throughout his essay, this growth is both "laudable and lamentable." It is laudable in that animal studies can provide space for a more sensitive understanding of the woeful animal condition in Western culture. However, it is also lamentable because academized animal studies de-politicize the animal condition and position nonhuman animals as objects to be studied as non-agential beings. Although CAS is intrinsically political, it does run the risk of losing its radical edge if scholars do not take care to remember that the studies we do therein are attached to real-world suffering.

CAS is, first and foremost, a flexible field of study rather than a set of rigid parameters and theories, which by its essence inevitably reticulates into other areas. Critical Animal Pedagogy (CAP) is an orientation that individual instructors of any field may adopt to help students and community members develop their own ideas, questions, and research into the nature of power and oppression. We do not want CAS to become a calcified academic area pursued by those already sold on the idea of animal liberation. If this were to happen, CAS could lose its applicability as an interdisciplinary theory that can influence understanding of the all-encompassing nature of oppression while also exposing the oppression that underlies Western commodity culture, from clothing to pharmaceuticals. Best and colleagues (2007) state a mission of CAS to advance "a holistic understanding of the commonality of oppressions, such that speciesism, sexism, racism, ablism, statism, classism, militarism and other hierarchical ideologies and institutions are viewed as parts of a larger, interlocking, global system of domination" (p. 5). They further eschew the academic institutionalization of CAS because it could lead to disengagement from community activists and from active practice of emancipatory strategies.

The purpose of this chapter, therefore, is to investigate the ways in which CAS can be used to expose and challenge power lines of domination and oppression. Through scholarship, personal experience, and practical examples, we hope to demonstrate that CAS can also be used as a lens through which other disciplines can view the world and its problems rhizomatically, in the sense developed by Gilles Deleuze and Félix Guattari. Deleuze and Guattari, coming from the respective fields of philosophy and psychoanalysis, famously critiqued the supposed stability and dogmatic nature of knowledge structures in academia and beyond. As they explain (2001), "The rhizome [unlike the rooted tree] connects any point to any other point, and its traits are not necessarily linked to traits of the same nature" (p. 1605) . . . "The tree imposes the verb 'to be,' but the fabric of the rhizome is the conjunction 'and . . . and . . . and . . .' This conjunction carries enough force to shake and uproot the verb 'to be'" (p. 1609). Their focus on multiplicity and the non-hierarchical nature of knowing sets a paradigm for the epistemology upon which CAS is founded, for its focus is not just on the single animal question ("to be") but on the ways in which the animal question leads to, and springs from, questions about the emancipation of other oppressed groups: women, people of color, people with disabilities, those of the LGBTQIA community, and so on—in other words, the "and . . . and . . . and . . ." of which Deleuze and Guattari write. The rhizome provides an apt visualization of the interconnectedness of oppression and the areas into which CAS scholars must encroach.

Interdisciplinarity as a Forgotten Life Praxis

From a macro-perspective, the divide between disciplinarity and interdisciplinarity in higher education is comparable to the ways in which human animals view themselves. Undoubtedly, the traditional disciplines have evolved as separate areas due to historical, cultural, and methodological reasons. This fragmentation is reflected not only in academic disciplines but also in other life activities where we compartmentalize and divide the world into discrete components. This trend has become more dominant with the physical development of production systems and the adoption of a (Henry) Fordist industrialized approach to areas such as health and education, and it is often difficult for us to really experience how societies in the past, and a few societies today, integrated the many aspects of their lives. The practice of one's spirituality, for example, was not restricted to certain times or places, although there were special celebrations and sacred sites. Rather, it was lived as a moment-to-moment experience with no division between the sacred and profane. In a similar way, we once were, as oral communities still are today, far more integrated with our environment on a phenomenological level, perceiving rocks, trees, nonhuman animals, wind, and rain as parts of a living, speaking environment of which we too are a part.

Our segmentation of the world has offered us many advantages, particularly in relation to the trade and distribution of goods and services. However, some groups have become significantly more materially advantaged than others in an increasingly frenetic, globalized, technologized world, and we are rapidly destroying our environment and the living communities of the Earth. Segmentation has also severely restricted our understanding of ourselves as members of the Earth community, paradoxically limiting our discernment that our understanding is itself severely limited! We know not that we know not. Of course, despite our much divided world, we do not segregate our personal activities in such a way, but continually integrate them without necessarily noting the ways in which they interconnect. We engage in relationships, we write, we have our histories, we listen to others' histories, we discuss social problems and politics, spirituality, sporting interests, child development, health, the law, we buy and sell, synthesizing our own viewpoints and opinions based on what we think we know and what we learn from others.

As such, the very idea of single disciplines or distinct life components is somewhat of a myth. As humans, we live interdisciplinary lives, although we often try to distinguish work life from personal life and to segment our roles as parents, children, siblings, activists, workers, writers, readers, teachers, and so on. We hope that the arguments we make within this chapter might have far-reaching applications for the individual reader's own sense of self and his or her place in the webbed nature of reality, as well as for social justice activists and the future of CAS.

Defining Interdisciplinarity

As academics, it is common to think of ourselves as belonging to certain disciplines or carrying out work in a particular field. This is useful in many ways, as we share colleagues' specialized, in-depth work and the development of research tools. However, it can also be a process which limits our perspectives on the world, on what is acceptable (conforming to our discipline), and what is not (differing from our discipline). Single disciplinary studies also carry the danger of limiting our creativity to a very narrow area. Further, in many ways, we fool ourselves into thinking that any one field of inquiry can ever be unmoored from other disciplines from which we consciously and unknowingly borrow.

In Les's workshops where he assists researchers with developing their papers for publication, it was at first thought that the most useful workshops would be those where researchers from similar fields came together. This way they could share a common professional language and understanding and so assist each other as experts using shared knowledge bases. However, his experience has been very different. He has found that, for example, microbiologists can have a great deal to say about education and agriculturalists about traditional healing. To be sure, this interaction is unpredictable, to say the least, but it is also very exciting and creative.

In Kim's Modern World Literature class, where students are assigned Etel Adnan's 1975 novella *Sitt Marie Rose*, she includes a historical presentation on the Lebanese Civil War and a fictional film depicting the personal losses of that war. This history lesson and film analysis, connected to a war that lasted from 1975 to 1990, necessitates understanding of and shines light upon contemporary issues in the Middle East. When teaching the Surrealists, she is compelled to visit a colleague from the French Department to make sure she is pronouncing Breton, Éluard, and Rimbaud correctly. The seemingly routine task of analyzing a work of literature is, when done thoughtfully, a trek through other disciplines.

Before delving deeper into *inter*disciplinarity, it first helps to define "discipline." Stephenson, Lawson, Carrington, Barton, Thorsnes, and Mirosa (2010) propose this explanation:

> We believe that disciplines are particular sets of ways of constructing, checking, holding and passing on knowledge. Disciplines are in part distinguished by the contexts in which they are applied, and the classes of problems to which the discipline directs its inquiries. (p. 272)

Disciplines differ in the techniques they use and the perspectives from which they see the world. Stephenson and colleagues (2010) further state, "In many ways, the academic disciplines are like nation states of the intellectual world, with their own territories, languages, cultures and governance arrangements. These features can limit the ability of disciplinarians to communicate easily with other disciplines" (p. 272). Like nation-states, these disciplines are often closed off from each other and a style of nationalism develops within. On any given college or university campus, it is not unusual for professors from one department to have little or no interaction with those from other departments. Repko (2008) notes that the fields are distinguished by "the questions the disciplines ask about the world, their respective perspective worldview, the set of assumptions they employ, and the methods they use to build up a body of knowledge" (p. 4).

Disciplines as we understand them today arose in the early nineteenth century, what Thompson Klein (1990) refers to as the "formalization of the pursuit of knowledge in various fields" (p. 22); hence, individuals pursued focused degrees in economics, English, history, medicine, mathematics, and so forth. It wasn't until the early- to mid-twentieth century that a crisis arose in higher education to challenge such formalized learning. Augsburg (2006) explains that fragmented knowledge, changing student demographics, and an increasingly complex, technologized world demanded a new interdisciplinary approach to learning (p. 9). Thus was born IS. Or, should we say, *re*born. Ancient Greeks and Romans are credited with developing a type of interdisciplinary curriculum. The Greek *enkuklios paedeia* and the Roman *orbis doctrinae* emphasized "the belief that an educated person is one who has surveyed the disciplines," and Roman philosopher Marcus Tullius Cicero developed "the concept of the *doctus orator* (the man who combines extensive knowledge of all sciences with wide experience of the problems of everyday life)" (Thompson Klein, 1990, p. 23). In sum, from its earliest inception, Western culture has seen the benefit of studying various disciplines, identifying where they intersect, and assuring that such study has real-world significance.

To wit, Buller (2008), writing from a geographical perspective, points out that an apparent single entity can be many things: "What is a sheep—a source of revenue, an organic and self-renewable resource, a grazing unit, a system of biochemical transfer leading to patterns of muscle and fat development, the symbol of a nostalgic rural economy and society when things were 'better' and slower-paced or even an actor in a spatialised socionatural network?" (p. 395). He goes on to make the point that "the argument here is that interdisciplinarity is more than a process of coming together (or coming between); it redefines or recontextualises the objects and the practices of study so as to permit interdisciplinary articulation" (p. 396). To understand interdisciplinary studies is to focus on the prefix "inter," as it alights on the area among fields, or what Repko (2008) terms "contested spaces," but it also promises to integrate those fields and "reconcile conflicting disciplinary insights" (p. 6). Of course, for CAS scholars, these ideological positions in themselves become subjects of study as we strive to understand the complex reasons for the oppression of nonhuman animals. Buller could just as easily have chosen human animals as the subject of the example with only minor changes, the point being the multifaceted nature of observers' perspectives on the subject in question. The validity of those perspectives is, of course, a matter for debate. A literary example of what Repko terms "contested spaces" arises when the Christian Bible is taught as literature, thereby allowing integration of history, theology, English, and other disciplines. IS, however, is not as simple as dipping one's toe into another field and analyzing the resulting ripples. In fact, Repko, Newell, and Szostak (2012) emphasize the differences between interdisciplinarity in the natural and social sciences, which are integrated "on the behalf of others," and the humanities that seek "to draw others . . . into the integrative process" (p. 301). But despite these differences of purpose, even the sciences and humanities can find and share "contested spaces." This has already happened, as when Singer (1975) published *Animal Liberation* to, among other things, contest the use of nonhuman animals by humans in a range of exploitative contexts. Although medical researchers supposedly work "on the behalf of others" (i.e., for human health), Singer's philosophical treatise, arising from the humanities, has attempted "to draw others . . . into the integrative process" (Repko, Newell, & Szostak, 2012, p. 301) by questioning, and thereby causing others to question, current medical ethics and offering new paradigms that include the elimination of animals as scientific subjects.

So, what, in concrete terms, is meant by interdisciplinarity? Schmidt (2007) proposes four types of interdisciplinarity and allied questions with respect to

1. epistemology concepts/theories: Are there truly interdisciplinary theories to be formulated or is it possible to have meta theories relating to theories across disciplines?
2. methodology methods/practices: How do we obtain knowledge across disciplines?
3. ontology objects (ontology): How do we see the nature of reality?

4. purpose setting/problem framing/problem solving: What is the intention in all of this as this will surely play a part in affecting the interdisciplinary methodology, etc.? (pp. 318–320).

As far as the disciplines themselves, Repko (2008) divides them into four distinct overarching categories: the natural sciences, the social sciences, the humanities, and the applied professions (p. 4). Much as we like to package the world into neat bundles for our own convenience, placing boundaries here and there, we easily forget how arbitrary these lines are. As a Buddhist might say, we use the sword of illusion to slice up reality. Not only do we forget that these boundaries are self-imposed, but our commitment to them may mean we fail to see a more comprehensive and multilayered picture.

For example, the problem of litter on a township street may be examined as a public administration problem, but its roots may also lie in the psychology of a people alienated from life in an economic system that worships conspicuous consumption and in the history of a shattered community. These issues might be reflected in the art on the walls, in the township music, in its theological understanding of faith, in the abuse of women, in levels of illness, in the exploitation of nonhumans, in xenophobia, and so on. There is no single point of explanation or entry into the problem of litter in the township. Rather, there is a web (or rhizomatic series of "and . . . and . . . and . . ."), a web of knowledge, action, and meaning. Similarly, it makes no sense to examine climate change as purely an issue of natural science, multifaceted though that is; rather, climate change is also political, historical, sociological, religious, literary, philosophical, economic, and cultural.

IS also lends itself to collaboration with colleagues from ostensibly different fields of study. In an early overview of IS, Thompson Klein (1994) comments on the opportunities for community and networking therein. In the past, educators were forced to go to the local library for resources, but now networking is seen as a "multilayered activity that encompasses familiar person-to-person forms of social contact through correspondence, telephone calls, and personal meetings as well as the rich resources of electronic communication" (p. 13). And now, about twenty years since Klein penned her commentary, educators have the additional communicative methods of Facebook, YouTube, and Skype.

In sum, a discipline may be viewed as a knowledge domain with its particular collected facts, theories, epistemologies, concepts, and methods (Repko, 2012, p. 4). In contrast, interdisciplinarity need not be confined to traditional disciplines but can include other "knowledge formations" such as indigenous knowledge, firsthand experiential knowledge, artisan knowledge, and so forth (Repko, 2012, pp. 10–11). From a social justice perspective, sympathy and emotion can also serve as knowledge bases. Donovan (2007) lauds Max Scheler's *The Nature of Sympathy* (1913/1926) as a seminal text that "elevates sympathy into a form of knowledge (*Verstehen*, or understanding) that he proposes as an epistemological alternative to the objectification of the Cartesian scientific mode" (p. 177). Sympathy as knowledge proposes a challenge to seventeenth-century philosopher René Descartes' infamous assumption that nonhuman animals are mere automata, thereby holding special significance for those who work toward animal liberation.

Scholars Crossing Borders

We feel well suited to write a chapter on CAS and IS because, despite our differing life paths, continents, and seemingly dissimilar disciplines, we both found ourselves on the board of the Institute for Critical Animal Studies (ICAS). Les is director of a center for creativity in South Africa and Kim teaches English composition and literature in the United States. Other board members have degrees in education, conflict resolution, geography, cultural studies, psychology, and so forth; still other board members are not academics but activists and political organizers (which is not to say the two positions—activist and academic—cannot ally). Seemingly singular and far afield, our interest in crossing theoretical borders led to our shared ideologies on nonhuman animal and other social justice concerns. Thus, we collaboratively engage in IS as part of the ICAS collective while also continuing our individualized research. Indeed, each person brings to a problem his or her own unique training, experiences, and cultural and experiential histories.

Les is trained as a biochemist and worked in hospital pathology labs before moving to the public health sector and from there to teaching sciences in a township school and eventually to a university. However, his PhD research, while drawing on his other experiences and training, used linguistic analysis of texts, research in social psychology, and the philosophy of critical realism, among other fields and disciplines.

His original intent was to look at farmed nonhumans to understand why humans abuse and slaughter them by the billions with very little moral consideration shown by most members of society. This work concerned carrying out textual analysis on articles in a farming magazine to look at ideological constructions and discourses. It also needed not only an understanding of sociolinguistics but also of social science theories of power, hegemony, and hermeneutics and a philosophical base for the ontology of the critical realist research. Naturally, he also needed to examine the various philosophical perspectives on nonhuman animals (particularly those related to ethics), language, and women, and some environmental and religious perspectives as well. Thereafter, looking at the different discourses that arose during his research, he found he needed to know a lot more about slavery of various kinds, making this a further area of his study. Using his training and experience in science, Les was able to examine the scientific and production discourses that dominated farming magazine articles.

Les's path then led to discourses of mass violence, genocide, and eventually to the work of Stanley Milgram, Philip Zimbardo, and Albert Bandura on, to use

Bandura's (1999) term, "moral disengagement." As the work from various areas came together, an overall picture began to emerge (and is still emerging), spreading outward, causing him to ask questions about political and economic systems, the environment, and spirituality, among other topics.

Kim's academic path, from her undergraduate to doctoral degree, was unwaveringly in English literature. As an undergraduate, she wrote her senior thesis on the American Harlem Renaissance poet Countee Cullen; as a master's student, she was a generalist, with special interest in Britain's Romantic poets. When entering her PhD program in English literature and criticism, she thought her education would pick up where it had left off, in traditional English fields. In contrast, her doctoral studies led to the production of her book *Women, Destruction and the Avant-Garde: A Paradigm for Animal Liberation* (*WDAG*) (2011). This text arose from a course in the burgeoning field of critical vanguard studies—analysis of sociopolitical artistic practitioners usually defined under the umbrella term "avant-garde"—as coined and developed by scholar Mike Sell. As Pedersen and Stănescu (2011) explain in *WDAG*'s introduction, the text

> can be read in many ways. It can be read as a feminist manifesto for the destruction of cultural conceptions and politics of female beauty . . . It can also be read as an educative account of the implications of the legacy of the avant-garde . . . Or it can be read as a deconstruction of rationality as an oppressive force . . . We, however, prefer to read the book as a passionately and sharply composed collage of negative spaces, which, like a surrealist artwork, generate new and unthought critical connections for animal liberation. (p. xi)

This commentary is not provided to be self-congratulatory or to promote Kim's book. Indeed, it is presented as much for what is in the excerpt as for what is missing: precisely, any mention of English literature. While there is some literary analysis involved, *WDAG* interweaves sociological constructs of identity, arguments in defense of anarchist political theory, and analysis of avant-garde performance art, surrealism, radical feminism, true crime, and popular culture. IS allowed Kim to discuss Jürgen Habermas's public sphere in the same chapter that analyzes the 2008 Disney film *Beverly Hills Chihuahua*. And CAS allows for a book that considers a multifaceted, multidisciplinary approach to human animal, nonhuman animal, and environmental liberation. As a volunteer, Kim's path was similarly surprising. While she had always wanted to be more involved in animal advocacy, her avocations began as a crisis counselor and medical and legal advocate for survivors of sexual violence and domestic abuse. Quite often, women fleeing issues of domestic violence stayed in or returned to the site of abuse because they had companion animals to attend to. Again, life itself is not so easily divided into human and nonhuman animal issues.

Once finishing her PhD, Kim put theory into practice by joining a grassroots animal rights group in Minneapolis, Minnesota. Soon, however, the abuse and exploitation of nonhumans led her to consider the oppressive culture from which those problems spring. Now, in addition to her animal advocacy work, she also volunteers within the prison system with juveniles and recently paroled sex offenders. These efforts began with an interest in helping nonhuman animals, with the "and... and... and..." leading to her working alongside others who fall victim to inherently oppressive and authoritarian governmental and social structures.

With this, we return to the nonhuman animal question. Benson (1992), writing more than seventy years ago in the classic *The Outermost House*, anticipates the danger of our restricted vision and the warping effects it can have in respect to nonhuman animals: "Remote from universal nature, and living by complicated artifice, man in civilization surveys the creature through the glass of his knowledge and sees thereby a feather magnified and the whole image in distortion" (pp. 24–25). Our goals as CAS scholars and activists must be to see the "whole image" and then take action.

Multifaceted Problems I:
An Interdisciplinary Approach to Rhinoceros Poaching

What we are really describing with interdisciplinarity is an integrated way of understanding and seeking to solve a problem or problems. Issues looked at from only one perspective might seem relatively clear within a certain set of ossified answers drawn from within a particular discipline. However, from an interdisciplinary perspective, the picture may be very different. Further, it offers problem solvers the ability to reconsider where power lies and who is providing answers to difficult questions. By confronting issues outside of our proclaimed areas of training, we also confront those who are making decisions both for us and for the nonhuman animals and environments who/that also populate our planet. As such, interdisciplinarity questions governments, organizations, and experts who allow exploitation and injustice to flourish. It is intrinsically political. This multifaceted and often surprising method of considering problems is illustrated in a recent case involving rhinoceros poaching in South Africa.

Rhino poaching is an increasing problem in the country despite well-run and organized wildlife areas and "game parks" (Nunns, 2012; Worldwide Fund for Nature, 2012). It might be expected that this problem is specifically the province of conservation authorities, as this is their specialized area and that they, with their expertise, knowledge, and skills concerning wildlife, should be able to understand the problem best and implement workable solutions. However, a recent prosecution of rhino poachers suggests a much more intricate web of connections and quandaries (Carte Blanche, 2011, n.p.).

Essentially, the allegations are these: rhino horn attracts very large sums of money as a handle for daggers, as medicine, and as an aphrodisiac—although this latter use is disputed (Ellis, 2005). There is an illegal trade in the horn, and because it is so marketable and sells for large sums of money, people are willing to kill the rhino and cut off the horn. The horn then has to be exported from South Africa to a place where it is sold, often the Middle or Far East.

One syndicate found an ingenious way to obtain the rhino horn on an apparently legal basis. While trade in rhino horn itself is illegal, it is not illegal to hunt rhino in South Africa, and when this happens, the hunter is allowed to take a trophy—usually the head including the horn or just the horn. This syndicate used sex workers from Thailand to pose as clients who wanted to hunt rhinos. The syndicate applied to the nature conservation authorities on behalf of their clients (each client is allowed to shoot one rhino a year) for permits. The provincial conservation authority issued the permits and these women went on "their" hunt. The women had never used rifles before and were certainly not skilled in shooting rhino. However, on each hunt, a professional hunter must, according to regulations, be present. It was this person who actually shot the rhino, although the women would later have their photographs taken with the dead animal bodies. Some of the women apparently cried when they realized what was happening to the rhinos. After the animal was killed, the horn was removed and mounted on a very simple wooden plinth for export as a legal trophy. Once out of the country, the horn could be sold as desired.

The case was actually investigated and prosecuted by the South African revenue service with the Hawks investigating team that not only tracked what the syndicate's main actor was doing but also noted that a number of parks officials were living well beyond their means and likely were involved in corruption.

There are many possible interdisciplinary (in its widest sense) facets to this case. The central problem might be framed as understanding the causes of rhino poaching and how to counter it, but there are other issues at play beyond the problem of the rhino horn trade. From a sociological feminist perspective, we can try to understand the exploitation of Thai sex workers, what their experiences are, the power differentials involved in the sex trade, the socioeconomic conditions that allow for this form of exploitation, the position of women in Thai society, and their ability to be moved across borders. From an ecofeminist perspective, we can explore the economic and political systems that promote the analogous constructions of animals and women as commodities for entertainment. Public administration studies might examine corruption at various levels and how it affects communities—and in this case, conservation workers—considering the reasons corruption flourishes and possible measures to prevent it. Criminologists, of course, could examine large crime syndicates, their reach, economic diversity, and political connectedness and how they affect social development. Legal tax theorists and specialists could analyze current tax laws and the effectiveness of their application as well as methods of investigation and prosecution and how tax evasion affects countries and communities. Conservationists might evaluate current legislation and ideologies around conservation and how they impact resource allocation for protection. These are only a few possible perspectives.

Most significant, a scholar from any of these disciplines would need to explore, to a certain extent, the other issues involved in rhino poaching. It is almost impossible to look at this matter from only one viewpoint, and it would be dangerous to leave the issue in the hands of a single discipline where researchers may not be willing to see it from various perspectives. Again, we return to the rhizome, and the list of "and . . . and . . . and . . ." that exposes power lines and webbed oppressions. From a CAS standpoint, the issue of rhino hunting would go beyond the exploitation of rhinoceros and into one or more of the other areas noted.

As already mentioned, the above ideas represent limited examples of disciplines that could investigate this particular scenario, but an integrated project with traditional and nontraditional disciplines might lead to a far better understanding of how this criminal activity works, conditions that make it possible, its overall effects on human animals, nonhuman animals, and society and possible means of prevention. This could generate significant new knowledges that would not be possible with individual-discipline investigations.

The CAS approach might also lead to a transdisciplinary understanding where a particular concept or concepts are understood as cutting across boundaries and applicable to the different disciplines in an overarching way. In the above example, power might be one such concept: the *powerlessness* of nonhumans who are hunted, women who are objectified, poor communities that are exploited and the *power* of government officials, men, crime syndicates, politicians, profit makers, and of the customers thousands of kilometers away who desire the animal fragment as trophy, medicine, or aphrodisiac. And as a field that does not detach itself from social justice issues, CAS can expose the lines of control with an aim to cease the oppression and domination of rhinos, women, and poor communities. As always, CAS remains grounded in action that springs from theory.

Interdisciplinary studies such as these are integral, as a scholar or activist researching the international sex trade may come across an article written by a CAS scholar and see the connections among women, animals, those from non-industrialized countries, the environment, and others. This is how the circle of compassion widens, when we find new pathways to ally the issue of animal exploitation with other examples of abuse and mistreatment.

Multifaceted Problems II:
Interdisciplinary and Literary Applications of CAS and CAP

As a community college English generalist and community volunteer, Kim has found new ways to integrate CAS into her own specialized discipline, while encroaching into other fields with an eye on a holistic approach to confronting oppression. This project has manifest in two ways: through activist outreach and by applying CAS and CAP to literary works that, up to this point, have not been analyzed with thought to the nonhuman animal question. The purpose of this section is to first show the potential for activist interdisciplinary outreach and then to show how CAS can be used as an interdisciplinary approach to pedagogy.

The outreach potential as an animal advocate appears obvious, as activists regularly attend protests and tables at events. However, there is a tendency to forget that educators have ready audiences (in Kim's case, about 100 students per semester) who can be challenged to look at both social issues and traditional literature in vibrant new ways with CAS as an interdisciplinary analytic lens. In this section, she provides some examples from her activism and pedagogy as encouragement to both expose and critique Western conceptions of "the animal" while also allowing viewers and listeners to see how nonhuman animal exploitation is inherently connected to other forms of subjugation.

Activist Outreach with Critical Animal Studies

In 2011, the Animal Rights Coalition (ARC), a group with which Kim volunteers, tabled at an event called Education Minnesota, a convention-conference directed toward kindergarten through high school teachers. Although ARC has a surfeit of material for science teachers about dissection in the classroom, along with pamphlets explaining why "pets" such as hamsters and guinea pigs should not be used in schools, they had no take-aways for teachers from other disciplines. Thus, Kim was tasked with developing English and social studies/history/civics lesson plans for middle school and high school teachers. In both cases, Kim was challenged with looking at other disciplines from a CAS perspective. While she does hold a PhD in English, she holds no education degrees; therefore, she is not officially qualified to teach middle or high school. However, the lesson plans she developed were popular among attendees. Although she developed four lesson plans, for the sake of space, only two are included here, and both attempt to emphasize how nonhuman animal oppression is allied with the subjugation of other historically oppressed groups.

1. The first is titled "Alice Walker 'Am I Blue?' Lesson Plan":

Grade Level: Middle to High School

Time Commitment: 2–3 class periods

Objective: This lesson plan uses Walker's short story to encourage students to consider the ways in which figurative language, word choice, and punctuation make writing meaningful. Students are then prompted to explore how literary devices relate to the story's theme and how that theme relates to their own lives.

Class Discussion Questions

1. Someone should read the second paragraph out loud. What pronouns are used in this paragraph? What pronouns are used to refer to Blue, the horse? Why does the pronoun change? (Note: A similar pronoun shift occurs when the horse named Brown is introduced.)

2. In what ways do paragraphs 7 and 14 relate to the title of this story? As you contemplate a response, consider the many meanings of the word "blue" and how those different meanings can change the implications of the title. Also consider her use of a question mark in the title.

3. According to the narrator, what does Blue have in common with African American slaves, Native Americans, and women from Japan, Korea, and the Philippines?

4. At the start of paragraph 17, what is the significance of the distinction that the narrator makes between Blue being "like a crazed person" and then "a crazed person"? In other words, Walker is first using a simile, a comparison using the words "like" or "as." Why did she use a simile and then alter it? What prevents others from seeing Blue and other animals as persons and people, rather than "like" persons and people? What does it mean to be a person?

5. Focus on Walker's use of *italics* and "quotation marks" in the second to last paragraph. Both are used here for emphasis, but what is she trying to emphasize, and how does the emphasis relate to what happens in the final paragraph of the story?

Small Group Work

—In the fifth paragraph, the narrator states that "human animals and nonhuman animals communicate quite well." As a group, make four lists: the first should provide examples of how humans communicate with other humans, the second should provide examples of how humans communicate with nonhumans, the third should provide examples of how nonhumans communicate with other nonhumans, and the final should indicate how nonhumans communicate with humans. What are the similarities and differences between human and nonhuman communication?

—In "Am I Blue?" the narrator develops a friendship with a horse before that horse feels betrayed by humans. Taking only about one minute, each person in your group should tell a story of a time in which he or she has felt a bond with a nonhuman animal. If you have never had such an experience, you can talk about relationships between humans and nonhumans that you have observed.

Individual Writing Activity

—Consider this quote from Alice Walker: "The animals of the world exist for their own reasons. They were not made for humans any more than black people were made for white, or women created for men." What does this quote mean to you? How does its meaning relate to Walker's "Am I Blue?"

2. The next lesson plan was offered to social studies, history and/or civics instructors, titled "Post–Civil War Lesson/Assignment Plan: An Exploration of Justice Movements in the United States":

Grade Level: Middle School

Time Commitment: 2–3 class periods if in a computer classroom *or* this can be a longer term research project

Objective: This lesson plan encourages students to explore the post–Civil War period as a founding era for the questioning of what and/or who counts as property. Specifically, this lesson asks students to investigate the children's and/or animal rights movements, and it would best be utilized in a history class that has just studied the Civil War, as students will need basic knowledge of slavery in the United States.

Complementary Material: 10 minute video by Eric Selman, co-author of *Out of the Darkness: The Story of Mary Ellen Wilson* (even better, have them read the book), about the start of the children's rights movement and its association with the American Society for the Prevention of Cruelty to Animals: http://www.youtube.com/watch?v=O8VSpIfEuKo

Foundational Questions for Class Discussion

1. What is *property*?
2. What are *rights*?
3. How were definitions of these concepts challenged during the Civil War?
4. Why did early Americans think they had the right to own other people? Where did that idea come from?
5. What is *racism*? (With that definition determined, students will then be introduced to the terms below that will likely be new to them, although they should be encouraged to figure out the meanings on their own based upon the meaning of the word "racism.")

Adultism: bias against children in favor of adults. Have students explain ways in which they feel adults have more rights than they do (whether justified or otherwise).

Speciesism: bias against other species of animal in favor of humans. Have students explain the ways in which humans have more rights than nonhumans.

Assignment:

—With this foundation laid, students will be tasked with researching and writing about the creation of either the American Society for the Prevention of Cruelty to Animals or the Society for the Prevention of Cruelty to Children. Ideally, at least half the class will focus on animals and the other half on children.

—Along with a historical overview, students should be asked to consider how the themes of American slavery—especially concerning property and rights—are also relevant to children's and animal rights organizations. Time permitting, students can also chose one contemporary children's or animal rights group, research it, and present their findings to the class.

Both of these lesson plans use CAS as a field and pedagogy to not only address traditional issues of human oppression but also to explore the ways in which that history is allied with the Western world's cultural views and treatment of nonhuman animals. To borrow from Pedersen (2009) again, these plans encourage students to "scrutinize and problematize a variety of power arrangements by which both humans and animals are currently [and historically] subjected to domination, marginalization, and exploitation" (p. 3). Such projects cannot be accomplished in a vacuum. Rather, they demand investigation of literature and history to come to insightful conclusions. Therein, issues of science also arise via eugenics, the belief that certain humans are genetically "more human" than others, as does contemplation of law and rights theory.

These lesson plans are also grounded in CAS, as they attempt to rewrite cultural narratives, as much as is humanly possible, from the nonhuman animal perspective. Best argues (2009):

> Whereas nearly all histories, even so-called "radical" narratives, have been written from the human standpoint, a growing number of theorists have broken free of the speciesist straightjacket to examine history and society from the standpoint of (nonhuman) animals. This approach, as I define it, considers the interaction between human and nonhuman animals—past, present, and future—and the need for profound changes in the way humans define themselves and relate to other sentient species and to the natural world as a whole. (n.p.)

Best's words emphasize the intent and import of these lesson plans, as they attempt to ease students, before they reach higher education, into an understanding of the "standpoint of (nonhuman) animals," which can only be understood, of course, from the human standpoint. The most efficient way to do that is to subtly ally the webbed oppressions of humans and nonhumans. This interdisciplinary approach also attempts to widen students' worldviews to observe the exploitation that has surrounded their history as human animals and the "hidden" histories of animal exploitation that continue into the present day, from their clothing, to their recreational interests, to the food on their plates.

Academic Outreach with Critical Animal Studies

As to CAS's future in the academy, it should be promoted as an interdisciplinary field, adaptable to any area of study. The human construct of "the animal" is always present, though often invisible, in literary texts. One goal of CAS scholars is to find "the animal" hidden in our cultural texts and return agency to nonhuman animals while also troubling human ideologies of what nonhuman animals are and how their histories intersect with those of humans. As English is Kim's field of expertise, she will use literature as an example of how CAS, as an interdisciplinary field, can be adapted as a theory and pedagogy.

In 1847, British writer Charlotte Brontë famously published the novel *Jane Eyre*. In this story of the eponymous heroine, Bertha Mason is the dark, exotic, frightening, Caribbean, Jamaican-born "madwoman in the attic" whom Brontë uses as a literary device and backdrop to the presumably more significant love story of Jane and Edward Rochester. As was common in the nineteenth century, Bertha provides a gothic (dark, mysterious, horrifying) element to a traditional Victorian novel. Then, in 1966, Dominican-born author Jean Rhys published *Wide Sargasso Sea*, a postcolonial novel providing a counternarrative to *Jane Eyre*. While postcolonialism is, itself, an interdisciplinary field with its own internal debates and controversies among its scholars and writers, when applied to literature, it is best defined as

> literary and cultural—and sometimes anthropological—studies . . . often used to refer to the consequences of colonialism from the time the area was first colonized. Such studies are generally concerned with the subsequent interaction between the culture of colonial power, including its language, and the culture and traditions of the colonized peoples. (Innes, 2007, p. 2)

In effect, postcolonial literature, whether written by the colonized or those from colonizing cultures, has attempted to give agency back to those who were subjects of imperialist domination, both as real individuals and within literary works that arose during the spread of European imperialism. *Wide Sargasso Sea* tells the story of Bertha Mason, thereby giving voice and power to a character who before was simply a means to a literary end. It tells the story of Antoinette Cosway, later renamed Bertha Mason by her English husband, an Anglo-Creole woman who lives through an unhappy childhood before being wedded to Rochester, moving to England, descending into madness, and being locked away in Rochester's attic as he seeks a more suitable wife.

Rhys's novel seemed to be the end of creating parallel plots to complement the imperialist underpinnings of *Jane Eyre*. This is where CAS and CAP are applicable. Pilot is another character in *Jane Eyre*, a Newfoundland dog framed as Rochester's loyal companion. What of *that* dog's life? How were dogs bred and domesticated in the nineteenth century and what does that say of the Western world's current infantalization, fetishization, and abuse of canines? What of Pilot's supposed natural subservience to Rochester and to humans in general? Similarly, what of the Newfoundland Nana in J. M. Barry's *Peter Pan*, "hired," or one could say "forced" by the Darling family to work as a governess for the family's children (much as was the poverty-stricken Jane Eyre)? Indeed, the very idea of breeding and naming canines is not without its problems and is ripe for further investigation.

These are but some examples of how CAS offers lively new ways to examine nonhumans not as tropes but as human constructs of what it means to be "animal," which always appears to suggest, in both literature and life, how can this creature be used to meet human ends? Our answers to these questions within our respective fields, and other fields upon which we may impinge, must be challenges to cultural assumptions as well. This means analyses not only for theory's sake but also for application to the broad objectives of the animal liberation movement and the development of CAS as a field and pedagogy. At this point, Kim's questions about a "postspeciesism" literary theory, at least as it applies to *Jane Eyre*, remains mere supposition. However, scholars are actively using such filters to widen the berth through which oppression and domination are analyzed.

For example, a chapter in the anthology *Confronting Animal Exploitation: Grassroots Essays on Liberation and Veganism* applies CAS to the short stories and novels of popular fiction writers. This innovative approach to CAS garners special acknowledgement in the anthology's afterword, by pattrice jones:

> Before I move on to talk about what we might learn from the book as a whole, I have to give a shout-out to Patrick McAleer's unique effort to read animal rights themes in Stephen King novels. While I don't know enough about those novels to have a clue as to whether he's on the right track, I do know that *millions* of people read Stephen King and that it might be useful to have this way to talk about animal rights with them. Lurking within every grassroots animal rights group are people who have ideas about how to talk about animal rights to people who are like them in some way or share some specific interest or viewpoint. We desperately need such creativity. (pp. 266–267)

As one who has read Stephen King's novels, Kim believes that McAleer is on the right track. Admittedly, the millions who read King's fiction are not reading King scholarship by the millions, but McAleer's interdisciplinary approach to popular fiction can inspire other scholars to read King's work in fresh ways and develop a more compassionate view of nonhuman animals in their personal lives.

McAleer (2013) acknowledges from the start that King's fiction may initially be a strange place to view as an "arena of social change." However, he notes that the well-known author, though regularly pegged as a master of horror, also uses his literature to confront issues of alcohol abuse, female oppression, child abuse, bullying, and other social problems. King's fictional work often includes nonhuman animals, and McAleer uses his essay, "Literary Analysis for Animal Liberation: Stephen King's Animal Kingdom," to move them from the margins to the centers of King's literary oeuvre, while acknowledging that such a reading may be far afield from King's original intent. McAleer (2013) notes about the purpose of his essay:

> So, as we approach the fiction of Stephen King with a critical eye cast towards the nonhuman animal characters that populate his fiction, we must read these texts with the intention of doing more than simply observing the presence of nonhuman animals. Much as how critical race studies are concerned with more than the mere presence of non-white characters in literature and other artistic expressions, the overarching theories of CAS help us to critically read and analyze the work of Stephen King and other forms of popular culture from an animal rights perspective so that, perhaps, action and positive change may occur. (p. 69)

What follows in McAleer's essay is an overview of King's canon that takes seemingly impotent literary tropes (nonhuman animals) and gives them primary positions through which one may consider their roles both in fiction and in life, arguing for a more sensitive and nuanced understanding of their fictional and cultural treatment, which are, of course, profoundly allied. McAleer's essay is a perfect example of how CAS can be used as a filter through which nonhuman animals are exposed as human constructs while also giving them power as beings independent of human ideologies and of value simply because they exist as independent entities, not as resources for the human animal and its cultural institutions.

Herein, we see the power of IS, CAS, and CAP to expose animal exploitation as bound to other forms of social oppression. The difference being that, finally, nonhuman animals are being noticed in a way that other subjugated groups have been in literary criticism and other academic disciplines. The potential here is truly without boundaries.

Conclusion

The interdisciplinary nature of CAS is a far cry from the elite academy, preferencing some knowledge above others, theory bound, enclosed within self-imposed limitations, and away from the real concerns of everyday life. We maintain that we cannot move toward a truer, more comprehensive understanding of the problems of power and oppression in their broadest incarnations without an interdisciplinary approach, an approach that offers so much, not the least of which might be emergent forms of knowledge and new knowledge groupings as-of-yet unthought. We write of knowledges so distinctly different in the same way that the properties of water could not be predicted, nor are they reducible to, the properties of hydrogen and oxygen. But our appeal is for far more than this. People do not engage in CAS just for idle interest, as an academic pastime, or a job passport; rather, CAS scholars are—and/or *must be*—deeply socially engaged. As in the proud histories of so many movements, their people care about what is happening in the world. Important things are at stake, there is real pain and suffering happening as we write these words—loss and devastation, perpetrators and victims, oppressors and the oppressed.

We need not only a melding of accepted disciplines and of traditional and nontraditional knowledge pursuits, but critically and without apology, we need our compassion, empathy, care, love, spirituality, hope, commitment, and solidarity to walk the road to liberation together. Only then can we truly speak of an interdisciplinary mission.

References

Augsburg, T. (2006). *Becoming interdisciplinary: An introduction to interdisciplinary studies.* Dubuque, IA: Kendall/Hunt.

Bandura, A. (1999). Moral disengagement in the perpetration of inhumanities. *Personality & Social Psychology Review, 3*(3), 193–209. Retrieved from the Academic Search Premier database.

Benson, H. (1992). *The outermost house* (First Owl Books Edition). New York: Henry Holt.

Best, S. (2009). The rise of critical animal studies: Putting theory into action and animal liberation into higher education. *State of Nature.* Retrieved from http://www.stateofnature.org/theRiseOfCriticalAnimal.html

Best, S., Nocella, A. J., Kahn, R., Gigliotti, C., & Kemmerer, L. (2007). Introducing critical animal studies. *Journal for Critical Animal Studies, 5*(1), 4–5.

Birke, L. (2012, July). Critical animal studies roundtable. *Minding Animals 2.* Lecture conducted from University of Utrecht, Utrecht, Holland.

Buller, H. (2008). The lively process of interdisciplinarity. *Area, 41*(4), 395–403.

Carte Blanche. (2011, July 31). *Rhino files 3 (part 1).* Retrieved from http://beta.mnet.co.za/carteblanche/Article.aspx?ID=4396

Crenshaw, K. (1991). Mapping the margins: Intersectionality, identity politics, and violence against women of color. *Stanford Law Review, 43*(5), 1241–1299.

Deleuze, G., & Guattari F. (2001). Kafka: Toward a minor literature. In V. B. Leitch (Ed.), *The Norton anthology of theory and criticism* (pp. 1593–1609). New York: Norton.

Donovan, J. (2007). Attention to suffering: Sympathy as a basis for ethical treatment of animals. In C. Adams & J. Donovan (Eds.), *The feminist care tradition in animal ethics* (pp. 174–197). New York: Columbia UP.

Ellis, R. (2005). Poaching for traditional Chinese medicine. *Save the Rhino.* Retrieved from http://www.savetherhino.org/rhino_info/threats_to_rhino/poaching_for_traditional_chinese_medicine

Innes, C. L. (2007). *The Cambridge introduction to postcolonial literatures in English*. Cambridge: Cambridge UP.

Institute for Critical Animal Studies (ICAS). (n.d.). Homepage. Retrieved from http://www.criticalanimalstudies.org/

ISLE: Interdisciplinary studies in literature and the environment. (n.d.) Homepage. Retrieved from http://www.asle.org/site/publications/isle/

jones, p. (2013). Afterword: Flower power. In K. Socha & S. Blum (Eds.), *Confronting animal exploitation: Grassroots essays on liberation and veganism* (pp. 263–280). Jefferson, NC: McFarland.

Journal of Interdisciplinary Studies. (n.d.). Why JIS? Retrieved from http://www.jis3.org/whyjis.htm

McAleer, P. (2013). Literary analysis for animal liberation: Stephen King's animal kingdom. In K. Socha & S. Blum (Eds.), *Confronting animal exploitation: Grassroots essays on liberation and veganism* (pp. 66–88). Jefferson, NC: McFarland.

Nunns, C. (2012, September 12). Vietnamese gangsters horny for poached rhino. *GlobalPost*. Retrieved from http://www.globalpost.com/dispatch/news/regions/asia-pacific/vietnam/120831/vietnamese-gangsters-rhino-horn-poaching

Pedersen, H. (2009). *Animals in schools: Processes and strategies in human-animal education*. West Lafayette, IN: Purdue UP.

Pedersen, H., & Stănescu, V. (2011). Introduction. In K. Socha, *Women, destruction, and the avant-garde: A paradigm for animal liberation* (ix–xi). Amsterdam: Rodopi.

Repko, A. F. (2012). *Interdisciplinary research*. Thousand Oaks, CA: Sage.

Repko, A. F. (2008). *Interdisciplinary research: Process and theory*. Los Angeles: Sage.

Repko, A. F., Newell, W., & Szostak, R. (2012). *Case studies in interdisciplinary research*. Los Angeles: Sage.

Schmidt, J. C. (2007). Knowledge politics of interdisciplinarity in the NSF's NBIC scenario. *Innovation, 20*(4), 313–328.

Singer, P. (1975). *Animal liberation*. Bournemouth, UK: Pimlico.

Socha, K. (2011). *Women, destruction, and the avant-garde: A paradigm for animal liberation*. Amsterdam: Rodopi.

Stephenson, J., Lawson, R., Carrington, G., Barton, B., Thorsnes, P., & Mirosa, M. (2010). The practice of interdisciplinarity. *International Journal of Interdisciplinary Social Sciences, 5*(7), 271–282.

Thompson Klein, J. (1994). Finding interdisciplinary knowledge and information. *New Directions for Teaching and Learning, 58*, 7–33.

Thompson Klein, J. (1990). *Interdisciplinarity: History, theory and practice*. Detroit: Wayne State UP.

University of California, Berkeley, College of Letters & Science. (n.d.). Homepage. Retrieved from http://ugis.ls.berkeley.edu/isf/

Worldwide Fund for Nature. (2012, August 21). TRAFFIC: "Loose horns," surging demand and easy money create "perfect storm" for rhino poaching. Retrieved from http://wwf.panda.org/wwf_news/?uNewsID=205992

PART IV

Radical Education

SEVEN

Radical Humility

Toward a More Holistic Critical Animal Studies Pedagogy

Lauren Corman and Tereza Vandrovcová

This chapter offers four primary contributions. First, we consider the relevance of intersectional theory and advocacy to Critical Animal Studies (CAS) pedagogy, and map some of the academic and activist approaches that inform the field, particularly animal ecofeminism and animal activism. (For a comprehensive overview of interdisciplinary fields that inform CAS, see Pedersen's [2010] "Critical animal studies and education research: A background.") In conjunction, we suggest some ways CAS can enhance its pedagogical techniques, which necessarily include the recognition of humans and nonhuman animals (or, said differently, humans and other animals) as teachers. We maintain that such recognition is vital for a more non-anthropocentric, anti-speciesist, and holistic pedagogy.

Second, we highlight the research and activism of Barbara Smuts and Sharon Núñez, respectively, as exemplary of how pedagogy can include nonhuman animals. Such experiential knowledge has the potential to influence not only how we conceive of the subjectivities of animals in our immediate contexts, but also how we think of other nonhuman animals, including those in factory farms and vivisection laboratories, where face-to-face encounters are less common for the majority of people.

Third, we address a pressing question raised by numerous educators who teach about animal exploitation: How do we navigate the challenges of showing graphic images? We explore possible strategies for the presentation and discussion of these materials, particularly in classroom settings. Many of us who teach about nonhuman animal issues are deeply conflicted about when and how to show certain disturbing videos and photos. These materials play a vital role in exposing students to the realities of animal abuse. Yet, students may experience negative emotions that can be demotivating when not handled sensitively. Thus, we examine contemporary research on the use of graphic images and education about emotionally charged issues, and suggest ways for mitigating students' potential negative reactions and emotional withdrawals.

Fourth, we review some strategies that we have found effective when teaching CAS. While still theoretically informed, the suggestions are primarily gleaned from Corman's experiences teaching numerous CAS undergraduate courses in Brock University's Sociology Department over the past four years. She also draws on her decade-long tenure with Toronto's Animal Voices radio show. Vandrovcová includes insights from her experiences teaching CAS and her role as a community organizer for events such as the Veggie Parade in Prague.

Overall, our chapter grapples with how subjectivity is rendered in CAS pedagogy and how we might integrate what is too commonly dismissed by dominant societies and cultures: marginalized human perspectives, animal subjectivities beyond suffering, and graphic representations of pain. CAS pedagogy requires us to pay attention to what is generally disregarded in the name of profit, convenience, and tradition. Resonating with the 10th principle of CAS, which stresses the importance of constructive critical dialogue and coalition building, we argue that centralizing marginalized human and nonhuman animal perspectives is necessary for a more fully realized solidarity-based alliance politics and pedagogy. Given the space limitations of the chapter and the breadth of the tenth principle, we chose to concentrate on the need for heterogeneous representations of animals' subjectivities in theory and activism, the expansion of intersectional analyses—which commonly presuppose only human social axes of "difference"—and the manifestation of these ideas specifically in CAS university pedagogy.

Voice and Dialogue

Years ago a colleague asked Corman bluntly, "Where are the animals in Critical Animal Studies?" Perhaps this seems like a ridiculous question, given that CAS seeks to foreground the lives of nonhuman animals and others who are oppressed. While the question might initially appear absurd, there is some truth in it. Her question in part relates to CAS's emphasis on intersectionality, which focuses on linked oppressions as a means of building solidarity among oppressed groups and as a move against single-issued analyses that fail to account for indivisible "entanglements of oppression" (Nibert, 2002).

While intersectionality in CAS is a crucial remediation, whose contribution and necessary continuation cannot be overstated, it largely has constructed an image of animals as suffering victims. Given intersectional theory's focus on linked oppressions, the shared forms of domination and suffering experienced by humans and nonhuman animals serve as major points of solidarity. CAS should retain its intersectional orientation while also taking the lead from Third World feminisms that stress resistance, agency, and richer forms of subjectivity that do not position women strictly as victims (e.g., Mohanty, 1988). From here, we can more directly conceive of ourselves as animals' allies rather than their saviors. New points of solidarity are possible. Such an approach is directly pertinent to how we engage in CAS pedagogy.

From its onset, CAS has sought to differentiate itself from mainstream animal studies (MAS) (Best, 2009; Best, Nocella, Kahn, Gigliotti, & Kemmerer, 2007). Unlike MAS, CAS stresses intersectional analyses: It explicitly emphasizes how different forms of domination, oppression, and power interlock and mutually reinforce each other. For example, in "Introducing Critical Animal Studies," founding members of ICAS argue in the fourth principle that the interdisciplinary field

> advances a holistic understanding of the commonality of oppressions, such that speciesism, sexism, racism, ableism, statism, classism, militarism and other hierarchical ideologies and institutions are viewed as parts of a larger, interlocking, global system of domination. (Best et al., 2007, p. 5)

According to Yuval-Davis (2006), intersectionality was first named in 1989 by feminist sociologist Kimberlé Crenshaw. However, the idea proliferated in the 1960s and 1970s in sociology more generally and by those who refuted the homogenized and overgeneralized claims of the Western women's movement, which took white middle-class women's experiences as universal. Notably, in the 1970s, the African American women's Combahee River Collective maintained that social and cultural axes, such as those related to race, class, and sexuality, occur simultaneously. In the 1990s, Collins's *Black Feminist Thought* further extended the reach of intersectional theory.

CAS's intersectional orientation also partially finds its roots in ecofeminism and "animal ecofeminism," in particular. Ecofeminism concentrates on critiquing, dismantling, and actively resisting interconnected and mutually supporting forms of oppression and domination, particularly the oppression and domination of women and of nature. Gaard (1996) characterizes "animal ecofeminism" as a tributary flowing from a broader stream of radical feminism. It presses for a "pluralistic feminism that includes concern for animals" (Adams, 2000, p. 63). Among other efforts, it addresses sexism and other forms of oppression manifest in the animal movements. (Animal ecofeminism has been accused of failing to address transphobia [Hammer, 2010], among other concerns [e.g., Plumwood, 2004].) Similarly, Kahn and Humes (2009) press for a new paradigm, "total liberation pedagogy," which "attempts to work intersectionally across and in opposition to all oppressions (including those of nonhuman animals) and for ecological sustainability" (p. 82). Like other pedagogues whose scholarship falls within the purview of CAS, they call for education about social justice and environmental sustainability to include animal advocacy.

Like animal ecofeminism and total liberation pedagogy, CAS is overtly political and strives to merge theory with practice (Best et al., 2007). The field heavily draws on the animal rights and liberation movements, which struggle to expose the egregious exploitation of nonhuman animals and to bring animals' interests into the sphere of moral concern. Rather than understanding activism as a potential threat to scholarship, either by introducing "bias" into our theory or by encumbering the field's legitimization within the academy, CAS recognizes that grassroots animal activism is vital for the creation of a robust field. We need to learn from activism, enrich its efforts, and stay in dialogical relationship with its campaigns and interventions.

While our educational efforts must acknowledge the work done by activists, they should also foreground critique (Best et al., 2007). This approach resonates with Paulo Freire's (2007) notion of "dialogical education," which actively solicits the perspectives of "the oppressed" but does not understand the mere proliferation of voice as the end goal. (Notably, founding members of CAS Anthony Nocella II [2004] and Richard Kahn [2003] extend a Freirean analysis in their efforts to develop holistic and anti-speciesist pedagogies, which put analyses of the environment and nonhuman animals in conversation with other anti-oppression politics and theories.) Critical engagement with the materials, analyses, and actions of the animal movements encourages dynamic and meaningful growth of both scholarship and activism. For example, to return to the question of nonhuman animal representation, many within the animal movements claim to be "the voice of the voiceless," a phrase that names the inability of exploited animals to affect large-scale change on their own. Yet, as pattrice jones (2005) astutely reminds us,

> Feminists would never tolerate men trying to run the movement against sexism. And, could you imagine what would have happened if, when I was doing anti-racist work, I had run around saying "I am the voice of the Black man"!?
>
> There are no such natural checks on self-importance in the animal liberation movement. We have people running around claiming to be "the voice of the voiceless" as if animals don't have voices of their own. That heroic attitude makes it easy to assume that you know what's best for the animals without stopping to wonder what they might say if you asked them and were able to understand their answers.

To enrich CAS, including its role within the animal movements, we need to bring issues of pain and suffering into our classrooms, activism, and art, while demonstrating that "the question of the animal" is not only intersectional but also complicated by the multiplicity of life and life experiences that cannot be reduced to victimhood and voicelessness. Instead of thinking of animals as voiceless, we must pay closer attention to their complex subjectivities in our work, including our pedagogy. Many social movements and social justice theories, particularly feminism and critical pedagogy, have long been preoccupied with questions of voice (Corman, 2012); that is, they center on how to move from object-oppression (expressed as "voicelessness," "silenced," etc.) to subject-liberation (expressed as "coming to voice," "having a voice," etc.) (Corman, 2012). More multifaceted representations of animals' subjectivities are necessary for CAS and the animal movements, including greater attention to the ways animals are voiced.

Although we cannot entirely escape the challenges of political representation, including potential misrepresentation and appropriation, we must strive to more fully integrate marginalized human and nonhuman animal voices into CAS pedagogy. As Armstrong (2002) argues, "Encountering the postcolonial animal means learning to listen to the voices of all kinds of 'other' [sic] without either ventriloquizing them or assigning to them accents so foreign that they never can be understood" (p. 417). CAS must work at the difficult juncture between recognizing that, in a certain sense, we are ethically called to represent animals, and at the same time we are forever limited in our ability to do so (see Bekoff, 2007). As environmental education researchers Oakley and colleagues (2010) attest,

> Incorporating nonhuman animals as stakeholders in our research raises particular challenges, of which there can be no guarantee of getting it "right." Putting animals on the agenda means asking questions on their behalf, with a recognition all the while of the messiness of the questions we will ask, the "answers" we might find, and the ways we will go about conducting our research and representing our findings. (p. 93)

We can never entirely know the subjective lives of animals (or humans, for that matter), and to pretend that we can is to contradict the anti-oppressive goals of CAS.

Corman attempts to enact this approach in her CAS pedagogy. For example, in the beginning of her Animals in Cross-Cultural Perspectives course, students study the social, cultural, and emotional lives of nonhuman animals. Later, when the class watches films that expose the wide-scale systemic violence done to nonhuman animals, the images are made that much more profound, as students recognize that the harm inflicted on nonhuman animals is not purely physical: Their families and their social and cultural bonds are broken; the abuse they endure is also psychological and emotional. This information is presented in conjunction with intersectional analyses of human cultural perspectives.

Orzechowski (2012) credits Corman's approach for helping to inspire his documentary *Maximum Tolerated Dose*, which offers nuanced portrayals of human workers and animals in the vivisection industry, illuminating not only animals' experiences of suffering but also their agency, capacity for pleasure, and emotional lives. This draws on earlier contributions that embody the CAS pedagogy we envision, merging intersectional analyses with scholarship typically associated with certain streams of cognitive ethology (e.g., Balcombe, 2007; Bekoff, 2007) and environmental education (e.g., Oakley et al., 2010; Warkentin, 2009). Examples of such work are Walker's (1988) "Am I Blue?" Davis's (1995) "Thinking Like a Chicken: Farm Animals and the Feminine Connection," Noske's (1997) *Beyond Boundaries: Humans and Animals*, Bell and Russell's (2000) "Beyond Human, Beyond Words: Anthropocentricism, Critical Pedagogy and the Poststructuralist Turn," and Best's (2007) "The Killing Fields of South Africa: Eco-Wars, Species Apartheid, and Total Liberation."

Despite such examples, those working within an intersectional framework, including many in CAS, often do not consider that cross-cultural analyses could include nonhuman animal cultures. Anthropocentricism permeates the idea of culture (see Noske, 1997), even by most who seek to "de-centre" the human subject. Similarly, society is often arrogantly presumed to be uniquely the domain of the human. In our discourses about resistance, we too often are deluded by the false assumption that only humans fight back (see Hribal, 2007, 2011). Further, many people do not think of nonhuman animals as teachers (see Smuts, 2001), and when we do, these lessons are too often marginalized rather than centralized. We have not yet really shaken our Western humanism or rigorously interrogated it in this regard. The question remains: How can we be better partners with animals in our efforts for liberation?

Humility and Listening

Below we draw on the salient work of psychology professor Barbara Smuts, and cofounder of the large abolitionist organization Igualdad Animal (Animal Equality) Sharon Núñez. Smuts' research on the social relationships of animals demonstrates powerful ideas about how to cultivate humility with the "more-than-human world" (Abram, 1996) so we may truly learn with nonhuman animals. Smuts has spent decades studying social relationships among nonhuman animals. Her research suggests ways in which we might form richer intersubjective relationships with nonhuman animals, ones based on profound mutuality, respect, and response. Similarly, Núñez's (2009) activism foregrounds her unique relationships with three rescued pigs and shows how attention to the individuality of animals deepened her commitment to animal advocacy.

As we open to the potential of intersubjectivity with nonhuman animals (and their intersubjectivity among themselves), the implications are profound not only for how we engage with animals in the proximal sense, but also how we regard animals who are confined and oppressed within exploitation industries. This suggests a shift away from the representation of nonhuman animals as strictly victims to the realization that animals can and do teach us if given the opportunity, thus illuminating a more fully realized non-anthropocentric and non-speciesist approach to pedagogy.

While Smuts does not explicitly situate her research within discourses of pedagogy, her insights offer great lessons for CAS education, particularly due to her dialogical engagements with nonhuman animals and her emphasis on their capacities as teachers. Echoing ecofeminists' concern with how specific contexts should inform ethical engagements (e.g., Gaard, 2001), Smuts demonstrates the need to move beyond species-based generalizations and to embrace an understanding of animals as unique beings with individual subjectivities who shape the worlds around them. During their Animal Voices interview, Smuts (2009) discussed with Corman a striking example of a nonhuman animals' pedagogical capacity. Smuts recounted the negative consequences that can occur when people fail to closely pay attention to the sociality of nonhuman animals, including our relationships with them.

The following interview excerpts illustrate Smuts' resistance to predetermined anthropocentric scripts used to interpret nonhuman animals' behavior. Discipline, for example, can be harshly and unfairly meted out as a response to so-called behavioral problems of animals. These behaviors can be animals' attempts to reasonably communicate a concern or discomfort. They demonstrate agency and a capacity to resist certain conditions and treatment. Smuts (2009) outlines how popular prescriptive dog training advice harmed her relationship with Safi, one of her dogs, and how they eventually built a stronger relationship based on responsiveness and humility. She examines the interactions with Safi in her article, "Between Species: Science and Subjectivity" (2006), and reflects on the transformative effect of her attentive approach. The experience with Safi is emblematic of her methodology.

Smuts recalls that her relationship with Safi, a black female German shepherd, was generally very harmonious. Their relationship was strained sometimes, though: a few times Safi growled when Smuts was sitting on the couch and once when she approached Safi while she was lying on the floor. Smuts' friend, a dog trainer, directed her to immediately "squash this behaviour." She insisted that Safi's behaviour was an attempt to dominate Smuts and warned that without forceful correction, Safi's behaviour could escalate into something quite dangerous:

> And they suggested that I do this thing that is now on some popular TV programs: It's called "the alpha roll" and supposedly it's something a high-ranking wolf might [do to] interact with a subordinate wolf in a way where the subordinate wolf ends up rolling over on the back and exposing the belly, and that ritual communication between wolves where the one who is on the bottom is acknowledging the higher status of the one on the top. So people have sort of taken this behaviour in wolves and tried to translate it whole to the human/dog relationship where the human, they say, has to act like the alpha wolf in order to maintain control over their dog and control is really emphasized.

Unsure how to address the Safi's behaviour, Smuts tried the alpha roll after Safi growled. She held her down, and was supposed to look scarily into her face, and wait for Safi's body to go limp. "But as soon as I looked into her eyes I let her go because I just—I saw surprise, and fear, like, 'Why is this person, who I get along with so well suddenly doing this horrible thing to me?'" recalled Smuts. She never tried the technique again, and instead chose to pay very close attention to the contexts that disturbed Safi. She quickly realized that these situations often had to do with quickly moving toward her. The growls were a way of saying, "Don't move like that," and likely related to previous physical abuse she had experienced. Smuts learned to speak to her from across the room and approach her slowly. Safi stopped growling and did not try to "dominate" Smuts again:

> It wasn't about dominance. It wasn't about control. It was her way, in her language, of communicating to me that she was uncomfortable with something that I was doing and I think it's really important that our dogs be allowed to communicate with us, in their language, and that we try to understand what that individual is saying . . . That particular individual in that particular context as opposed to saying that every time a dog growls at a person it's because they want to dominate them and the appropriate response is control. Dogs are so—there's so much more going on—and they say so much to us with their bodies and their sounds and I think so much of it just flies right by the average dog owner. They just don't even notice and so, eventually, the dog has to do something, you know, really—that you have to notice because nobody's been listening. (Smuts, 2009)

Smuts is willing to see her dogs as teachers whose behaviours provide pedagogical instruction in their relationships. Her story disrupts the assumption that animals are subordinate, irrational, and solely instinct driven.

Smuts' central dedication to recognizing and treating Safi as an individual, not merely an embodied manifestation of a particular species or breed, is significant. She regards this nonhuman animal as a subject who is not a shallow caricature or a mere representative of an entire species, somehow made fully comprehensible through manuals. By opening up to Safi as a subject, with a particular history, she approaches her dog with radical humility. She conceives of Safi's behaviour not as a sign of obstinacy or dominance but as a legitimate and reasonable attempt to communicate. Infused throughout Smuts' narrative is her commitment to dialogical exchange. She discusses Safi's "embodied communication" (2006) as language. What might typically be conceived as a behavioural problem is instead interpreted as a communicative gesture.

Smuts notes the tremendous ability for nonhuman animals to improve our own skills in social relationships. We can allow them to positively change us. For Smuts, relationships with nonhuman others centrally hinge upon paying attention. The deep sense of presence with nonhuman animals defines Smuts' methodology and permeates her research (e.g., 2001, 2006). In that place of presence, of paying attention, of embodied listening, people actually hear the voices of nonhuman animals. Smuts' capacity to listen well to nonhuman others also enables her to represent animals as voiced. Animals are understood as specific individuals, with particular pasts that inform their experiential knowledge, which they then bring into their social engagements with others. Smuts suggests a connection between Safi's past experience and the request that her current behaviour implies: Although Smuts does not know Safi's history, Safi certainly knows. Because Smuts is willing to pay attention, she hears and then shapes her own behaviour accordingly. In light of such knowledge, Smuts does not render her as a helpless victim. Her appreciation of Safi's trauma instead shapes how their relationship unfolds. Safi's past—actively expressed (though also seemingly with some restraint!)—informs Smuts' knowledge of the present. Smuts does not position herself as the voice of the voiceless. Safi speaks; Smuts listens.

Yet, it is not just Smuts who changes; Safi also modifies her behaviour. Receiving the communication of a valid concern, Smuts realizes that the onus is upon her to actively interpret Safi's growls. By dropping the training advice and the associated dominance narrative, Smuts comes into relationship with Safi, and Safi then changes her behaviour toward Smuts once the message is received and action is taken. This is the dialogical dance of deep relationship, precisely the kind of relationship and exchange that humanist scholars deny. We see here that animals, when given the opportunity to engage across species, also participate in dialogue. The anthropocentrism of the liberal humanist subject does not hold, and cannot hold, in the context of such profound interspecies relating. The Western notion of the human subject acting upon a passive world, where humans alone are subjects, is clearly a ruse. "Animals . . . are constantly learning over the course of their own lifetimes through actively engaging with their environments," states Warkentin (2009, p. 31).

Smuts' approach has far-reaching ramifications not only for our relationships with domesticated animals in our immediate contexts but also for animals outside of these more immediate settings. Smuts concludes "Between the Species" with a plea that we generalize her methodology:

> We humans relinquish personhood over and over due to our failure to recognize the subjectivity and individuality of members of other species. To take back our personhood in relation to other animals changes everything. Anyone who seriously engages in this task comes to realize that our planet is replete with opportunities to form personal relationships with many different kinds of beings. Even if most of us end up forming bonds only with domestic animals, it is important to fully digest the fact that millions and millions of potential nonhuman friends exist in our forests and oceans, savannas and swamps. Radically rethinking our relations with other species can change the future; for example, in the context of an endangered species, what if we expanded our concerns about the disappearance of an abstract category to include the concrete reality of death by starvation or disease or poaching of multitudes of feeling, thinking, *relational* beings [author's emphasis]. (2006, p. 125)

Such insights are certainly not just emerging from within the Academy. For example, in her interview with Animal Voices, activist Sharon Núñez (2009) poignantly brings animals' suffering and pain into public discourse. For example, she reflects on the pigs at the open rescue site: "All the mothers of the pigs were in crates where they could hardly move. They couldn't turn around. They couldn't even touch their babies" (2009). She also highlights the pigs' specificity and unique subjectivities as a vital part of her discourse. Indeed, that specificity vitally enriches her advocacy and, consequently, her representations. As shown below, the pathos of the wide-scale suffering of pigs within factory farms is made more potent when considered alongside the individuality of those who were rescued. Although she was already vegan and involved in different animal groups, it was Núñez's experience of bearing witness to animal suffering and her personal relationships with pigs that greatly intensified her passion and dedication to advocacy:

> I'd say a major change for me . . . has been going to the factory farms and seeing images, real images of what real animals are undergoing today. A major change for me was the rescue of six piglets. Three of them unfortunately died [from sickness]. But three of them are still alive. And these three piglets are now three pigs that weigh about 200 kilograms each, and they are amazing individuals, each one with their personality. They are wonderful beings who deserve respect. I love them and I see them weekly, and they have changed my life. I mean, knowing them, knowing what individuals that are just the same as them undergo and suffer every day has made me understand that some people must dedicate their lives, or dedicate most of their time, to changing the plight of animals.

She later elaborated on the specific nonhuman animals she has known through the rescue, highlighting their individuality.

> It's very important for activists and people in general to get to know individual animals. There's not really a common characteristic for these three pigs. They're three different individuals. One of them is very social, and likes to be around people, and likes to be with the other pigs. . . . Mark is very shy. He loves to be around people also, and he loves to get people's attention. Gracie is . . . well, she isn't very shy. She's always the first one to go to the food, and she's a bit violent with the other pigs, because she always wants to get her way, and do what she wants. Getting to know them from the time they were babies to now. . . . It's something that's changed my life. Some friends, or some people after meeting these pigs, have decided to stop eating meat, and some of them have decided to take animal rights activism more seriously.

Núñez then touched on the unexpected and inexplicable role that meeting animals can play in intensifying one's commitment to advocacy. We again hear in her account how relationships with individuals strengthen her resolve to act on behalf of all animals.

> I think it's surprising when ... how a person who is passionate about animals can become even more passionate about animals. Every different individual I meet makes me more passionate about fighting for animals. . . . It's very important to feel compassion and love for animals, and I think this is one of the most important things for an activist, because that's what gives you strength to work on a daily basis, or at least that's what happened to me.

Echoing Smuts, Núñez stresses the importance of face-to-face and embodied relationships with nonhuman animals not only as inspiration for herself but also (hopefully) for others. She is an animal activist who directly enters animal exploitation facilities and removes animals from harm and captivity. Her organization has done a number of high profile open rescues: These involve documenting industries such as factory farms and freeing animals. Her friendships with rescued animals, which are shaped through their individual subjectivities, are transformative.

Núñez's relationships with the rescued pigs are intensely dialogical, and we see that they have changed her and informed how she educates others about animals. Her recognition of these nonhuman subjectivities, experienced through direct interactions with three survivors, deepens her awareness of suffering and invigorates her activism. She recognizes the rescued pigs' influence on her life, expressed as a kind of two-way dynamism. Not only do these pigs possess the agential capacity to influence Núñez but they also actively seek out human and nonhuman social relationships. These relationships are either fostered, as with Mark who loves (and receives) human attention, or frustrated, as with caged pigs who cannot reach their babies, for example. Centrally, their will to enact such desires motivates her both through witnessing its denial within factory farms and its actualization within sanctuary. The pigs provide information that she would not have otherwise, and because of her attention and responsiveness, they change how she understands animals and they galvanize her activism.

Presence and Pain

Involving animals and their subjectivities in CAS pedagogy is vital but not risk-free. A major challenge is to mediate the experience of witnessing through photos or films animal abuse in order to inspire students' critical thinking and to support their protest against violence. In such instances, part of the teacher's responsibility is to provide emotional and intellectual guidance as students struggle with the information.

Messages about animal suffering in human societies can be presented through a variety of media, such as written texts, but pictures and videos of animals' pain and suffering play a crucial role. In *The Psychology of Environmental Problems*, Winter and Koger (2004) note that "if we cannot see something we are not likely to find it important" (p. 160). Munro (2005) adds that images of suffering animals "move people to act against a perceived injustice" (p. 183).

The importance of graphic imagery in opening people's minds and connecting their attitudes with their actions was recently confirmed by the Video Comparison Study conducted by the Humane Research Council in the United States (HRC, 2012). In this study more than 500 respondents aged 15–23 viewed one of four short videos promoting veganism (one of which, *Farm to Fridge*, contained graphic images, while the others dealt with environmental and health issues) and provided their feedback, such as whether the video encouraged them to consider dietary changes. Of the four videos, *Farm to Fridge* was the most effective, although it had a lower engagement rate (i.e., more people stopped watching the video before it was completed). This video used graphic imagery of farmed animal abuse and appealed to ethics, in contrast to the others that appealed to environmental and health concerns.

Visual messages can have positive effects on people's attitudes toward animal rights, but they can also deter them. Graphic images and videos can convey a message that no words can; yet we should be cautious about how we present and discuss these materials because of the wide range of emotions they can elicit. Problems of animal cruelty are often bound with negative emotions such as anger, fear, depression, grief, shame, and guilt (Jasper, 1997, p. 114). These emotions can lead to the critical review of our treatment of animals and can inspire us to take constructive action. However, sometimes they also arouse students' defense mechanisms or anxiety. There are many difficulties involved in presenting graphic material; fortunately, there are also ways to diminish negative impacts. Below we consider some key challenges associated with the presentation of graphic images of animal suffering, as related to isolation, emotional withdrawal, defense mechanisms, and prescriptive moral judgments. In conjunction, we outline some possible ways forward.

The first problem is that negative emotions that arise from witnessing animal abuse, such as depression, shame, or anger, can intensify when we lack opportunities to share them with others. As the famous artist and animal rights activist Sue Coe states in her interview "Witness to Slaughter" with Heller (2012):

> It's not my stomach I worry about; it's my mind, or wherever my soul is located, because it gets broken every time animals suffer. When I make art, I make more witnesses, and when there are enough witnesses, the horror stops. Insanity comes from isolation, feeling you are alone in seeing what most do not. (p. 21)

Feelings of isolation and negative impacts on mental health are major reasons we need to speak with students about these feelings, to support their participation in the animal advocacy movements and also to emphasize the importance of their work in this field.

Also, we should be cautious about inadvertently discouraging students from activism by unintentionally flooding them with huge amounts of information that require significant time and effort to process. Shepherd and Kay (2012) present several studies on public reaction to important social problems, such as environmental, energy, or economic issues. They found that the more worried people were about an issue, the more they intentionally avoided information about it. Also feeling that a topic seems to be too complex or overwhelming predicted an increased motivation to avoid learning more about an issue. As the authors argue, "Participants who felt that the issue was 'above their heads' reported an increased desire to adopt an 'ignorance is bliss' mentality" (p. 275). Shepherd and Kay add that "the psychological processes that are instigated when issues are seen as both severe and complex may limit any criticism of the current system and its decision-making process" (p. 276).

Therefore, it is important to provide satisfactory information about the reality of animals used for human purposes and possible strategies for addressing these issues when we present disturbing materials in the class. For example, we can give advice about getting involved in different forms of activism, making different consumption choices, and dialoguing with others about these issues. We must also stress gains in animal movements and give people a sense of hope that progress is possible.

Another problem associated with presenting graphic materials is the defense-mechanism phenomenon, in which people respond to painful emotions or thoughts with denial and other defensive strategies. According to Lertzman (2008), the images and videos that induce anxiety can lead people "unconsciously to deny or pretend the problem is not there, or that it is the responsibility of someone else." It is thus crucial to find the right ways both to inform and inspire and to stimulate action: "People heal and make change when they feel supported, understood and challenged" (2008). We can help reduce anxiety and intervene in the negative experiences of witnessing animal cruelty by focusing on possible future change and by emphasizing the agency of every participant to positively impact the world.

Further, the presentation of graphic images should avoid pressure to change students' opinions in a certain direction, such as becoming vegan. If they feel pressure to accept specific values or attitudes it may cause the reaction known as "psychological reactance," which is activated whenever people feel a restriction put upon their actions or opinions (Brehm, 1966). According to Brehm, when people feel forced to change their attitudes or consumer behaviors their reactions are exactly the opposite: they will lock in their existing position. Open discussion in which every opinion is recognized can help mediate this automatic reaction.

Such "reactance" can be created when students with differing a priori assumptions are divided into opposing groups. In a recent study Coleman (2011) conducted on moral conflicts, he found that "when participants were given both pro and con information on an issue, and then engaged in a discussion with someone who held an opinion opposite to their own, they typically ended up stuck in their original position, angry and fed-up." Yet when they discussed multiple perspectives on the issue, they were much more open and able to learn. Therefore it is important to foster the space for students' own individual decision making.

Winter and Koger (2004) studied why people resist messages about the environmental crisis. As with witnessing animal cruelty, these messages cause emotions such as anxiety or sadness. Taking a Freudian perspective, they recommend that people work with these emotions and experience them more fully. In classrooms we can help students to increase their awareness about their feelings and help them to find the ways in which they tend to "minimize, distort, deny or intellectualize them" (p. 50). Our defense systems are automatic and habitual but once we allow ourselves "to experience the fullest degree of sadness, energy is lined up and available for redirection" (p. 51). Rust (2008), who is also engaged in environmental issues, noted that overwhelming guilt about the damage we have done can make us very defensive. She warns of blocking our feelings, because then we could "lose touch with the urgency of crisis" (p. 160), or the urgency of animal cruelty in this case. It is important to help students work with their negative emotions.

To decrease risks of burnout and depression we can help students learn stress management techniques such as cognitive therapy. Cognitive therapist Burns (1999) claims that negative thoughts create our bad moods and cause depression and that by learning to restructure them we can change our moods. He offers a list of ten cognitive distortions or common errors such as "All-or-Nothing Thinking," "Overgeneralization" or "Disqualifying the Positive" (p. 33). He recommends using the Triple Column Technique, which helps to recognize distorted thoughts and substitute more rational and less upsetting ones.

Sztybel (2005) brings Burns's insights into the realm of animal advocacy, and gives concrete advice about how to substitute common negative cognitive ideas about animal rights with positive ones by using the Triple Column Technique. In the first column, Sztybel discusses "toxic thought," such as, "animal rights is overwhelmingly hopeless . . ." (p. 5). In the second column he describes the cognitive errors, such as "disqualifying the positive [in which the person] ignores both progress made and what is in progress behind the scene . . ." (p. 14). In the third, he offers a substitute thought or a rational self-defense against negativism, for example, that changes at the micro-level adds up to macro-changes and that we should focus on what we as individuals can do.

It is important to inform students about the violence done to animals and to mediate their experiences of animal suffering. However, we should be aware of potential negative impact of graphic materials. We must find a balance between informing them about depressing realities and providing possible solutions. We need to allow students to share and analyze their emotions.

Enacting CAS Pedagogy

In our last section, we present some strategies for CAS pedagogy that we find useful. Our recommendations are based on an enactment of the ideas detailed above, our own experiences learning about these issues, and our efforts in classrooms and other educational contexts, such as the radio show and other forms of public outreach. However, given the space limitations, we focus on CAS and postsecondary classes. While our synopsis is incomplete, we hope it might serve as a starting point for those who are new to CAS pedagogy and as an additional pool of ideas for those already in the field. We have organized our strategies into five key clusters, though ideas described in each overlap: (1) the importance of context, (2) bringing nonhuman animals into the conversation, (3) intersectionality of oppressions, (4) working with graphic images, and (5) incorporating activism.

The Importance of Context

It can be quite a profound experience to introduce the term "pedagogy" and discuss its influence in students' lives. It is remarkable but not surprising that many undergraduate students, who have spent decades within institutional learning facilities, often do not know the word "pedagogy" or that it is even a process or set of ideas to engage and to question.

Typically, Corman begins each CAS course with an introduction to pedagogy and a brief lecture about its history. Even the idea of the classroom, the position of the professor at the front, and so on is discussed. This can help "make strange" some of the taken-for-granted assumptions and show students that while pedagogy may seem abstract, it is something that they are already engaged in and certainly have opinions about. Starting with the immediate context of the classroom can set the tone for the rest of the course in which everyday assumptions are critiqued. Hierarchies in the typical classroom setting become more transparent, while students are encouraged to think of themselves as both students and teachers.

Although Corman finds this a useful strategy, it is not one that can be uncritically embraced: Given that the instructor is a woman who appears young, power in the classroom can be skewed negatively and some students already will be less inclined to take the course seriously. While critiques of power in the classroom are crucial, how this is done depends on many factors, including one's own diverse social location.

Beyond discussions of pedagogy and the classroom space, appreciation of the numerous contexts in which the students are embedded is necessary. For example, if students are geographically situated in an economically depressed area, that will bear on their experiences generally and also their educational experiences. Providing ways for students to talk about their lives in a safe and supportive environment will make the course materials and pedagogical approach more responsive and meaningful to them. Including opportunities for students to reflect on their personal relationships with nonhuman animals can help ground theory about human-animal relationships and institutional uses of animals. Writing exercises, discussions, and anonymous surveys, among other exercises, can improve the solicitation of such information and help professors tailor materials.

Recognition of students' social locations is also important. Initiating discussions early in the class about white privilege and racism indicates to students from the onset that self-reflection and personal critique will be part of the courses and that such issues are indivisible from questions relating to nonhuman animals. For example, Corman typically begins her courses with a video, such as antiracist educator and hip hop radio host Jay Smooth's (2011) TEDx Talk "How I Learned to Stop Worrying and Love Discussing Race."

Smooth humorously describes difficulties of discussing race and illustrates that while we must take individual responsibility for our privilege and fight racism, we have been socialized to think about race in certain ways and ongoing work is needed: we must continually deconstruct and resist the racist discourses that daily bombard us. Inclusion of such material early in the term can facilitate expectations about how to engage with ideas. The Smooth video is used to inspire a conversation and to introduce students to the field of CAS, which maintains that nonhuman and human oppressions are linked. It also helps shift discussions of oppression away from individual analyses (i.e., racist people are just "bad" people) to ones about underlying systemic and structural causes and the interests they serve. This can decrease defensiveness and help students address their own privilege.

Given that non-Native students in North America are raised within settler colonialist societies, it is important to include First Nations' perspectives in course materials. While CAS is a progressive field that offers a major challenge to much of the existing academy, it is not the only alternative voice regarding human-animal relations. Exposure to a diversity of First Nations' perspectives disrupts the stereotype of a monolithic indigenous worldview. For example, Margaret Robinson (2010) points to the many ways in which Mi'kmaq culture has long identified the agency of nonhuman animals, an idea that is significant for CAS.

Bringing Nonhuman Animals into the Conversation

Indigenity is not restricted to people, and students should be encouraged to educate themselves about indigenous nonhuman animals and other species within their local ecologies, as well as habitat loss and extinction. Such information can help challenge hierarchical thinking and place humans within a larger, horizontal web of life. Research about indigenous wildlife, in combination with exercises in which students explore outside—if access is available—and identify animals (and their traces) emphasizes that the world is shared with nonhuman others. In both rural and urban areas, students can keep a weekly journal about the animals they encounter, from squirrels to spiders. CAS courses should stress that nonhuman animals possess their own unique worldviews and experience their own ways of knowing. The research of Fawcett (2000), Watson (2006), and Whitehead (2010), among others, lends itself to this goal. Exercises that inspire inquisitiveness and reverence for life complement discussions about exploitation under capitalism.

As argued above, it is paramount for students to learn about nonhuman animals' societies, cultures, and emotional capacities. Rather than simply being lighthearted distractions, dialogue about the complex and diverse subjectivities of nonhuman animals can increase empathy toward them, while refusing to flatten their existences to pure victimhood. This can deepen understandings of nonhuman animal oppression by demonstrating that harm enacted through objectification and exploitation is not only physical but also psychological and emotional. Further, when students recognize that animals resist, conversations shift from discourses of charity and human heroism—although liberations should certainly be lauded and discussed—to more humble orientations of potential ally and partnership. The research of Hribal (2007), Noske (1997), and Warkentin (2009) bolsters such efforts.

Intersectionality of Oppressions

Perhaps the most unifying and defining characteristic of CAS is its commitment to situating nonhuman animal issues within intersectional analyses. In the classroom, this commitment can be enacted in a variety of ways. Texts that elucidate how human and nonhuman oppression reinforce and complicate each other should be centralized. That is, analyses that demonstrate how various forms of oppression do not occur in isolation help develop more robust and holistic analyses. Examples are Birke (1994), Deckha (2007), and Patterson (2002), as well as many contributors to this volume. (Weil [2004] offers advice about discussing these issues with children through texts such as *The Power and Promise of Humane Education*. However, despite its significant contribution in general and to CAS in particular, humane education theories also have a number of limitations, such as rendering of oppression through a "liberal and materialist lens" and the tendency to dichotomize oppressed and oppressor [Humes, 2008, p. 70].)

Working with Graphic Images

Vandrovcová outlined above some of the current research about the presentation of graphic images and ways in which negative responses may be mitigated. As noted, graphic images are invaluable for educating about nonhuman animal exploitation. However, it is extremely challenging to introduce students to these disturbing materials, and educators are frequently torn about how to offer these materials and how to help students process them. For Corman, films such as *Earthlings* (2005) are sometimes played at the beginning or midway point of a course, depending on the narrative arc of the curriculum (i.e., the trajectory of the underlying thesis of the course). Students in her third-year undergraduate Animals in Cross-Cultural Perspective course watch a film on industrial animal use midterm, after students have studied animals' social, cultural, and emotional lives.

Overwhelmingly, students have expressed that the previous weeks' information enhances their understanding of the pain and suffering presented in the film. Alternatively, students in her fourth-year undergraduate course Animals and the Law watch *Earthlings* in the second week because it is important for them to immediately confront the suffering that animal law attorneys and others are mobilizing against. Given that Brock University's Department of Sociology is progressive and tackles many issues of oppression across its curricula, it is easy to build upon existing frameworks. Again, context is important and educators should be responsive to the particularities of each situation.

Regardless of what or when images are shown, students should have opportunities to discuss their thoughts and feelings about the materials. At times even stopping a film before it is finished may be helpful if a break is needed. Encouraging dialogue in small and large groups, immediately after and later, is a good idea. Opportunities for discussion with the teacher in private can aid students who are reluctant to publicly share their feelings. Also, critical dialogue about the images themselves should be part of the processing of the information. For example, it is worthwhile to ask students to reflect on questions such as, what are the limitations of the material? How are humans, animals, and the environment socially constructed? What questions should be explored further?

Incorporating Activism

As part of the field's dedication to accessibility and to honouring activism, advocates' perspectives should be included within CAS courses through a range of materials and means. For example, educators can invite activists to give guest lectures, teach materials created by activists, speak about their own activism, encourage activist involvement, and legitimate non-academic perspectives through the presentation of materials generated by nonscholars. Students should be informed about local forms of activism and ways to get involved. Further, support should be provided for students who become active, if they are not already. Basing curricula around local case studies engages students who often have direct knowledge about these issues. These case studies strongly illustrate the relevance of the curricula and show that these issues are very much part of a larger public dialogue. Campus activism can be a great opportunity for students as well, as they are familiar with the institutional context and may know the network of people who are involved.

Exposure to activism should not be restricted to local issues and initiatives. Indeed, animal activism is international. Integrating information about global activism underlines the fact that the animal movements are not strictly Western. Inclusion of international perspectives on activism frequently expands students' consciousness about animal issues. These perspectives powerfully demonstrate the need to pay close attention to grassroots voices regarding what issues are most urgent and what will produce positive gains. Awareness that effective activism is informed by an understanding of specific (social and other) contexts should be part of drawing attention to how Western forms of animal activism have been vehicles for racism and cultural imperialism. Articles and other media should be incorporated to attune students to these issues (Hamanaka & Basile, 2005; Harper, 2010).

In closing, we would like to underscore a point that is likely obvious to critical pedagogues but is worth explicitly mentioning: Soliciting students' feedback is not just beneficial but is also ethical. Educators who claim to care about students' opinions, but who do not seek them out and incorporate suggestions into their teaching as appropriate, forget an original imperative of critical pedagogy: "To resolve the teacher-student contradiction, to exchange the role of the depositor, prescriber, domesticator, for the role of student among students would be to undermine the power of oppression and serve the cause of liberation" (Freire, 2007/1970, p. 75).

Conclusion

CAS pedagogy is not about imposing knowledge on the so-called ignorant masses. Following Freire (2007/1970), we greatly resist the banking model of education that separates the world into teachers and students, wherein the former deposits knowledge into the latter. We are all perpetual students and teachers. Self-righteousness and shaming do not belong in CAS pedagogy. Self-reflection about our own biases is key.

As such, while CAS pedagogues continue to refuse single-issued analyses, we must also cast a critical gaze on our own approaches. As we have argued, an intersectional and anti-oppression commitment should stay central to CAS, but it should also be expanded to include human and nonhuman animals' subjectivities in richer and more complex ways. Rather than simply being pleasant diversions from discussion of violence and abuse, pedagogy that includes the diversity and depth of animals' lives—in conjunction with more conventional intersectional analyses—disrupts the tendency to reduce experiences to victimhood. This expanded CAS model shifts our discourses from charity and pity to the possibility of more humble and holistic alliance.

We also stress the importance of providing information about animal abuse in classrooms and the need to be cautious about how we present and discuss materials. The negative feelings that can arise from graphic media can demotivate students but they can also inspire them to constructively act. Therefore, we suggest encouraging open discussion, offering possible solutions, and teaching stress management techniques.

We envision CAS pedagogy as a process rather than as a set of fixed rules. By staying flexible and changing approaches as needed, based on context and new information, we carry forward a dedication to open-ended conversations. There is no such thing as a perfect political subject who somehow arrives fully immunized from oppression. We are both committed to anti-oppressive politics, but we also know that our understandings and analyses will always develop.

Special Thanks

We would like to acknowledge some of the mentors who have greatly influenced our pedagogy. Corman thanks Leesa Fawcett, Constance Russell, and Rae Sikora. Vandrovcová thanks Hana Rýdlová, Petr Lupač, and Oleg Suša.

References

Abram, D. (1996). *Spell of the sensuous: Perception and language in a more-than-human world.* New York: Random House.

Adams, C. (2000). Animal rights. In C. Kramarae & D. Spender (Eds.), *Routledge international encyclopedia of women: Global women's issues and knowledge* (pp. 6–63). New York: Routledge.

Armstrong, P. (2002). The postcolonial animal. *Society & Animals, 10*(4), 413–419.

Balcombe, J. (2007). *Pleasurable kingdom: Animals and the nature of feeling good.* New York: Palgrave Macmillan.

Bekoff, M. (2007). *The emotional lives of animals: A leading scientist explores animal joy, sorrow, and empathy—and why they matter.* Novato, CA: New World.

Bell, A., & Russell, C. (2000). Beyond human, beyond words: Anthropocentrism, critical pedagogy, and the poststructuralist turn. *Canadian Journal of Education, 25*(3), 188–203.

Best, S. (2009, Summer). The rise of critical animal studies: Putting theory into action and animal liberation into higher education. *State of Nature: An Online Journal of Radical Ideas.* Retrieved from http://www.stateofnature.org/?p=5903

Best, S. (2007). The killing fields of South Africa: Eco-wars, species apartheid, and total liberation. *Fast Capitalism, 2*(2). Retrieved December 12, 2010, from http://www.uta.edu/huma/agger/fastcapitalism/2_2/best.html

Best, S., Nocella, A. J., Kahn, R., Gigliotti, C., & Kemmerer, L. (2007). Introducing critical animal studies. *Journal for Critical Animal Studies, 5*(1), 4–5.

Birke, L. (1994). *Feminism, animals, and science: The naming of the shrew.* Buckingham: Open University Press.

Brehm, J. W. (1966). *A theory of psychological reactance.* New York: Academic.

Burns, D. (1999). *Feeling good: The new mood therapy.* New York: Avon.

Coleman, P. T. (2011). Climate change, partisanship and conflict: What's a weather-beaten nation to do? *Psychology Today, 11.* Retrieved from http://www.psychologytoday.com/blog/the-five-percent/201110/climate-change-partisanship-and-conflict-what-s-weather-beaten-nation-d

Collins, P. (1990). *Black feminist thought: Knowledge, consciousness, and the politics of empowerment.* London: HarperCollins.

Corman, L. (2012). *The ventriloquist's burden? Animals, voice, and politics.* Unpublished doctoral dissertation. York University, Toronto.

Crenshaw, K. (1989). Demarginalizing the intersection of race and sex: A black feminist critique of antidiscrimination doctrine, feminist theory and antiracist politics. *University of Chicago Legal Forum*, 138–167.

Davis, K. (1995). Thinking like a chicken: Farm animals and the feminine connection. In C. Adams & J. Donovan (Eds.), *Animals & women: Feminist theoretical exploration* (pp. 192–212). Durham, NC: Duke University Press.

Deckha, M. (2007). Animal justice, cultural justice: A posthumanist response to cultural rights in animals. *Journal of Animal Law & Ethics*, Vol. 2, 189–230.

Fawcett, L. (2000). Ethical imagining: Ecofeminist possibilities and environmental learning. *Canadian Journal of Environmental Education, 5*, 134–147.

Freire, P. (2007/1970). *Pedagogy of the oppressed* (M. B. Ramos, Trans.). New York: Continuum.

Gaard, G. (2001). Tools for a cross-cultural feminist ethics. Exploring ethical contexts and contents in the Makah whale hunt. *Hypatia, 16*(1), 1–26.

Gaard, G. (1996). *Ecofeminism now!* Medusa Productions. [Video]. Retrieved from http://www.youtube.com/watch?v=BTbLZrwqZ2M

Hamanaka, S., & Basille, T. (2005). Racism and the animal rights movement. Retrieved from http://www.satyamag.com/jun05/hamanaka.html

Hammer, I. (2010, February 19). The biotic woman: Talking about transphobia and ecofeminism with Ida Hammer. Retrieved from http://bitchmagazine.org/post/the-biotic-woman-talking-about-transphobia-and-ecofeminism-with-ida-hammer

Harper, A. B. (2010). *Sistah vegan: Black female vegans speak on food, identity, health and society.* Brooklyn, NY: Lantern.

Heller, S. (2012). Witness to slaughter. *Print, 66*(2), 20–22.

Hribal, J. (2011). *Fear of the animal planet: The hidden history of animal resistance.* Oakland, CA: AK.

Hribal, J. (2007). Animals, agency, and class: Writing the history of animals from below. *Human Ecology Review, 14*(1), 101–112.

Humane Research Council [HRC]. (2012). Video comparison study: Youth response to four vegetarian/vegan outreach videos. VegFund.

Humes, B. (2008). Moving toward a liberatory pedagogy for all species: Mapping the need for dialogue between humane and anti-oppressive education. *Green Theory and Praxis: The Journal of Ecopedagogy, 4*(1), 65–84.

Jasper, J. (1997). *The art of moral protest: Culture, biography and creativity in social movements.* Chicago: University of Chicago Press.

jones, p. (2005, April). *The power of grassroots movements.* Paper presented at the first Grassroots Animal Rights Conference, New York. Retrieved from http://www.bravebirds.org/GARC1.html

Kahn, R. (2003). Paulo Freire and eco-justice: Updating pedagogy of the oppressed for the age of calamity. Retrieved from http://getvegan.com/ecofreire.htm

Kahn, R., & Humes, B. (2009). Marching out from Ultima Thule: Critical counterstories of emancipatory educators working at the intersection of human rights, animal rights, and planetary sustainability. *Canadian Journal of Environmental Education, 14*, 179–195.

Lertzman, R. (2008, June 19). The myth of apathy. *Ecologist, 34*(4). Retrieved from http://www.theecologist.org/blogs_and_comments/commentators/other_com ments/269433/the_myth_of_apathy.html

Mohanty, C. (1988, Autumn). Under Western eyes: Feminist scholarship and colonial discourses. *Feminist Review, 30*, 61–88.

Munro, L. (2005). *Confronting cruelty: Moral orthodoxy and the challenge of the animal rights movement (human-animal studies)*. Leiden: Brill Academic.

Nibert, D. (2002). *Animal rights/human rights: Entanglements of oppression and liberation*. Lanham, MD: Rowman & Littlefield.

Nocella, A. (2004). Understanding the ALF: From critical analysis to critical pedagogy. In S. Best & A. Nocella (Eds.), *Terrorists or freedom fighters?: Reflections on the liberation of animals* (pp. 195–201). New York: Lantern.

Noske, B. (1997). *Beyond boundaries: Humans and animals*. Montreal: Black Rose.

Núñez, S. (2009). *Pushing the envelope: Animal rights in Spain*. [Interview audio file]. Retrieved from Animal Voices website, http://animalvoices.ca/2009/02/17/pushing-the-envelope-animal-rights-in-spain/

Oakley, J., Watson, G., Russell, C., Cutter-Mackenzie, A., Fawcett, L., Kuhl, G., . . . Warkentin, T. (2010). Animal encounters in environmental education research: Responding to the "question of the animal." *Canadian Journal of Environmental Education, 15*, 86–102.

Orzechowski, K. (2012). *Maximum tolerated dose*. [Documentary]. Canada: Decipher Films.

Patterson, C. (2002). *Eternal Treblinka: Our treatment of animals and the Holocaust*. New York: Lantern.

Pedersen, H. (2010). Critical animal studies and education research: A background. In *Animals in schools: Processes and strategies in human-animal education* (pp. 1–15). West Lafayette, IN: Purdue University.

Plumwood, V. (2004). Ecofeminism. In L. Code (Ed.), *Encyclopedia of feminist theories* (pp. 150–153). New York: Routledge.

Robinson, M. (2010, November 14). Indigenous veganism: Feminist natives do eat tofu. *Scavenger*. Retrieved from http://www.thescavenger.net/animals/indigenous-veganism-feminist-natives-do-eat-tofu-237794-504.html

Rust, M. J. (2008). Climate on the couch: Unconscious processes in relation to our environmental crisis. *Psychotherapy and Politics International, 6*(3), 157–170.

Shepherd, S., & Kay, A. C. (2012). On the perpetuation of ignorance: System dependence, system justification, and the motivated avoidance of sociopolitical information. *Journal of Personality and Social Psychology, 102*(2), 264–280.

Smooth, J. (2011). How I learned to stop worrying and love discussing race. Retrieved from http://www.youtube.com/watch?v=MbdxeFcQtaU

Smuts, B. (2009). *Paying attention to the noise: Barbara Smuts' research with dogs, wolves, and nonhuman primates*. [Interview audio file]. Retrieved from Animal Voices website, http://animalvoices.ca/2009/08/25/paying-attention-to-the-noise-barbara-smuts'-research-with-dogs-wolves-and-nonhuman-primates/

Smuts, B. (2006). Between species: Science and subjectivity. *Configurations, 14*(1), 115–126, 191. Retrieved from http://search.proquest.com.alpha2.latrobe.edu.au/docview/217782903?accountid=12001

Smuts, B. (2001). Encounters with animal minds. *Journal of Consciousness Studies, 8*, 5–7, 293–309.

Sztybel, D. (2005). Coping with animal rights stress: A cognitive therapy tool for fighting stress caused by being a witness to speciesism. Retrieved from http://davidsztybel.info/x-coping.pdf

Walker, A. (1988). Am I blue? In I. Zahara (Ed.), *Through other eyes: Animal stories by women* (pp. 1–6). Freedom, CA: Crossing.

Warkentin, T. (2009). Whale agency: Affordances and acts of resistance in captive environments. In S. McFarland & R. Hediger (Eds.), *Animals and agency: An interdisciplinary exploration* (pp. 23–43). Leiden: Brill.

Watson, G. (2006). Wild becomings: How the everyday experience of common wild animals at summer camp acts as an entrance to the more-than-human world. *Canadian Journal of Environmental Education, 11*, 127–142.

Weil, Z. (2004). *The power and promise of humane education*. Gabriola, BC: New Society.

Whitehead, H. (2010). Conserving and managing animals that learn socially and share cultures. *Learning & Behavior, 38*(3), 329–336.

Winter, D., & Koger, S. (2004). *The psychology of environmental problems* (2nd ed.). Mahwah, NJ: Lawrence Erlbaum.

Yuval-Davis, N. (2006). Intersectionality and feminist politics. *European Journal of Women's Studies*, 193–209.

EIGHT

Engaged Activist Research
Challenging Apolitical Objectivity

Lara Drew and Nik Taylor

In this chapter we address the eighth principle of Critical Animal Studies (CAS) which points to the need to "reject pseudo-objective academic analysis by explicitly clarifying its normative values and political commitments." We argue that to make claims of non- or apolitical scholarship is itself an ideological sleight of hand. We recognise that we are not the first to make this claim but point out that it is rarely considered vis-à-vis human-animal scholarship, outside of CAS approaches (see, e.g., Best, Nocella, Kahn, Gigliotti, & Kemmerer, 2007). We explain precisely what is *critical* about Critical Animal Studies, namely the fact that the concept of the intersectionality of oppression is central to all work in this oeuvre and argue that once this is fully realised, the very idea of writing "objectively" can only be seen as a myth promoted on behalf of the institutions with a vested interest in maintaining the anti-animal status quo.

Introduction

This chapter stems from our experiences as both activists and scholars and, while we do not discuss this directly, it underpins what follows. We wanted to write this chapter because we feel strongly that activism and scholarship can be complementary. More, we also feel that claims to the contrary—that research must of necessity be objective—are highly problematic for numerous reasons and we return to this argument in some detail below. When nonhuman animals are thrown into the mix, as they are for both of us who locate our intellectual homes in two different disciplines, in community education (LD) and sociology (NT) combined with CAS, respectively, these issues become even more pertinent. How we think about animals impacts how we treat them and, as a consequence, the ways in which animals are constructed, ignored, or otherwise marginalised by academic thinking becomes a significant part of how they are configured in modernity and thus within capitalism itself. Disentangling the ways animals are produced and constituted discursively and literally within capitalist enterprises—and we include here the knowledge enterprise as well as other institutions that construct, deconstruct, use, and abuse animals—thus becomes of paramount importance for both activists and scholars.

At this point it is worth a quick note on terminology. We recognise that language matters. We also recognise that the category "animal" is a constructed one designed to underscore difference, human versus animal. However, we also need to make our writing clear and readable. As such we have opted to use the term "animal" even though we find it highly problematic, not least because it condenses a vast array of other beings, essentially all of those considered to be not human, into one category. Similarly, fields such as Animal Studies (AS), Anthrozoology, and Human-Animal Studies (HAS) are fraught with difficulty (e.g., HAS underscores the very binary between humans and other species that many working under that rubric are trying to ameliorate). Furthermore, the abstract ways in which animals are conceptualized by some within these fields are also problematic, particularly from a CAS point of view, which rejects the idea that animals are nothing more than analytical tools in an intellectual endeavour. In our view, CAS is always and inherently politically engaged. For us CAS scholarship is both political and academic and it always grounds animals in the forefront by recognizing that modern capitalist societies exist only in and through their exploitation of other animals. Further we believe that scholarship (of whatever ilk, and this extends beyond any form of animal studies across all disciplines) can never be objective and neutral. Instead we see scholarship as ideologically oriented and driven. The current chapter, for instance, is driven by a belief in the basic tenets of CAS and a critical appraisal of the use of nonhuman animals within modern society informed by a desire to liberate them.

Our aims in this chapter, then, are multiple. We want to open a space for debate about activism and scholarship, and while we are broadly supportive of activism within scholarship, we are not blind to the tensions this invokes, not least because of claims from within the academy that scholarship must be objective and apolitical. Our own intellectual location at the intersection of poststructuralism, posthumanism, and CAS leads us to reject such ideological boundary-policing assertions and see them as inextricably attached to the interplay of power-knowledge. We thus recognise the important role that discourse plays in constituting knowledge itself as well as determining the topics and issues deemed worthy of investigation. We begin this chapter by considering the idea of neutrality in research. Pointing to similarities with feminist arguments regarding the inclusion (or exclusion) of women into research, we consider the ideological role that the notion of objectivity has in debates about scholarly work in general and (critical) animal studies in particular. We then move on to consider the role that CAS has in attending to this debate, and in beginning to suggest ways forward, we address the contribution that radical education and "research as resistance" can play.

CAS, Neutrality, and Ethics

Feminists have long held that notions of objectivity in research are not only an impossibility but also an idealised version of the research process that rests upon a rationalized, masculinist, liberal humanism (see, e.g., Harding, 1987; Smith, 1987; Stanley & Wise, 1993). Moreover, the way in which this is policed—academically and culturally—produces a hierarchy of knowledge which favours white, Western, human-centred ways of knowing the world. We are thinking here, for example, of the various prescripts one must adhere to as an academic in order to be published in peer-reviewed journals, an integral part of an academic career that often has little to do with engaging the general public or other stakeholder groups in informed debate. Additionally, appeals to objectivity preclude, or at least obfuscate, considerations regarding the need to be attentive to the voice of those "researched." In AS this is particularly problematic given that our "subjects" of research do not actually have a voice that is recognised in modern cultures or modern academic research. In essence this makes questions about the research procedure even more important and forces us to rethink not only taken-for-granted ways of seeing the world but the very methods we use to investigate it, and we return to this later in the chapter. For now it is enough to highlight the similarities between the CAS project and some of the earlier feminist work on epistemology.

Like earlier feminist work (e.g., Stanley & Wise, 1993), CAS encourages explicit clarification of its normative values and political commitments. These normative and political commitments involve a critique of capitalism, imperialism, oppression, and hierarchy in all their forms. CAS is underpinned by animal liberation, which in essence argues that nonhuman animals should not be considered objects to be subjugated and dominated by humans but that all life has intrinsic value. In other words the recognition of sentience in other beings should be central to human treatment of them and this should be noncommodified sentience. Thus the animal liberation movement (ALM) seeks to actively challenge the impoverished moral status of nonhuman animals while at the same time arguing against the notion that nonhuman animals are property (Best & Nocella, 2006). However, CAS rejects the single-issue focus of other animal protection approaches and includes a larger social justice framework that also rejects, for example, homophobia, racism, sexism, classism, ableism, speciesism, and so on (e.g., Nocella, Bentley, & Duncan, 2012). In other words, the liberation position seeks total liberation and views the oppression of humans, animals, and Earth as interlinking issues and while it is recognised that different oppressed groups hold different histories and daily experiences, CAS scholars point out that these experiences are generally rooted in a similar system of oppression as a result of the overarching system of domination. As Nibert (2002) clarifies further "the oppression of various devalued groups in human societies is not independent or unrelated; rather, the arrangements that lead to various forms of oppression are integrated in such a way that the exploitation of one group frequently augments and compounds the mistreatment of another" (p. 4). CAS scholars point to the institutionalization and normalization of intersected oppressions and locate them within a broader neoliberal capitalist paradigm. Therefore, CAS promotes an intersectional approach to social change by challenging all forms of oppression and domination and asks that we begin to challenge taken-for-granted assumptions about nonhuman animals under capitalist systems.

The normative and political commitments of CAS are underpinned by anti-capitalist and anti-hierarchical positions that inherently stand in opposition to domination and hierarchical power relationships. Again, there are clear parallels with certain feminist concerns and approaches here. Domination is held to be reflected in economic, social, and political institutions that are both based on, and create, hierarchical, standardized, and authoritarian structures. Domination is also reflected in the depths of our mental apparatus that reinforces binaristic and hierarchical thinking and ways of acting (Bookchin, 2005; Foucault, 2000). Power manifests itself in part through various discourses that support binary and hierarchical modes of thought by normalizing them. In turn, such modes of thought, precisely because they are considered normative, underpin institutions and approaches. However, power is not simply played out in the arena of the symbolic but also materially, and it is here that real animals (and humans for that matter) are subject to a variety of abuses and oppressions. This is why CAS scholars must attend to the lives of real animals as well as to the embedded daily practices that impact upon these lives. Such hierarchy and imposed authority are directly linked to a capitalist mindset that encourages individualism, competition, and a general lack of concern for other beings. In turn, this reinforces a preoccupation with the exchange-value of products. As Torres (2007) reminds us,

> The true conditions of production are covered, difficult to determine, and superseded by the exchange value of a particular product. When this happens, we can all essentially behave as though the conditions of production are immaterial. (p. 36)

As Torres correctly points out "the production of goods is about *social relationships*" (p. 15, italics in original) and when we, as a capitalist, consumer society, focus exclusively on the end product, we neglect (purposefully) to consider the relationships that go into that production. This neglect is purposeful as uncovering the true treatment of beings in this chain of commodities would uncover unsavoury practices that would force us to rethink our role in it as well as its very existence. This is particularly the case for nonhuman animal beings, who, caught up in the animal industrial complex (Noske, 1987, for an up-to-date reworking, see Twine, 2012) become "nothing more than living machines, transformed from beings who live for themselves into beings that live for capital. Capital has literally imprinted itself upon the bodies of animals" (Torres, 2007, p. 11).

As Bookchin (2005) states, "A world so completely tainted by hierarchy, command, and obedience articulates its sense of authority in the way we have been taught to see ourselves: as objects to be manipulated, as things to be used" (p. 450). Western societies are bombarded by ideas of profit and efficiency with nonhuman and human animals viewed as objects and resources to be used. The idea of the legitimacy of human dominance through hierarchy is so entrenched, and so much a part of us and our interactions with each other, that this is projected onto the rest of the ecosystem, which is then rendered as a resource for humans to use as they see fit. Underscored by an intellectual heritage that encourages beliefs in human supremacy, the right (or in fact the necessity) to control nature in order to prove our own civility (Elias, 2000) and supported by myriad discourses that convince us that this is the natural order of things, this becomes increasingly hard to contest and resist. While exploitation can exist without capitalism, the structure and nature of modern-day capital has deepened and continues to exacerbate our domination over marginalised human groups, animals, and the natural world (Torres, 2007). CAS rejects the very logic of hierarchy and domination that includes not just capitalism and the state but also speciesism, patriarchy, racism, and any number of other manifestations of power disparity. Thus CAS's anti-hierarchical and anti-capitalist normative and political commitments are positions promoted not only in theory but also in practice as a way to encourage revolutionary change for both humans and nonhuman animals. The attention to the material, as well as symbolic, ways in which animals are used within modern societies and the clear links made to the economic rationales that underpin this treatment ensure that CAS scholars are mindful of real animals throughout their work and their activism. What is less clear, and is perhaps a future consideration for CAS scholars, is how to remain mindful that the methods we choose to use in our studies do not simply represent animals but are constitutive of beliefs about them in the first place. As Law (2004) reminds us methods are "enactments of relations that make some things (representations, objects, apprehensions) present 'in-here', whilst making others absent 'out there'" (p. 14). All scholars—including those of us who locate ourselves in CAS—need to be attendant to the fact that the methods used throughout the social sciences and humanities to study animals can inscribe differences between humans and animals (Taylor, 2012).

Overt acknowledgment of the political commitments that drive CAS scholarship may begin to mediate against this; however, this overt clarification may come under scrutiny as itself being ideological, because the academy inherently favours scientific "norms" such as "neutrality" and "objectivity." Given the deep entrenchment of societal institutions and capitalism it is hardly surprising that the academy plays such a role. In this respect the academy can be seen to be operating as an "ideological state apparatus" (Althusser, 1971) to underscore and promulgate the interests of the dominant class (here, we see the dominant class not only in socioeconomic class terms but also as those who have interests in maintaining the anti-animal status quo). However, the academy, perhaps more than any other institution in society, can offer a place for the development of new and critical ideas, and this is especially the case if it remains open to a dialogical relationship with activists. Ideas and new theories can inform action and in turn action can lead to the development of new ideas and theories. However, to achieve this, the academy has to accept, at least in principle, that all research is ideological and that claims to neutrality in research are nonsensical. As the sociologists of science remind us, all knowledge is a product of the outcome of social relations and contexts (e.g., Kuhn, 1996; Latour & Woolgar, 1979). Lather (1992) points out that research consisting of overtly based values and convictions that are openly opposed to the status quo is neither more nor less ideological than mainstream research. Instead, claiming positions of neutrality and objectivity mystify the intrinsic ideological nature of research that further legitimises the status quo (Lather, 1986), reproducing social inequality. Nothing can ever be totally impersonal, or totally independent, of the writer and it remains impossible for researchers to not influence (intentionally or unintentionally) their own research. Likewise, poststructuralism acknowledges that all points of view are inherently politically biased and inherently rejects objectivity (Peters & Burbules, 2004). Despite the growing acknowledgement that all research is positioned, the positivistic paradigm underpinning mainstream academia leads many within to still lay claim to neutrality and be intent on keeping ethical convictions to a minimum due to a belief that they taint the research process (see, e.g., Aronowitz & Ausch, 2000). This approach legitimises and privileges the interests of the status quo, including environmental and animal exploiters, silencing further the "voice" of nonhuman animals, and it is an approach CAS fundamentally opposes and explicitly rejects.

However, allowing these voices to be heard is not a straightforward issue and we have to be attentive to the fact that we, as researchers and scholars, as well as activists, create and construct our knowledge about this world, including the animals in it, as a part of the work that we do. It is not simply enough to claim the moral high ground and assume that because our ideological commitments are exposed and guide our work that we are necessarily making the voices of the silenced heard. To this end, we need to rethink fully our epistemological heritage and frameworks. It is not simply enough to add animals to existing frameworks as some within mainstream animal studies attempt to do, for example, those arguing that cruelty to animals needs to be taken seriously because it allows us to identify and prevent violence toward humans (for an overview, see Becker & French, 2004). We were struck by the following excerpt from Stanley and Wise's *Breaking Out Again* (1993):

> Most feminists, or rather feminist academics, seem to want to add women into what's already there—add women into courses or set up courses on women. Add women into this theory or into that theory . . . what they seem to want is to take away the sort of ripple of discontent on the surface of academic life called "women" and incorporate this. And then having done this everything will be all right. We can say "psychology is *really* a science, anthropology is a *truly* scientific discipline these days." What no one seems to want any more is to do something which disturbs the whole thing . . . If you take women seriously, if you make women's experience the central feature of what you're doing, then you just *can't* leave the rest undisturbed. And once you start saying this about women you have to start saying the same thing about children, about black people, about prostitutes. (p. 18)

While Stanley and Wise were here commenting on the attempt to add women into existing epistemological frameworks, this excerpt can readily apply to attempts to add animals into existing frameworks. It is clear that simply tacking animals on to existing research simply will not be successful any more than it was successful for the feminist agenda. Perhaps this, then, begins to approach the crux of the problem or the difference between CAS and other scholarship that addresses human-animal relations. Mainstream animal studies (MAS) has opened up the door to the inclusion of a consideration of animals within academic research, and while there are those within MAS who approach human-animal relations critically, there are also those who seek to study human-animal relations safely. The commonly used definition of cruelty to animals as "*socially unacceptable* behavior that intentionally causes unnecessary pain, suffering, or distress to and/or death of an animal" (Ascione, 2001, p. 1, emphasis added) is a good example. Overlooking culturally sanctioned acts of animal harm in favour of speciesist concentration on companion animals allows the problem behaviour (here limited to harm to companion animals) to be addressed without taking into account the systemic ways in which animal abuse is condoned and even encouraged. Presumably this is because the former allows us to adopt the "safe" approach of individualizing and pathologising animal abuse rather than seeing it as a deeply entrenched issue requiring far more radical solutions (Beirne, 1999; Cazaux, 1999; Taylor, 2011). In other words, this body of "safe" research seeks to do with animals what some of the early liberal feminists sought to do with women—simply tack them on to existing theories; to include them in our current theories without any real consideration of the radical places that this must logically take us to.

Current intellectual frameworks have a rich history based on human exceptionalism. From the Ancient Greeks onward humans have compared themselves to animals in order to prove their superiority and civility. While this has taken different forms at different points in time (the belief that only humans have tool use, language, culture, etc.), it has always been based upon the creation, maintenance, and repair of the supposedly pure distinction between human and all else (usually termed "Nature" or "animal"). Scholars have demonstrated how this pure distinction is a fallacy designed to privilege and elevate the human while at the same time justifying the myriad abuses of animals in society (Birke & Hockenhull, 2012). The posthumanist turn in the social sciences has encouraged (and perhaps been based on) a much needed perspective which decentres the ontological importance of humans (Twine, 2012). And once this decentring occurs we find ourselves in the enviable position of being able to consider animals—and crucially—their relationships to humans differently. As Benson (2011) points out, "If we have never been modern, as Bruno Latour suggests, neither have we (or the traces we leave behind) been human, if 'human' is meant to indicate a class of beings separate from all other living beings by an unbridgeable ontological or ethical abyss" (p. 4).

While the "animal turn" seen in academia in the last decade has led to exciting ideas such as that above, what is lacking, we feel, is following through where such ideas take us. As we take off the blinkers caused by the privileging of the human in Western thought and start to recognise that animal and human lives are inextricably intertwined, all too often we do not follow this train of thought through to its uncomfortable conclusions. Murray (2011) in her argument points out that "non-human animals incarcerated in modern factory farms, vivisection laboratories, the sport and entertainment industries and pet producing puppy mills are slaves" (p. 87), and that capitalism and animal abuse are inextricably intertwined. She argues that

> the formal subsumption of animals and extension of the power of the landowner over them marked the beginnings of both an *increase* in the numbers of non-human animal slaves in England, and the preconditions for an *intensification* of methods of production. It was a process that was constructed *in* and *through* already existing speciesist social relationships and one that furthered those social relationships. (p. 93)

She further argues that "rather than appearing as an *anomaly* opposite the capitalist system, the enslavement of non-human animals has become embedded in and an intrinsic component of the capitalist economy" (p. 95). Similarly, Benson (2011) points out, in his consideration of whether history can ever really include nonhumans, that "human society is not merely built on the backs of nonhuman animals; it is also built for and by animals" (p. 5).

Where these arguments differ from many of the abstract post humanists (e.g., Haraway, 2003), and what makes them to our mind intrinsically more critical, is that they extend the decentring of the human as an academic exercise into a political one. This is due to the recognition that arguments that human and animal lives are inextricably combined in ways that enrich our lives, histories, and societies necessitate harsh questions about the ways in which they are treated. Similarly, if we acknowledge the roles animals play in society then we have to consider our own complicity in establishing structures intended to facilitate their use and abuse. Finally, if we want to argue that epistemologically we have to include them in our thinking, then we must extend this to argue that we must also consider them ethically. This then leads to an awareness of the necessity of challenging traditional beliefs regarding animals, their position in society, and their relationships to humans. While traditional political activism is one way to do this, a complementary way is through education. This interweaving of activism and education forms the basis of activist scholarship.

In scholarly activist work, a way of challenging and resisting apolitical objectivity and clarifying political commitments is to engage in radical education frameworks. These frameworks are most commonly known as critical pedagogy (Freire, 1972; Giroux, 2001; hooks, 1994; Kincheloe, 2008; McLaren, 1995; Shor, 1992), popular education (Foley, 2004; Newman, 1994), and, more recently, ecopedagogy (Kahn, 2010). Although there are slight differences in the histories and meanings of the terms we will use the term "critical pedagogy" in reference to radical education throughout this chapter.

Critical pedagogy is a tradition in the field of radical education that encompasses community development, activism, and social change. It is a philosophy and practice of education that attempts to question and challenge domination, and the beliefs and practices that uphold such domination (Kincheloe, 2008). It is intrinsically connected with social justice in that it concerns itself with questions of how to transform inequitable and oppressive institutions and social relations. Its aims are to empower people who feel marginalised socially and politically and it encourages people to take control of their own learning to effect social change (hooks, 1994). In other words, this radical tradition is grounded in the notion of political struggle and social transformation.

Radical education frameworks are philosophies and practices that rest upon the breakdown of the objectivity and neutrality barriers. Those working within these philosophical frameworks recognise that all knowledge is produced in discourses of power, and radical education frameworks make it clear that there is no neutral ground (Meyer, 2011). Such frameworks rest upon the argument that all research is severely limited when it cannot reflect on its own presuppositions because of its insistence that they do not exist. The culture of positivism and the rationalist empiricism it gives birth to extends the internalisation of passivity through reinforcing the master-slave capitalist structure, an inherent driver of the status quo, which people become dependent on and trusting of. Positivism leads to passivity and conformity because ideologically it reinforces an authoritarian worldview underpinning methods of social control such as elitism, patriarchy, and speciesism, which are deemed the norm. This structure leaves people inherently vulnerable to the influence of the status quo that both alienates and controls. It further prevents people from making decisions themselves (by rendering them passive), thus restricting human freedom and autonomy. In other words, these power structures are repressive and deprive us of self-determination and autonomy, subordinating the individual for the needs of the ruling class (DeLeon, 2008). Positivism and objectivity reinforce this relationship and are tools that directly influence not only the master-slave dynamic but also a culture of passivity to benefit the system and those in power. Critical pedagogy inherently rejects worshipping the god of objectivity, and through recognition of impartiality of knowledge and knowledge formation, foregrounds a more ethical position, one that stresses the need to reject claims of "truth" while at the same time underscoring the necessity of being honest about the normative and political commitments that directly influence the creation of knowledge.

Critical pedagogy emphasizes active engagement in social justice, stressing the importance of moving beyond simply researching social problems. These frameworks not only encourage clarification of political commitments but also commitments in action that involve stepping out of the ivory tower and into the streets (Nocella, 2007). Radical education theories coalesce with the objectives of CAS and scholarly activist research that intentionally puts theoretically driven ideas to use. CAS seeks to go beyond using theories that are divorced from practice and to fully engage in praxis. Ideas alone do not make a difference to the oppressed and the suffering. Radical educational frameworks promote politicised research that seeks to move beyond purely stating ideological commitments and aims to be inclusive of the political and activist role more so. One of the central goals of CAS's political commitments is underpinned and informed by total liberation and transformation. In other words, intervention methods and ethical commitments, rather than just critique, are needed to challenge the root cause of a problem in order to alleviate social and ecological problems. Too often those in power positions in educational institutions undermine the critique of practices that lead to injustice and suffering in the name of objectivity and neutrality. In some cases, educational institutions do this while using their institutional mission statements that are saturated and labelled with the language of social justice (Kincheloe, 2011). On the one hand, educational institutions spout mission statements that may encourage equity and social justice; on the other hand, these institutions generally disapprove of work that is radical and resisting of the status quo. A well-known example of this is Ward Churchill, who was suspended and fired from the University of Colorado at Boulder in 2005. Churchill received public outcry over some of his academic work about American foreign policies (just after 9/11), which led to CU-Boulder launching an investigation on Churchill's background and academic work. Churchill was then fired due to plagiarism claims concerning some of his published work. He responded to this by filing a suit in state court arguing that he was actually fired for what he felt was protected free speech within his university. The University of Colorado in Boulder is a prime example of an institution that promotes social justice using labels of "sustainability" and "research" yet is resistant of work that radically questions the status quo. Educational institutions normalise voices that naturalise dominant perspectives through claiming the stance of objectivity and neutrality to further conceal the mechanisations of power (Kincheloe, 2011). By failing to address normative values and political commitments one has taken a distinct moral position inherently defending the global capitalist perspective perpetuating the status quo.

Therefore, as CAS seeks to be both political and academic, an important task of CAS is to criticise the workings of those who appear and claim to be apolitical. As Chomsky (1996) argues, it is the responsibility of academics and intellectuals to be engaged politically and to promote politicised research. Those who appear neutral or independent are those who tend to exercise political violence obscurely (Foucault, 2000). Thus, this political violence needs to be unmasked. It therefore remains an ethical duty to disclose normative and political commitments (Meyer, 2011) and, in the CAS context, to point out the interconnections between such positivistic ways of viewing the world and planetary and nonhuman animal suffering due to corporate greed and knowledge control. Activist-scholars must deliver a jolt to dominant epistemologies to expose these deceptions. Liberatory and resistant radical education frameworks can be used as a way for activist-researchers to openly engage in resistance politics, to ally with the oppressed (both human and nonhuman animals) and are ways to engage in social and political struggle. Therefore, we argue, CAS, as both a scholarly and activist field, must work with these frameworks to counteract those who become seduced by the sirens of political neutrality. CAS must promote politicised research and activism, and radical education frameworks in the role of activist, teacher, researcher, and knowledge worker provide the opportunity to do so authentically.

However, although we argue that the activist-scholarly role can be complementary, it is a given that it can be seen as inherently contradictory given the destructive role that universities tend to play in the promotion of global capitalism and exploitation of humans and nonhuman animals. Academia is an institution that is hierarchical and essential to capitalism and therefore is fundamentally at odds with CAS normative and political commitments. We are all too aware that the educational system maintains the power in the hands of one social class at the expense of others (Foucault, 2000). As Flecha (2008) states:

> The nature of critical pedagogies forces us to confront our own positioning as scholars within bourgeois educational institutions as we recognise that, before, perhaps, we can claim that our work is "radical", we must consider our own complicity in the commodification of knowledge and the proliferation of bourgeois values. (p. 15)

With this in mind we need to facilitate rigorous self-awareness as activist-scholars to ensure we understand the forces that construct our consciousness and produce our subjectivities, particularly within contemporary Western culture. So as CAS situates itself in a scholarly activist role, CAS activist-scholars must remain conscious of their positioning and the difficulties of working and participating in an institution that has a vested interest in maintaining the anti-animal status quo. This almost always involves working under considerable pressure to conform. Resisting this pressure can have profound consequences ranging from ostracism to dismissal (Kincheloe, 2011).

In acknowledging this inherent contradiction, we argue CAS, through clarifying its political commitments, can play a role in dismantling the dominant ideology and act as a way within the institution to resist the status quo. Working within the institution with a radical framework offers the opportunity for activist-scholars to promote CAS goals and commitments. Integrating CAS theory into the classroom and building an active connection that involves staff and students with community groups and social movements would be two key ways to achieve this. This means forging alliances through action with other oppressed groups (both human and nonhuman animals) and making direct and authentic connections to the world beyond the classroom in theory and practice. Staff and students then become active participants in the creation of knowledge for action and change in not only the classroom but also the community environment. This facilitates an active, not a passive, relationship to the world. So utilising radical education frameworks not only encourages an opposition to apolitical scholarship but also a mandatory commitment to openly engage in resistance politics and to do so with others who share similar points of view (e.g., feminist, environmental and critical race scholars). We do not mean to embed ourselves within the professionalization discourse within the institution but to openly engage in politics both in the institution and the streets. As Nocella and Kaltefleiter (2011) argue, "Social change has never been possible by people playing it safe or trying to be collegial" (p. 213). Thus we see a way forward for activist-scholars to make use of radical education frameworks to lay the groundwork for political change for both human and nonhuman animals; this is a way that utilises social justice and radical education frameworks as well as considers the place of research as resistance.

Research as Resistance

While recognising the problems CAS faces due to being partly embedded within the academy, we believe research itself can, in similar ways to (radical) education, be a powerful tool for social change. Similarly, we also recognise that it can be just as powerful in maintaining the status quo and silencing others. However, we argue that research can be used as a tool of resistance to empower and liberate if it provides access to alternative perspectives that lay the groundwork for structural change. Research informed by such principles can be used as a tool of resistance and change by exposing the dominant and repressive ideologies of existing social systems (Lewis, 2012). This may involve research within social movements where the researcher is participatory in approach and active within the movement. It also requires that the researcher-academic presents a political and ethical viewpoint in the interest of marginalised and oppressed groups. This may involve, for example, conducting research on the very use, treatment, and exploitation of nonhuman animals while actively participating in ethical practice and social action that rejects the exploitation of nonhuman animals. Potts and Brown (2005) argue that "committing ourselves to anti-oppressive work means committing to social change and to taking an active role in that change" (p. 255). Activist-academics who conduct research committed to social justice view it as a method that can expose the intersected nature of domination and oppression in order to oppose, resist, and transform it.

In particular, research that is used as a tool of resistance is generally participatory based, seeking to work with the participants rather than on or for them. This participatory process often values local knowledge and seeks to empower marginalised communities from repressive systems to strengthen their capacity to generate new knowledge (O'Leary, 2010). For as Lewis (2012) confirms, "Activist research is firmly political in its orientation and has embedded within it relationships based on dialogue with participants" (p. 228). A dialogical approach insists that everyone involved in the conversation participates as equal and co-learners (Freire, 1972). In other words, everyone in this process becomes a co-creator of knowledge, which is the essence of activist and social justice methodologies. Instead of the researcher typically being the creator of new knowledge, the participants included are the incubators instead. Further, Routledge (2009) argues that this reflects activist academic practice that "prioritizes grounded, embodied political action, the role of theory being to contribute to, be informed by, and be grounded in such action, in order to create and nurture mutual solidarity and collective action—yielding in the end a liberatory politics of affinity" (pp. 90–91). Thus, from a CAS perspective, research has a direct political purpose and requires a personal and explicit commitment to social justice that challenges the status quo in its processes as well as its outcomes. Of course, this raises unique challenges within CAS given that many of the participants we wish to work with, or on behalf of, are nonhuman. We believe it is possible to hold to the tenets of social justice frameworks, however, but urge the CAS community to engage with the difficult question of how—precisely—to bring animals in to the research that we do. This may take the form of including ethologists in our research (see, e.g., Balcombe, 2011) and making it truly interdisciplinary, or it might follow more novel routes and work within multispecies methodological frameworks (e.g., Kirksey & Helmreich, 2010). Without including them we risk falling into the trap of arguing that our approach is better simply because our moral ground is higher. While it is tempting to believe this is enough—and in many cases it may be (e.g., slaughterhouses, animal experimentation)—it is still the case that we need to ensure our arguments are grounded clearly in information regarding real animals and their well-being.

A slightly different activist-academic methodology that has a social justice orientation using an anti-oppressive angle is through the work of narrative. Narrative is a form of political expression through storytelling that can provide space for those that are marginalised and silenced, whether the voice being heard belongs to human or nonhuman animals (Nocella & Colling, 2012). In the case of nonhuman animals, they cannot narrate accounts of their suffering in the same way that humans can (Best, 2011), yet their voices and stories can be represented through narrative research to expose their enslavement in factory farms, vivisection labs, and other places of cruelty. Through this process, nonhuman animals can communicate in various ways by telling us of their suffering. For example, pigs in farms resist by escaping their pens and speak by screaming when their babies are taken from them. Cows will call loudly for days and even weeks after their calves have been taken from them. Showing these narratives provides space for nonhuman animals to be heard and for their stories to be represented and told. Hribal's (2011) work represents the narratives of nonhuman animals in zoos and animal theme parks and depicts the escapes and attacks of animals as intentional as they represent actions that express their own desire for freedom. These types of political stories express a political viewpoint by making direct criticisms of social structures that reinforce this exploitation. So the use of narrative has traditionally been used to bring forward the voices of those who have been silenced (Kimpson, 2005) and this method allows for nonhuman animals voices to be heard in some capacity.

Both narrative and other social justice methodologies reflect an opportunity for resistance that directly challenges conventional modes of research. This stems from dialogical encounters that work toward the empowerment of the marginalised as they act to construct their own knowing, and attempt to create and activate their own strategic plan for emancipation. This removes the temptation to dictate answers to problems and instead encourages people's own thinking through critical questioning in a community context (Freire, 1972). A working example of this is the Indigenous Resiliency project that was undertaken in Redfern, Townsville, and Perth (Australia) (Somers & Maher, 2009). The research project worked with young indigenous Australians to explore young people's perspectives on resilience in relation to blood-borne viruses and sexually transmittable infections. This project was not only guided by the primary researchers but also intentionally engaged young indigenous people (peer researchers) to help develop and conduct the project. This approach allowed indigenous youth to engage in knowledge building and action concerning sexually transmitted infections and blood-borne viruses, allowing them the chance to influence change within their community. This is one of many examples that is inherently dialogical and intrinsically radical that places value on subjective elements in experience, privileging these personal experiences as foundational for the creation of knowledge. This approach could be used in CAS by conducting qualitative research in marginalised groups, such as women and people of colour, and social movements, such as the animal liberation movement. This would work through dialoguing with activists or those marginalised by drawing on their subjective experiences (through dialogical interviews) and directly constructing knowledge based on these experiences and dialogues. This then potentially empowers activists or those marginalised by giving them direct control of the knowledge being built. These techniques remain in stark contrast to positivistic methods that claim the researcher as the only expert with the power to create knowledge, where participants are treated as objects and have no involvement or control in the research process (Potts & Brown, 2005). In this way, then, activist-academic methodologies directly attack positivistic hierarchical power relations that CAS inherently rejects.

Further, using a CAS angle, if we are to promote liberating research methodologies then the university's role in knowledge production needs to be challenged and critically reflected upon. We must pay attention to, and shift, how power relations work in and through the process of doing research (Potts & Brown, 2005) and "this includes recognising our own privilege and working to dismantle unjust systems that keep us in that privileged space" (p. 258). As Lather (1991) argues, often our efforts to liberate through our research continue to reinforce relations of dominance. Again, using the example of research on indigenous Australians generally involves them being examined and measured with the intention of producing new insights and knowledge aimed for community change, yet this knowledge becomes commodified (Potts & Brown) and is often used as a form of social control. Picking up on the notion of power and knowledge and the intrinsic relationship between the two, knowledge can be oppressive in how it is constructed and used (Potts & Brown). In other words, so called community-based research projects that are intended to benefit those who are marginalised have become tools of social control. So instead of putting the ownership of knowledge into the hands of those who directly experience marginalisation, this power of knowledge is placed in the hands of those who are privileged, reinforcing relations of dominance even if the original intention is liberation. So as CAS scholars-activists, we must work to expose the political nature of knowledge and unmask the dominant forces that shape our work. We must encourage emancipatory and liberatory knowledge that can be acted on to facilitate resistance in the academic sphere (Casas-Cortés & Cobarrubias, 2007; Lewis, 2012). In order to facilitate liberatory knowledge, CAS research would require activists and marginalised groups to be directly involved in the research process to place the ownership of knowledge back in the hands of activists and marginalised groups. This process would then facilitate a type of resistance to the re-creation of oppressive knowledge.

We have argued here that claims of neutrality and objectivity within the research process are expressions and workings of power. We have further argued that activist-scholars within CAS, in adopting approaches like those of radical education frameworks, can make clear their political and ideological orientations and, in doing so, can be mindful of the ways in which they are themselves implicated in the construction of knowledge. We are aware that our ideas are not straightforward or unproblematic and that much remains to be discussed. We have not, for example, considered the methods that our social justice approaches might take, and the role nonviolent direct action can play within them. Space precludes a thorough examination of these issues that are taken up by others in the current volume.

References

Althusser, L. (1971). Ideology and ideological state apparatuses. In *Lenin and philosophy, and other essays* (B. Brewster, Trans.; pp. 127–189). London: New Left.

Aronowitz, S., & Ausch, R. (2000). A critique of methodological reason. *Sociological Quarterly, 4*(4), 699–719.

Ascione, F. (2001, September). Animal abuse and youth violence. *OJJDP: Juvenile Justice Bulletin,* 1–1.

Balcombe, J. (2011). Concluding remarks. From theory to action: An ethologist's perspective. In N. Taylor & T. Signal (Eds.), *Theorizing animals: Re-thinking humanimal relations* (pp. 281–289). Boston & Leiden: Brill Academic.

Becker, F., & French, L. (2004). Making the links: Child abuse, animal cruelty and domestic violence. *Child Abuse Review, 13*(6), 399–414.

Beirne, P. (1999). For a nonspeciesist criminology: Animal abuse as an object of study. *Criminology, 37*(1), 117–147.

Benson, E. (2011). Animal writes: Historiography, disciplinarity and the animal trace. In L. Kalof & G. Montgomery (Eds.), *Making animal meaning* (pp. 3–16). East Lansing: Michigan State University Press.

Best, S. (2011). *Animal agency: Resistance, rebellion and the struggle for autonomy.* Retrieved from http://drstevebest.wordpress.com/2011/01/25/animal-agency-resistance-rebellion-and-the-struggle-for-autonomy/

Best, S., & Nocella, A. (2006). *Igniting a revolution: Voices in defense of the earth.* Oakland, CA: AK Press.

Best, S., Nocella, A., Kahn, R., Gigliotti, C., & Kemmerer, L. (2007). Introducing critical animal studies. *Journal for Critical Animal Studies, 5*(1), 4–5.

Birke, L., & Hockenhull, J. (2012). *Crossing boundaries: Investigating human-animal relationships.* Boston & Leiden: Brill Academic.

Bookchin, M. (2005). *The ecology of freedom: The emergence and dissolution of hierarchy.* Oakland, CA: AK Press.

Casas-Cortés, M., & Cobarrubias, S. (2007). Drifting through the knowledge machine. In D. Graeber & S. Shukaitis (Eds.), *Constituent imagination: Militant investigations/collective theorization* (pp. 112–126). Oakland, CA: AK Press.

Cazaux, G. (1999). Beauty and the beast: Animal abuse from a non-speciesist criminological perspective. *Crime, Law & Social Change, 31*(2), 105–126.

Chomsky, N. (1996). *Powers and prospects: Reflections on human nature and the social order.* Sydney: South End.

DeLeon, A. (2008). Oh no, not the "A" word! Proposing an "anarchism" for education. *Educational Studies, 44*(2), 123–141.

Elias, N. (2000). *The civilizing process. Sociogenetic and psychogenetic investigations.* Blackwell: Oxford.

Flecha, R. (2008). Heartless institutions: Critical educators and university feudalism. *International Journal of Critical Pedagogy, 1*(1), 1–6.

Foley, G. (2004). *Dimensions of adult learning: Adult education and training in a global era.* Crow's Nest, NSW: Allen & Unwin.

Foucault, M. (2000). *Power: The essential works of Foucault, 1954–1984* (J. Faubion, Trans.). New York: New Press.

Freire, P. (1972). *Pedagogy of the oppressed.* London: Penguin.

Giroux, H. (2001). *Theory and resistance in education. Towards a pedagogy for the opposition.* Westport, CT, & London: Bergin & Garvey.

Haraway, D. (2003). *The companion species manifesto: Dogs, people and significant otherness.* Chicago: Prickly Paradigm.

Harding, S. (1987). *Feminism and methodology.* Bloomington: Indiana University Press.

hooks, b. (1994). *Teaching to transgress: Education as the practice of freedom.* New York: Routledge.

Hribal, J. (2011). *Fear of the animal planet: The hidden history of animal resistance.* Oakland, CA: AK Press.

Kahn, R. (2010). *Critical pedagogy, ecoliteracy, and planetary crisis.* New York: Peter Lang.

Kimpson, S. (2005). Stepping off the road: A narrative (of) inquiry. In L. Brown & S. Strega (Eds.), *Research as resistance: Critical, indigenous and anti-oppressive approaches* (pp. 73–96). Ontario: Canadian Scholars.

Kincheloe, J. (2011). Critical pedagogy and the knowledge wars of the twenty first century. In K. Hayes, S. Steinberg, & K. Tobin (Eds.), *Key works in critical pedagogy: Joe Kincheloe* (pp. 285–406). Netherlands: Sense.

Kincheloe, J. (2008). *Critical pedagogy.* New York: Peter Lang.

Kirksey, S., & Helmreich, S. (2010). The emergence of multispecies ethnography. *Cultural Anthropology, 25*(4), 545–576.

Kuhn, T. S. (1996). *The structure of scientific revolutions* (3rd ed.). Chicago: University of Chicago Press.

Lather, P. (1992). Post-critical pedagogies: A feminist reading. In C. Luke & J. Gore (Eds.), *Feminisms and critical pedagogy* (pp. 120–137). New York & London: Routledge.

Lather, P. (1991). *Getting smart: Feminist research and pedagogy with/in the postmodern.* New York: Routledge.

Lather, P. (1986). Issues of validity in openly ideological research: Between a rock and a soft place. *Interchange, 7*(4), 63–84.

Latour, B., & Woolgar, S. (1979). *Laboratory life: The construction of scientific facts.* Princeton, NJ: Princeton University Press.

Law, J. (2004). *After method: Mess and social theory.* London: Routledge.

Lewis, A. (2012). Ethics, activism and the anti-colonial: Social movement research as resistance. *Social Movement Studies, 2*(1), 227–240.

Meyer, E. (2011). Critical ontology and teacher agency. In K. Hayes, S. Steinberg, & K. Tobin (Eds.), *Key works in critical pedagogy: Joe Kincheloe* (pp. 219–226). Netherlands: Sense.

McLaren, P. (1995). *Critical pedagogy and predatory culture: Oppositional politics in a postmodern era.* London: Routledge.

Murray, M. (2011). The underdog in history: Serfdom, slavery and species in the creation and development of capitalism. In N. Taylor & T. Signal (Eds.), *Theorizing animals: Re-thinking humanimal relations* (pp. 87–106). Boston & Leiden: Brill Academic.

Newman, M. (1994). *Defining the enemy: Adult education in social action.* Sydney: Stewart Victor.

Nibert, D. (2002). *Animal rights/human rights: Entanglements of oppression and liberation.* Lanham, MD: Rowman & Littlefield.

Nocella, A. (2007). Unmasking the animal liberation front using critical pedagogy: Seeing the ALF for who they really are. *Journal for Critical Animal Studies, 5*(1), 1–10.

Nocella, A., Bentley, J., & Duncan, J. (2012). *Earth, animal and disability liberation: The rise of the eco-ability movement.* New York: Peter Lang.

Nocella, A., & Colling, S. (2012). *Love and liberation: An Animal Liberation Front story.* Williamstown, MA: Piraeus.

Nocella, A., & Kaltefleiter, C. (2011). Anarchy in the academy: Staying true to anarchism as an academic-activist. In R. Haworth (Ed.), *Anarchist pedagogies: Collective actions, theories, and critical reflections on education* (pp. 200–217). Oakland, CA: PM.

Noske, B. (1997). *Beyond boundaries: Humans and animals.* Montreal, New York, & London: Black Rose.

O'Leary, N. (2010). *The essential guide to doing your research project.* London: Sage.

Peters, M., & Burbules, N. (2004). *Poststructuralism and educational research.* Lanham, MD: Rowman & Littlefield.

Potts, K., & Brown, L. (2005). Becoming an anti-oppressive researcher. In L. Brown & S. Strega (Eds.), *Research as resistance: Critical, indigenous and anti-oppressive approaches* (pp. 255–286). Toronto: Canadian Scholars.

Routledge, P. (2009). Toward a relational ethics of struggle: Embodiment affinity, and affect. In R. Amster, A. Deleon, L. A. Fernandez, A. J. Nocella, & D. Shannon (Eds.), *Contemporary anarchist studies* (pp. 82–92). New York: Routledge.

Shor, I. (1992). *Empowering education: Critical teaching for social change.* London: University of Chicago Press.

Smith, D. (1987). *The everyday world as problematic: A feminist sociology.* Boston: Northeastern University Press.

Somers, J., & Maher, L. (2009). The indigenous resiliency project: A worked example of community based participatory research. *NSW Public Health Bulletin, 20*(7–8), 112–118.

Stanley, L., & Wise, S. (1993). *Breaking out again: Feminist ontology and epistemology.* London: Routledge.

Taylor, N. (2012). Animals, mess, method: Post-humanism, sociology and animal studies. In L. Birke & J. Hockenhull (Eds.), *Crossing boundaries: Investigating human-animal relationships* (pp. 37–50). Boston & Leiden: Brill Academic.

Taylor, N. (2011). Animal abuse and criminology: The contribution and the challenge. *Critical Criminology, 19*(3), 251–263.

Torres, B. (2007). *Making a killing: The political economy of animal rights.* Oakland, CA: AK Press.

Twine, R. (2012). Revealing the 'Animal-Industrial Complex'—A concept & method for critical animal studies? *Journal for Critical Animal Studies, 10*(1), 12–39.

PART V

Taking It to the Streets

NINE

From the Classroom to the Slaughterhouse

Animal Liberation by Any Means Necessary

Jennifer Grubbs and Michael Loadenthal

The advancement of a Critical Animal Pedagogy (CAP) is predicated on the examination and eradication of speciesist pedagogies. Academics who challenge these oppressive pedagogies are mapped within a spectrum of discourses that examine power and subsequently labeled within a binary of "good scholar–bad scholar." The hegemonic animal welfarists enjoy the privileges of being the "good academic," while those who adopt an anti-speciesist methodology and endorse confrontational tactics are rhetorically constructed as the latter. There are those who critique speciesism but do not support direct action, and those who care nothing of the species binary but would illegally remove a dog or cat from an abusive home. Regardless, activists and academics in support of confrontational tactics are constructed as the ideological-other and tactically radical. Similar to the intersectionality of systems of oppression, systems of repression intersect at the juncture of academia and activism. The experiences of leftist academics are stratified within neoliberal academic capitalism, the individualistic knowledge-as-commodity corporate university. The political landscape of dissent is manipulated through the architecture of industry-sponsored legislation. Thus, the ghettoization (symbolically and respectfully referring to the removal and isolation of Jews to an island in Venice called *Ghèto*) of Critical Animal Studies (CAS) scholars coincides with the terrorization of animal liberationists. The rhetoric used to redefine "dissent" as "terrorism" in the 2006 U.S. Animal Enterprise Terrorist Act (AETA) makes no distinction between the quantitative research churned out by anarchist anti-speciesist academics and the torched leather factory in Salt Lake City, Utah—both can, in the language of the law, "damage or interfere with the operations of an animal enterprise." Through an interrogation of these processes, we define our roles as academics committed to defending animal liberation by whatever means necessary.

The following chapter takes on the challenge of bridging the personal with the political. It attempts to do so by interrogating an investigative tradition and praxis not yet solidified within the academy. Personal experiences, told through anecdotal tales, contextualize the terrain of academic and activist repression. We attempt to remedy the jargon-ridden theoretical groundings of this chapter with a satirical conclusion: a communiqué. The communiqué captures our disdain for oppressive pedagogies and capital-driven legislation that marginalize and silence animal liberationists. Despite the inspiring and lengthy history of animal liberation actions in the last half century, there remains a gaping hole in academic literature on this storied past. There are a plethora of government-sponsored treaties that attempt to define property destruction and animal rescues as terrorism, and heaps of publishers anxious to print yet another Animal Studies (AS) paper praising the contradictory practice of "humane" exploitation. But the theoretical articulations sympathetic with animal liberation are systematically excluded through the channels of academic capitalism. Scholars face a disincentive to devote serious analytical attention to defining and defending animal liberation. This chapter, as part of the larger CAS efforts, recognizes the revolutionary significance of animal liberation. Although it may make us a bit unpopular and solidifies our typecast roles as "radical," we unabashedly encourage and endorse the theoretically significant methodologies of animal liberation by whatever means necessary. In academia, the endorsement of both legal and illegal direct action in opposition to speciesism is certainly not smiled upon. Universities serve animal products in their cafeterias, many have animals in vivisection labs, and further use animal cadavers in medical school classrooms. Sure, other "radical" challenges to hegemony are frowned upon, but the holistic, intersectional critiques of ideology we promulgate call into question the very essence of contemporary academia: capitalism, speciesism, classism and privilege, systemic racism, gender and sexual normativity, and so on. We support a revolution that challenges all of these structures of oppression in the name of total liberation. It is not about who is labeled the most radical or which radicals are most repressed. It is about how the structure of academia marginalizes those challenging its modern-day form.

Reflexivity: Examining Our Roles as Authors

We approach CAS as vegan activists, but also as doctoral students advancing anti-speciesist anarchist theory in the social sciences. Our dual roles as community organizers and budding academics are further complicated by our positions in the anthropocentric departments in which we reside. Throughout our tenure as students, we articulated academic defenses of direct action and animal liberation in our respective fields: anthropology and conflict analysis & resolution. We undertake these projects with the intent to challenge anthropocentric notions of justice only as a human right. At times, that has made our research seem irrelevant by and off-putting to our peers. Graduate instructors have called our public endorsement of animal liberation misguided and naïve. While colleagues apply for grants subsidized by the National Institutes of Health, National Science Foundation, or federal government agencies, we remain resolute in our decision to seek funding from ethical (nonvivisectionist, nonmilitaristic, etc.) sources. Our attempts to engage in collaborative projects that advance anti-speciesist thought are often met with disinterest from those who perceive our work as unimportant. Alas, we happily reside in the marginalized corners of our disciplines that intersect with CAS.

Our work has argued that intersectionality, as described by feminist and critical race scholars for decades, is a project that must continue to extend its logic outward to ever expanding spheres of inclusivity. Kimberlé Crenshaw (1989, 1991), along with many feminists writing about the relationship between systems of power, argued that constructed forms of identity, privilege, and oppression exist at the intersections. Within this pursuit, we argue that speciesism functions in relation to other systemic oppressions (e.g., sexism, racism, ethnocentrism, ableism, etc.) as a constructed hierarchy enforced through violence and the threat of violence. This point, made through a careful and measured line of argumentation, serves to forcibly interject an anti-speciesist politic into an already established sphere of intersectional-critical race-Black-ecofeminist thought. Our hope is that once such an interjection has occurred conceptually, one's decision to selectively oppose some binaries (e.g., racism, sexism) and not others (e.g., speciesism) can be seen as disingenuous, self-serving, and an articulation of a violently asserted privilege. This strategy relies on the inability of academia to refute newly acknowledged spheres of inclusivity; in other words, once it is properly argued that speciesism exists as a constructed, violent, and oppressive hierarchy, it rapidly becomes the impetus of the forward-thinking academic to develop points of praxis to avoid participation in such a system. Such a shift in consciousness remains far from simple, and while intersectional scholars are eager to locate new manifestations of human oppression (e.g., ableism, sizeism, transphobia), challenges to speciesism remain marginalized within a context of guilt and individual culpability. Unlike sexism, racism, ethnocentrism, and homophobia, which occur at the categorical system level, one's interplay with speciesism is experienced in the bodily reality of the day-to-day by all human animals regardless of sexual, gender, racial, ethnic, or other identities. It is lived through the foods we eat and the products we purchase.

This effort to draw linkage between divergent academic discourses has extended to our roles as vegan activists seeking to advance coalitions with anti-authoritarian movements challenging capitalism and the state. This work has developed over the years to take many forms. To cite a few examples, we seek to present anti-speciesist and pro-direct action projects (e.g., Animal Liberation Front, Stop Huntingdon Animal Cruelty) at otherwise nonvegan anarchist convergences such as book fairs, conferences, and skill shares. We cater leftist events provided the function agrees to be exclusively vegan. We write and present about vegan parenting in a variety of venues and, whenever possible, find ways to intertwine our pro-Animal Liberation Front (ALF) message into a number of non-animal liberation–themed anarchist and leftist pursuits. In general, we try to find ways to advance anti-speciesist and pro-direct action sentiments into leftist and academic projects at sites where they might otherwise be relegated to the stack of causes. Thus, instead of simply dropping leaflets at the info table, we attempt to also elaborate and situate our politics into our workshops, presentations, and written work. This praxis highlights our pursuit to challenge single-issue politics, instead choosing speciesism as a pivot point for exposing and analyzing a host of coercive and violent sociopolitical systems. For example, Jennifer has inserted her politics into academic conference organizing and department functions through catering. These menus have been shifted from campus-catered animal products to locally sourced vegan food prepared in her home. One of the avenues in which this effort is channeled is via the field of critical animal studies.

CAS Principle 9 and the Role of Academia

The emergent field of critical animal studies (CAS) must assert itself firmly as an advocate for radical social change, not simply as an analytical, investigative, and theoretical pursuit. Scholars choosing to associate themselves with the CAS label do so with the foreknowledge that association carries with itself the linkage between research and practice. CAS principle 9 states that an affiliated individual:

> Openly supports and examines controversial radical politics and strategies used in all kinds of social justice movements, such as those that involve economic sabotage from boycotts to direct action toward the goal of peace. (Best, Nocella, Kahn, Gigliotti, & Kemmerer, 2007, p. 5)

This benchmark must be understood as a challenge to our sense of academic safety and observer isolation; in other words, an interruption of the uncontested space one typically occupies when viewing a social movement externally and without self-exposure. In order to exemplify these tendencies, one can explore resistance to the AETA, as well as support for the campaigns of economic sabotage carried out by the clandestine activists of the ALF and its allies. As these sites of animal advocacy occupy different positions in terms of illegality, publicity, and resulting isolation, they will be discussed separately.

Within these two tendencies a tension exists. For the first camp of critical scholars, they seek to expose and critique the state-corporate-speciesist alliance, providing necessary analysis, interpretation, and decryption for the matrices of oppression. In the second camp of scholarship, we find academics speaking in support of illegal direct action, not simply pontificating on the motivations of the clandestine actors. Unfortunately, for the sake of developing a culture of support for direct action, most critical animal scholars fall into the first camp and function as individuals competing in the marketplace of the university and the publishing house. Most academics of the activist variety have situated themselves firmly in the first position of explaining and diagramming oppression instead of linking themselves to the opposition, against the oppressive institutions. In this explanatory camp, we find legal scholars discussing the AETA, gender theorists dissecting the sexual politics of meat (Adams, 2010), and bioethicists exposing the practices of industrial animal agriculture. In the latter position, that of advocacy, we see a dwindling collective of activists defending controversial tactics, debunking the terrorization of animal activists, and producing knowledge that serves to contextualize the often misconstrued actions of underground activists. As a new generation of postgraduate scholars emerges, we must ensure that our ranks swell with critical rhetoricians and thinkers that serve to advance revolutionary, systemic challenges to speciesism, domestication, commodification, and environmental degradation.

In the current moment of state repression riding the coattails of 9/11, far too few academics, professors, and scholars publicly associate themselves with direct action, and an even further few stand firmly in support of the ALF or in a position against speciesism. Those that do are often marginalized in a matrix of professional scorn and juridical punishment. The examples are numerous and include David Pellow, Scott DeMuth, Rik Scarce, Richard Kahn, and Stephen Best, as well as a growing number of pre- and postgraduate activist-academics struggling to enter into the open market of the academy. Pellow and Best have had their academic research interrogated by their universities and their activist involvement called into question. Scarce refused to provide information from his doctoral research on animal liberation and spent four months in jail on a contempt order. Certainly, there is privilege in having a PhD and being employed at a university, and there is a rhetorical and physical distance between the roles of activist and academic. However, there are many forms of repression, and it is not in our interest to stack which type of oppression is worse. The circular game of doing so deters attention away from structures of oppression and privilege. Modes of oppression aside, this is a troubling trend.

In the last few years, the world has been witness to an unprecedented upswell in sustained campaigns of decentralized, clandestine, direct action throughout the world. No longer are liberation-aimed sabotages, vandalisms, arsons, and animal "thefts" confined to the United States, Britain, Western Europe, and Scandinavia. In the Barack Obama era, we have seen (quite literally) the explosion of direct action networks throughout Mexico, Chile, Greece, Argentina, Russia, Switzerland, the Netherlands, and parts of South America, Eastern Europe, and Southeast Asia! These newly emergent networks have risen and taken shape in a particularly challenging time for advocates of political violence. Not only is the largess of the state's military and policing apparatus allowed free reign to quell revolutionary acts of political "violence," but these underground saboteurs, vandals, liberationists, and fire starters have been rapidly recast as terrorists in an era in which terrorism has taken the boogeyman place once occupied by communism and fascism.

Creating False Binaries: Activist v. Terrorist

At this juncture, one can keenly pinpoint the relationship between the politics of total liberation and the praxis informed by activist-academics. The total liberation framework must be understood as distinct from reformist, welfarist, and other animal rights frameworks. While a working definition of the politics of total liberation is part of an ongoing, living process, one can say it is the attempted articulation of a holistic, liberatory politic where intersecting forms of domination are challenged. It is a struggle against "domination of all kinds" (Best, 2009, p. 199). It is here, at the intersection of terrorism and resistance, that one witnesses the taxonomy of the state's rhetoric. The United States, in its own war on dissent, has managed to succinctly reframe the discourse through the prosecution of nonviolent saboteurs through legislation designed to combat terrorism. Examples of this include not only the federally mandated AETA but also scores of state-level analogues that draw rhetorical and legal linkages between animal enterprise interference and terrorism. This criminalization of dissent, termed the "Green Scare" by activists, has served to create a political line in the sand, a demarcation that separates acceptable forms of activism (e.g., petitioning, voting, permitted marches, etc.) from those strategies and tactics deemed as terrorism.

Furthermore it is precisely this illogical language of statecraft that activist-academics have been quick to adopt, proudly proclaiming support for social justice movements as long as they avoid so-called militant, aggressive, or dangerous tactics. A scholar may write in praise of a daytime picket in front of a foie gras seller and then distance him- or herself from another set of activists who return to that facility at night and set fire to it. This is hypocritical. These types of hypocrisies serve the state's agenda of separating the "good" protestor from the "bad" protestor—the activist from the terrorist. Of course one must surround their strategic evaluations in a set of ethics. Examining the ALF's guidelines, once can see that these meet the CAS principles in a number of key ways. According to the North

American Animal Liberation Press Office's (2012) frequently asked questions, the ALF guidelines are:

1. To liberate animals from places of abuse, i.e., laboratories, factory farms, fur farms, etc., and place them in good homes where they may live out their natural lives, free from suffering.

2. To inflict economic damage to those who profit from the misery and exploitation of animals.

3. To reveal the horror and atrocities committed against animals behind locked doors, by performing direct actions and liberations.

4. To take all necessary precautions against harming any animal, human and non-human.

5. Any group of people who are vegetarians or vegans and who carry out actions according to these guidelines have the right to regard themselves as part of the ALF.

Like CAS principles, ALF guidelines are not a grab bag from which one can pick and choose. In order for an activist to adopt the ALF moniker, all five must be followed. If an actor finds issue with one of the guidelines and seeks to act outside of them, the actor ceases to qualify for his or her ALF affiliation.

The ALF guidelines contain an explicit endorsement of property destruction (2) as well as prohibitions against targeting human life (4). In other words, when someone writes, "I support animal liberationists, but not when they break windows," this is outside of CAS and ALF principles. Similarly, it would be outside of the ALF guidelines to declare, "Our ALF cell advocates detonating explosives during the circus to kill or maim the handlers," because such an action does not "take all necessary precautions against harming any animal, human and non-human." Thus, to be "in solidarity" with the ALF is to support not only the protection of all life but also to maintain support for the tactics and strategy of direct action. It is needlessly divisive to create fissures in our movement by, for example, separating academics in support of sabotage via glue and paint from those in support of sabotage via fire. These criminal nomenclatures are the sport of prosecutors and juridical statesmen, not those who claim to serve the cause of total liberation. If we choose to herald the men and women with the Sea Shepherd Conservation Society who bravely fight whaling fleets, we cannot turn our backs on the equally brave Mexicans who have used fire and explosives to destroy sites of exploitation. Both have inflicted economic sabotage and avoided harming human and nonhuman life, and it is this principle that we stand behind, not the tactical decision making of individual underground cells.

The Privilege of Confronting Speciesism

It is important to remember that as critical animal scholars and total liberationists, we are against constructed hierarchies of all forms, be they species, sex, gender, race, ethnicity, ability, and so on. This need is especially clear when seeking to draw out a working definition of the total liberation framework. Nicoal Sheen has offered one such explanation via her role as a North American Animal Liberation Press Officer. In a 2012 interview Press Officer Sheen explained total liberation, stating:

> Total liberation provides agency for all. Every single being on this planet deserves their liberation and freedom from social constructs that limit who we are, how we live and how we interact with each other—human and other-than-human. Total liberation is not concerned with single issues politics, which only serves to stifle the progress of social justice. Total liberation does not dabble in "When our liberation is achieved, we will then fight for your liberation." Total liberation as a concept and in praxis recognizes that our oppression is inextricably linked and must be fought on all fronts. (pp. 1–2)

In this manner, total liberation is against single-issue agendas and the leveraging of one's freedom at the expense of another's. The tendency for activists and academics to segment their analytical critique to a particular manifestation of coercive hierarchy—while ignoring and thus reinforcing others—is a performance of privilege and runs counter to the spirit of solidarity we seek to foster as revolutionary architects. Similarly, one can identify privilege when activism is seen as something that is relegated to a specific portion of life, a job of sorts, as this implies that an individual possesses enough time, energy, and resources to act outwardly beyond their own needs for survival. The anti-hierarchical logic within critical animal scholarship extends to challenging such hierarchies created between legitimate, legal forms of resistance and illegal forms, between the privilege of speaking from within the academy and the nonprivilege of smashing the windows of a leather factory. As the latter act contains not only a lack of privileged protection but also an included risk, one can clearly witness the issue of repercussions and risk as they relate to modes of struggle.

To be speciesist is a privilege because one can benefit from a speciesist culture that views nonhumans as commodities from which humans can benefit. Speciesism is a constructed privilege, yet resistance to it can sometimes draw from other hierarchical and oppressive relationships. For example, attention is brought to the nonhuman animal skin trade through the exploitation of human female bodies, and activists may graphically display the mass slaughter of nonhuman animals for food alongside disembodied images of other species' collective traumas from the North American slave trade, genocide of native peoples, and the Nazi Holocaust. The animal rights organization People for the Ethical Treatment of Animals (PETA) infamously promulgates misogynist campaigns such as "I'd rather go naked than wear fur," and the PETA.XXX website eroticizes animal advocacy. There are hardline vegan subcultural products including music and sloganeering that draw from masculinist and homophobic language and a meat substitute form of lifestyle (read Whole Foods) that plays on classism by directing vegan dollars toward an increasing variety of "fake meats" and away from the food politics of agriculture and artificial processing that should function as an integral part of a vegan critique of our contemporary food system. In essence, veganism becomes the province of a moneyed minority who can afford expensive foods. Thus, veganism is rendered apolitical through sizeist, racist, and classist discourses that replace ideological critiques with green capitalism. Systematically, anti-speciesist beliefs are treated as a complementary lifestyle that may or may not accompany further analyses of oppressive structures. Animal exploitation is the temporality for humans, either strategically undermined or intentionally abandoned.

These sorts of tradeoffs, where an activist exploits racism, sexism, and so forth to confront speciesism, serve to further isolate anti-speciesists as single-issue warriors. In this way, even resistance to speciesism serves to further construct privilege and oppressive ideology. Scholars that rank oppressions while serving as the "voice" of the anthropomorphized "voiceless," and activists who remove clothing in protest of fur, do so by relying on oppression itself. Rather than disrupt intersectional systems of oppression, these single-issue campaigns hegemonically fragment them into isolated structures and isolate oppression into specific instances or individual structures rather than interconnected systems of oppression. Such an act is hegemonic in so far as it creates more tension between single-issue campaigns rather than facilitates coalitions. Coalition building across movements has been slow to address these shortcomings, and critical awareness of these matrices remains a challenge to anti-speciesist advocates.

Through intermovement resistance, U.S. suffragists, many of whom were also vocal opponents of vivisection, were challenged on their exclusionary agenda of female suffrage rather than suffrage as a human right. Suffragists such as Elizabeth Cady Stanton ardently defended that suffrage be awarded to white women as a matter of superiority. In the generation that followed, feminists were splintered over issues including class, sexuality, gender performance, and race. Second wave events like the Michigan Womyn's Music Festival served as privilege markers predicated on single-issue politics. Resistance to the privileged and exclusionary mainstream feminism grew as the critiques became more prevalent. Women's Studies departments proper have slowly transformed into Women's, Gender, and Sexuality Studies and Critical Race, Gender, and Sexuality Studies departments. Feminist thought, as an academic discipline and movement, has been critiqued for its narrow focus and continues to evolve in response. Women of color have challenged the feminist tendency to isolate structures of oppression into single-issue identity politics. Scholars such as Kimberlé Crenshaw, Patricia Hill Collins, and Elizabeth Martínez articulate structural oppression within the realm of intersections, arguing that systems such as sexism, racism, classism, and heterosexism intersect and diverge in ways that shape individual experiences. Contemporary intersectional feminist scholar A. Breeze Harper created the Sistah Vegan Project and has helped facilitate rich discussions about experiences with racism and classism, journeys to vegan practices, holistic health, and how white privilege operates within the mainstream U.S. vegan movement.

U.S. ecofeminists in the 1980s, such as Marti Kheel, Carol Adams, pattrice jones, and Greta Gaard, laid the groundwork for an academic feminist discourse that consistently critiqued speciesism. Their work advanced critiques of animal exploitation in terms of racialized sexual politics, the ways in which other-than-humans are situated within gendered and sexualized systems of commodification. Rather than argue feminism to be a monolithic movement, vegan ecofeminist thought promotes coalition building and praxis. Adams creates links between visual rhetoric, linguistics, and animal exploitation, whereas jones makes salient connections between homophobia, critical race theory, and anti-speciesist thought. Kheel and Gaard created a feminist discourse that interrogated the spectrum of anti-speciesist activism. Although ecofeminists promote praxis, there is still much debate regarding acceptable means of resistance.

In efforts to challenge academic privilege, scholars can utilize their positions to queer social movement discourse. Critical animal scholars hold the ability to craft intersectional interdisciplinary positions in defense of animal liberation that challenge neoliberal institutionalized activism. From direct rescue to property destruction, animal liberation is both rhetorically significant and effective. The exclusion of animal liberation in academic texts demonstrates a devaluation of this important mode of resistance. Perhaps single-issue animal advocacy groups that function as corporations afford mainstream acceptance because of their limited analysis. For example, the American Society for the Prevention of Cruelty to Animals (ASPCA) fetishizes "pet" animals such as cats, dogs, and horses, while ignoring vivisection, animal farming, skin trades, toxicity testing, and so on. Further, single-issue academics do not threaten the multitudes of privilege vis-à-vis ignoring how speciesism facilitates sexism, classism, racism, ableism, and others. Thus, critical animal scholars are tasked with creating intersections and forging coalitions between and among movements, linking theoretical work to social justice movements outside of the academy and defending a spectrum of animal advocacy and liberation strategies.

Single-issue feminist thought, similar to single-issue animal advocacy, misses the point. The shifts in feminist thought and advocacy emerged through decades of difficult dialogues. These dialogues relied on the practice of both reflexivity and accountability. We must constantly examine the ways in which our social justice work is positioned within a world of omnipresent oppression. It remains crucial that as we craft theory and engage in justice movements, we think about how our work is situated. The mere privilege of species is awarded to all humans engaging in animal liberation, but there is privilege awarded to academics that solely treat animal liberation as a theory and direct action solely as a research population. As critical animal scholars, we must remain critical. We are critical not only of how species privilege is constructed and operationalized but also how institutions create pedagogies of resistance. Liberation pedagogies should not be limited to the temporarily set legal parameters. As time has shown, acceptable forms of exploitation change. Domestic violence and human slavery are no longer legal means of human relations in the United States, and those who resisted such oppressions in the past, often engaging in then-illegal activities, are seen as heroic today. In other words, today's terrorist may be tomorrow's freedom fighter.

The ALF and Its Press Office

In attempting to pinpoint a locale where liberationist theory meets practice, the ALF provides an inspiring example. The ALF challenges state-sponsored capitalism with their disregard for private property. Property itself is conceptualized within an anarchic-Marxist framework, concluding that the transformation of animal into commodity or property itself is inherently exploitative. The use of direct action as a mechanism to expose violence while upholding a strictly nonviolent policy has effectively challenged the state's monopoly on violence sanctified by the police and military (Weber, 1919). At the disruption of such large sites of capital, animal industries often turn to the government for protection from the ALF's exposing of the corporate-state incestuous interdependency. This is evident in lobby groups such as the American Legislative Exchange Council (ALEC) and its role in drafting and pushing the repressive Animal Enterprise Terrorism Act. Accordingly, the state has responded to the ALF with violent political repression designed to fragment the movement through fear.

Though the ALF as a movement, network, and strategy has no formalized framework outside of the guidelines noted above, it exists as a rare example of praxis that advances the politics of total liberation while avoiding the selling out of other struggles. The ALF does not remove animals from fur farms by exploiting sexism, nor does it burn down slaughterhouses through the use of racially exploitative incendiary devices. Actions are not exclusive to a specific national location or economic class, nor are they restricted by dichotomies such as city versus rural, first world versus developing world, and so on. While critiques can certainly be made of ALF tactics as dependent on some forms of privilege (e.g., physical ability, citizenship status, etc.), these are no different than critiques of engagement with other forms of illegality. For the ALF, the anonymous nature of the actions—the "masking" of the actor—flattens the identity of the saboteur. The gender, racial, ethnic, and age demographics of ALF members is thus impossible to determine outside of those that have been caught by police. Since the vast majority of ALF actions have not been solved, it is unclear what a typical ALF activist looks like. From those that have been arrested or accused of ALF, ELF, and associated affiliations, approximately half are female, and large portions are nonwhite and from non-English speaking countries.

As academics decrypting the intricacies of systemized animal oppression, we hold the privilege to not only critique farming, biotechnology, and fashion but also to defend those that take action at the targets of our criticism. We, as scholars in defense of animal liberation, should embrace the privilege of our soapboxes to defend the ALF underground from our podiums located aboveground. In liberatory struggles of the past, one is reminded of (mostly female) members of the German left press who wrote in support of the actions of the Red Army Faction, or even the work of Naomi Klein in her supportive and documentary work regarding the anti-globalization movement. If one requires an example of how this can be accomplished contemporarily, we can examine the North American Animal Liberation Press Office as one avenue to both articulate and legitimize the use of direct action.

The Press Office can serve as a centered hub for a decentralized network of clandestine actors. As the Officers distribute, explain, and defend the actions of underground animal liberation cells, academics in support can lend their authoritative voices in chorus to reinforce, contextualize, and further nuance the acts reported. It is here that we can use the infrastructure of the Press Office to meld our traditional academic structures such as conferences, journals, print publications, and formal educational opportunities. If one were to search for these things in the current academic pool of materials, they would find that nearly all of the "authoritative" voices discussing the ALF are either government counterterrorism reports or academic journals discussing the ALF from a threat assessment perspective. Further, it is difficult to find a faculty biography within an academic department that demonstrates a research agenda in support of animal liberation by whatever means necessary.

The sparse number of academics writing in defense of animal liberation outside of the nonprofit industrial complex are stratified within the academy. Universities are explicit with funding distribution and departmental hires that demarcate interdisciplinary CAS work. Under the politically repressive days of the USA Patriot Act, Grand Juries, and the AETA, research agendas face coercive structural hurdles such as the Institutional Review Board, university collaboration with the FBI for surveillance, and contractual—rather than tenured—research and teaching agreements. Although some academics may support a spectrum of tactical approaches to animal liberation, and many of us may frequent the Press Office website, there remains a gap in presence. We are expected to leave our balaclavas at home, put a cardigan over our "Free Walter Bond" t-shirts, eat our seitan in secret, and write about hegemonic animal welfare. The academic boat must not be rocked. But this academic marginalization is about more than compulsory speciesism, it is about capitalism as well.

Academic Capitalism: Compulsory Speciesist Thought

There are many products and processes that define contemporary academia: classroom instruction, the curriculum vitae (CV), the tenure process, the doctoral dissertation, publications, conference papers, and so on. Each insists on the compartmentalization of our work into productive individual bodies. What could serve as a transformative site of intellectual collectivism has been coopted into a neoliberal machine fueling academic capitalism. Academic capitalism is defined through Marx's framework of commodification: the transformation of students into consumers, professors into producers of knowledge, and knowledge itself as a commodity—known as tuition, which is actualized as commodity—the college degree. We, as academics, are asked to produce goods (books, journal articles, and courses) that have an exchange-value for the university. Our value is determined by the academic capital prescribed to these goods: the sales of our books, the prestige of the journals in which we publish, and the stature of conferences we attend. Thus, in order to be valued, to have a job within the academy, we are expected to compete with one another—to be fragmented into, again, productive individual bodies (aka units of production). The job-hiring process in academic departments is predicated on our adoption of neoliberal academic capitalism. Departmental calls for hire epitomize the subjection into these processes.

The following job listing from a university in the Washington, D.C. area demonstrates what is used to assess applicants:

> Biology–Endocrinology, Associate or Full Professor
> The Department of Biology at American University invites applications for a tenured position at the advanced Associate or Full Professor level, to begin Fall 2011. We request: A PhD in Endocrinology or a closely related field; an established record of research including evidence of significant external funding and a strong publication record; and substantial teaching experience are required . . . Applicants are encouraged to: Send a curriculum vitae, letter of application, three letters of reference, and samples of written work to (American University, 2011)

This listing highlights what the academy values: an established record of individual research, evidence of individual external funding, a significant individual publication record, and substantial individual teaching experience. Again, it is all about the productivity of the individual.

But before someone can even apply for these positions, they must earn a PhD, an even earlier subjection into neoliberal academic capitalism. Exploited teaching and research assistants are asked to work twenty hours a week, often not provided with health insurance, and prohibited from negotiating their contracts. So when job announcements like this appear, recent graduates scurry around to compile all of their individual accomplishments. By capital necessity, even the most critical scholars find themselves subjected to the neoliberal academy. The ability to collaborate among critical discourses and movements are impeded by the capital control of the academy itself. Through a process of intellectual commodification, the ability to produce and consume critical thought is marked by privilege. The attributes used to demarcate critical thought from academic critical thought are marked by the capital value of thought itself. In the competition-driven neoliberal academy, intellectual thought is constrained by a market-driven individualism.

Thus, the academy serves as a conditioning conduit into academic capitalism and neoliberal individualism. It should come as no surprise, then, that CAS is expected to operate as a single-politic discipline. Critical voices are always easier to silence if there are fewer. Further, isolated activist-scholars pose a decreased threat to compulsory speciesism. Through a series of formative experiences, we have been socialized within the neoliberal academy that regards our pro-direct action work as marginal, rendering it threat rather than theory.

Examining Our Own Marginalized Histories

Jennifer wrote on the intersections of speciesism with anthropocentric oppression. She was isolated in both of her master's programs: communication and women's, gender, and sexuality studies. The approval process for her master's projects was hindered because of an anti-speciesist agenda. The inclusion of the ALF was further met with hostility from faculty unwilling to serve on the committee. One of the recommendations she received from her Women's Studies Thesis Review Committee was: "Jennifer, can you please demonstrate why the 'animal issue' is something we, as feminists, should care about? Women are being exploited all over the world. Why worry about Wilbur the pig?" In these departments, speciesism did not register within the acceptable spectrum of intersecting systems of oppression. As her work has progressed over the years, the blatant endorsement of direct action animal liberation has continued to raise brows. One colleague put it frankly when he said, "Your work seems cool, but it's a shame you do *this kind* of work. All those years of study, and you will just end up teaching from a prison cell." Without ever reading her work, many colleagues assume it is atheoretical terrorist apologia.

The subjection to academic capitalism continued when she attended her first doctoral program interview. Through a series of questions, she was asked to reduce years of research to a two-minute advertisement. Once admitted, her research became candidly referred to as "animal stuff," and was relegated into the realm of fringe anthropology. Despite the emphasis on intersectionality, her research was consistently reduced to a single politic. Her colleagues had no interest in collaborating with the person doing "animal stuff," and federal-funding agencies refused to support a scholar who unabashedly endorsed animal liberation. She had hoped to enter the academy and queer the boundaries of species. She hoped to challenge the individualism of neoliberal academic capitalism through collaboration. As a culmination of these experiences, Jennifer's doctoral dissertation examines the multitude of ways animal liberation advocates experience repression.

Michael, in his master's studies, sought to develop a data-driven defense of the Animal and Earth Liberation Fronts and faced similar obstacles and ostracizing. Despite the fact that his research design, pre-research literature review, and methodology were approved, when it came time to meet with respondents and generate findings, tokenism and sensationalism became roadblocks and scorn. This resistance to pro-ALF, pro-direct action research developed in two forms. First, despite the protections afforded by respondent anonymity and informed consent, after conducting interviews and pulling quotes, Michael was told by his advisor that he must hand over complete transcripts of the conversations or risk being accused of fabricating materials. Since the interviews involved respondents' discussing clandestine, criminal activities, delivering anything short of select quotes from entirely anonymous respondents was not an option. During this negotiation between the researcher and his advisor, Michael stood his ground, made the conflict public, and was able to deliver only those sections that quotes were taken from, and only after a process that anonymized the respondents.

While these challenges to methodology were overcome, additional resistance was encountered during the writing period. While his department initially appeared excited about the prospect of a student conducting quantitative analysis of ALF/ELF "attacks," when these data were used to conclude that these movements categorically were not engaged in terrorism, the study received a less than enthusiastic audience. The study concluded that not only did the criminal actions of the ALF/ELF not fit within the taxonomic catch-all of "terrorism" but that the criminalization of dissent felt by these networks was due to the challenges they presented to the institutions of speciesism, the protection of private property, and the state's regulation of dissent. In sum, when the study of direct action was perceived to be contributing to the prevention of such "attacks," the dissertation was viewed as a worthy contribution to the fields of terrorism studies and security studies, but when it became apparent that the aim was not prevention, Michael's work was quickly reframed as a leftist student pushing some special interest, irrelevant, activist agenda—more terrorist apologia.

It is inherently queer to disrupt the normative tropes of hierarchy that naturalize speciesism. But there is also something quite queer about challenging our roles as academics, maintaining transparent dialogue through collaboration, and refusing to accept that theory is a mere commodity. Rolling up our sleeves and getting in the thick of it can only fulfill this commitment. At our own institutions, we were disturbed by the reliance on campus catering through the Aramark Corporation. The company has refused to allow employees to unionize; employees are paid below minimum wage through contractual loopholes; and, finally, Aramark serves heaps of unethical cuisine. After a few conversations with the department chair and writing a conference paper about food politics and praxis, we found ourselves talking more than doing. Jennifer nominated herself as the coordinator for food and beverage for the queer linguistics conference, Lavender Languages, held at Washington, D.C.'s American University. With Michael, she ordered two coffee vats, stocked up on almond milk, and began cooking. The Department of Anthropology endorsed the decision to completely circumvent campus catering and serve exclusively local vegan food at all department meetings, conferences, and miscellaneous events. This has meant late nights of boiling pasta, early mornings of brewing coffee, and a lot of difficult conversations about what intersectionality actually means. It does mean Jennifer's well-intentioned efforts are exploited, as she and Michael are the people shopping, cooking, and attending to food and refreshments all weekend. Change needs to start somewhere, and ideally the model will expand into a collective of department members focused on reducing complicity in exploitative practices.

For animal liberation advocates, so much is at stake, and so much more is at stake for the animals themselves. We need to challenge these neoliberal processes that are being pressed onto us. When we return from a CAS conference and add the presentation to our CV, it is yet another reminder of how we are complicit in the value of our academic capital. Perhaps it would transgress individualism if we imagined departmental CVs or a collective CV for graduate cohorts. This would create a large document that presents what our work as a department amounts to, rather than productive individual beings. We must actively disengage these practices through collaborative work and transparency. Chandra Mohanty and Jackie Alexander serve as excellent examples of this trend in feminism, coauthoring and co-presenting at conferences. Mohanty and Alexander remained transparent when institutions tried to pit one against the other by inviting both to apply for tenured positions. Through a commitment to collaboration, they have written and presented extensively about the neoliberal academy.

Both activist and academic bodies are conditioned within our current politically repressive moment through coercion and fear to work alone, to move away from collectivity. Anthropocentric academic departments fear the inclusion of critiquing speciesism and the endorsement of the ALF because of its indictment of humanism. Activists fear the prison industrial complex, academics fear the academic industrial complex. Agent provocateurs infiltrate general assemblies, grand juries coerce snitching, and terrorist enhancements increase sentences for our incarcerated. Tenure is used as leverage, research data is subpoenaed during criminal investigations, and funding is systematically denied. Violence through capitalism has and is institutionalizing the exclusion of anti-speciesist non-state actors, activists, and academics alike.

By whatever means necessary, we endorse animal liberation. Perhaps our research condoning illegal direct action will be more difficult to sell on the job market. Perhaps our colleagues will rate us poorly on departmental merit reviews because they resent the almond milk in their coffee. Regardless, we continue to occupy the academy as anti-speciesist intersectional insurgents, by whatever means necessary.

Conclusion

Having presented what the authors hope is a compelling case against single-issue politics and academic isolationism, the following is an attempt to challenge the chorus of naysayers and constructively contribute to an emergent politic of intersectional, liberatory struggle. In order to accomplish this task, the authors have chosen to pen a communiqué of sorts that seeks to scorn the scornful and praise the praise-worthy. While we recognize the presumptive, bombastic, and arrogance of such an approach, we chose to proceed with it anyway. Perhaps we see ourselves as students, lecturers, and organizers during the day, and clandestine insurgents conspiring revolution in the night.

What does it mean to be the defenders of those that choose the window-breaking hammer, the bomb, the clandestine liberation, and the spark of a flame? What does it mean to speak in favor of "militants" from John Brown, to the Warsaw Uprising, or, more contemporarily, those that tucked away their laptops and jumped across the fence to liberate puppies at Italy's Green Hill breeders?

In crafting this chapter, we reminisced about formative experiences with both activism and academia. Our personal experiences inform the ways in which we [de]construct theory and the politics we advocate. Michael spent weekends working with his dad, a Philadelphia cheesesteak cook, who later worked in the kitchen of a New Jersey prison. Jennifer's father was a butcher in high school and later worked as a police officer until the mid-1980s. Our personal is our political. The decision to advocate direct action animal liberation has meant confronting our own privilege and realizing the ways in which animal exploitation permeates our collective memory. Our parents worked in the types of places the ALF has targeted. We balance the hypocrisies that come with loving our fathers, condemning their past jobs, and endorsing smashed butcher-shop windows.

The act of writing collaboratively challenges the neoliberal individualism in academia. As children, we are taught that problem solving is a team effort. Two heads are better than one. This logic does not have a place in academic capitalism, where the CV is a brag rag of individual accomplishments. We chose to coauthor this piece as part of a larger politic that resists isolationism. Collaborative projects foster transparency and community accountability, while creating space for horizontal presses and publications. This piece reflects our commitment to working together for radical change rather than career advancements. Our politics must be reflected in not only the theory we collectively write but also the larger nexus of publishers and funding agencies. As knowledge producers, we should ask ourselves: How would our work fare if we applied the Stop Huntingdon Animal Cruelty campaign's model of secondary and tertiary targeting? The model calls into question the intentionality of our work, from who we work with, to who funds our research, to where we publish.

The steps taken that transform thought to text, text to publication, and publication to conference presentation must remain part of a reflexive practice. The ways in which we craft theory also provide a space to demonstrate solidarity with animal liberation actions. Rather than conclude with a few summative pages, we creatively engage in direct action. Although ours is from the privilege of a computer, it remains consistent with our support of direct action. What follows is a communiqué-in-the-works, a starting point for us to collectively build from. Let us be creative with the means we take to queer our academic place of privilege. Let us ensure our research that quantifies direct rescues and collates communiqués does not service the state's euphemized war on [animal] terrorism. Our roles as academics are twofold. We occupy and perpetuate a system of privilege that commodifies and privatizes intellectual thought. But those spaces are ours to reclaim, the walls of the ivory tower filled with neocolonial, racist, classist, sexist, and speciesist theories are ours to smash.

Atop an Activist-Academic Soapbox: A Communiqué of Sorts

To the students from Chile, Colombia, Britain, Canada, and elsewhere who took to the barricades to attack austerity!

To the Mexican eco-insurrectionists who pen communiqués to claim bombings while quoting Stirner, Kaczynski, Nietzsche, and Orwell with precise footnotes!

To the graduate students banging their heads against the walls of their classrooms!

To the teachers, from kindergarten to postgraduate, that inspire social war!

On a day soon to be actualized, we shall unite and revolt. We are the masses, those churning out commodities that alienate us from our bodies. Our thought is transformed into capital; the labor of teaching is only valued as part-and-parcel to the degree, our contracts determined by customer (also known as student) evaluations, and the frequency we publish with prestigious presses. The commons were stolen and sold on the market without our consent. Our classrooms have been replaced, our courses turned cyborg through blackboard templates.

We joined the academy with optimism that it bred revolution. Instead, we have seen how the privileged walls of the Tower constrain thought and action. Our colleagues scoff at the ever-so-complicated pronunciation of "speciesism" while the deans capitalize on our veganism as part of their green initiative. Students declare their love for animals in between sips from their Starbucks skim milk lattes. Conferences about exploitation structurally create class barriers through scheduling during work hours and expensive membership and attendance fees. Universities are fed, cleaned, and maintained by underpaid, non-unionized, contract workers who oftentimes are denied benefits.

In order to defend animal liberation, these hegemonic practices in the academy must cease.

Single-issue politics reproduce systems of power and create a competitive environment for critical scholars. Rather than fight one another for space on the soapbox, we must think bigger. The entire landscape of this academy needs to be re-envisioned. It is ineffective to argue one type of power is worse than another: "power over" is always exploitative. Power is constructed and situated at intersections. Neoliberal individualism must be replaced with collaborative collectivity. The terrorists are those alienating us from our colleagues, our thoughts, and our teaching.

With all of this in mind, we formed a cell and made a plan of attack.

During the early hours of the morning, at approximately 03:00, clandestine agents of the Something-Or-Other Liberation Front (SooLF) entered the facility located at _____ St., _____ USA, and left behind four time-delay incendiary devices. Before placing the devices, we ensured that nothing living remained inside, and as we disappeared into the night with armfuls of jubilant four-legged friends, we could smell the cleansing aroma of sweet, liberatory vengeance!

We hope that our actions are understood by the wider society as more than an act of isolated criminality but instead as another salvo in an ever-accelerating social war for animal liberation! We submit this action as a gesture of solidarity with those facing repression by the state and those that remain caged.

The raid last night was the work of a small cell of friends who decided that enough was enough, talk was cheap, and that direct action gets the goods. Despite seeing our former allies turn snitch, and friends exposed to be agents of the state, we trod on in our collaborative struggle against capitalism, speciesism, and the state. To those out there that feel isolated and alone, do not be discouraged. All you need to be a hero is a pair of bolt cutters, a pry bar, accelerant, and a map. If there are enough of you together, form a cell and strike! But if you find your vegan potlucks are a party of one, do not let this be a barrier to getting active. We should not be afraid to trust our comrades just as we should not be afraid to act alone. If the state makes us suspect our lovers are spies, then they have already won, but if we can run with a free heart and a wild spirit, then no cage can contain us!

The state likes to call us "eco-terrorists," "extremists," and other such nonsense, but we know enough to understand why. In 1939, an infamous Chinese authoritarian revolutionary, known for his murderous reign, wrote:

> It is good if we are attacked by the enemy, since it proves that we have drawn a clear dividing line between the enemy and ourselves. It is still better if the enemy attacks us wildly and paints us as utterly black and without a single virtue; it demonstrates that we have not only drawn a clear dividing line between the enemy and ourselves but have achieved spectacular successes in our work. (Tse-Tung, 1968, p. 15)

It has been at the historical moments when we have been most successful that the state has painted us in the blackest of lights. We are the ones that closed Consort Beagle Kennels (1997), Hill Grove Farm (1998), Shamrock Farms (2000), Regal Rabbits (2000), Newchurch Farm (2006) and have pushed Huntingdon Life Sciences to the brink of collapse (any day now). We are the ones that have bankrupted fur stores and foie gras sellers, stole the Silver Spring monkeys (1981), and burned Vail's ski lodges to the ground (1998). If success is the mark separating an "activist" from a "terrorist," then we deserve the title wholeheartedly, but if the term is used to separate the single-issue law abiders from the revolutionary adoptees of the brick and the bomb, then we proudly stand in support of the latter.

Not only do we stand in support of total liberation, we also stand proudly shoulder-to-shoulder with the accused. When we teach our children of the heroes of our time, we will tell the stories of Ronnie Lee, Robin Webb, Marie Mason, Daniel McGowan, Josephine Overaker, Rod Coronado, and the late Barry Horne. When the cops and courts call our friends "terrorists," it is our duty to redirect that accusatory hand at the real terrorists—the state and speciesist capitalism. As the masked liberationists so famously said, "The earth is not dying, it is being killed, and those who are killing it have names and addresses." These are the real terrorists, those that send terror into the hearts of the living—the vivisectionists, butchers, animal "handlers," and "farmers," and so on. We will also teach our children these names. We will teach them about Monsanto, Covance, Tyson Foods, Cargill, Ringling Brothers, Sea World, Novartis, and that fucking clown Ronald McDonald.

We will teach our children that terrorists are corporations that terrorize and that real heroes wear masks and seek justice in the night.

We need to make sure that our actions reflect the world we want to create and stand in stark opposition to that which we despise. Let us use our cells as experimental laboratories for developing new ways of coexisting with one another. Use these small microcosms to practice participatory decision making, positive anti-authoritarian collaboration, noncoercive divisions of labor, and emancipatory communication. If we only see ourselves as animal liberationists, Earth liberationists, class warriors, and so on, we will remain isolated, which only serves to aid the interests of the state. We must begin to see our strikes outside of a single-issue campaign mindset. Single-issue agendas cease to address systemic intersections of power, and in fact help to sustain institutional mechanisms by normalizing our isolationism. For many of us who are, were, or will be students of "higher" education, we understand that, like single-issue campaigning, academic disciplines function to fragment research and teaching into easily digestible units appropriate for standardized blocks of instruction time. Like the stalls and pens that ensnare our animal nations, these methods of academia cage our desires to learn and explore.

We must always remain committed to the cause of liberation despite the venue. We seek to insert anti-speciesist and anti-capitalist polemics within otherwise sterile and centrist avenues of the academy, resisting the tendency for our colleges to pigeonhole us as the "animal rights lady," or the "pro-violence guy." When scholars speak of ecofeminism, critical race theory, and intersectionality, we will remind them that oppression does not start and stop at the human race but extends to all creatures. We will defend the role of animal liberation to the academy while we are simultaneously attacked by other activists. We will endure the accusations of careerism, grandstanding, and armchair radicalism. Further, while we publicly champion the cause of freedom from atop our respective soapboxes, we must constantly stay grounded in the myriad of struggles in which we interact.

In closing, we proclaim total solidarity with those in the academy that sacrifice and struggle for liberation. Since we know that this communiqué, and others like it, will be seen by the relative few, it is up to teachers, professors, students, and researchers to further these debates in the classroom, the journal page, and the book chapter. We need critical scholars to explain to cynics why a charred leather factory is a beautiful thing or while thousands of minks escaping into the woods deserves heroic commemoration.

We all have our roles in this war. Some of us open cage doors, some of us light fires, some of us glue locks, and some of us explain these things to our students. Some of us do it all. Know that just because someone dons a cardigan and speaks from a podium does not mean they cannot sport a balaclava after the school bell chimes.

We are here to say loud and clear, from the classrooms to the slaughterhouse, "At the expense of our funding, at the expense of our prestige, at the expense of our freedom, animal liberation by any means necessary!"

Direct solidarity with comrades Tamara, Tortuga, Fede Buono, Braulio Duran, Abraham López, Adrian Magdaleno, Giannis Dimitrakis, Yiannis Dimitrakis, Gabriel Pombo da Silva, Marco Camenisch, Eric McDavid, Marie Mason, Daniel McGowan, and Walter Bond, along with those unnamed and imprisoned from the ALF, Earth Liberation Front, Informal Anarchist Federation, Revolutionary Struggle and beyond.

Direct solidarity with all anarchist prisoners in Mexico, Chile, Greece, Italy, the United States, Switzerland, and the world! We are all accomplices.

In memory of Barry Horne, Xosé Tarrío, Mauricio Morales, and Avalon!

Until they all burn!

STRUGGLE!!! STRUGGLE!!! STRUGGLE!!! UNTIL THE END!!!

For the expansion of the social war on all fronts!!!

For the destruction of everything that dominates us!

For Total Liberation!

For international anarchist coordination!*

Signed:

The "We Are Your TAs/GRAs/interns/students Cell"

Tongue and Cheek Parody Unit

Something-Or-Other Liberation Front (Anytown, USA)

Note
All closing statements cobbled together and shamelessly plagiarized from the words of the Mexican insurrectionists.

References
Adams, C. J. (2010). *The sexual politics of meat: A feminist-vegetarian critical theory, 20th anniversary edition* (Rev. ed.). New York: Continuum.
American University. (2011). Current full-time faculty openings. American University. Retrieved from http://www.american.edu/hr/Ft-Faculty.cfm
Animal Enterprise Terrorism Act of 2006, S.3880 109th Congress. (2005–2006). Text as of November 16, 2006. Retrieved from http://www.govtrack.us/congress/bills/109/s3880/text
Best, S. (2009). Rethinking revolution: Total liberation, alliance politics, and a prolegomena to resistance movements in the twenty-first century. In R. Amster, A. DeLeon, L. Fernandez, A. Nocella, & D. Shannon (Eds.), *Contemporary anarchist studies: An introductory anthology of anarchy in the academy* (pp. 189–199). New York: Routledge.
Best, S., Nocella, A. J., Kahn, R., Gigliotti, C., & Kemmerer, L. (2007). Introducing critical animal studies. *Journal for Critical Animal Studies, 5*(1), 4–5.
Crenshaw, K. (1991). Mapping the margins: Intersectionality, identity politics, and violence against women of color. *Stanford Law Review, 43*(5), 1241–1299.

Crenshaw, K. (1989). Demarginalizing the intersection of race and sex: A black feminist critique of antidiscrimination doctrine, feminist theory, and antiracist politics. *University of Chicago Legal Forum*, 139–167.
North American Animal Liberation Press Office. (2012). Frequently asked questions about the North American Animal Liberation Press Office. Retrieved from http://animalliberationpressoffice.org/NAALPO/f-a-q-s/#5
Sheen, N. (2012, August 13). Total liberation provides agency for all—Press Officer Nicoal R. Sheen. Retrieved from http://animalliberationpressoffice.org/NAALPO/2012/08/13/nicoal-r-sheen-total-liberation-provides-agency-for-all/
Tse-Tung, M. (1968). To be attacked by the enemy is not a bad thing but a good thing. *Quotations from Chairman Mao Tse-Tung*. Peking, Beijing: Foreign Languages Press.
Weber, M. (1919, January). *Politik als beruf (politics as a vocation)*. Lecture presented at the Free Students Union, Munich University. Retrieved from http://www.ne.jp/asahi/moriyuki/abukuma/weber/lecture/politics_vocation.html

TEN

Taking It to the Streets

Challenging Systems of Domination from Below

Richard J. White and Erika Cudworth

Anarchism is the goal that we pursue: the absence of domination.
—Gustav Landauer

Drawing on anarchist theory and practice, this chapter carries forward the invitation to "take it to the streets" by focusing on ways to provoke the individual consciousness to think critically and act constructively, to challenge systems of exploitation, injustice, domination, oppression, torture, and killing that concern humans and nonhuman animals. In this way, the chapter emphasises the fact that anarchist praxis has much to offer the excellent contribution that Critical Animal Studies (CAS) has brought to understanding the interlocking nature of systems of power and domination.

The principal aim of this chapter is to invite the reader to make new—or renewed—engagements with anarchist theory and praxis as a framework with which to better confront, challenge, and subvert the exploitative and violent interlocking systems that underpin the treatment of both humans and nonhuman animals in society. Drawing on the approach adopted by important anarchist thinkers, particularly the geographer Élisée Reclus, our intention is to stir the emotional registers of the individual reader and provoke action by emphasizing the ways in which the suffering and death of nonhuman animals is thoroughly embedded in ordinary spaces of the everyday. This chapter emphasizes the micro-geographies of domination by positing individuals and their local milieu as a central locus of power that can be harnessed to resist and dismantle entrenched systems of interspecies domination. In not abstracting dominion to being "out there"—as driven by the macro "capitalist" economy or enforced by "democratic" political elites—this chapter firmly situates meaningful spaces of transformation as being embedded in (1) routine and local sociospatial relations and (2) in the here and now. This call for the liberation of all animals, both human and nonhuman, emphasizes the broader community and ties that transcend species boundaries. Meaningful change and true liberation are not obtainable by asking permission from the representatives of the market (e.g., corporations) or the state (e.g., political elite). Rather, the most effective sites of resistance and power will be those that emerge from the individual operating beyond the market and the state through bottom-up strategies of resistance. This bypassing of the capitalist market and the state is a very Landauerian position in so far as it emphasizes:

> The State (as) a condition, a certain relationship between human beings, a mode of behavior; we destroy it by contracting other relationships, by behaving differently toward one another . . . We are the State and we shall continue to be the State until we have created institutions that form a real community. (Landauer, 2010/1909, p. 214)

The invitation to take it to the streets is important because it encourages a decentered sociospatial ethical framework(s) of analyses to be thought through from below (emphasizing most strongly in this chapter those spaces of hope that are embedded from the individual and his or her community). This is an important and necessary development for many reasons not least of which is framing systems of domination with reference to specific spaces and places. As Springer, Ince, Picerill, Brown, and Barker (2012) argue: "Social transformation is, of course, necessarily a spatial project, and a spatial dimension to the effective critique of existing structures is an important element of imagining and forging spaces for new ones" (p. 1593). Thus, when contemplating strategies of resistance, a local milieu should be sought, one which places particular emphasis on the roles and responsibilities of the individual and the community as having the potential to be(come) meaningful sites of resistance that can effectively challenge interspecies domination. This emphasis on the intimate connections, the intimate and meaningful connections that humans make with nonhuman animals, brings with it a welcome range of new possibilities and spaces for radical change. Individual and community levels have been evident in many transformative actions and strategies that animal activists or organizations have advanced. As Italian social anarchist Giovanni Baldelli (1971) observes: "A truly anarchist and social revolution will not be the work of revolutionaries but of society itself" (p. 24).

While noting that veganism—not vegetarianism—is the proper moral baseline of nonviolence, the chapter pays particular attention to anarchist geographer Élisée Reclus and his conscious-raising paper "On Vegetarianism" (1901). Linking violence with ugliness, Reclus advances a range of powerful subjective and emotional arguments that speak to individual readers and provokes them to act appropriately: "Ugliness in persons, in deeds, in life, in surrounding Nature—this is our worst foe. Let us become beautiful ourselves, and let our life be beautiful!" Such an appeal is an extremely important one to pursue within a challenge to systems of domination in our society; part of this challenge is acknowledging how focusing attention onto the human scale avoids talking about animal suffering in the quantifiable and abstract and prevents overly reifying animal abuse as being imposed from the meta-ideologues of the state and capitalism.

The chapter concludes with the question of appropriate anarchistic strategies of change. How can or should we think about building new and constructive anti-capitalist and anti-hierarchical bridges between and within our existing academic, activist, policy making, and wider communities, while resisting and rejecting violence as a means of successfully challenging systems of domination? Here particular attention is paid toward the importance of having consistency between the means by which we challenge systems of domination for the ends that result in liberation and parity.

Critical Animal Studies, Anarchism, and Human-scale Resistance

What are the dominant, routine, normalized, everyday experiences that underpin the majority of interactions of human and nonhuman animals in industrialized Western society? There are, of course, wonderful examples of life-affirming, interspecies relations embodying compassion, feeling, care, nurture, reciprocity, and unconditional love, yet as Pedersen and Stănescu (2011) argue, "The actual life situation of *most* nonhuman animals in human society and culture, [i]s physically and emotionally experienced with its routine repertoire of violence, deprivation, desperation, agony, apathy, suffering, and death" (p. ix).

The statistics that can be marshaled to underpin this animal condition invoke numbers of truly staggering and unimaginable proportions: at least 55 billion land-based nonhuman animals are deliberately killed in the farming industry (Mitchell, 2011). Indeed, this figure is projected to increase substantially with an extra 360 million cattle and buffaloes, 560 million extra sheep and goats, and 190 million extra pigs needed by 2030 to match growing consumer demand (Food and Agriculture Organization, 2002). In Great Britain, more than 3.79 million scientific procedures on living nonhuman animals were started in 2011; this is an increase of more than 68,000 from 2010 (Home Office, 2012). A cruel irony in itself, such overwhelming statistics negate the reality of abuse by encouraging greater distance and detachment from the reader of the statistics toward the individual nonhuman killed or exploited under such appalling circumstances. In an attempt to arrest this emotional and empathetic detachment and inject meaning and resonance to these abstract numbers, Les Mitchell (2011), when contemplating the annual 55 billion land-based nonhuman animals killed in the farming industry, observes that

> This is over 150 million individuals each day or the equivalent of the populations of South Africa, Zambia, Zimbabwe, Malawi, Mozambique, Namibia, Botswana, and Angola (US Census Bureau, 2010). Except for a very tiny minority, all the nonhumans in the industry will meet with a violent death at a relatively young age; all will have been confined during their lives; many will have been mutilated; numerous females will have been repeatedly made pregnant but their young taken away shortly after birth; family structures will have been destroyed. (p. 38)

This (imagined) emphasis on the killing fields also serves another purpose—to emphasize the all too concrete real geographies of violence, suffering, trauma, and abuse thoroughly embedded in space and place: violence is neither disembodied nor abstract; it occurs, as this chapter will emphasize, *somewhere to someone.*

Yet set in the context of this appalling background of extreme, and increasing, systematic exploitation and abuse of nonhuman animals, there have been highly celebrated developments across broad swathes of academia in the last twenty years of new interdisciplinary fields of study that have been increasingly referred to as signaling an "animals turn" in academia. In terms of the particular constellations of meanings and interpretations that have been generated by this interest in animal life, Wheeler and Williams (2012) emphasize:

> In the case of animal studies . . . these questions seem very often to be about ethics—about our place, and the place of animals, in other words—in a long mutually shaping symbiosis of human and more-than-human relationships. The growing interest in animal life, both without and within us, alongside the growing understanding that all this life is semiotic, might suggest that what we are attempting to think about is life, mind and minding, and thus ethics, from a wider than human perspective. (p. 5)

Thus, we know far more about the uniqueness and complexity of animal life than ever before; it appears that the right "ethical" questions are being raised that would problematize—at the very least—the dominant cycle of violence and suffering that defines most animals' experiences, but these are having no impact on destabilizing the everyday systems of domination that result in the jarring statistics noted above.

Importantly, an intense frustration and disillusionment with the disconnect between theory and action in mainstream animal studies has been constructively channeled into the birth of CAS, which has developed and matured into an important and vital field of interdisciplinary praxis, particularly so in the last ten years. To draw a distinct line in the sand between the former and the latter, Best, Nocella, Kahn, Gigliotti, and Kemmerer (2007) argue for the development of a critical approach to animal studies, one that perceives that relations between human and nonhuman animals are now at a point of crisis implicating the planet as a whole. This dire situation is evident most dramatically in the

> intensified slaughter and exploitation of animals (who die by the tens of billions each year in the United States alone); the unfolding of the sixth great extinction crisis in the history of the planet (the last one being 65 million years ago); and the monumental environmental ecological threats of global warming, rainforest destruction, desertification, air and water pollution, and resource scarcity, to which animal agriculture is a prime contributor. (p. 4)

In contra-distinction, "mainstream" animal studies was characterized by Best and colleagues (2007) as

> an abstract, esoteric, jargon-laden, insular, non-normative, and apolitical discipline, one where scholars can achieve recognition while nevertheless remaining wedded to speciesist values, carnivorist lifestyles, and at least tacit—sometimes overt—support of numerous forms of animal exploitation. (p. 4)

Dismantling traditional hierarchies and boundaries among academic-activist policy making and wider communities, the burgeoning field of CAS has been both extensive and impressive in depth and content. Within diverse bodies of literature, there has been a focus on problematizing anti-specialist praxis by harnessing intersectional studies to challenge the multiple overlapping sites of oppression that are relevant to better understanding both human and nonhuman animal conditions. In recent years, research that has brought to the surface significant intersections have emerged from inter- and cross-disciplinary contributions from a range of angles, including ecofeminism, queer theory (Grubbs, 2012), disability studies, feminist critical race studies, and sentience studies. Exploring and understanding the common roots of oppression is important for many reasons. Anarchist Brian Dominick, in his influential pamphlet *Animal Liberation and Social Revolution* (1997), argued that "the more we recognize the commonality and interdependence of our struggles, which we once considered quite distinguished from one another, the more we understand what liberation really means" (p. 5).

Ah! Anarchism: though a long-held source of inspiration in both vision (a reverence for all life) and organization (not least evidenced by a strong commitment to decentralized and leaderless internal structures) for several animal liberation activist communities and groups, most notably the Animal Liberation Front, there exists some gaping anarchist-shaped holes in the literature that seeks to critically analyze and explore the role of capital and the state (through political economy) in the context of interspecies modes of exploitation and domination in contemporary society. To give just one illustration of this, the recently published and much welcomed book *An Introduction to Animals and Political Theory* focused on the "the question of how political communities ought to govern their relations with non-human animals" (Cochrane, 2010, p. 1). Here the most prominent schools in contemporary political theory—utilitarianism, liberalism, communitarianism, Marxism, and feminism—were used to explore questions of justice and ethics. However, anarchist (political) praxis was not deemed important enough to even merit a footnote. There are, of course, some notable exceptions to this dearth of such critical analyses (see Bookchin, 1980; Dominick, 1997; Torres, 2007) that have utilized pluralistic anarchist and ecological critiques to underpin a range of detailed, persuasive arguments about the broad nature of domination, power, and hierarchy.

Anarchism and Domination

Attempts to capture a definite, neatly packaged reading of anarchism are futile. As Iain McKay (2008) observes:

> Anarchism is a socio-economic and political theory, but not an ideology. The difference is very important. Basically, theory means you have ideas; an ideology means ideas have you. Anarchism is a body of ideas, but they are flexible, in a constant state of evolution and flux, and open to modification in light of new data. (p. 18)

That said, there is a naturally a broad range of common qualities embedded in anarchist praxis, not least of which is the interrogation of power relations and, where these are found to be unjust and unsupportable, a commitment to confronting and dismantling them. This has led to an almost exclusive focus on the state as the culprit for all that ails society. In some cases, this misunderstanding has arisen due to influential anarchists proposing a rather narrow reading of what anarchists are/ anarchism is. George Woodcock (1986), for example, argued that "anarchism is the doctrine which contends that government is the source of most of our social troubles . . . and by further definition, the anarchist is the man (sic) who sets out to create a society without government" (p. 11). While this is a suitable definition, we feel that it lacks inclusivity.

Consequently, we encourage a more complete, "thicker" definition of anarchism, one that understands that "anarchist thought has mobilised not only around opposition to the state and capitalism, but in opposition to all forms of external authority and thus all forms of domination" (White & Williams, 2012, p. 1629). At all times, however, and particularly in any critical discussion of humans and other animals, it is fundamental to acknowledge that, as Wieck (1971) argues: "Anarchists have always insisted on the priority of life and action to theory and system" (p. 10). It is this unconditional respect for life and the intense hatred of violence, exploitation, and injustice—particularly when exacted upon the most defenseless and innocent—that burns brightly at the core of anarchism. Baldelli (1971) illustrates this wonderfully:

> Anarchism is a purity of rebellion. A pig who struggles wildly and rends the air with his cries while he is held to be slaughtered, and a baby who kicks and screams when, wanting warmth and his mother's breast, he is made to wait in the cold—these are two samples of natural rebellion. Natural rebellion always inspires either deep sympathy and identification with the rebelling creature, or a stiffening of the heart and an activation of aggressive-defensive mechanisms to silence an accusing truth. This truth is that each living being is an end in itself; that nothing gives a being the right to make another a mere instrument of his purposes. The rebel against authority holds to this truth everything that concerns him and recognizes no other judge than himself (sic). (p. 17)

The radical, but logical, juxtaposition contained in this quote at once emphasizes the connected experiences and speaks of natures that unite humans and nonhuman animals. The commonality and overlap in the face of suffering and violence is one that has been emphasized repeatedly by some of the key thinkers and visionaries of anarchism; hence, the importance of intersectionality was acknowledged long before the term was conceived. Given this "purity of rebellion," it is particularly disappointing to note the lack of consideration of the animal condition within the corpus of anarchist writings. This disappointing lack of acknowledgment has been captured by Socha (2011) when she argues that a "proper contemplation of anarchist traditions leads to concern for animals. Can a society whose abiding objective is freedom from violence, hierarchy, and oppression confine, slaughter, dominate, eat and wear other sentient creatures?" (p. 15). The answer, although it seems self-evident to those attuned to the animal condition, goes ignored and unspoken by the average human being, even those who are part of the animal turn in academia.

To begin to address this lacuna here, we want to now appeal to two individuals in particular—Peter Kropotkin and (especially) Élisée Reclus—to highlight the importance of those anarchists who have incorporated nonhuman animals into their critiques of power, ethics, and (human) nature. Reclus is particularly important for emphasizing the direct lessons that we can draw from the way in which we view and engage with nonhuman animals, and more important, how these relationships can be meaningfully transformed ("become beautiful") by appealing to our own agency and choice in everyday decisions and actions.

Anarchism and the Nonhuman in Kropotkin and Reclus

The body of work left by key anarchist figures such as the geographers Kropotkin and Reclus continue to enjoy well-deserved recognition and influence in terms of their critiques of the market and the state. Less acknowledgment and attention, however, has been paid toward their writings that reposition humans as being a part of, rather than apart from, nature; and both observe commonalities between human and animal communities.

In his most celebrated work *Mutual Aid*, Kropotkin (1998/1901) noted how few animal species exist by directly competing with each other compared to the numbers who practice "mutual aid," and that those who do are likely to experience the best evolutionary prospects:

> Wherever I saw animal life in abundance, as, for instance, on the lakes where scores of species and millions of individuals came together to rear their progeny; in the colonies of rodents; in the migrations of birds which took place at that time on a truly American scale along the Usuri; and especially in a migration of fallow-deer which I witnessed on the Amur, and during which scores of thousands of these intelligent animals came together from an immense territory, flying before the coming deep snow, in order to cross the Amur where it is narrowest—in all these scenes of animal life which passed before my eyes, I saw Mutual Aid and Mutual Support carried on to an extent which made me suspect in it a feature of the greatest importance for the maintenance of life, the preservation of each species, and its further evolution. (p. 18)

It is unlikely, he continues to argue, that humans, "a creature so defenceless . . . at his beginnings should have flourished so successfully without co-operation" (p. 74). Thus sociability is inherent in the success of humans as a species. Drawing upon the work of anthropologists, Charles Darwin's observations, and his own examination of nonhuman animal sociality, Kropotkin argued that from the earliest times, humans were social rather than individualistic and that they are dependent on "the support they found in their surroundings" (p. 154). The evolutionary narrative that Kropotkin weaves through his empirical investigation is not one of a path toward fixed things, but a process of relationships. Species is not a fixed taxonomy but about the recognition of what Darwin called "differentiations." Mutual aid is an organizing force across a range of species, as a "factor of evolution" that enables species, including humans, to flourish. As Marshall (2010) notes, anarchists "consider society to be a self-regulating order which develops best when least interfered with" (p. 13), and this order, for Kropotkin, is not exclusive to the human animal.

While Kropotkin's key contribution is the notion of humans as embedded in relationships with other species, and as animals among many others, Reclus provides a more explicit challenge in terms of the need to confront the animal question as intrinsic to anarchist projects. In this and in countless other ways, Reclus's ethical maturity and clear sightedness clashed directly with the conservative and deeply speciesist moral codes of the society in which he lived:

> An area in which Reclus was far in advance of his time, and in which he anticipated current debate in eco-philosophy and environmental ethics, is his effort to raise both ethical and ecological issues concerning our treatment of other species. His ideas are important in view of the fact that he was not only a pioneer in ecological philosophy but also an early advocate of the humane treatment of animals and of ethical vegetarianism. (Clark & Martin, 2004, p. 33)

It is important to note that it is highly probable that Reclus did eat a vegan diet but referred to it as vegetarianism. As Wrenn (2011) notes: "Historically, the Western vegetarian movement did generally eschew the consumption of all nonhuman animal products . . . and the modern vegan movement was initiated with the establishment of The Vegan Society in Britain in 1944" (p. 16). Writing in the first issue of the *Vegan News*, Donald Watson (1944), cofounder of the UK Vegan Society, argued:

> The unquestionable cruelty associated with the production of dairy produce has made it clear that lacto-vegetarianism is but a half-way house between flesh-eating and a truly humane, civilized diet, and we think, therefore, that during our life on earth we should try to evolve sufficiently to make the "full journey." (p. 1)

Certainly an appropriate and consistent moral baseline emerging from a critical (anarchist) understanding of the exploitation of nonhuman animals in contemporary society would advocate for veganism rather than vegetarianism.

When one seeks to understand how Reclus attempts to raise human consciousness toward nonhuman animals, what becomes particularly interesting and important is the way in which he doesn't appeal directly to the language of rights, but rather encourages personal, subjective, and emotional connections to be made by the reader. In "On Vegetarianism," for example, Reclus appeals to overcome exploitation of nonhuman animals by appealing first to his reader's emotional registers, rather than developing an argument based on so-called rational, scientific calculus (rights-based theory, etc.). In doing so, Reclus appeals to the individual, as the site of contest and action, to act differently. The root causes of violence and domination are not solely "out there" in wider society. Our use of nonhuman animals teaches us many (un)comfortable truths about ourselves and of those whom we identify in society. What is also striking is that the central arguments here are founded on personal and intimate reflections, which strike the heart of the reader far more effectively and intensely than by appealing to the more abstract, quantified statistics of untimely death involving billions of nonhuman animals, an argument that we argued above. By illustration, Reclus (1901) offers this reflection:

> Other pictures cast their shadows over my childish years, and, like that glimpse of the slaughter-house, mark so many epochs in my life. I can see the sow belonging to some peasants, amateur butchers, and therefore all the more cruel. I remember one of them bleeding the animal slowly, so that the blood fell drop by drop; for, in order to make really good black puddings, it appears essential that the victim should have suffered proportionately. She cried without ceasing, now and then uttering groans and sounds of despair almost human; it seemed like listening to a child. And in fact the domesticated pig is for a year or so a child of the house; pampered that he may grow fat, and returning a sincere affection for all the care lavished on him, which has but one aim—so many inches of bacon. But when the affection is reciprocated by the good woman who takes care of the

pig, fondling him and speaking in terms of endearment to him, is she not considered ridiculous—as if it were absurd, even degrading, to love an animal that loves us? (p. 1)

The crux of Reclus's approach is not to appeal to impersonal quantitative and aggregated spaces of species abuse with which to illustrate this suffering. Rather, he seeks to personalize the encounter in such a way that encourages the reader to empathize closely with the memory, while also (hopefully) reflecting meaningfully on their individual experiences of similar examples of horrors—of the massacres that are "the primary condition of our daily food" (p. 2) and revealed by the "petty incidents of life" (p. 2), be they in private spaces (the slaughterhouse) or public: "Butchers display before the eyes of the public, even in the most frequented streets, disjointed carcasses, gory lumps of meat, and think to conciliate our estheticism by boldly decorating the flesh they hang out with garlands of roses!" (p. 3). Undoubtedly, Reclus's (distressing) childhood experiences and encounters of (violent) human-nonhuman animal encounters (e.g., Reclus talks about fainting at the sight of the blood dripping from an enormous carcass on the slaughterhouse yard) encouraged a more complex, richer, and nuanced reading of the human condition to emerge. This is no accident, which becomes obvious when we pay attention to the organization of contemporary spaces and the positioning of those places where animal (ab)use occurs. In so many words, "out of sight means out of mind"; in contemporary Western culture, these spaces of violence and suffering are regularly hidden from the public's view. Such a deliberate spatial separation, as Adams (1990) argues, furthers dissolves any concern or identity with other consumable "food" animals:

> The action of fragmentation, the killing, and the dividing is elided. Indeed patriarchal culture surrounds actual butchering with silence. Geographically, slaughterhouses are cloistered. We do not see or hear what transpires there . . . the knowledge that the slaughterhouse offers is knowledge we do not want to know. (p. 49)

For most people, their experience of animal corpses will not be displayed in butcher shop windows, but rather becomes further broken down, sanitized, and displayed as neatly cellophane-wrapped lumps of flesh in their supermarket's refrigerator section.

Important, by intending to similarly provoke the reader to undergo a critical (and more disturbing) process of questioning, of consciousness-raising, Reclus also allows for the possibility that the individual is capable of making different (moral) choices: to celebrate beauty and reject ugliness in (their) relations with nonhuman animals and transform their actions and attitudes to these ends. This acknowledgment of agency is tremendously important in many ways, not least of which is it legitimizes the multiple micro-spaces of power that can be utilized to influence society constructively from the bottom up, rather than unnecessarily externalize the engines of change by rarifying them as the preserve of either "the state" or "the market."

"Is it Vegan?": Intersectionality, Feminist Politics, and Everyday Life as Models for Liberation

For Dominick (1997), "Only a perspective and lifestyle based on true compassion can destroy the oppressive constructs of present society . . . This to me is the essence of anarchy" (p. 17). Yet the idea of a compassionate lifestyle has often been dismissed as nonpolitical, consumerist, or bourgeois, a series of everyday practices that are not clearly embedded in challenging systemic dominations. Here, we suggest that this separation of the micro-politics of everyday living from the apparently macro-politics of contestation associated with social movements is a false distinction. Rather, daily lives involve continuous decisions that form part of challenges to multiple and overlapping systems of domination.

An example of such a critique can be found in the work of the social ecologism of Murray Bookchin, who has taken forward the anarchist concern with nonhuman life expressed by Kropotkin and foregrounded in Reclus. Bookchin (1980, 1991/1982) has written extensively about the linked dominations of humans based on different kinds of socially constituted hierarchy (race, age, gender, class, caste, wealth, and so on) with the domination of the nonhuman lifeworld. But while Bookchin does account of a wide range of interlinked forms of social domination, he is scathing of a politics that emphasizes lifestyle or personal transformation, seeing this as antithetical to sustained collective resistance and protest against injustice. He dismisses "deep ecology" as "wilderness reverence" and ecological feminism as essentialist. Both these ecologies are understood to be tainted by mysticism (1991/1982, pp. xv–xix). "Mystical ecologies," as he puts it, are open to incorporation into commoditization and are ill placed to challenge the commodification of human and other natures. Bookchin's insistence on a political ecologism that challenges capitalism is admirable, yet his caricatures of other ecologisms are inaccurate. For example, to reduce ecofeminism to a position that glorifies motherhood and celebrates feminist witchcraft is wholly unreflective of the range and breadth of ecofeminist theorizing and concerns (see Cudworth, 2005). Further, Bookchin's depoliticizing of the politics of everyday life is at odds with the ideas of other left or anarchist writers and activists (see Vaneigem, 2003/1967) and an anathema to the theories and practical politics of feminism and its insistence about the false dichotomy of personal and public worlds (Fraser, 1989).

The questioning of linked forms of social domination has a long legacy in postcolonial and feminist theory, and in particular in ecofeminist work (Alaimo, 2000). Bookchin uses an overarching notion of hierarchy to discuss different kinds of domination but in his account, the forms of domination run in parallel, emerging at different times. Feminist work has often focused, however, on the relationships between and across different kinds of social domination. Some of those attempting to understand the cross-cutting of multiple social inequalities with gender have used the term "intersectionality" to emphasize the ways social differences and dominations are mutually constitutive. The social effects of, for example, race and gender are not simply an overlapping of inequalities. Gender relations, through intersection, change the very properties of race (McCall, 2005). While the term "intersectionality" emerged from Black feminism in the United States (Crenshaw, 1991), this focus on multiple inequalities and forms of social domination has been a characteristic of socialist feminist writing (Walby, 1990, 2009) as well as ecofeminism (Cuomo, 1998; Sturgeon, 2009). Certainly, feminists, particularly ecological ones, have made links between the intersected oppressions of humans and the oppression of the rest of the animal world (Adams, 1990; Gaard, 1993; Plumwood, 2004). An important characteristic of feminist politics has been the linking of everyday practices to political awareness and mobilization. As the well-known British feminist sociologist Ann Oakley puts it:

> Feminist defences of animals and attacks on "corpse eaters" are tied to the principle of accountability for what we do to others bodies . . . Some 80 per cent of animal rights and environmental campaigners are women . . . Research on environmentalism suggests that a sense of community with others may be nearly as important as concern over the biosphere in generating environmentalist politics. Caring *about* follows from caring for: caring labour and emotional connection are intimately related. (2002, p. 134)

In the UK, the largest all-women political campaign to arise since the suffrage movement occurred just prior to the outbreak of war in 1914 and was generated by women protesting against the upgrading of Britain's nuclear "deterrent" in the form of the Women's Peace Camp at Greenham Common, in Berkshire. The camp lasted from 1981 to 2000 with campers facing evictions, arrests, charges of criminal damage and trespass, local opposition, and vigilante attacks, alongside the inclement English weather. Sasha Roseneil (1995) has suggested that while not feminist in inception, the all-women protest camp became increasingly embedded in feminist politics over time and drew on a range of tactics of protest and contestation. As important as these were, what Roseneil calls the "internal mode of action" of the camp was key to its longevity and the radical nature of its challenge. This was characterized by redefining "domestic tasks," everyday challenges to patriarchal normativity, and the practices of shared decision making.

In the feminist space of Greenham, the ethos of nonviolence implied that no meat would be eaten, cooked, or brought to camp, and many of the campsites (situated at the various gates of the Greenham air force base) were also vegan rather than vegetarian. Gifts of food for the campers were greeted with a recurring question: "Is it vegan?" Here the politics of everyday life are a crucial element of the praxis of contestation, and there is no separating the individual or lifestyle politics of abstention from the consumption of food derived from nonhuman animals and the protest against militarism and nuclearism.

Challenging Systems of Domination by Becoming Beautiful

When contemplating effective and appropriate strategies for change, it is important that the means and the ends are consistent. For example, a future anarchist world based on the principles of nonviolence must strive wherever possible and appropriate to ensure that these principles are deeply embedded in the means to these ends. As Baldelli (1971) remarked:

> The tree is known by its fruit but the so-called ends of political organizations and movements seem never to manage to ripen. Let the tree be judged then, by what it feeds upon, the so-called means. To say that the end justifies the means is to acknowledge that the means, judged separately, are unjust . . . What will not be permissible tomorrow is permitted today in order that it is not permissible tomorrow. This is to declare today's humanity in some way inferior to tomorrow's, and to burden the latter with a debt of gratitude unasked for and more likely to be cursed than blessed. (pp. 19–20)

While the notion of "becoming the change you wish to see in the world," as Mohandas Gandhi famously stated, is very much present in the writings of those such as Gustav Landauer, it has been an important element of anarchist thinkers outside the West. For Gandhi, political means were key to challenging forms of domination for they are "ends in the making." Gandhi constantly emphasized the extent to which nonviolent resistance—or *satyagraha* (see Sharp, 1979)—was essential for the realization of political transformation (Bondurant, 1959). The realization of Gandhi's (1954) stateless society (based on communal ownership and village decision making in local federations of village organizations) was the goal of the Sarvodaya movement of "gentle anarchists" after Gandhi's death (Ostergaard & Currell, 1971; Ostergaard, 1985). Geoffrey Ostergaard (1989) notes that Gandhian anarchism extends the notion of community beyond the human to nonhuman animals, and in Gandhi's view, abstention from eating animals and animal products was part of the means to the realization of freedom (or self-governance, as he would have preferred).

This chapter has sought to impress on the reader the notion that change is something that can—indeed, *must*—begin by questioning the relationships that the individual has with nonhuman animals. Where these relationships are exploitative and life-denying rather than life-affirming, they must be addressed by the deliberate, alternative actions of that individual. In the context of "normalized" animal exploitation and (ab)use, this activism could easily become embedded in the regular and the everyday; this means not simply in consumer choices (what to eat, to drink, to wear) or decisions about which animal rights organizations to support, but also in more active, deliberate, and positive forms of engagement such as regularly volunteering at local animal sanctuaries, drawing attention to spaces of animal abuse through public demonstrations, or participation in events challenging animal abuse directly (i.e., joining the local hunt saboteurs out in the field). Important, the urgent need to transform existing relationships of domination is also encouraged by focusing on change at the individual level. As Tom Cahill (1989) argues, "The anarchist sees the question of change as an immediate one, not something to be postponed until practical pressing matters are dealt with in an effective, but amoral, way" (p. 235).

Toward the end of *Animal Like Us*, philosopher Mark Rowlands (2002) discusses several varieties of animal rights activism (pp. 177–178), many of which are directly relevant to the message of "taking it to the streets." He argues that the most immediate and direct way to act on a street-level is for individuals to strive to make the necessary lifestyle changes where nonhuman animals are concerned. These changes must be consistent with one's conscience and actively promote an ethics of nonviolence. Embracing veganism is a huge step in that direction, as is becoming educated about animal rights issues and talking publicly about them. However, these changes in themselves are not enough. A greater intersectional consciousness should also be recognized in action, one that acknowledges the multiple forms of oppression and where the individual takes pro-active steps to avoid "fuel(ing) the fires of other injustices" (Kemmerer, 2011 p. 4).

Rowlands also considers a third category of activism: direct action through civil disobedience. Civil disobedience can, and has repeatedly been, a powerful weapon to provoke wider social change. From the anarchist perspective, as has been argued, it is important that the means and the ends are consistent, and that all nonviolent strategies of resistance have been considered and harnessed wherever possible and appropriate. Rowlands (2002) considers more extreme forms of civil disobedience in turn and develops a powerful conclusion to this consideration:

> Many of the positive actions we can take on behalf of animals are morally legitimate even if they are illegal, because the laws that they flout are fundamentally unjust. *Acts of rescue* should be distinguished from *attempts to change society*. Acts of rescue can justifiably involve violence, but only if this is necessary for self-defense and proportionate to the violence used against you. Animal rights terrorism, however, the most extreme form of animal rights activism, is not morally acceptable. Extreme acts such as these are best understood as attempts to change society, since they would be ineffective as acts of rescue. But, as attempts to change society, their use of violence is morally wrong. (p. 194)

Rowlands's thoughts about violence and the distinction between acts of rescue and attempts to change society in this context are interesting but perhaps can be applied more consistently in some contexts than others. For example, feminists working with domestic violence at a women's rescue shelter would say rescue is absolutely political and about changing society. Providing safe spaces for women and children is not separable from challenging the legitimacy of violence used in the home.

In the area of animal rescue, however, the waters are muddier. In the UK, for example, those working in companion animal rescue would usually say their work is nonpolitical, as they are focused on the enforcement of existing animal protection laws, while those rescuing laboratory animals understand their actions are founded upon law breaking and political liberation. For Ghandian Sarvodaya activists, or for the peace protesters at Greenham Common, there is no separation between ends and means, the public and the private, everyday acts of resistance and forms of public civil disobedience. In both cases, nonviolence was both the means and the "ends-in-the-making." Where nonhuman animals are concerned, a world must surely be overturned and/but this transformation begins with us, in the spaces and places of our communities.

Conclusions: Becoming Beautiful, Becoming Active

Animal liberation is human liberation. This chapter has sought to emphasize the immense solidarity that underpins life—human and nonhuman—and encourage a personal interpretation of animal abuse that is identifiable, qualitative, and real by arguing that this needs to be contextualized and situated not in the abstract and quantitative world of statistics, but instead in the individual, the community, and the everyday rituals and practices that underpin the individual with important ethical choices to make.

This focus has many important implications, but we have highlighted three in particular. First, the individual is a necessary and important site of transformative power that must be utilized to confront the interlocking nature of systems of power, abuse, and domination that underpin humans and animals in society. The second proposition is that change must begin now, as the Earth is locked into a potentially catastrophic series of interconnected crises. Every second counts, just as every life counts. There can be no more postponing to another day a revolution in our attitudes toward nonhuman animals. As Best (2011) writes,

> If every moment is pregnant with revolution, this is an especially pivotal time in history, a crossroads for the future of life. As the social and ecological crisis deepens, with capitalism surging, species vanishing, oceans dying, resources diminishing, and the catastrophic effects of global climate change now immanent and irreversible, windows of reasonable political opportunity for the production of an alternative social order are rapidly closing. The actions that humanity now collectively makes or fails to take will determine whether the future is more hopeful or altogether bleak. (pp. xxiii–xxiv)

Acknowledging the interconnection of Earth, human, and nonhuman animal liberation, Reclus's (1901) demand is universally held for those who want to live in a beautiful anarchist world of nonviolence, justice, and empowerment for all:

> We no longer want to hear the bleating of sheep, the bellowing of bullocks, the groans and piercing shrieks of the pigs, as they are led to the slaughter. We aspire to the time when we shall not have to walk swiftly to shorten that hideous minute of passing the haunts of butchery with their rivulets of blood and rows of sharp hooks, whereon carcasses are hung up by blood-stained men, armed with horrible knives. We want some day to live in a city where we shall no longer see butchers' shops full of dead bodies side by side with drapers' or jewellers,' and facing a druggist's, or hard by a window filled with choice fruits, or with beautiful books, engravings or statuettes, and works of art. We want an environment pleasant to the eye and in harmony with beauty. (p. 5)

We owe this to our fellow earthlings, and ourselves, as well as future generations who stand to inherit this beautiful and magnificent Earth.

Finally, thinking constructively about decentralized bottom-up strategies of resistance, there are many exciting possibilities of praxis that are being—and waiting to be—enacted in the everyday. In terms of academic-activism, while writing "can function as critical direct action though its close attention to the present" (Thrift, 2005, p. 11), there are very real limits and constraints that the (so-called) activist in the academy faces. Wherever possible, the radical academics, anarchist or otherwise, must invest considerable time and resources into integrating themselves beyond the academy and into the streets by working collaboratively and actively with others. This will hopefully result in new and stronger bridges that can connect activist, educational, policy making, and broader public communities, which in turn will potentially realize new spaces of hope for the urgent action that must be harnessed to effectively change and overcome dominate-submissive relationships between humans and nonhuman animals. Having argued that the act of writing can only go so far, the intention of this chapter has been to do more than expand the body of animal liberationist–anarchist writing but to take it to the streets. If this chapter has helped provoke new ideas between writing and activism through raising consciousness, suggesting new connections, and inspiring constructive ideas that can be meaningfully perceived and engaged (by the individual) then it will have made a small but important and necessary contribution.

References

Adams, C. J. (1990). *The sexual politics of meat*. Cambridge: Polity.
Alaimo, S. (2000). *Undomesticated ground: Recasting nature as feminist space*. Ithaca: Cornell University Press.
Baldelli, G. (1971). *Social anarchism*. Harmondsworth: Penguin.
Best, S. (2011). Introduction. Pathologies of power and the rise of the global industrial complex. In S. Best, R. Kahn, A. J. Nocella II, & P. McLaren (Eds.), *The global industrial complex: Systems of domination* (pp. ix–xxv). Plymouth: Lexington.
Best, S., Nocella, A. J., Kahn, R., Gigliotti, C., & Kemmerer, L. (2007). Introducing critical animal studies. *Journal for Critical Animal Studies, 5*(1), 4–5.
Bookchin, M. (1991/1982). *The ecology of freedom: The emergence and dissolution of hierarchy*. Montreal: Black Rose.

Bookchin, M. (1980). *Towards an ecological society*. Montreal: Black Rose.
Bondurant, J. (1959). *The conquest of violence: The Gandhian philosophy of conflict*. Oxford: Oxford University Press.
Cahill, T. (1989). Co-operatives and anarchism: A contemporary perspective. In D. Goodway (Ed.), *For anarchism: History, theory, and practice* (pp. 235–358). London: Routledge.
Clark, J. P., & Martin, C. (2004). *Anarchy, geography, modernity: The radical social thought of Élisée Reclus*. Oxford: Lexington.
Cochrane, A. (2010). *An introduction to animals and political theory*. Basingstoke: Palgrave.
Crenshaw, K. W. (1991). Mapping the margins: Intersectionality, identity politics, and violence against women of colour. *Stanford Law Review, 43*(6), 1241–1299.
Cudworth, E. (2005). *Developing ecofeminist theory: The complexity of difference*. Basingstoke: Palgrave.
Cuomo, C. (1998). *Feminism and ecological communities: An ethic of flourishing*. London: Routledge.
Dominick, B. A. (1997). *Animal liberation and social revolution: A vegan perspective on anarchism or an anarchist perspective on veganism*. Baltimore: Firestarter. Retrieved from http://zinelibrary.info/files/animalandrevolution.pdf
Food and Agriculture Organization of the United Nations. (2002). World agriculture: Towards 2015/2030: Summary report. Retrieved from ftp://ftp.fao.org/docrep/fao/004/y3557e/y3557e.pdf
Fraser, N. (1989). *Unruly practices: Power, discourse and gender in contemporary social theory*. Cambridge: Polity.
Gaard, G. (1993). Living interconnections with animals and nature. In G. Gaard (Ed.), *Ecofeminism: Women, animals, nature* (pp. 1–12). Philadelphia: Temple University Press.
Gandhi, M. K. (1954). *Sarvodaya*. Ahmedabad: Navajivan.
Grubbs, J. (2012). Guest editorial: Queering the que(e)ry of speciesism. *Journal for Critical Animal Studies, 10*(3), 4–6.
Home Office. (2012). Statistics of scientific procedures on living animals, Great Britain 2011. Retrieved from http://www.homeoffice.gov.uk/publications/science-research-statistics/research-statistics/other-science-research/spanimals11/spanimals11snr?view=Binary
Kemmerer, L. (2011). Introduction. In L. Kemmerer (Ed.), *Sister species: Women, animals and social justice* (pp. 1–43). Chicago: University of Illinois Press.
Kropotkin, P. (1998/1901). *Mutual aid: A factor of evolution*. London: Freedom.
Kropotkin, P. (1987). *The state: Its historic role*. London: Freedom.
Landauer, G. (2010/1895). Anarchism-socialism. In G. Kuhn (Ed.), *Revolution and other writings: A political reader* (pp. 70–74). Oakland, CA: PM.
Landauer, G. (2010/1909). The party. In G. Kuhn (Ed.), *Revolution and other writings: A political reader* (pp. 206–212). Oakland, CA: PM.
Marshall, D. (2010). *Demanding the impossible: A history of anarchism*. Oakland, CA: PM.
McCall, L. (2005). The complexity of intersectionality. *Signs, 30*(3), 171–180.
McKay, I. (2008). *An anarchist FAQ: Vol. 1*. Edinburgh: AK.
Mitchell, L. (2011). Moral disengagement and support for nonhuman animal farming. *Society & Animals, 19*, 38–58. Retrieved from http://www.animalsandsociety.org/assets/462_mitchellsa.pdf
Oakley, A. (2002). *Gender on planet earth*. Cambridge: Polity.
Ostergaard, G. (1989). Indian anarchism: The curious case of Vinoba Bhave, anarchist "saint of the government." In D. Goodway (Ed.), *For anarchism* (pp. 201–216). London: Routledge.
Ostergaard, G. (1985). *Non-violent revolution in India*. New Delhi: Gandhi Peace Foundation.
Ostergaard, G., & Currell, M. (1971). *The gentle anarchists*. Oxford: Clarendon.

Pedersen, H., & Stănescu, V. (2011). Series editor's introduction: What is "critical" about animal studies? From the animal "question" to the animal "condition." In K. Socha (Ed.), *Women, destruction, and the avant-garde: A paradigm for animal liberation* (pp. ix–xi). Amsterdam: Rodopi.

Plumwood, V. (2004). Ecofeminism. In R. White (Ed.), *Controversies in environmental sociology* (pp. 43–60). Cambridge: Cambridge University Press.

Reclus, É. (1901). On vegetarianism. Retrieved from http://theanarchistlibrary.org/library/Élisée-reclus-on-vegetarianism.pdf

Roseneil, S. (1995). *Disarming patriarchy: Feminism and political action at Greenham*. Milton Keynes, UK: Open University Press.

Rowlands, M. (2002). *Animals like us*. London: Verso.

Sharp, G. (1979). *Gandhi as a political strategist*. Boston: Porter Sargent.

Springer, S., Ince, A., Picerill, J., Brown, G., & Barker, A. J. (2012). Reanimating anarchist geographies: A new burst of colour. *Antipode, 44*(5), 1591–1604.

Socha, K. (2011). *Women, destruction, and the avant-garde: A paradigm for animal liberation*. Amsterdam: Rodopi.

Sturgeon, N. (2009). *Environmentalism and popular culture: Gender, race, sexuality and the politics of the natural*. Tempe: University of Arizona Press.

Thrift, N. (2005). *Knowing capitalism*. London: Sage.

Torres, B. (2007). *Making a killing: The political economy of animal rights*. Edinburgh: AK.

Vaneigem, R. (2003/1967). *The revolution of everyday life* (D. Nicholson Smith, Trans.). London: Rebel.

Walby, S. (2009) *Globalization and inequalities: Complexity and contested modernities*. London: Sage.

Walby, S. (1990). *Theorizing patriarchy*. Oxford: Basil Blackwell.

Watson, D. (1944). *Vegan News, 1*. Retrieved at http://www.ukveggie.com/vegan_news/

Wheller, W., & Williams, L. (2012). *The Animals Turn*. Retrieved from http://www.lwbooks.co.uk/journals/newformations/pdfs/76_intro.pdf

White, R. J., & Williams, C.C. (2012). The pervasive nature of heterodox economic spaces at a time of neoliberal crisis: Towards a "postneoliberal" anarchist future. *Antipode, 44*(5), 1625–1644.

Wieck, D. (1971). Preface. In G. Baldelli, *Social anarchism* (p. 9). Harmondsworth: Penguin.

Woodcock, G. (1986). Anarchism: A historical introduction. In G. Woodcock (Ed.), *The anarchist reader* (pp. 11–56). Glasgow: Fontana.

Wrenn, C. (2011). Resisting the globalization of speciesism: Vegan abolitionism as a site for consumer-based social change. *Journal for Critical Animal Studies, 9*(3), 9–27.

AFTERWORD

From Animal Oppression to Animal Liberation

A Historical Reflection and the Growth of Critical Animal Studies

Karen Davis

After we met as hunt saboteurs in the mid-1980s, I had a conversation with a fellow animal rights activist who said, "Ten years ago when I started doing this, I thought we'd end sport hunting in no time. I thought reason would prevail. It seemed so obvious." Likewise, philosopher Peter Singer, whose 1975 book *Animal Liberation* sparked the modern animal rights movement, told a group of us in the 1990s that in the early 1970s when he was working on the book, "My expectation ranged all the way from having mass support for goals such as getting rid of factory farming. But that hasn't happened."

Decades later, our campaigns against factory farming and sport hunting continue, along with all of our other campaigns to liberate nonhuman animals from human oppression. We stopped the Hegins Pigeon Shoot in Pennsylvania in the 1990s, but Pennsylvania gun clubs continue to round up and shoot tens of thousands of pigeons each year purely for fun. Thus far, efforts to prohibit these sadistic massacres have failed in the state legislature even though pigeon shoots are illegal under the state anticruelty law. The 7.5 billion chickens slaughtered annually for food in the United States in the mid-1990s has climbed to 9 billion, and analysts predict that the number of farm animals slaughtered on a global scale each year could double from 65 billion to more than 100 billion animals by 2050 (Davis, 2009, p. v). We may have reduced the number of nonhuman primates used in laboratory experiments, but the numbers of equally sentient birds, rats, and mice (and countless other species) experimented on in laboratories around the world are astronomical, as are the megatons of fish pulled traumatically from their water homes for sport and consumption every single day. It can be difficult for even the most dedicated animal rights advocate to bear constantly in mind the fact that each and every one of these billions of anonymous beings is an individual who is experiencing his or her own life as intimately as each of us experiences our own individual existence. Animal liberationists must never forget this fact. We must do everything possible to inscribe it in society's consciousness through all of the avenues of teaching and advocating available to us. One of those avenues arose in the early 2000s: critical animal studies (CAS). CAS was developed by academic-activists who critiqued the oppression of nonhumans as victims within higher education, most especially in research labs. Its founders demanded a more holistic approach to understanding nonhuman animal oppression by finding roots of solidarity with human-focused groups such as the Black Panther Party and the American Indian Movement. Since their creation, I strongly supported both CAS and the Institute for Critical Animal Studies (ICAS) because I believed in (1) the mission of the field and organization and (2) in the foundational text, *Terrorists or Freedom Fighters? Reflections on the Liberation of Animals* (Best & Nocella, 2004). In turn, ICAS has supported my work by always inviting me to their conferences and also awarding me in 2009 the book of the year for *Prisoned Chickens: Poisoned Eggs*. In the early 1980s, that is not where I saw the movement going—indeed, we thought that animal abuses would rapidly decline. I did not foresee the animal rights–liberation movement drawing from the field of critical race theory to consider how Crenshaw's groundbreaking essay "Mapping the Margins: Intersectionality, Identity Politics, and Violence Against Women of Color" (1991), which explores "the race and gender dimensions of violence against women of color" (p. 1242), would become a foundational work from which animal activists should draw their ideas. CAS made these connections, thereby offering activists and scholars a broader platform for understanding the webbed nature of oppression. There was an energy developing in the animal rights movement that was moving toward intersectionality and to be conscious of more social justice movements. ICAS and those friends of ICAS were the ones really pushing that great energy. In 2007, the United Poultry Concerns (UPC) held its seventh Annual Conference at New York University Law School, which proved to be one of the most intersectional events in the modern day animal rights movement. The Conference on the topic of "Inadmissible Comparisons" asks:

> Can the Holocaust be compared with African American slavery or the Native American genocide? Can any of these experiences be related to those of animals on today's factory farms? Recently, a number of writers and thinkers have sought to draw parallels between the suffering of one group of individuals and another, and incurred the wrath of those who consider their experience unique. This conference explores why such comparisons are offered and asks whether they should or should not be made. It examines the rhetoric and images of those comparisons and the agendas that might lie behind them, while

interrogating the need for comparative thinking in the first place. (United Poultry Concerns, n.p.)

This conference came a year after Ashanti Alston, former Black Panther Party member, and many other radical and revolutionaries spoke at the Institute for Critical Animal Studies conference at Syracuse University. Other speakers at UPC's seventh Annual Conference included Charles Patterson, Carol J. Adams, pattrice jones, Andrea Smith, and Roberta Kalechofsky. Conferences are a great place to build friendships and build new critical ideas, organizations, projects, books, and movements.

Despite new critical pathways such as CAS, many activists understandably become consumed with rage and despair. Activists grow exhausted and burn out, confronted with the never-ending horror, day in day out, of our species' relentless assault on other species, our own species, and the environment. While I have never burned out, I did drop out once before returning to the animal rights movement for good. In 1974, I joined a tour to the Magdalen Islands in the Gulf of St. Lawrence that was designed to show islanders and the Canadian government that tourism was a better way to make money from baby harp seals than clubbing them to death for the fur trade and sport. (To this day, the effort to stop the slaughter of the harp seals continues.) What I unexpectedly witnessed on the ice floes off Grindstone Island during that tour caused me to withdraw from further activity for animals for ten years. I felt I could not handle the trauma of reflecting on animal agony at the hands of humans on a daily basis.

This was not the first time I had felt this fear. In college in the 1960s, a similar experience beset me. Having become active on campus in the American civil rights movement, my discoveries about Hitler and Stalin in my history classes—of whose atrocities I had learned nothing in high school—led to an obsession so overwhelming that I had to drop out of school, unable to cope with the knowledge of the human-engineered suffering and death of concentration camp prisoners and slave labor camp victims with whom I identified to the point of requiring psychiatric therapy. The plight of nonhuman animals posed a comparable sanity risk.

That said, one spring day in the early 1980s, I walked anxiously across Lafayette Park in Washington, D.C., in response to a newspaper ad for World Laboratory Animals Day. As I looked at the photographs of animal victims of head transplants and burn experiments, I pledged on the spot that never again would I abandon animals to the iniquity of our species because "I couldn't bear their suffering" (Davis, 2011, pp. 132–136).

Trying to educate people and get them to care about animals in the empathic and ethical way that is needed to end the horror can be psychologically devastating. Animal liberationists are up against attitudes and behaviors that will not yield easily or quickly. For many people, the idea that it is as morally wrong to harm animals intentionally as it is to harm humans intentionally borders on heresy. The idea that animals could suffer unjustly in being forced into unnatural patterns of behavior and condemned to live in inimical conditions imposed by an alien species (ourselves in our fascist aspect) threatens the age-old assumption that nonhuman animals and all things on Earth exist (were made) for us to manipulate as we please. Hostility among human groups is an integral part of human history, but just as feuding individuals and nations come together against a common enemy, so humans unite in defense of human supremacy over all other forms of life. The boundary between human and animal is inviolable (Davis, 2005, p. 2). I believe that my conclusion mirrors the mission and beliefs of the ICAS, with ICAS adding a focus on the environment as a living organism that is sacred as well.

In reality, however, those boundaries between human and animal are continuously blurred, the sanctity of them cast aside. Theriomorphy, in which humans and nonhuman animals are blended, takes many forms. Human and nonhuman animals share a common evolutionary heritage and sentience, and we share many similar and identical interests and behaviors. Meat eaters incorporate animals into themselves by eating them. Human infants' first milk in many parts of the world is from a lactating cow or goat, and many people are theriomorphic as a result of cross-species organ transplantations.

So-called bestiality—sexual relations involving human and nonhuman animals—as Dekkers observes in his book *Dearest Pet: On Bestiality* (1994), is "omnipresent—in art, in science, in history, in our dreams" (p. 5). In myth and religion, animals are frequently employed by the gods to impregnate women. In this regard, Dekkers writes,

> Jesus Christ, himself the Lamb of God, had absolutely no need to be ashamed of his origins, since the dove which had fathered him in Mary was a god as well as a dove. Like the children of Leda and her swan [in Greek mythology], he is at the same time the product of bestiality (man x animal) and of theogamy (god x man). The same ambiguity is found in other religions. (p. 10)

A similar ambiguity appears in Western science. Animals are substituted for humans in biomedical research, which is based on the assumption that other animal species can double for humans as sources of information about the human condition. Inflicting human diseases on nonhuman animals in search of a cure, however modern this may seem, is essentially a type of purification ritual. Through the ages, people have sought consciously or unconsciously to rid themselves of their impurities (diseases, sins, and vices) by symbolically transferring their impurities to sacrificial victims—innocent victims known as scapegoats. Often, these victims are represented as having both human and nonhuman attributes. In Christianity, Jesus is the sacrificial lamb who takes away the sins of the world. In the Hasidic custom of *kaparos* (atonements), adherents transfer their sins and punishments symbolically to chickens, their "doubles," who are then conveniently slaughtered in place of the sinners.

In short, the boundaries we establish, abolish, or redefine, between human and nonhuman animals, are essentially arbitrary and self-serving. Yet, even so, these strongholds and strangleholds of thought are being challenged by the evolving Western philosophic and scientific tradition, and by the growth of animal liberation forces around the world. As has frequently occurred with other liberation movements throughout history, higher education has been one of the areas of fiercest challenge (i.e., most, if not all, research universities have Women's Studies, Critical Race Studies, and Latino/a Studies departments and majors). Today, we now find animal studies—a cross-disciplinary field that, finally, thinks about animal species other than humans—gaining popularity in academia. However, as Pedersen and Stănescu (2011) point out, it is a "mild irony that so much of animal studies is invested in human/animal intersubjectivities and 'encounters' when most nonhuman animals, at least those we have not yet tamed, coerced, or domesticated into docility and dependence, are likely to flee as far away from us as possible if they had a chance" (p. x). In other words, disciplines such as animal studies and human-animal studies are often disengaged with the political repercussions of their fixation on the "animal"; there is no inherent demand in those fields that humans stop eating and wearing nonhumans, at least as a starting point. CAS stands in strong defiance against the face of such uncritical theorizing. As are animal and human-animal studies, I look forward to CAS growing as a discipline in higher education while maintaining its focus on street-level activism as well.

Outside the academy, modern experiences and the advancing sciences of animal cognition and ethology are causing many people to rethink their attitudes and assumptions about the complexity and subtleties of experience within other species. In the last quarter of the twentieth century, the creation of farm animal sanctuaries in North America and Europe provided fresh opportunities for people to get to know chickens and turkeys and other food animals differently from the demeaning stock versions of these animals. Meanwhile, the avian sciences are debunking the prejudice against birds in general, and ground-nesting birds such as turkeys and chickens in particular, as primitive. Avian scientists are developing a whole new birdbrain nomenclature based on the now overwhelming evidence that birds' brains are complex organs that process information in virtually the same way as the human cerebral cortex, findings summarized by the Avian Brain Nomenclature Consortium in *Nature Neuroscience Reviews* (2005).

Without overestimating the progress, there is reason to speculate hopefully that our traditional presumptions are evolving, albeit at a tragically glacial pace, toward the view that nonhuman animals are kin to ourselves and that they, like us, are endowed with dignity, value, and autonomy in their own right. In his essay

"Against Zoos" (1985), Jamieson writes: "Morality and perhaps our very survival require that we learn to live as one species among many rather than as one species over many. To do this, we must forget what we learn at zoos" (p. 117). I would expand the argument to cover all forms of subjugation and incarceration of other sentient species: circuses, farms, state fairs, and others.

Although proclamations and analyses are not enough, college classrooms and scholarly publications provide crucial opportunities to inculcate animal liberation sentiments, arguments, and desires in the consciousness of humanity. But we must beware of romanticism in all of its aspects. In a recent post, "Animal Aesthetics," Texas State University historian McWilliams (2012) offers a sobering look at some of the hard realities that the animal liberationist must face without faltering. He describes a recent tour of the English and Irish countrysides, "where the aesthetics of animal life are the ruling theme of existence." McWilliams writes of how, embedded in these cultures, "one finds layers and layers of aesthetic (rather than moral) meaning lodged between what is real and what is right." He explains:

> These barriers are more than stubborn obstructions to achieving justice for animals. They are overwhelmingly perceived by those who passively build them not as barriers, but as positive aspects of a vernacular culture that you question, quite honestly, at your peril. The connection between rightness and reality, at this point in time, is virtually impossible for the people living in these cultures to conceptualize, much less make. Trying to convince a sheep farmer living on a family farm outside of Oxford to scrap his operation on moral grounds is as likely as the moon turning to cheese. Cheese! See, there's no escaping this insidious lexicon of abuse.

None of this, McWilliams hastens to assure us, is to say that animal liberationists should give up or become crushed with despair. Not at all. It is simply a reminder, as he notes, "that when we claim to pursue our Sisyphian brand of activism for selfless reasons," we had better mean it.

As I said earlier, I have been advocating for animals and animal rights, nonstop, for thirty years, ever since that critical moment in Lafayette Park in Washington, D.C., on World Laboratory Animals Day when I pledged to fight for animals instead of shunning my obligation to them. Little did I know then that seven years later, in 1990, I would launch an organization dedicated to promoting the compassionate and respectful treatment of chickens and other domestic fowl. In the late 1980s, I was warned by some animal advocacy leaders that an organization devoted to chickens would never fly, and a well-meaning scholar of animal ethics mourned my "defection" from the "high road" of strictly scholarly pursuits.

All of this pessimism was unfounded. Through United Poultry Concerns, I created the perfect opportunity to integrate the intellectual, ethical, and visceral elements of my calling on behalf of animals and animal liberation. Our chicken sanctuary will always protect me from burning out because I could never abandon the birds whom I have come to know and love, and who need me to fight for them. Similarly, my interest in conceptual analyses of the human-animal relationship and ideas on how to transform this relationship constructively is complementary and invigorating. It is hard to drop out once one sees oneself as an advocate with a case to put before the public. What matters is making the most of the opportunity of being on the right side of justice and compassion for animals, and for all abused beings, while we are living.

This book is a vital contribution to that challenge. Each chapter is purposely written collaboratively to signify that we cannot confront and end oppression alone. Even solitary liberators are working within a community of like-minded individuals who support any work that leads to freedom for the oppressed. I started my activism in the civil rights movement and now work as a scholar and advocate to not only provide sanctuary for abused birds but to challenge human perceptions of them. These beginning and ending points are not so far apart. Human liberation should not be held distinct from nonhuman animal liberation. Critical animal studies is continued proof that activism, scholarship, and the many expressions of domination are not distinct entities, and we must continue to fight oppression in whichever way it manifests.

References

Avian Brain Nomenclature Consortium. (2005). Avian brains and a new understanding of vertebrate brain evolution. *Nature Neuroscience Reviews, 6*, 151–159.

Best, S., & Nocella II, A. J. (2004). *Terrorists or freedom fighters?: Reflections on the liberation of animals*. New York: Lantern.

Crenshaw, K. W. (1991). Mapping the margins: Intersectionality, identity politics, and violence against women of colour. *Stanford Law Review, 43*(6), 1241–1299.

Davis, K., (2011). From hunting grounds to chicken rights: My story in an eggshell. In L. Kemmerer (Ed.), *Sister species: Women, animals, and social justice* (pp. 127–140). Urbana: University of Illinois Press.

Davis, K. (2009). *Prisoned chickens, poisoned eggs: An inside look at the modern poultry industry*. Summertown, TN: Book Publishing Co.

Davis, K. (2005). *The holocaust and the henmaid's tale: A case for comparing atrocities*. Summertown, TN: Book Publishing Co.

Dekkers, M. (1994). *Dearest pet: On bestiality* (P. Vincent, Trans.). New York: Verso.

Jamieson, D. (1985). Against zoos. In P. Singer (Ed.), *In defense of animals* (pp. 108–117). New York: Basil Blackwell.

McWilliams, J. (2012, July 21). Animal aesthetics. Eating plants blog. Retrieved from http://jamesmcwilliams.com/?p=1806

Pedersen, H., & Stănescu, V. (2011). Series editor's introduction: What is "critical" about animal studies? From the animal "question" to the animal "condition." In K. Socha (Ed.), *Women, destruction, and the avant-garde: A paradigm for animal liberation* (pp. ix–xi). Amsterdam: Rodopi.

United Poultry Concerns (UPC). (2007). 7th Annual Conference. Retrieved May 26, 2013, from http://upc-online.org/forums/120306forum.html

LIST OF CONTRIBUTORS

Alessandro "Alex" Arrigoni, PhD, was born in 1971 in Italy. He pursued his undergraduate degree in philosophy, with his thesis, *Animal Rights: Toward a Civilization Without Blood*, published in 1998. In 2006, he received his doctorate at Siena University on the topic of human and nonhuman animal relationships from a zoo-anthropological perspective. In 2007, Alex co-presented the exhibit *Zoomania: Animals, Hybrids and Monsters in Human Cultures*. Currently, he works for an Italian association that fights for people with disabilities' rights and is described in his chapter in *Earth, Animal, and Disability Liberation: The Rise of the Eco-Ability Movement* (2012).

Sarat Colling has a degree in writing, rhetoric, and discourse and is pursuing a master's in critical sociology at Brock University. Her research interests include critical animal studies, animal geographies, anarchism, and transnational feminism. Her current work examines the experience and representations of animals who have escaped from factory farms and slaughterhouses. Sarat has volunteered for environmental, animal, and social justice organizations in BC and Ontario. She is the founder of *Political Media Review* and coauthor of *Love and Liberation: An Animal Liberation Front Story*.

Lauren Corman teaches critical animal studies in the Department of Sociology, Brock University, St. Catharine's, Canada. She is currently completing her PhD in environmental studies at York University. She was a host and producer of the animal advocacy radio program and podcast, "Animal Voices," on CIUT 89.5 FM in Toronto from 2001 to 2009, a show she still happily guest hosts. Her research focuses on human and nonhuman voices, subjectivities, and resistances. Her interdisciplinary scholarship and activism draws on a variety of anti-oppression theories, especially those that link animal liberation struggles with other social justice and environmental concerns.

Erika Cudworth is Senior Lecturer in International Politics and Sociology at the University of East London, UK. Her research interests include international political theory, social intersectionality and gender, and human relations with non-human animals. Her current work on animals is on the relationship between "domination and affection" in human lives with companion dogs, theorizing human violence against non-human domesticate animals and the eroticisation of species domination. She is author of *Environment and Society* (Routledge, 2003), *Developing Ecofeminist Theory: The Complexity of Difference* (Palgrave, 2005), and *Social Lives with Other Animals: Tales of Sex, Death and Love* (Palgrave, 2011).

Karen Davis, PhD, is president of United Poultry Concerns (http://www.www.upc-online.org), which promotes compassionate and respectful treatment of domestic fowl. Her articles have appeared in *Animals and Women*, *Terrorists or Freedom Fighters*, and the *Encyclopedia of Animals and Humans*. Her books include *Prisoned Chickens, Poisoned Eggs: An Inside Look at the Modern Poultry Industry*, *More Than a Meal: The Turkey in History, Myth, Ritual, and Reality*, and *The Holocaust and the Henmaid's Tale: A Case for Comparing Atrocities*. She was profiled in the *Washington Post* and is in the U.S. Animal Rights Hall of Fame "for outstanding contributions to animal liberation."

Lara Drew is a PhD candidate at the University of Canberra (Australia) in Education. Her research examines the radical strand of the Animal Liberation Movement and seeks to show through narrative stories and visual imagery how activists learn as they work informally through practices of activism. Lara's other research and writing interests include radical education, anarchism, prison abolition and anti-capitalist positions. Lara is a project director for the Oceania Institute for Critical Animal Studies chapter, is a committee member of Animal Liberation ACT, a non-profit animal rights grassroots organisation, and participates in various other grassroots campaigns for animal liberation.

Amy J. Fitzgerald is an associate professor in the Department of Sociology, Anthropology, and Criminology at the University of Windsor in Ontario, Canada. Her areas of interest and specialization include critical animal studies, green criminology, gender studies, and environmental sociology. More specifically, her research focuses on the perpetration of harms (criminal and otherwise) by humans against the environment and nonhuman animals. She has published articles and books on the coexistence of animal abuse and intimate partner violence, sport-hunting culture, and harms produced by the human and "pet" food industries.

Carol L. Glasser received a BA at Tulane University and PhD in sociology at the University of California, Irvine. Her current research focuses on the intersections of feminism and animal rights and the role of radicalism in the animal rights movement. She is currently research director at the Humane Research Council, a nonprofit organization that conducts research to support animal protection organizations. Carol also serves on the editorial team of the *Journal for Critical Animal*

Studies, is on the board of Band of Mercy, a Los Angeles–based grassroots organization, and participates in various grassroots campaigns for animal liberation.

Jennifer Grubbs is a doctoral student in anthropology at American University, specializing in race, gender, and social justice. She is currently a coordinator for the Working Group Committee on Humane Research with the Institute for Critical Animal Studies. Her past research includes an autoethnography of farm sanctuary, a Marxist-anarchist analysis of animal industries, and a feminist analysis of animal slavery. Her current research expands on the intersectionality of oppression, the animal liberation movement, and the capitalist mode of production. As a vegan anti-capitalist anarchist, she uses her academic position to queer the normative nonsense that happens in that ivory tower.

Melanie Joy, PhD, is a Harvard-educated psychologist, personal-relationship coach, professor of psychology and sociology at the University of Massachusetts, Boston, and celebrated speaker. She has written a number of articles on psychology, animal protection, and social justice, which have been published in a variety of journals and magazines. Joy is the leading researcher on carnism, the psychology of eating meat, and has been interviewed for numerous magazines, books, and radio on her work, including the BBC, NPR, PBS, and ABC Australia. She has presented her work at national and international academic and grassroots conferences.

Stephanie Jenkins received her BA in philosophy at Emory University in 2003, her MA in philosophy from Pennsylvania State University in 2007, and her dual PhD in philosophy and women's studies from Pennsylvania State University in 2012. Her dissertation, *Disabling Ethics: A Genealogy of Ability*, argues for a genealogy-based ethics that departs from traditional bioethical approaches to disability. Her research and teaching interests include twentieth-century continental philosophy, especially French, feminist philosophy, disability studies, critical animal studies, and ethics.

Ronnie Lee has been active in the animal protection movement for more than forty years. He is best known for being one of the founders of the Animal Liberation Front, and in his younger days he spent a total of nine years in prison for direct action against the industries of animal persecution. Since being released from his last prison sentence in 1992, he has been involved in various campaigns and educational efforts against animal abuse and now believes that a combination of vegan outreach and political campaigning is essential for the achievement of animal liberation.

Michael Loadenthal is an anarchist organizer and academic insurgent based in Washington, D.C., and has been an involved with a number of anti-authoritarian and anti-capitalist projects in the United States and abroad. In 2010, he completed a master's degree at the Centre for the Study of Terrorism and Political Violence (University of St. Andrews, Scotland), focusing his dissertation on the Animal/Earth Liberation Front. He has authored numerous works under a variety of pseudonyms, taught "Terrorism and Political Violence" at Georgetown University, and is currently a doctoral student at the Institute for Conflict Analysis and Resolution (George Mason University, Virginia).

Atsuko Matsuoka is an associate professor at the School of Social Work, York University. Her research has addressed the importance of intersectionality of oppression among immigrants and refugees and care for ethnic older adults. Focusing on intersectionality of oppression, she developed restorative justice-based mediation among older ethno-racial minority immigrant women as an alternative intervention for elder abuse, and currently she is implementing a recovery approach–based mental health program with ethnic older adults. She has coauthored a book on the Eritrean diaspora, titled *Ghosts and Shadows: Constructions of Identity and Community in an African Diaspora* and a Japanese book, *Critical Social Work and Analysing Practice through Deconstruction: Experiential Learning*. She integrates anti-speciesism into social work education and is a board advisor for a nonprofit organization, Social Workers for Animals, which aims to transform social work for all. She has written a number of papers in the area of critical animal studies.

Les Mitchell, PhD is the director of the Hunterstoun Centre of the University of Fort Hare, South Africa, and the director of the Institute for Critical Animal Studies Africa. He is a Fellow of the Oxford Centre for Animal Ethics and has worked in pathology, community health, and education in the UK, Tanzania, Zambia, Zimbabwe, Malawi, and South Africa. He has published scholarly articles in a range of journals as well as contributing chapters to books and coediting *Living by Voices We Shall Never Hear*. His research interests include critical realism, nonhuman animal ethics, discourses, power, genocide, moral disengagement, relevant education, open education, and alternatives to violence.

David Nibert is professor of sociology at Wittenberg University, where he teaches animals & society, global change, social stratification, and law and society. His published works include *Domesecration: Animal Oppression and Human Violence* and *Animal Rights/Human Rights: Entanglements of Oppression and Liberation*. He co-organized the section on Animals and Society of the American Sociological Association and serves as a member of the section council. His research interests include the historical and contemporary entanglement of the oppression of humans and other animals.

Anthony J. Nocella II, PhD, an intersectional academic-activist is a Visiting Professor in the School of Education at Hamline University and Senior Fellow of the Dispute Resolution Institute at the Hamline Law School. Dr. Nocella has published more than fifty scholarly articles or book chapters; cofounded eco-ability and critical animal studies; cofounded and is director of the Institute for Critical Animal Studies; is the editor of the *Peace Studies Journal*; and has published more than fifteen books. His areas of interest include social justice education, disability studies, Hip Hop, transformative justice, and peace and conflict studies. His website is www.anthonynocella.org.

Sean Parson is an assistant professor of politics and international affairs, and sustainable communities at Northern Arizona University. His current research is on radical environmental political theory, anarchist social movements, and resource politics. In addition to academia Sean has been involved in Food Not Bombs, the Northwest Forest Defense movement, climate justice activism, and is currently working with the Repeal Coalition. He is finishing a book manuscript on Food Not Bombs and their struggle against the City of San Francisco. When not writing, grading, or teaching he spends most of his time taking his best friend, Diego, out on hikes.

David N. Pellow is professor of sociology at the University of Minnesota. His teaching and research focus on ecological justice issues in the United States and globally. His books include *The Slums of Aspen: Immigrants vs. the Environment in America's Eden* (with Lisa Sun-Hee Park), *Resisting Global Toxics: Transnational Movements for Environmental Justice*; *The Silicon Valley of Dreams: Environmental Injustice, Immigrant Workers, and the High-Tech Global Economy* (with Lisa Sun-Hee Park); and *Garbage Wars: The Struggle for Environmental Justice in Chicago*. He has served on the boards of directors for the Center for Urban Transformation, Greenpeace USA, and International Rivers.

Arpan Roy is a graduate student of anthropology at California State University, Los Angeles, where he is writing a thesis on anarchist-activists in Israel. He has conducted fieldwork in Israel, the West Bank, and in the occupy movement in Los Angeles. His activist interests include animal rights, anti-capitalism, indigenous rights in India, and Palestine solidarity. Arpan is also bridging the gap between academia and activism through documentary filmmaking projects and in helping organize an upcoming interdisciplinary conference in Los Angeles that will bring activists and scholars together to discuss the importance of a political culture.

Kim Socha, PhD, is author of *Women, Destruction, and the Avant-Garde: A Paradigm for Animal Liberation* and is a contributing editor to *Confronting Animal Exploitation: Grassroots Essays on Liberation and Veganism*. She has also published on topics such as composition pedagogy, critical animal studies, Latino/a literature, and surrealism. Kim is a professor of English and an advocate for animal liberation and social justice at the Animal Rights Coalition, Institute for Critical Animal Studies, and the Minnesota branch of the National Organization for the Reform of Marijuana Laws.

John Sorenson is a professor in the Department of Sociology at Brock University in Canada, where he teaches Critical Animal Studies, as well as courses on globalization and on antiracism. His books include *Animal Rights*; *Ape*; *Culture of Prejudice* (with Judith Blackwell and Murray Smith); *Ghosts and Shadows: Constructions of Identity and Community in an African Diaspora* (with Atsuko Matsuoka); *Disaster and Development in the Horn of Africa*; *African Refugees* (with Howard Adelman); and *Imaging Ethiopia*. A forthcoming book is *Thinking the Unthinkable: New Readings in Critical Animal Studies*. He is currently the editor of the *Journal of Critical Animal Studies*.

Vasile Stănescu is the co-general editor of the Critical Animal Studies book series published by Rodopi Press. He serves as the associate editor for the *Journal for Critical Animals Studies* (JCAS). Stănescu has reviewed texts for *Ethics and the Environment*, *Society and Animals: The Journal of Human-Animal Studies*, *Critical Sociology*, and the book series Key Themes in 20th and 21st Century Literature and Culture. He is currently a PhD candidate at Stanford University where he teaches a course titled "Eating Animals."

Nik Taylor, PhD, is currently a senior lecturer in sociology at Flinders University in Australia. She published widely on human-animal relations on issues such as links between human- and animal-directed violence, and humane education and animal-assisted therapy. Nik is the managing editor of *Society & Animals*; a charter scholar of the Animals and Society Institute; a participant in the Australian Animals Study group; and an associate member of the New Zealand Centre for Human-Animal Studies. Nik is also an editorial board member of *Anthrozoos* and *Sociology*.

Tereza Vandrovcová is a doctoral candidate in sociology at the Faculty of Arts, Charles University in Prague, Czech Republic. She aspires to establish critical animal studies in the Czech Republic. Her book *Animal as an Experimental Object: a Sociological Reflection* (in Czech) was published in 2011. She also co-organized the 2nd International European Critical Animal Studies Conference in Prague. In 2013 she became co-director of the Institute for Critical Animal Studies Europe. She teaches anthrozoology at the Faculty of Humanities, Charles University in Prague. Her research interests include critical animal studies, bioethics, qualitative methodology, and sociology of science.

Adam Weitzenfeld is an independent scholar and animal liberation activist. Adam has been active in the animal liberation and vegan movements since 2004. He has worked at animal sanctuaries, taught classes, and given talks on animal ethics, cofounded AR and vegan organizations, and presently maintains the critical animal studies blog HEALTH (http://eco-health.blogspot.com), where he writes on food justice, the vegan movement, and radical politics. His work is indebted to ecofeminist theory, *Satya*, *Animal Voices*, *Vegans of Color*, and *The Vegan Ideal*. Adam earned a bachelor's degree in environmental ethics from Beloit College and a master's degree in philosophy from the University of North Texas.

Richard J. White, PhD, is a senior lecturer in economic geography at Sheffield Hallam University, UK. Richard's main interdisciplinary research and writing has drawn attention to the prevalence of "anarchist" spaces of work and organization in society. Engaging anarchist notions of justice and intersectionality, his research also explores ways of tackling the violent systems that underpin the lived experiences of many humans and other animals in society. Richard currently serves on a range of editorial boards, including the Critical Animal Studies Book Series with Rodophi Press. He was the editor-in-chief of the *Journal for Critical Animal Studies* between 2008 and 2012. Richard can be contacted at Richard.White@shu.ac.uk

🐋 INDEX 🐋

Abalone Alliance, 63
Ableism, xx, xxvii, 44, 70, 74, 147, 161, 181, 188
Abolitionism, 18
Academic repression, xxx
Acampora, Ralph, 15
Adams, Carol, 14, 16, 33, 34, 35, 54, 55, 82, 83, 188, 211, 223
Adorno, Theodor, 57, 58
Africa, John, 60
Agamben, Giorgio, 8
Ageism, xx, 44
Agency, 37
Ahmadahy, Zainab, 68
Alston, Ashanti Omowali, 62
American Indian Movement, 60
American Legislative Exchange Council, 189
Anarchism, xxii, xxix, xxxiv, 37, 63, 64, 68, 101, 120, 180, 182, 189, 200, 202, 203, 204, 206, 207, 208, 212, 214, 215, 216, 217, 230, 231, 232, 233, 234, 235
Animal abuse and domestic violence, 35, 120, 230
Animal care ethics, 16
Animal Enterprise Terrorism Act, xxx, 179–180, 182, 183, 184, 189, 190
Animal exploitation and women, ix, x
Animal Industrial Complex, x, xi, 40
Animal Liberation Canada/USA, 44
Animal Liberation Front, xiii, xxix, xxx, 44, 54, 182, 183, 184, 185, 189, 190, 192, 193, 194, 195, 200, 206, 229, 232
Animal resistance, 65–67, 140, 171

Animal studies, xxii, xxiii, xxiv, xxvi, xxvii, xxviii, 14, 77, 92–93, 104, 111, 113, 137, 159, 160, 164, 180, 205, 206, 225
Animal turn in academic studies, 18–20, 165, 208
Animal Voices (radio program), 136, 141, 144, 229, 235
Animals and Society (journal), 93
Animals as food, xi, 41, 42, 58
Anthropocentrism, 3–7, 30, 31, 45, 53, 74, 75–77, 78, 79, 81, 135, 140, 141, 143, 181, 192, 194
Anti-Vivisection League, 69

Baldelli, Giovanni, 203, 207, 214
Band of Mercy, xxix
Bears, 51, 65, 68
Best, Steve, xxii, xxiii, xxvi, xxvii, xxx, xxxi, xxxiii, 19, 42, 43, 45, 51, 52–53, 54, 56, 69, 74, 93, 94, 96, 99, 101–106, 108, 111, 112, 113, 127, 128, 137, 138, 140, 158, 160, 171, 182, 183, 184, 205, 206, 216, 222
Biocentrism, 39, 53
Birds, 12, 18, 60, 64, 81, 209, 221, 225, 226, 227
Black Panthers, 56, 60, 62, 222, 223
Boas, Franz, 91
Bookchin, Murray, 162, 212
Brock University, xxiii, xxvii, 94
Brown, John, 54, 60
Buffaloes, 204

Calarco, Matthew, 9
Capitalism, x, xi, xix, xx, xxvi, xxx, xxxi, 13, 14, 19, 38, 40, 41, 43, 51, 52, 60–64, 67,

77, 78, 151, 159, 160, 162, 163, 165, 168, 179, 180, 182, 187, 189, 191, 192, 193, 194, 195, 197, 198, 204, 207, 212, 216, 234
Carnism, xxxiii, 3, 20–24, 231
Cats, xxiv, 31, 60, 69, 188
Center on Animal Liberation Affairs, xxii, 94
Chavez, Cesar, 61
Chicago Brown Berets, 60
Chickens, 11, 23, 41, 61, 66, 80, 81, 82, 140, 221, 222, 225, 226
Chinese Business Association of Toronto, 44
Chomsky, Noam, 168
Churchill, Ward, 61, 168
Clamshell Alliance, 63
COINTELPRO (Counter Intelligence Program), 61
Colling, Sarat, 171
Collins, Patricia Hill, 137, 187
Combahee River Collective, 137
Cooper Jackson, Esther, 62
Coronado, Rod, 59, 198
Cows, ix, 41, 53, 65, 66, 171, 204, 224
Crenshaw, Kimberle, 112, 137, 181, 187, 222
Critical Animal Studies and mainstream animal studies, xxviii, 94–95, 137, 164, 205–206
Critical Animal Pedagogy 113, 123, 124, 129, 130, 179,
Critical Animal Studies pedagogy 149–153, 166–169, 179
Critical Animal Studies, principles of, xvii, xxvi, xxvii–xxix, xxxiii, 95, 96, 106, 107, 184, 185
Critical feminist theory, xxxiii, 29, 31–33
Critical race studies, xxiii, xxxiii, 29, 31, 36–37, 130, 169, 181, 187, 188, 199, 206, 222, 225

Daly, Mary, 55, 56
Darwin, Charles, 209
Davis, Angela, 62
Decolonization, xxxiii, 51, 52, 56, 57, 58, 59, 60, 70
Deleuze, Gilles, 58, 113, 114
Derrida, Jacques, xxv
Descartes, Rene, 52, 92, 119
Direct action, xiv
Dogs, xiii, xxiv, 12, 31, 51, 60, 68, 69, 92, 129, 141, 142, 179, 188

Dominick, Brian, 206, 212
Donovan, Josephine, 14, 16, 118
Dunayer, Joan, xxi, 12

Earth First!, 44
Earth liberation, 43, 51, 106
Earth Liberation Front, 190, 193, 200, 232
Eco-ability, xxxii
Ecofeminism, 14, 17, 31, 33–35, 43, 54, 55, 56, 63, 122, 135, 137, 138, 141, 181, 188, 199, 206, 212, 213, 230, 235
Ecopedagogy, xxii, xxviii, 166
Einstein, Albert, xxii
Entanglements of oppression, 59
Environmental justice, 37–39
Epstein, Barbara, 63

Factory farms, xxix, xxx, 42, 52, 61, 69, 79, 80, 81, 135, 144, 145, 165, 171, 185, 221, 222, 229
Fanon, Franz, 56–57, 58
Federal Bureau of Investigation, xxix
Feminism, 13, 14, 18, 31–35
Fisher, Linda, 58
Food Not Bombs, xxi, 63, 233
Foucault, Michel, 84
Francione, Gary, 12, 17, 18
Frankfurt School, 57
Freedomways, 62
Freire, Paulo, 89, 90, 91, 138, 153
Fur trade, 59

Gaard, Greta, 55, 137, 188
Gandhi, Mohandas, xxii, 214
Garner, Margaret, 65–66
Gigliotti, Carol, xxvii, 45, 52, 74, 94, 111, 137, 158, 182, 205
Global warming, xi
Goats, ix, 59, 82, 204, 224
Graeber, David, 101
Green criminology, 39–42
Green Hill breeding facility, 51, 68–70
Groundless solidarity, 64, 68
Guattari, Felix, 58, 113, 114
Guinea pigs, xxix, 124

Habermas, Jurgen, 91, 120
Hales, Jennifer, 58
Hampton, Fred, 60

Haraway, Donna, xxiv, 17
Harper, Amy Breeze, xxxii, 58, 97, 188
Harris, John, xxv
Holocaust, xx, 44
hooks, bell, 91, 97
homophobia, 43, 161, 181, 188
Horne, Barry, 198, 200
Horses, 9, 10, 125, 188
Hribal, Jason, 65, 151, 171
Humane education, xxii, 151, 234
Humane meat, 23, 79, 80, 81, 83
Humane Society of the United States, xxx
Humanism, xxxiii, 3–15, 19, 43, 58, 140, 160, 194
Humanitarian League, xxvii, xix, xx
Huntingdon Life Sciences, 51, 198

Institute for Critical Animal Studies, xxii, xxiii, xxvi, xix, xxxi, xxxii, 94
Intersectionality, xix, xx, xxii, xxv, xxvi, xxxii, xxxiii, xxiv, 31–36, 42, 43, 59, 140, 149, 151, 153, 158, 161, 179, 180, 181, 187, 188, 192, 194, 195, 199, 206, 208, 212, 213, 215, 222, 230, 231, 232, 233, 235
ISLE (Interdisciplinary Studies in Literature and the Environment), 111

JOIN Community Union, 60
jones, patrice, 129, 138, 188, 223
Journal for Critical Animal Studies, 61, 96
Journal of Applied Animal Welfare, 93
Journal of Interdisciplinary Studies, 111

Kahn, Richard, xxii, xxiii, xxvii, 45, 51, 74, 94, 102, 111, 137, 138, 158, 166, 182, 183, 205
Kalechofsky, Roberta, 22
Kemmerer, Lisa, xxvii, 45, 52, 74, 94, 111, 137, 158, 182, 205, 215
Kheel, Marti, 83, 188
King, Coretta Scott, 62
King, Dexter Scott, 61
King, Martin Luther, Jr. xxviii, 28, 51, 61, 106, 62
King, Stephen, 110, 129, 130
Klein, Naomi, 190
Kropotkin, Peter, 208, 209

Latour, Bruno, 165

Lee, Bobby, 60
Lee, Ronnie, xxix, 198
Legambiente, 69
Locavorism, 79, 80, 81, 83
Luke, Brian, 16

Malcolm X, 60
Marshall Bioresources, 51
Martinez, Elizabeth, 188
Marx, Karl, xxv, 191
Marxism, 112, 189, 207, 231
Mason, Marie, 198
Mauss, Marcel, 90, 91
McCance, Dawne, xxv
McGowan, Daniel, 198
Mice, 221
Militarism, xxvii, 14, 62, 63, 106, 113, 137, 214
Military Industrial Complex, x, xi
Misogyny, xx, 186
Mohanty, Chandra, 194
Monkeys, xxiv, 57
MOVE, 60

Nana, 129
Newton, Huey, 60
Niagara Action for Animals, xxiii
Nibert, David, 41, 161
Nocella, Anthony II, xxii, xxiii, xxvii, xxx, xxxi, 45, 50, 61, 74, 94, 111, 137, 138, 158, 160, 161, 167, 169, 171, 182, 205, 222
Nonviolence, xxix, xxx, 62, 63, 173, 184, 189, 203, 213, 214, 215, 216
North American Animal Liberation Press Office, 44
Noske, Barbara, 34, 40, 66–67, 140
Nunez, Sharon, 135, 140, 144, 145

Oakley, Anne, 213
Occupy, xxxii, 106, 69, 98, 234
October 4th Organization, 60
Operation Bite Back, 59
Overaker, Jospehine, 198

Patterson, Charles, 223
Pedersen, Helena, xxvi, 77, 112, 119, 120, 127, 135, 225
People for the Ethical Treatment of Animals, xx, 82, 186, 187,

Pets, 8, 35, 40, 69, 124
Pigeons, 221
Pigs, ix, xxiv, 11, 24, 80, 92, 140, 144, 145, 171, 192, 204, 208, 210, 211, 217
Pilot, 129
Plumwood, Val, 9
Postcolonialism, 38, 56, 67, 68, 128, 139, 212
Posthumanism, xxiv, xxxiii, 3, 10, 12, 13, 14, 17, 18, 19, 20, 159, 165

Queenie, 66
Queer, xxiii, 55, 58, 64, 67, 81, 82, 188, 193, 194, 196, 206

Racism, x, xiv, xx, xxvi, xxvii, xxxii, xxxiii, 9, 11, 14, 29, 30, 36, 37, 38, 43, 44, 45, 59, 61, 69, 74, 77, 81, 106, 112, 113, 126, 137, 150, 153, 161, 162, 180, 181, 187, 188, 234
Rainbow Coalition, 60, 61
Rats, 221
Regan, Tom, 12
Reclus, Élisée, 53–54, 202, 203, 208, 209, 210, 211, 212, 216
Religion, xxi
Rhinoceros, xxxiv, 121–123
Rising Up Angry, 60
(Royal) Society for the Prevention of Cruelty to Animals, xxii, xxix
Ryder, Richard, 30

Safi, 141, 142, 143,
Salatin, Joel, 80, 81, 83
Salt, Henry, xix, xx
Sanbonmatsu, John, 11, 19
Sartre, Jean-Paul, 9
Scarce, Rik, 102, 183
Scrub jays, 65
Seale, Bobby, 60
Sex workers, 55
Sexism, xx, xxvi, xxvii, xxxiii, 9, 11, 14, 28, 29, 30, 33, 35, 38, 43, 44, 45, 106, 112, 113, 137, 138, 161, 181, 187, 188, 189
Shakur, Assata, 56
Sharks, 44
Sheep, ix, 82, 116, 204, 217, 226
Sims, James Marion, 67
Singer, Peter, xix, xxv, 11, 12
Smith, Andrea, 223

Smuts, Barbara, 140–143, 145
Socha, Kim, xxi, 208
Solidarity, xxvi, xxviii, xxxi, xxxiii, 51, 52, 56, 59, 62, 63, 64, 67, 68, 70, 74, 77, 83, 106, 110, 131, 136, 137, 170, 185, 186, 196, 197, 199, 200, 216, 222, 234
Sorenson, John, xxiii, 94
Speciesism, x, xvii, xx, xxi, xxvi, xxvii, xxxiii, 3, 10, 11, 12, 13, 15, 18, 19, 20, 21, 29–31, 33, 35, 38, 39, 43, 44, 45, 55, 57, 61, 69, 78, 81, 84, 102, 106, 113, 127, 129, 137, 161, 162, 167, 179–183, 186–188, 191, 192, 193, 194, 197, 231
Speciesism and racism, x, 11, 20, 61
Speciesism and sexism, x, xxxiii, 3, 11, 20
Stepanian, Andy, 62
Stop Huntingdon Animal Cruelty, 62, 182, 196
Stănescu, Vasile, 77, 79–80, 82, 83, 120, 204, 225
Subjectivity, xxvii, 8, 9, 65, 66, 99, 136, 137, 140, 141, 143

Terrorization, xxxiii, 179, 183
Theriomorphy, 224
Tolstoy, Leo, xxii
Total liberation, xxii, xxvi, xxviii, xxx, xxxi, xxxii, xxxiii, xxxiv, 19, 24, 25, 42–45, 51–74, 106, 111,137, 138, 140, 161, 167, 180, 184, 185, 186, 189, 198
Transphobia, 55
Turkeys, 225
Turtles, 64, 65
Twine, Richard, xxviii

United Poultry Concerns, 222, 223, 226, 230

Vegan Society, 210
Veganism, xiii, xiv, xx, xxviii, xxi, xxxiii, 4, 21–25, 34, 61, 62, 63, 74–83, 97, 100, 103, 104, 106, 107, 129, 144, 146, 147, 180, 181, 182, 185, 187, 188, 194, 197, 203, 210, 212, 213, 215, 231, 232, 234, 235
Vegetarianism, xiii, xx, xxi, xxx, 34, 53, 185, 203, 209, 210, 213
Vivisection, xiv, xxix, 8, 51, 67, 69, 70, 92, 99, 102, 103, 135, 139, 165, 171, 180, 181, 187, 188, 198

Walker, Alice, 62, 124–126, 140
Watson, Donald, 210
Webb, Robin, 198
White Lightning, 60
Wild justice, 65
Wolfe, Carey, 12, 13
Woodcock, George, 207
Wor Kuen, 60
World Trade Organization, 54

Young Lords, 60
Young Patriots, 60

Zapatistas, 64, 91

Studies in the Postmodern Theory of Education

General Editor
Shirley R. Steinberg

Counterpoints publishes the most compelling and imaginative books being written in education today. Grounded on the theoretical advances in criticalism, feminism, and postmodernism in the last two decades of the twentieth century, Counterpoints engages the meaning of these innovations in various forms of educational expression. Committed to the proposition that theoretical literature should be accessible to a variety of audiences, the series insists that its authors avoid esoteric and jargonistic languages that transform educational scholarship into an elite discourse for the initiated. Scholarly work matters only to the degree it affects consciousness and practice at multiple sites. Counterpoints' editorial policy is based on these principles and the ability of scholars to break new ground, to open new conversations, to go where educators have never gone before.

For additional information about this series or for the submission of manuscripts, please contact:

>Shirley R. Steinberg
>c/o Peter Lang Publishing, Inc.
>29 Broadway, 18th floor
>New York, New York 10006

To order other books in this series, please contact our Customer Service Department:
>(800) 770-LANG (within the U.S.)
>(212) 647-7706 (outside the U.S.)
>(212) 647-7707 FAX

Or browse online by series:
>www.peterlang.com

www.ingramcontent.com/pod-product-compliance
Ingram Content Group UK Ltd.
Pitfield, Milton Keynes, MK11 3LW, UK
UKHW022238230426
12048UKWH00018BA/1334